LAW, JUSTICE, DEMOCRACY, AND THE CLASH OF CULTURES

The Cold War ideological battle with universal aspirations has given way to a clash of cultures as the world moves concurrently toward globalization of economies and communications and balkanization through a clash of ethnic and cultural identities. Traditional liberal theory has confronted daunting challenges in coping with these changes and with recent developments such as the spread of post-modern thought, religious fundamentalism, and global terrorism.

  This book argues that a political and legal philosophy based on pluralism is best suited to confront the problems of the twenty-first century. Pointing out that monist theories such as liberalism have become inadequate and that relativism is dangerous, the book makes the case for pluralism from the standpoint of both theory and its applications. The book engages with such thinkers as Spinoza, Kant, Hegel, Rawls, Berlin, Dworkin, Habermas, and Derrida, and with several subjects that are at the center of current controversies, including equality, group rights, tolerance, secularism confronting religious revival, and political rights in the face of terrorism.

Michel Rosenfeld is the Justice Sydney L. Robins Professor of Human Rights at the Benjamin N. Cardozo School of Law, where he is also Director of the Program on Global and Comparative Constitutional Theory. He is the co-editor-in-chief of *International Journal of Constitutional Law* and the author or co-editor of numerous books, most recently *The Oxford Handbook of Comparative Constitutional Law* (2012) (co-edited with Andras Sajo) and *The Identity of the Constitutional Subject: Selfhood, Citizenship, Culture and Community* (2010). Among his many honors, Rosenfeld received the French government's highest and most prestigious award, the Legion of Honor.

Law, Justice, Democracy, and the Clash of Cultures

A PLURALIST ACCOUNT

MICHEL ROSENFELD

Benjamin N. Cardozo School of Law
Yeshiva University

CAMBRIDGE
UNIVERSITY PRESS

CAMBRIDGE UNIVERSITY PRESS
Cambridge, New York, Melbourne, Madrid, Cape Town,
Singapore, São Paulo, Delhi, Tokyo, Mexico City

Cambridge University Press
32 Avenue of the Americas, New York, NY 10013-2473, USA

www.cambridge.org
Information on this title: www.cambridge.org/9780521703420

First published 2011

Printed in the United States of America

A catalog record for this publication is available from the British Library.

Library of Congress Cataloging in Publication data
Rosenfeld, Michel, 1948–
    Law, justice, democracy, and the clash of cultures : a pluralist account / by Michel Rosenfeld.
        p.   cm.
    Includes bibliographical references and index.
    ISBN 978-0-521-87872-2 (hardback) – ISBN 978-0-521-70342-0 (paperback)
    1. Political rights.   2. Human rights.   3. Justice, Administration of.   4. Equality before the
    law.   5. Pluralism.   6. Liberalism – Political aspects.   7. Jurisprudence.   I. Title.
    K3240.R695   2011
    320.01′1–dc22   2011012266

ISBN 978-0-521-87872-2 Hardback
ISBN 978-0-521-70342-0 Paperback

Contents

Introduction   *page* 1

PART I   LIBERAL JUSTICE AND FLEETING SPECTERS OF UNITY

1. Reframing Comprehensive Pluralism: Hegel versus Rawls   23
    1.1. The Problematic Nexus Between Unity and Plurality   23
    1.2. The Kantian Revolution: Severing Unity from Plurality   27
          1.2.1. Adapting Kant: The Pure Social Contract Proceduralist
                  Approach   29
          1.2.2. Rawls's Kantian Contractarianism in A *Theory of Justice*   31
          1.2.3. Habermas's Dialogical Kantian Proceduralism   34
    1.3. Teleological Monism: The Utilitarian Alternative   35
    1.4. The Allure and Limitations of Value Pluralism   37
    1.5. The Hegelian Dimension of Comprehensive Pluralism   42
    1.6. From the Modern to the Post-Modern and from Homogeneous
          to Heterogeneous Societies   51
          1.6.1. The Modern versus the Post-Modern   52
          1.6.2. The Contrast Between Homogeneous and
                  Heterogeneous Societies   57
    1.7. Comprehensive Pluralism and the Priority of the Good over
          the Right   59
    1.8. Comprehensive Pluralism and Rawls's *Political Liberalism* 62

2. Equality and the Dialectic Between Identity and Difference   68
    2.1. The Dialectic of Equality: A Three-Stage Progression   70
    2.2. From Liberalism to Pluralism   77
    2.3. The Dynamic Between Identity and Difference   82
    2.4. Single-Status Society and the Federalization of Difference 86

v

2.5. Accommodating Cultural Difference Within Pluralism
     and the Dialectic of Equality   88
2.6. Designing a Legal and Institutional Framework to
     Accommodate Cultural Difference   90

3.   **Human Rights and the Clash Between Universalism
     and Relativism: The Case of Minority Group Rights**   92
     3.1. Human Rights and the Confrontation Between Universalism,
          Particularism, and Relativism   95
     3.2. The Constitutional Protection of Minorities and the Conflict
          Between Individual and Group Rights   99
     3.3. Minority Rights Under the U.S. Constitution   103
     3.4. Comprehensive Pluralism, the Constitution, and Group Rights 109
     3.5. Comprehensive Pluralism and the Nexus Between Human
          Rights and Constitutional Rights   115

     PART II   E PLURIBUS UNUM?

4.   **Spinoza's Dialectic and the Paradoxes of Tolerance: Can Unity
     Be Willed out of Necessity?**   125
     4.1. Spinoza and Tolerance: Paradoxes and Contradictions   126
     4.2. From Marx and Hegel to Spinoza   130
     4.3. Spinoza's Dialectic of Tolerance in Political Context   133
     4.4. Spinoza's Theory and Tolerance and Pluralism in a Post-
          Modern World   144

5.   **The Clash Between Deprivatized Religion and Relativized
     Secularism: The Constitutional Conundrum**   149
     5.1. The Secular versus the "Areligious"   151
     5.2. The Constitutional Treatment of the Relationship Between
          Religion and the State in Comparative Perspective   154
          5.2.1. The Constitutional Models   155
          5.2.2. Lessons from Constitutional Jurisprudences   156
          5.2.3. Recent Historical Changes and New Trends   161
     5.3. A Pluralist Account of the Constitutional Treatment of the
          Relationship Between Religion and the State   164
     5.4. The Pluralist Constitutional Approach to Religion as Superior
          to Its Liberal Counterpart and as Means to Unity
          Amidst Diversity   178

6. **Dworkin and the One Law Principle: Can Unity Be Imposed Through an Interpretive Turn?**   182
    6.1. Dworkin's Thesis and the One Law Principle   183
    6.2. Dworkin, His Rivals, and the Distinction Between Principle and Policy   185
    6.3. Counterfactual Reconstruction and Dworkin's Theory of Interpretation   191
    6.4. Evaluating Dworkin's Interpretive Enterprise: Moving from Concept to Conception and Law as Integrity   197
    6.5. Contrasting Dworkin's Theory and Pluralism in Terms of the One and the Many   204

    PART III   CAN PLURALISM THRIVE IN TIMES OF STRESS?
    ON GLOBALIZATION, TERROR, AND THE CLASH OF CULTURES

7. **Rethinking Political Rights in Times of Stress: Can Pluralism Thwart the Progression from Stress to Crisis?**   211
    7.1. A Pluralist Conceptual Framework for Political Rights   212
        7.1.1. Constitutional Framework and Pluralist Politics   215
        7.1.2. Political Rights and the Struggle Between Self and Other   217
        7.1.3. Pluralism and the Distinction Between Ordinary Times, Times of Crisis, and Times of Stress   221
    7.2. Liberal, Republican, and Communitarian Approaches to Constitutional Democracy and Political Rights   223
        7.2.1. Liberalism's, Republicanism's, and Communitarianism's Overriding Values and Pluralism   223
        7.2.2. Comparing Liberal, Republican, and Communitarian Political Rights   227
    7.3. Pluralism and the Derivation of Political Rights   233
        7.3.1. Pluralism and Limited Liberalism, Republicanism, and Communitarianism   234
        7.3.2. Relational and Contextual Pluralist Political Rights in Action: The Example of Free Speech   236
    7.4. Pluralist Political Rights in Times of Stress   238
        7.4.1. Hate Speech and Militant Democracy   239
        7.4.2. The War on Terror   244
        7.4.3. Pacted Secession   246
    7.5. Final Appraisal on the Room for Pluralism in Political Rights During Times of Stress   248

8. **Derrida's Deconstructive Ethics of Difference Confronts Global Terrorism: Can Democracy Survive the Autoimmune Ravage of the Terror Within Us?**   251
   8.1. Derrida, Deconstruction, and the Ethics of Difference   253
   8.2. Global Terrorism's Challenge to the Ethics of Difference   255
   8.3. Derrida's Deconstruction of Globalization, Tolerance, and Democracy   260
   8.4. Assessing the Ethics of Difference's Account of Global Terrorism   263
   8.5. Global Terrorism and the Contrasts Between Pluralist Ethics and the Ethics of Difference   266

9. **Habermas's Discourse Ethics of Identity and Global Terror: Can Cosmopolitanism, Post-Nationalism, and Dialogue Downsize the Terrorist Threat?**   271
   9.1. Terrorism's Challenge to Habermas's Conception of Modernism   271
   9.2. Global Terrorism and the Post-National Rule of Law Cosmopolitan Order   274
   9.3. Habermas's Analysis of Global Terrorism in the Context of Discourse Theory   280
   9.4. A Critique of Habermas's Assumptions Regarding Global Terrorism and Consequent Implications for Habermas's Post-National Discourse-Theory Model   287
   9.5. Coping with Global Terrorism Beyond the Ethics of Identity: Pluralism as an Alternative to Habermas's Proceduralism   290

10. **Conclusion: The Hopes of Pluralism in a More Unified and More Fragmented World**   297

Bibliography   309
Index   317

Introduction

The clash of ideologies that dominated the era of the Cold War has given way to a clash of identities. At the highest levels of abstraction, the Cold War conflict between liberal capitalism and Marxist communism, as fierce and ideologically charged as it was, was one among two contenders that were equally anchored in the legacy of the Enlightenment and equally committed to universalism. In a nutshell, the project of the Enlightenment consists in adherence to the rule of reason and to promotion of equal liberty for all, and both liberal capitalism and Marxist communism have been *ideologically* aligned with this project though their respective interpretations of its key terms were, to be sure, widely divergent.

Liberal capitalism and Marxist communism appeal to reason and eschew metaphysical claims, and though their conceptions of liberty and equality are in conflict, they both adhere to the view that every human being is ultimately inherently equal to every other human being and that all human beings are equally entitled to liberty. Moreover, whereas liberal capitalism may be strongly committed to negative liberty and Marxist communism dependent on positive liberty[1] to be fully realized through the revolution of the proletariat, and whereas these two ideologies may greatly diverge along the spectrum that extends from purely formal equality to full material equality, they both fully coincide in their universalism.

Liberal capitalism presents itself as optimal for everyone everywhere, and so does Marxist communism. Liberal capitalism may be more open to diversity than Marxist communism as the former is generally tolerant of religion, cultural differences, and a broad array of individual lifestyles, whereas the latter has been historically inimical to all of the above. Nevertheless, the primacy of liberal capitalism remains as supreme as that of Marxist communism. Religious diversity may be welcome by the liberal capitalist, but her tolerance cannot extend to those religious precepts that require actual interference with the liberal capitalist agenda. In short, both of the

---

[1] For a discussion of the distinction between negative and positive liberty, see Berlin 1970: 118–72.

ideologies in question claim the entire globe as their relevant and legitimate sphere of application and influence.

With the demise of Soviet communism and the end of the Cold War, it seemed logical that liberal capitalism would proceed to practical implementation of its universal vision on a worldwide scale. In part, this has been accomplished through spread of a process of globalization that comprises the deployment of an ever more comprehensively global economy aspiring to a single market that reaches into every corner of the world, and to completely unimpeded worldwide mobility of capital and labor. This is to be complemented by evolution to a fully integrated worldwide system of communication capable of sustaining a veritably global public sphere. At the same time, however, the actual process of universalization of liberal capitalism has been accompanied by a corresponding process of increasing fragmentation and particularization. That latter process is best exemplified by the proliferation of identity politics, whether based on ethnic differences – such as those that led to violence in, and to the breakup of, former Yugoslavia – or cultural/ideological ones – such as the numerous clashes between religious fundamentalists and secularists in various parts of the world. Paradoxically thus, the more the world becomes bound together, the more people, ideas, and goods migrate, the more it also becomes violently split and divided. Globalization thus appears to go hand in hand with balkanization.

Globalization and balkanization do not merely coincide but seem mutually dependent and mutually reinforcing. This is made manifest by the post-communist resurgence of nationalism. As one observer puts it,

> Nationalism is typically a reaction to feelings of threatened identity, and nothing is more threatening in this respect than global integration. So the two go together . . . although they push in opposite directions. (Beiner 1995: 3)

Identity politics relies on severing the self from the other, based on some particularities or differences that resist all bridging or universalization. Moreover, the centrifugal thrust fueled by the juxtaposition of rapidly disaggregating parts seems prone to being propelled much farther by the politicization of religious fundamentalism. Indeed, if balkanization contradicts globalization by refusing equal liberty to those it casts as ethnically or nationally different, as Habermas observes, religious fundamentalism projected into the political arena for its part, refuses to play by any plausible conception of the rule of reason (Borradori 2003: 72).[2]

---

[2] This is not to imply that the precepts of fundamentalist religion are necessarily contrary to reason. Rather, whether or not such precepts are amenable to justification according to the rule of reason, the religious fundamentalist would reject appeal to reason as delineated by the Enlightenment as a means of justification. For example, there may well be plausible arguments against a right to abortion that may appeal to reason. The religious fundamentalist, however, is one who insists that the prohibition is

Taken together, identity politics and religious fundamentalism challenge the project of the Enlightenment, in general, and liberalism, in particular. Ethnic-based identity politics stands against the Enlightenment's call for universalization and challenges liberalism's individual-regarding conception of equal liberty and justice (Rosenfeld 1998: 216), by insisting on often incompatible group-regarding equality and justice. Religious fundamentalism, on the other hand, negates downright both the Enlightenment project as a whole and liberalism in all its facets. Furthermore, whereas identity politics with its stress on the differences that set each self against others is inherently anti-universalist, religious fundamentalism can certainly have universalist aspirations. For example, certain religious fundamentalists, such as those that have endorsed Jihadist global terror, believe it to be their duty to spread their religion worldwide, by force if necessary.[3]

If the trend toward identity politics were not coupled with an equally powerful trend toward transnational economic, legal, and political integration (Rosenfeld 2008), one could perhaps envisage a world made up of an increasing diversity of identity-based groups co-existing without interacting with one another throughout the globe. In such a scenario, each identity-based group would have internal autonomy to pursue its own normative objectives and would limit opening toward other groups to what would be strictly necessary to maintain peace among virtually exclusively inward-looking neighbors with commonly agreed borders designed to keep each of them separate from the others. In such a universe, dealings within the same community, or intra-communal dealings, would be maximized, and those among different communities, or inter-communal ones, minimized. Mono-ethnic, mono-religious, mono-cultural, and mono-linguistic nation-states would be the ideal, and each time a new identity group would form it could sever its ties to the larger group with which it happened no longer to identify through peaceful secession, thus gaining autonomy for self-government, self-fulfillment, and self-realization. In short, pursuant to this scenario, the world would tend toward peaceful subdivision into the smallest viable identity-groups operating according to the principles of internal autonomy and external non-interference based above all on reciprocal non-involvement.

Transnational integration, which is taking place to some degree on a worldwide basis, and which is particularly far along in Europe, however, strongly militates against the achievement of any ideal approximating peaceful coexistence and mutual indifference among tightly woven thoroughly homogeneous atomistic group-based entities. As is particularly clear within the ambit of the European Union (EU), the

---

justified *because* it is imposed by his religion, which, he asserts, is in exclusive possession of the truth and of moral certainty.

3 See Habeck 2006.

Westphalian nation-state is under siege from above as well as from below (Rosenfeld 2008). Basque or Catalan separatism may threaten the unity of Spain, but the integrity of its sovereignty, as understood in Westphalian terms, also seems compromised by the professed supremacy of EU law as decreed by the EU's European Court of Justice (ECJ) sitting in Luxembourg over inconsistent national law (Id.).

Transnational integration combined with infra-national division and compartmentalization call for combination of new poles of (external) identification and of (internal) differentiation. In other words, as the need for greater convergence on a transnational scale joins the need for greater room for divergence on a national and infra-national scale, appropriate standards of legitimacy and normative validity adapted to these new circumstances are called for. On the one hand, a plurality of non-unified and non-fully integrated legal regimes proliferate. For example, whereas the ECJ claims supremacy for EU law over inconsistent member-state law, several member-state constitutional courts, such as the German, have rejected such supremacy in principle though not, as of this writing, in practice (Rosenfeld 2008:419). Because no formal institutional mechanisms are in place to deal with such conflicts, a citizen of an EU member-state has no protection against inconsistent or even contradictory legal obligations stemming from two separate legal regimes to which that citizen is equally bound.[4] On the other hand, international courts, such as the International Criminal Court (ICC), and transnational Courts, such as the ECJ and the ECtHR, dispense supranational justice, and both supra-national and infra-national arenas of democracy multiply – even if not always in a full-fledged way as attested by the EU's oft noted "democratic deficit".[5]

These shifts in the locus and context of law, justice, and democracy necessitate the articulation of normative standards of validity and legitimation that properly account for the proliferation of, and novel forms of interaction among, rapidly shifting poles of identification. Liberalism tailored to the needs of the Westphalian nation-state no longer seems up to the task. Ought such liberalism be perfected or rather superseded? And if no longer viable, should liberalism be replaced by a single integrated set of overall normative criteria? Or, by a plurality of them better suited for a division of tasks among the new multiplicity of intersecting levels and arenas of intersubjective dealings? Has the time come for abandoning what may likely prove a futile quest for overall unity and consistency?

---

[4] See Garlicki 2008 pointing out that an EU citizen is actually subject to at least three distinct potentially contradictory legal regimes: that of that citizen's member-state as interpreted by the latter's constitutional court; that of the EU as interpreted by the ECJ; and that of the European Convention on Human Rights (ECHR) as interpreted by the European Court of Human Rights (ECtHR) sitting in Strasbourg.
[5] *See* Resnik 2008:40; Kumm 2008: 135.

The challenge posed by politicized religious fundamentalism[6] is more radical and more daunting than that posed by ethnic-based identity politics. The latter need not entail a wholesale repudiation of liberalism. Catalan or Quebecqwois separatists can certainly consistently retain a liberal outlook within Cataluna or Quebec while simultaneously asserting identity-based group rights respectively against Spain or Canada. A religious fundamentalist, however, cannot compromise in any way when it comes to the prescriptions of his religion, and must therefore demand that the polity and that all public and private institutions within it comply with the applicable norms imposed by his religion. There may be overlaps between a fundamentalist religion and Enlightenment norms (e.g., the religious assertion that human beings are all created equal by God, that they all possess a soul, and that God has made them free to choose between good and evil, may be understood as sharing a great deal in common with the Enlightenment's commitment to equal liberty for all), but to the religious fundamentalist such overlaps carry no normative implications. There is no room for compromising with, or for opening toward, proponents of the Enlightenment project just because of even significant overlaps such as those mentioned earlier. Indeed, for the religious fundamentalist it is only exactly *what* the true religion prescribes and *because* it does so that counts. Everything else must be dismissed, and there is no room for give and take, even in the political arena, with proponents of other religions or with those who embrace secularism.[7]

The most radical challenge is that posed by "crusading" or by "Jihadist" religions that proclaim the divine right to eliminate anyone or anything that stands in their path to achieving the universal spread of true religion. This challenge, however, is also the one that is easiest to meet from a normative standpoint. The belligerent

---

[6] Non-politicized religious fundamentalism, in contrast, may well be accommodated within the ambit of a liberal constitutional polity so long as it remains focused intra-communally and so long as its precepts are not grossly violative of the liberal state's public policy, such as would be, for example, forbidding all medical treatment for children with life-threatening diseases. Moreover, a distinction must be drawn, for present purposes, between religious fundamentalism as a *religious* matter and as a *politico-constitutional* matter. From a religious standpoint, a "fundamentalist" is someone who interprets holy texts literally; from a politico-constitutional standpoint, in contrast, a "religious fundamentalist" is one who considers his or her religion as the repository of absolute truth *and* who insists that the state be ruled exclusively pursuant to the dictates of the true religion. Unless otherwise specified, "religious fundamentalism" will be used throughout in its politico-constitutional meaning.

[7] There may be exceptions regarding religious fundamentalism's utter intolerance toward other religions and toward non-religious ideologies, but such exceptions must be exclusively grounded in the teachings of the true religion. For example, for an ultra-orthodox Jew, whereas the state of Israel must be ruled exclusively according to Jewish religious law, the *halacha*, the *halacha* itself allows for Jews in the Diaspora to recognize the legitimacy of the state in which they live so long as the latter complies with the set of norms known as the "Noachide laws." See Stone 1991. See also March 2009, for an interesting discussion of the contemporary debate among Muslim religious authorities concerning whether or not the Shariah permits Muslim minorities in non-Muslim countries to interact in the political arena with public authorities and other non-Muslim civil society and political actors.

religious fundamentalists, be they radical Christian fundamentalist abortion clinic bombers in the United States or Al Qaeda Islamic fundamentalist global terrorists, pose an existential threat to all others, be they religious or secular. Accordingly, the normative imperatives against such a belligerent stance in the name of religion are clear: Intolerance and, if absolutely necessary, even the use of violence are called for, consistent with all plausible conceptions of the individual's right to survival and to self-defense. More generally, whether a belligerent ideologically intransigent group be religious or secular – those who seek genocide or ethnic cleansing based on an ideology of ethnic purity are no different, for present purposes, than those who assert a religion-based mandate to kill the infidel – any such group ought to be equally fought. Moreover, the normative apparatus furnished by traditional liberalism is amply sufficient to provide an adequate normative framework to all those who face an existential threat posed by religious or ethnocentric fanatics. Indeed, whatever bias it may have in favor of the individual and against the group, traditional liberalism suffices – based on its commitment to individual freedom and to freedom of association for peaceful purposes – to offer both the individual and the group, whether secular or religious, the requisite normative and institutional backing needed to secure survival and ward off the above mentioned existential threats. In other words, whatever divisions they may otherwise have regarding individual versus group rights, or regarding secularism versus state-sponsored religion, all non-belligerent groups in a multi-ethnic, multi-cultural, and multi-religious polity can equally rely on traditional liberalism to provide all the necessary and sufficient normative ammunition required in their confrontations against all variants of belligerent fundamentalism.

Paradoxically, it is not belligerent fundamentalism but non-belligerent religious fundamentalism and certain kinds of politicized or re-politicized religions that pose a much more formidable challenge to the asserted legitimacy of traditional liberalism, or even to that of the somewhat less fully encompassing political liberalism elaborated by Rawls (Rawls 1993). As one observer has noted, there has been a "deprivatization" of religion since the 1980s (Casanova 1994: 3) that involves two interrelated processes: the "repoliticization of the private religious and moral sphere" and the "renormativization of the public economic and political spheres" (Id.: 5–6). This combined with the spread of "strong" religion (Sajo 2009) has amounted to a frontal attack against the separation between the realm of faith and that of reason, which had stood as one of the pillars of the Enlightenment.

Strong de-privatized religion challenges the neutrality of the secular state and traditional liberalism's suitability as a viable normative framework for legitimate relationships between the state and religion (Rosenfeld 2009: 2336–7). If freedom *of* religion requires allowing religion to implement its edicts and norms in the public sphere lest we end up with a vacuous "naked public square" (Neuhaus 1984), then freedom *from* religion becomes compromised. Moreover, to the extent that conflicts between religions exist within a polity, not only does freedom from religion for the non-religious becomes threatened but so does freedom from (the dominant) religion for a significant portion of the religious population within the polity. Thus, for example, if a state were to promote and implement Christian norms and values, then that state might not only impinge on atheists and agnostics but also on Muslims and Jews, inasmuch as certain key precepts of Christianity may be in conflict with those of Islam and Judaism.

The politicization of strong religion is likely to differ from ethnic-based identity politics to the extent that the former may well have universalist aspirations whereas the latter, for the most part, does not. For instance, some politicized religions seek the imposition of a ban on abortion throughout the polity even though other religions and the vast majority of the non-religious within that same polity deem abortion permissible and the right to it desirable, or even necessary to the achievement of equal liberty. On the other hand, as already suggested, the Catalans and the Quebecquois tend to be consistently internally liberal and harbor no design to impose the dictates associated with their distinct identity beyond the bounds of the space traditionally reserved for their intra-communal dealings. There are, of course, religions that are compatible with liberalism and religions that do not have universalist ambitions – at least in the sense of not seeking to subject all within a multi-religious polity to their own norms and values – as there are identity groups that are illiberal and even some that resort to ethnic cleansing or to genocide. The point, however, is that all the previously mentioned religions and identity-based positions, with the exception of liberal religions fully compatible with the secular state and with the Enlightenment-based divide between faith and reason, pose a serious challenge to traditional liberalism, though each type of group involved may do so differently and to a different degree. In any case, the moral, legal, and political legitimacy of the liberal state as deployed in its Westphalian framework is profoundly called into question.

Not only, is the institutional value and legitimacy of liberalism under severe challenge, but so are its epistemological foundations. Epistemologically, liberalism is wedded to the modern mindset and approach to the factual and normative issues that confront the polity. Modernism, in turn, is closely associated with the traditional Enlightenment conception of the rule of reason and with the sharp divide between faith and reason. Both of these, however, have been radically attacked by post-modern thought. The post-modern movement defies meaningful encapsulation as it encompasses a diverse and complex array of views expounded by a large number of very different authors. Nevertheless, for present purposes, suffice it to focus on a small number of generally applicable key points. The post-modern challenge builds on the "disenchantment of reason" fueled by the transformation of the Enlightenment's design to implant the rule of reason into the mere instrumentalization of reason. The rule of reason aims at discovery and institutionalization of a universally justifiable rational order. What has led to the "disenchantment of reason," however, has been recourse to reason and scientific methodology for purposes of advancing the narrow interests of the powerful, fostering colonialism and neo-colonialism, exacerbating differences in wealth, and the like (Habermas 2001: 130, 138–40). The reduction of reason to instrumental reason thus seems to turn the means of the Enlightenment against its ends, and particularly against the pursuit of liberty and equality for all.

Whether or not postmodernism is altogether incompatible with the project of the Enlightenment, conceived as one that evolves and adapts over time, is a matter of dispute that will be further addressed in Part III. For now, what is most important are the consequences that postmodernism draws from the instrumentalization of reason. As the latter becomes pervasive, the usefulness and legitimacy of the rule of reason as regulator of the normative order that presides over the relevant social and political institutions diminish to the point of leaving a great vacuum. Social actors become alienated and retreat into subjectivism because recourse to reason has left them powerless to achieve justice in the face of the ravages spread by instrumental reason. This fosters a multiplication of purely subjectively grounded conceptions of the good that escape from the constraints of modernism or of the traditional Enlightenment-based rule of reason (Id.: 58, 88, 140). Post-modern subjectivism, therefore, appears as particularistic and as prone to leading to endless fragmentation and to relativism in law, morals, and politics. In other words, as post-modern discourses proliferate, the clash between conflicting visions of justice and disparate conceptions of the good becomes increasingly magnified with no readily apparent common denominator available to carve out common grounds, or to mediate between the ever-increasing sets of differences that seem irremediably at odds with one another.

Although postmodernism does not entail or call for balkanization, it fits comfortably with the processes of particularization and identity formation that pave the way to balkanization. Moreover, by weakening modernism's refusal to cede the public sphere to religion, postmodernism unwittingly clears the stage for (re)politicized religion to begin (re)capturing what modernism had set as the exclusive preserve of secularism. Also, the retreat of modernism ironically sets the public stage for the deployment of politicized religions that are universalist in their religious outlook as well as in their political agenda, including belligerent crusading or Jihadists fundamentalist religions.

On the one hand, the relativism associated with postmodernism favors a process of balkanization within the normative realm. Every norm, value, or conception of the good is only justifiable from the perspective of those who identify with it and are already committed to it. Just as in the case of balkanization in the context of nationalism, balkanization in the realm of norms prompts relativization and hence devaluation of the norms embraced by all those who make up the "other," and to overvaluation, if not absolutization, of the norms to which one is oneself committed. Accordingly, the coupling of relativism with subjectivism linked to postmodernism results in a dialectic defined by the mutually reinforcing conflict between an ever more fragmented, atomized, and relativized realm of intersubjective and inter-communal dealings and an ever more isolated, narcissistic, all-encompassing, and solipsistic realm of subjective and intra-communal (self) dealings.

On the other hand, a post-modern world marked by increasing solipsistic isolation is demoralizing, and particularly so in light of the great spread and intensification of inter-communal dealings brought about by globalization. One becomes more and more enclosed within one's own truth while at the same time being forced to interface with an increasing number of others who all deny or devalue one's own truth. This predicament provokes, in turn, a yearning to escape from one's solipsistic prison, and, consistent with the dynamics of postmodernism, two seemingly separate moves emerge as promising. The first of these consists in projecting one's own subjective normative perspective outward and, as a consequence, imagining it as being universal; the second, in internalizing a normative perspective coming from "the outside," thus escaping one's merely subjective prison by imagining what is obtained from others as being worthy of being shared with them *because* it is universal.[8]

It now becomes apparent how normative balkanization and the drive toward overcoming, or compensating for, the utter isolation it begets under post-modern conditions favors the rise of particular religions conceived (from the inside) as universal, which claim the right to exclusive rule over all facets of the life of the polity. Relativization casts the ideology of secularism, once privileged under modernism, as one more merely subjective value system. This sets secularism as just one more ideology, one more metaphysical position, and hence the equivalent of one more, among a large number of, competing religions.[9] This allows for a de-relativization of religions that were doubly relativized under modernism through subordination to secularism and through relegation to the private sphere. Furthermore, each particular thus de-relativized religion can now cast itself as universal not only inwardly (as a large number of religions, even under conditions of modernism, do) but also outwardly in the public arena that is typically populated by numerous other religions and non-religious ideologies. At the same time, in the context of pervasive postmodern existential loneliness and anxiety, a de-relativized particular religion that aggressively promotes itself as universally encompassing looms as especially enticing to those who seek to escape from the strictures of their own subjective isolation.

[8] Unless what is internalized coming from others is cast as universal, escape from subjective solitude would only lead to subservience to the arbitrary (viewed from the outside) value order of others.

[9] It is noteworthy, in this respect, that secular public education has been characterized by religious fundamentalists as preaching the "religion" of "secular humanism." See *Smith* v. *Bd. Of Sch. Comm'rs*, 827 F.2d 684 (11th Cir. 1987) (U.S. Federal Court of Appeals).

Finally, such a religion appears perfectly suited to confront and to counter globalization. Globalization aims at universalization by uprooting the particular and leveling
or submerging differences. De-relativized and de-privatized religion, in contrast,
projects *its* particular as the universal and wields its universalized particular against
the systematic uprooting of identities deployed by the process of globalization in
its quest for a uniform worldwide market unimpeded by the vicissitudes of local
cultures.

Consistent with this analysis, and with the claim advanced by Habermas that
global Jihadist terrorism is a byproduct of the implantation of the global economy
(Borradori 2003: 66), it becomes clear how fundamentalist religious terrorists could
seek to arrogate to themselves the task of systematically countering globalization.
Identity politics cannot defeat the opening of markets by itself as the violence that
the push to globalization inflicts on particular identities and cultures can be met
arguably only through violence. From a post-modern perspective, the two instances
of violence involved could be regarded as equivalent (leaving aside, for the moment,
whether they would be equally condemnable or merely equally relativized due a
total absence of means to evaluate any normative stance from the outside); from
a religious fundamentalist Jihadist perspective, however, the global terrorist's violence would be in the service of the truth and against those bent on uprooting and
dismantling it.

As already mentioned, the struggle against belligerent fundamentalist religion
is easily normatively justified for all those who do not share the latter's perspective. Leaving aside whether postmodernism is necessarily wedded to relativism, and
whether it can *systematically* justify moral condemnation of, and armed struggle
against, belligerent fundamentalist religion and the global terrorism associated with
it – questions that will be addressed in Chapter 8 – it seems obvious that neither
the disenchantment of reason not the retreat to subjectivism would deter the post-
modernist from siding in this confrontation with liberalism as the lesser of two evils.
On the other hand, so long as the realm of intersubjective and inter-communal
interaction is not reducible to that of the war pitting belligerent fundamentalist
religion against all others, postmodernism does pose several serious challenges to
liberalism.

Two of these challenges are particularly acute and troubling in the context of
the contemporary multi-ethnic, multi-religious, and multi-cultural polity. The first,
already alluded to, is the dislodging of secularism from the pedestal on which it
stood during the modern era tracing back to the Enlightenment. The second challenge, in turn, is posed by postmodernism's rejection of the possibility of devising
neutral state institutions to mediate and do justice among the conflicting conceptions of the good typically present within the contemporary polity. As will be further
discussed in Chapter 1, what distinguishes the postmodern from the modern polity is

that whereas they both harbor a multiplicity of competing conceptions of the good, the modern polity is one that perceives its unity and legitimacy safeguarded by a set of neutral norms that provide criteria of justice that are neutral as between all relevant conceptions of the good. From a post-modern perspective, however, no such neutral norms or institutions, be they procedural or substantive, can be found with the consequence that the source of unity and legitimacy of the modern liberal state is no longer available. The post-modern polity is one that (self) perceives itself as lacking neutral tools to preserve justice and unity amidst a continuous clash among competing conceptions of the good.

Whether or not one shares the post-modern perspective, these two post-modern challenges, both of which originate from within a *participant* rather than an *observer* perspective, raise serious questions concerning the relevance of liberalism in the context of the normative life of the contemporary polity. In other words, even if one dismisses postmodernism from a philosophical standpoint, the fact remains that the former privileged position of secularism is now severely challenged and that there is little faith that neutral criteria can be found to promote justice in the multicultural polity.

As liberalism no longer seems adequate to meet the two post-modern challenges discussed earlier, are there any viable alternatives? Can peace and justice be legitimately maintained in a well functioning normatively coherent multi-ethnic, multi-religious, multi-cultural polity in which secularism can no longer be credibly privileged and in which no neutral grounds of unity and harmony can be found? What are the implications of the concurrent trends toward greater *external* harmonization through globalization of markets and ever more pervasive international and transnational regulation and toward *greater* internal differentiation through exacerbation of identity politics in settings where mass migration of labor and other factors cause a proliferation of clashing identities? What are the consequences of the apparent loss of legitimacy of liberalism for democracy, law, ethics, and politics?

Polities that comprise a multitude of competing conceptions of the good – as is the case for virtually all contemporary polities – are pluralistic-in-fact. In an earlier work, I argued that for polities that are pluralistic-in-fact "pluralism-as-norm," and in particular a conception of it that I labeled "comprehensive pluralism," offers the best available alternative for settling questions of justice, morals, ethics, and legitimacy (Rosenfeld 1998). Specifically, I emphasized that comprehensive pluralism is preferable to liberalism – understood here in the narrower sense of philosophical liberalism as opposed to liberalism as ideology, or as framing the broad political and institutional instrumentalities associated with modernism and the Enlightenment project – in two key respects. First, comprehensive pluralism lacks liberalism's bias toward the individual and is hence better suited to deal with group-based claims and group-regarding concerns such as those involved in identity politics (Id.: 213).

Second, comprehensive pluralism rejects liberalism's claims to neutrality, and is thus better suited than liberalism in the context of post-modern polities where appeals to neutrality tend to ring hollow.

I have also argued that comprehensive pluralism is preferable to republicanism and communitarianism, the two principal competitors to liberalism in contemporary legal, moral, and political philosophy grounded in the legacy of modernism and of the Enlightenment. Republicanism shifts the focus from liberalism's concentration on individual self-realization and self-fulfillment to the paramount valorization of self-government. To achieve self-government, one must "be forced to be free" to use Rousseau's famous expression (Rousseau 1947: 15), meaning that one must sacrifice the quest for individual self-fulfillment in the private sphere to assume the duties of the citizen who is responsible to partake in the governance of his or her polity through pursuit of the latter's common good or, to refer again to Rousseau, general will. Comprehensive pluralism rejects the paramouncy of self-government and considers the latter as one good among many. Moreover, whereas republicanism may be well suited to a city-state such as Rousseau's Geneva, it seems particularly problematic in an era of globalization and balkanization. Indeed, the more global governance becomes, the less influence the individual citizen is likely to be able to have. Conversely, as polities become increasingly internally balkanized without any prospect of overcoming pluralism-in-fact, the more difficult it will become to articulate a polity-wide common good or general will.

Communitarianism places pursuit of the communal good above all and thus opposes a group-regarding bias to liberalism's individual-regarding bias. Communitarianism is viable both in a Marxist communist setting and in a liberal capitalist one, though its contours are bound to vary significantly depending on whether it is linked to the former or the latter. In a liberal capitalist setting, communitarianism provides an antidote to the general liberal individualist emphasis, by stressing that ultimately individuals can only have meaningful lives and achieve their aspirations in communities. Accordingly, the market economy that fosters individualism must be complemented by institutional arrangements that enhance communal solidarity. Ultimately, communitarianism is biased in favor of the group, making comprehensive pluralism preferable to the extent that it does not harbor such a bias. In complex pluralistic societies, there are bound to be conflicts that pit the individual against the group, and normative criteria for resolving such conflicts are likely to be more authoritative if they lack all bias as between the two antagonists. As the concurrent trend toward globalization and balkanization evolves, certain groups tend toward greater homogeneity (e.g., solidification of ethnic identity in the face of vast waves of immigration), whereas others veer toward greater heterogeneity (e.g., Germany's society has become more diverse through integration of its Turkish origin minority). Under such circumstances, both individual-based and group-based biases seem bound to exacerbate difficulties, thus making recourse to comprehensive pluralism more desirable.

One of the important byproducts of the post-modern attack on modernism is the serious undermining of the legitimacy and appeal of philosophical monism. Monistic theories adhere to the view that there is a single source of validity and legitimacy for all normative issues (Rosenfeld 1998: 206). Utilitarianism is thus a monist theory as it sets the maximization of utilities as the ultimate criterion of normative validity, and so are most conceptions of liberalism, such as those of Kant, John Stuart Mill, Rawls, or Habermas, as well as republicanism and communitarianism. Moreover, the erosion of monism is but the other side of the coin of postmodernism's already alluded to witting or unwitting promotion of relativism.

Monism whether based on a deontological theory that claims universal validity and neutrality among all conceptions of the good, or on a teleological theory that postulates the ultimate validity of a single unified conception of the good, seems far from convincing in a world propelled toward globalization and balkanization. Relativism, in contrast, seems thoroughly plausible but highly dangerous. If all values and all norms can only be justified from the conception of the good from which they emanate, and if the prevailing conceptions of the good span a very broad spectrum and often clash with one another, this results in a complete lack of commonly shared normative criteria.

If one follows the logic of relativism strictly, then tolerance becomes the equivalent of intolerance, freedom of coercion, and equality of subordination. And this is particularly dangerous and unattractive for our own times as it might lead to the conclusion that Jihadist global terrorist is the moral equivalent of the Quaker pacifist so long as the terrorist can appeal to a normative justification *within* a particular collectively shared interpretation of Islam just as the pacifist can rely for her stance on publicly established Quaker precepts.

Under these circumstances, pluralism seems preferable both to monism and to relativism. I have argued, moreover, that comprehensive pluralism offers a systematic and unified approach that not only avoids the pitfalls of monism and relativism, but also allows for the greatest possible peaceful coexistence among the widest possible range of conceptions of the good (Rosenfeld 1998: 199–224). Pluralism, in general, and comprehensive pluralism, in particular, however, confront very high hurdles as it is very difficult to remain halfway between monism and relativism without eventually veering into one or the other. I have attempted to clear these hurdles by conceiving comprehensive pluralism dialectically as engaged in a dynamic in which it tends to draw closer to relativism in the course of its attack on monism, and, conversely, it tends to veer in the direction of monism in its determined rejection of relativism (Id.: 208–13), all the while remaining fully distinct from both of these.

This latter challenge continues to persist in light of arguments made by critics and of important changes in circumstances in the decade that followed the initial elaboration of comprehensive pluralism. One of the most challenging criticisms, expressed by Frank Michelman, is that to remain cogent comprehensive pluralism must either ultimately end up prescribing a Rawlsian overlapping consensus – and hence amount to a monism in disguise – or a mere modus vivendi – and thus retreat to relativism with an unsubstantiated hope that mutual acceptance and cooperation might nonetheless prevail (Michelman 2000). One the other hand, the expansion and exacerbation of the conflict between globalization and fragmentation, which certainly originated prior to the advent of the twenty-first century, but which came to occupy center stage after the September 11, 2001, global terrorist attack on the United States, raises new and serious questions concerning the viability or desirability of pluralism.

Just as the legitimation of liberal capitalism may depend on the existence of conditions of moderate scarcity, so too the appeal of pluralism may well be restricted to conditions of relatively moderate divergence among competing conceptions of the good. In short, pluralism may be particularly attractive for multi-cultural Canada, but entirely inappropriate in the context of a clash of civilizations (Huntington 1996), or of global terrorism and mutual intolerance between strong religion and secularism (Sajo 2009; Haarscher 2009). As already underscored, liberalism *suffices* to validate the struggle to safeguard the legacy of the Enlightenment against belligerent fundamentalism be it religious or ethnocentric in origin. But is not liberalism *necessary* as well as *sufficient* in the twin struggle against the intransigent would-be destroyers of Enlightenment values, and in favor of expanding coordination to free the Enlightenment project from its Westphalian moorings and propel it to completion on a global scale? If the answer were in the affirmative, then pluralism would, at best, become superfluous and, at worse, downright dangerous and counterproductive.

While recognizing that, under the conditions of a war of all against all, pluralism would become problematic and even perhaps of little practical use, I will argue and seek to make the case, throughout this book, that comprehensive pluralism is still best suited to meet the principal challenges that have come to the fore since September 11, 2001. Based on the conviction that there is a close dynamic nexus between theory and practice, I will endeavor to further clarify, deepen, elaborate, and expand the theoretical underpinnings and implications of comprehensive pluralism and test these against salient new practical concerns and challenges that confront the current era of globalization and fragmentation.

Keeping in mind the inextricable links between theory and practice, this book concentrates on two principal further elaborations of comprehensive pluralism that will expand and somewhat modify my previous account of it. The first of these elaborations relates to the theoretical underpinnings and contours of comprehensive pluralism; the second, to its practical applications under recent conditions pitting greater divergence against greater convergence.

In my initial account of comprehensive pluralism I stressed that *if* a society is pluralist-in-fact, *then* comprehensive pluralism affords the best available means of normative legitimation and validation (Rosenfeld 1998: 200–8). I also focused primarily on comprehensive pluralism's potential regarding inter-communal relationships. In what follows, I will endeavor further to explore comprehensive pluralism's potential and argue that it bests all its plausible rivals under all the conceivable conditions that may be encountered by contemporary societies. Accordingly, I will maintain that comprehensive pluralism is best regardless of whether or not a polity finds itself under conditions of pluralism-in-fact. As we shall see, this latter proposition is important because of its theoretical implications, even if it has little practical effect given that all contemporary polities ultimately seem to be pluralistic-in-fact. Moreover, the theoretical implications in question will become manifest in the exploration of the potential of comprehensive pluralism for intra-communal dealings. Finally, to further explain and buttress my claim that comprehensive pluralism remains distinct from both monism and relativism, I will briefly compare and contrast it to value pluralism as articulated by Isaiah Berlin (Berlin 1970: 167–72) and subsequently expanded as a theory of contemporary moral philosophy (Galston 2009: 803).

From the standpoint of practical applications, the focus of analysis will concentrate on new problems that have surged since September 11, 2001, or on new perceptions that have emerged since that date with respect to problems that had been identified earlier. How does comprehensive pluralism fare in light of the changes brought about by globalization, fragmentation, and balkanization; global terror and the reactions to it; the difficulties surrounding de-relativized and de-privatized religion; the exacerbation of conflicts between the individual and the group; the tensions between legal unity and the rapidly growing plurality of layered and segmented, often inconsistent, and, at times, even contradictory, legal regimes (Rosenfeld 2008)?

I will argue that comprehensive pluralism affords the best available means to salvage and redirect the project of the Enlightenment conceived as an ongoing dynamic process evolving over time that adapts, meets certain challenges, and puts them behind it, only to confront new ones that require further retooling and fine-tuning. It is thus true that the role of reason can no longer be the same after the spread of the disenchantment referred to previously. But that does not necessarily imply that other conceptions or uses of reason may not be available to work hand in hand with adaptation of comprehensive pluralism to meet the aforementioned new challenges that confront it. Furthermore, in its trajectory since the times of the French Revolution, the project of the Enlightenment has advanced the pursuit of liberty and equality for all through the eradication of particular inequalities and though removal of certain obstacles to liberty, and has embraced certain conceptions of liberty and equality, such as the liberal one, to the exclusion of others. Keeping in mind the victories achieved, the directions taken, the persisting problems yet to be solved, and the new challenges that must be confronted, there is no apparent impediment to teaming up the project of the Enlightenment with comprehensive pluralism to carry forward the ongoing quest for equal liberty.

The book is divided into three parts. Part I, entitled "Liberal Justice and Fleeting Specters of Unity," concentrates on the increasingly insurmountable difficulties that liberalism confronts in an ever more plural world. Part I consists of three chapters. Chapter 1, "Reframing Comprehensive Pluralism: Hegel versus Rawls," situates comprehensive pluralism in relation to value pluralism and emphasizes the former's dialectical nature, its Hegelian roots, and its dynamic concurrent struggle against monism and relativism. Specifically, when properly viewed in its full dialectical potential, comprehensive pluralism emerges as neither collapsible into a monistic Rawlsian "overlapping consensus" nor into a relativistic "modus vivendi." Chapter 2, "Equality and the Dialectic Between Identify and Difference," provides a plural-ist account of the dynamic between self and other and between identity and diffe-rence, which has played a central role in conceptions of equality since Aristotle's injunction to treat "equals equally and unequals unequally" (Aristotle 1980: bk. V). Liberals have typically had difficulty with difference, tending to equate equality with identity. This poses particular problems for plural societies and for group equality claims. Based on a critique of work by Jeremy Waldron, which tackles these diffi-culties from a liberal perspective, this chapter reconceives equality dialectically into three successive stages, the first linking difference to inequality, the second, equality to identity, and the third, equality to difference. Chapter 2 concludes by drawing implications from this dialectic approach and suggests how a pluralist approach can lead to the overcoming of liberal shortcomings. Chapter 3, "Human Rights and the Clash Between Universalism and Relativism: The Case of Minority Group Rights," builds on the analysis of the dynamics of equality in the Chapter 2 for purposes of a critique of the culture wars concerning the universality of post–World War II human rights. Emphasizing that when viewed in a pluralist light, the dichotomy between universalism and relativism is a false one, the chapter concludes that human rights are neither universal nor merely relative. Furthermore, by focusing on the clash between individual rights and (minority) group rights, Chapter 3 highlights the differences between pluralism and liberalism and those between liberalism and communitarianism. Based on that analysis, the chapter argues for the superiority of pluralism over even complex and nuanced conceptions of liberalism, such as that advanced by Will Kymlicka.

Part II is entitled "E Pluribus Unum?" and it zeroes in on three very different attempts to find unity amidst diversity. On the surface, there may seen to be little connection between Spinoza, the constitutional protection of religious pluralism, and Dworkin's famous claim that there is a single right answer for every hard case. On a deeper level, however, all three deal with the key concept of tolerance and with the necessity to reconcile unity and plurality in ways that imply the constant work of a dialectic of inclusion and exclusion. Chapter 4, "Spinoza's Dialectic and the Paradoxes of Tolerance: Can Unity Be Willed out of Necessity?," examines Spinoza's advocacy of tolerance, which is puzzling in view of his absolute devotion to reason and to the indissoluble unity of the universe implicit in his pantheism. Nonetheless, and even though he often equates religion with superstition, Spinoza advocates widespread religious tolerance. Spinoza was not a pluralist, but his defense of tolerance is particularly relevant for a contemporary pluralist because of Spinoza's dialectical approach and because he justifies tolerance neither on the basis of skepticism nor on that of moral relativism. Moreover, Spinoza lived in a period of intense religious conflict and as an excommunicated Jew in a Christian society was well acquainted with both intra-communal and inter-communal intolerance. Spinoza's dialectic is particularly relevant to comprehensive pluralism for unlike Hegel's or Marx's it lacks any assumption of an inexorable march to ever-greater progress and integration. Two of Spinoza's insights are particularly instructive for pluralists: First, though there is one truth and it is discoverable through reason, religion can provide different, even if partial, insights into the same truth; and, second, in a world that is in fact divided, albeit because of passion and prejudice, tolerance achieved through self-constraint and acceptance of diversity may be the best means to preserve political peace and unity.

Chapter 5, "The Clash Between Deprivatized Religion and Relativized Secularism: The Constitutional Conundrum," tackles the constitutional problems raised by the endeavor to preserve freedom *of* religion and freedom *from* religion in light of the politicization of strong religion and the relativization of secularism discussed earlier. These problems underscore the inadequacy of liberalism under current circumstances and pose a daunting challenge to comprehensive pluralism. I will argue that comprehensive pluralism can meet that challenge and point the way to the best available constitutional means to promote peace among conflicting religions.

Chapter 6, "Dworkin and the One Law Principle: Can Unity Be Imposed Through an Interpretive Turn?," deals with Dworkin's much maligned "one right answer" for every hard case thesis, which is easily attacked if taken out of context but which has much to offer if taken in its full and proper setting. Dworkin's project is a hermeneutic one. He seeks to reconstruct adjudication in hard cases in relation to a systematic commitment to an equal concern and equal respect principle interpreted from within a liberal egalitarian vision that resembles that of Rawls. Dworkin accepts that the world is pluralistic-in-fact and seeks to construct unity out of diversity focusing on the practical task of adjudication through creative deployment of a counterfactual liberal imagination. Ultimately, however, Dworkin's project fails, and the one-answer thesis cannot be vindicated both for internal and external reasons. Dworkin's liberalism like all liberalism is monistic and hence intolerant of non-liberal viewpoints. Moreover, Dworkin's reconstructive hermeneutics is so bound to his egalitarian-liberalism that it proves unacceptable even to proponents of other strands of liberalism such as libertarian-liberalism. The lesson from a pluralist standpoint is that Dworkin's too restrictive reconstructive hermeneutics must give way to an approach that is more accommodating of diversity so as not to unduly foreclose acceptance or accommodation of a wide range of conceptions of the good.

Part III is entitled "Can Pluralism Thrive in Times of Stress? On Globalization, Terror, and the Clash of Cultures." Its purpose is to provide a critical assessment of the ways in which globalization, global terrorist fundamentalism, and further intensification of identity politics, in a world that is increasingly wired together, threaten the viability of Enlightenment-based normative theories and of the institutional mainstays of contemporary constitutional democracy. This critical assessment will proceed by placing dramatic recent developments in historical perspective and by examining some of the most salient theoretical reactions to them.

Chapter 7 is entitled "Rethinking Political Rights in Times of Stress: Can Pluralism Thwart the Progression from Stress to Crisis?" The reaction to global terrorism and the waging of the "war on terror" (e.g., through legislation that greatly enhances the powers of the state such as the U.S. Patriot Act, through curtailment of civil liberties, or through extensive domestic surveillance) has posed significant threats to fundamental rights and to democratic institutions. Through focus on a broad conception of political rights, this chapter places these in a historical and a pluralist perspective in light of recent exigencies. From a pluralist standpoint, politics involves striving to achieve a proper balance between identity and difference among self and other (or, more precisely, selves and others). Moreover, for politics to function adequately, a sufficient level of overall identity must be maintained in relation to the polity taken as a whole among all those who interact as selves and others within such polity. A distinction can be drawn between ordinary times, times of stress, and times of crisis, according to whether the requisite overall identity is under no significant threat, under pressure but with no present danger of unraveling, or under palpable threat of dissolution. After articulating a pluralist perspective on politics in times of stress, Chapter 7 compares the latter to its liberal, communitarian, and republican counterparts and argues for the superiority of pluralism. The focus on times of stress is exemplary because recourse to pluralism seems more urgent and easiest justified when unity is more fragile without being on the brink of tearing. Moreover contemporary circumstances, as the chapter will indicate, often give rise to conditions of stress making them to a significant degree typical of the age.

The next two chapters tackle two different diagnoses of global terrorism and two different normative and practical approaches to it, one based on an ethics that places greater emphasis on difference, and the other, on an ethics of identity. Furthermore, both of these theoretical approaches are steeped in the Enlightenment and claim that they offer ways of coping with the threats posed by global terrorism that are consistent with maintaining and furthering the project of the Enlightenment. Chapter 8, "Derrida's Deconstructive Ethics of Difference Confronts Global Terrorism: Can Democracy Survive the Autoimmune Ravage of the Terror Within Us?," provides a critical pluralist assessment of Derrida's diagnosis and normative appraisal of global terrorism. Derrida claims that global terrorism defies meaning and that it forms part of what is the equivalent of an autoimmune disease within the body politics of Western democracies, and above all the United States. Furthermore, Derrida condemns global terrorism from the standpoint of his deconstructive ethics of difference, which requires reaching to, and caring for, the other in all his or her singularity. The autoimmune metaphor is important as global terrorism highlights that the other can be as easily within as without. On the other hand, pluralism reveals that Derrida's ethics of difference is ultimately unsatisfactory. Global terrorism need not be meaningless, and no cogency or systematic condemnation of it can issue from an ethics allowing for an infinite proliferation of singularities, and thus becoming, for all relevant purposes, the functional equivalent of relativism.

Chapter 9, "Habermas's Discourse Ethics of Identity and Global Terror: Can Cosmopolitanism, Post-Nationalism, and Dialogue Downsize the Terrorist Threat?," assesses Habermas's diagnosis and assessment of global terrorism from the standpoint of an ethics of identity. Whereas Derrida regards global terrorism as posing an internal threat to the project of the Enlightenment, Habermas deems such terrorism to pose an external threat. As previously noted, for Habermas global terrorism goes hand in hand with globalization, but it could be overcome if economic globalization were complemented with an appropriate set of supra-national constitutional norms and political institutions. Consistent with Habermas's conception of communicative ethics, the combination of cosmopolitan governance, transnational government, and constitutional patriotism could lead to a proper constraining and legitimation of globalization. From that perspective, global terrorism stems from gross material inequities rather than from any clash of cultures. Accordingly, such terrorism represents a breakdown in communications which is amenable to redress. Viewed from a pluralist perspective, however, Habermas's communicative framework achieves unity and identity at too great a price and unduly reduces religious fundamentalism to a mere symptom of economic resentment. Moreover, this has important consequences not only in terms of the meaning and handling of global terrorism but also in terms of the viability of transnational purportedly unifying normatively regulative devices such as constitutional patriotism.

Chapter 10, "Conclusion: The Hopes of Comprehensive Pluralism in a More Unified and More Fragmented World," assesses the potential of pluralist solutions to the issues examined throughout the preceding inquiry and details how such a pluralist approach may help rechart and redirect the project of the Enlightenment. This chapter will also detail how pluralism, for all its virtues, is also limited, and how fundamentalist fanaticism, if fully unleashed, could well end up destroying pluralism in a war to the end between a self and another that are radically and irreversibly estranged from one another.

PART I

Liberal Justice and Fleeting Specters of Unity

1

Reframing Comprehensive Pluralism

Hegel versus Rawls

1.1. THE PROBLEMATIC NEXUS BETWEEN
UNITY AND PLURALITY

At a very basic level, pluralism is inevitable. So long as the "I" remains distinct from the "Thou," the self from the other, perspectives must remain, in some meaningful sense, plural. The implications from this observation, however, are far from obvious. On the one hand, it follows from the fact that the relationship between self and other – be they two individuals, rival tribes or nations, or contending ideologies aspiring to universality such as liberal capitalism and Marxist communism – is irreducible, and that therefore pluralism can go "all the way down." On the other hand, the fact of pluralism in this barest of all manifestations does not appear to carry any palpable normative implications. Does the fact that one is always confronted with a plurality of perspectives entail any moral, political, or legal "ought"? Arguably, not. Indeed, one can cogently argue that the differences between self and other are normatively irrelevant and that what counts is that they are both selves entitled to equal dignity. In that case, *normative* pluralism would be unjustified. Or, conversely, one can insist that overlooking the differences between self and other could only lead to injustice and subordination as one would inevitably end up favoring some over others, thus making normative pluralism the only legitimate alternative.

Viewing the matter from a normative perspective, pluralism – at least the fact of pluralism – must be taken into account when one encounters and interacts with a stranger. This is vividly illustrated by reference to the advent of the independent market for the exchange of goods. As Max Weber puts it, "the market was originally a consociation of persons who are not members of the same group and who are, therefore, 'enemies'" (Weber 1968: 672). Because market transactions are among strangers, they cannot come within the purview of any one of the respective communal norms of those who have traveled away from home to exchange goods. I cannot impose my own customs and mores on a stranger with whom I wish to exchange goods, and I cannot subject that stranger to the authorities within my own community, should something go wrong with the proposed exchange we are about to carry out. To fairly account for the plurality of unshared communal normative commitments spread among all the strangers involved, market transactions must therefore be subjected to norms that transcend those not shared by all those who have come to market. And, the normative regime laid out by modern contract law presumably fills that need and supposedly allows for market exchanges that are fair and efficient (Rosenfeld 1985: 811–14).[1]

Free markets and modern contract law are historically linked to the advent of the ideology of individualism, itself inextricably bound to the emergence of modern Western civilization (Dumont 1977: 4). Individualism contrasts sharply with the organicist and collectivist ideology that prevailed in the Middle Ages, according to which the individual did not live for her sake but to perform specific functions for the common good (Lukes 1973: 46). Medieval society was "one whole and was indivisible, and within it the individual was no more than a part" (Ullmann 1967: 42). Consistent with this distinction, medieval ideology was anti-pluralistic, and modern individualism is necessarily pluralistic (in fact). Indeed, within the perspective of individualism, every individual relates to others as a "stranger" inasmuch as each individual constitutes a world unto herself in that she is the master of her own desires, priorities, commitments, objectives, and, to use Rawls's expression, "plan of life" (Rawls 1971: 92–4). Thus, every other individual's aspirations and objectives are "alien" to me, and, conversely, I remain estranged from others to the extent that they cannot comprehend or appreciate my desires, commitments, goals, and aspirations as I do.

Whereas the ideology of the Middle Ages requires normative negation of plurality, that of individualism mandates a normative accounting and accommodation of plurality. An individual should be at a minimum allowed, and at best encouraged, to develop and pursue a plan of life of her own and differences among individual plans of life ought to be, in principle, respected. The difficult question is to find the appropriate normative framework that would best enable the plurality in question to flourish. Is monism as embodied in liberalism, in general, or in Kantian morality or utilitarianism, in particular, preferable? Or, is pluralism more likely ultimately to prove the normatively superior way to give plurality its due?

The answers to these questions are far from obvious, for unless one resorts systematically to relativism – which, as already stressed, would be highly undesirable –

---

[1] The market not only allows strangers to interact but also transforms into strangers all those who come to exchange. This is exemplified by the English doctrine of "sale in market overt." According to this rule, all sales at an open market or fair are valid even if a merchant sells property he has stolen to a bona fide buyer. This creates an exception to the general rule under English property law that a victim of theft can recover her property from an innocent buyer who obtained the said property from the thief (Rosenfeld 1985: 887). Accordingly, communally grounded English property law gives ground to "stranger"-based contract law in every open market or fair on English soil.

accommodating plurality requires finding a plausible and legitimate way to reconcile and harmonize unity and diversity. This latter problem similarly confronts the free market economy as envisaged by Adam Smith, which goes hand in hand with the modern ideology of individualism, and with any normative framework that might offer the best available set of moral and legal precepts to properly sustain plurality and individual singularity.

In Adam Smith's view, what sets the market in motion is the convergence of multiple atomistic would-be traders guided exclusively by self-interest to the utter disregard of the common good or public interest (Smith 1976: 18).[2] Moreover, at least initially, each individual comes to the market with his own subjective appraisal of what he seeks to obtain though a market exchange.[3] Accordingly, the market confronts two sets of divergences due to plurality among its participants; conflicting individual self-interests; and inconsistent attributions of use value to goods available for trade among various would-be traders.

In Smith's vision, plurality must be preserved for the market to function, for if self-interest were replaced by altruism and differences in use value were erased, the impetus for exchange and competition would be destroyed. On the other hand, the plurality at the individual market participant level is complemented by unity at the level of the market as a whole. As Smith sees it, competition fueled by conflicting self-interests yields the common good as what he terms "an invisible hand" transforms a series of discrete contractual market exchanges fueled by a plurality of interests and aims into a maximization of wealth that inures to the benefit of all (Id.: 477). Moreover, the incommensurable plurality of subjective use values is translated in the course of contractual market exchanges, for Smith, into a common language of intersubjective exchange values (Id.: 32) or, to put it in contemporary terminology, the market functions by systematically transforming the plurality of inputs it encounters into a unified and fungible whole through monetarization. Moreover, what is crucial, for our purposes, is that the Smithian market needs to preserve at once both plurality, as expressed in use- values, and unity, as manifested in exchange values, in order to function.

The Smithian market preserves both plurality and unity in their full integrity in a harmonious whole that is held together by a constant dynamic that binds plurality to unity, in part, through the "invisible hand," and, in part, through a nexus

---

[2] As Smith famously put it, "it is not from the benevolence of the butcher, the brewer, or the baker, that we expect our dinner, but from their regard to their own interests. We address ourselves, not to their humanity but to their self-love" (Smith 1976: 18).

[3] Once a market is well established, traders may only be concerned with maximizing wealth, becoming totally indifferent concerning what is traded in order to achieve that aim. Initially, in contrast, presumably one goes to market to trade apples for oranges because, as a matter of personal taste or need, one prefers oranges to apples.

between use value and exchange value.[4] The perfect Smithian market is, of course, a counterfactual ideal that no real-life market can closely approximate. As stressed over two hundred years after the formulation of Smith's economic theory, "there has never been and almost certainly there never will be a modern consolidated democracy in a pure market economy" (Linz & Stepan 1996: 11). More importantly, in the context of the present inquiry, even on the assumption of a perfect market economy, nothing homologous springs to mind in the realms of morals, law, and politics. Significantly, even Smith's own moral theory predicated on sympathy toward the other (Smith: 1976) is at odds with the "morals" of the Smithian market where replacing self-love and self-interest by sympathy would be disastrous (Rosenfeld 1985: 876). More generally, it is difficult to imagine, even counterfactually, a coherent equivalent to the "invisible hand" or to the seamless fluidity that binds use value to exchange value in Smith market economy applicable to the realms of morals, law or politics.

In the absence of a systematic construct akin to the Smithian market, two alternatives loom as plausible for purposes of developing the best possible normative framework for morals, law, and politics, consistent with individualism and with the project of the Enlightenment. The first alternative is predicated on monism, and it primes unity over plurality; the second, on pluralism, and it places greater emphasis on plurality than on unity as such. Both of these, however, must adequately account for that which they seem to relegate to the second position, namely plurality for monism, and unity for pluralism.

There are two predominant monistic approaches: the deontological one that emerges from the revolutionary theory of morals elaborated by Kant and the teleological one, most notoriously developed in the theory of utilitarianism. Kant's theory and utilitarianism will be briefly examined, respectively, in Sections 1.2 and 1.3. I will next briefly explore the version of pluralism that seems to best fit with individualism and liberalism, namely value pluralism as articulated by Isaiah Berlin, and I will assess how it manages to account for the nexus between unity and plurality (Section 1.4). After concluding that neither monism nor value pluralism is the optimal alternative, I will lay out the case for comprehensive pluralism and emphasize its Hegelian roots and allegiances (Section 1.5). After that, I will briefly revisit the distinction between the modern and the post-modern and between homogeneous and heterogeneous polities from the perspective of *participants* as opposed to *observers* (Section 1.6). I will then underscore the implications of comprehensive

---

[4]   The precise relationship between use value and exchange value has remained rather elusive, and
     Adam Smith shed little light on it (Samuelson 1976: 438). What is important for our purposes, however, is that there would be no impulse to trade in the market in the absence of use value, and no
     rational unified and systematic market without exchange value.

pluralism's embrace of the good over the right and defend it against critics such as Habermas (Habermas 1998a: 405) and Michelman (2000) (Section 1.7). Finally, I will seek to demonstrate that, if properly understood in terms of its Hegelian dynamics, comprehensive pluralism remains distinct from, and more suited to contemporary needs than, Rawls's most pluralistic among his philosophical accounts, namely that concerning an "overlapping consensus" in his *Political Liberalism* (Rawls 1993) (Section 1.8).

1.2. THE KANTIAN REVOLUTION: SEVERING UNITY FROM PLURALITY

Kant proposes to dispel the normative conundrum posed by the confrontation between the need for unity and the fact of plurality, by sundering the realm of the right from that of the good, and by granting priority to the former over the latter (Kant 1969). What allows Kant systematically to keep separate the realm meant to be ruled by unity from that ruled by plurality is the deployment of the categorical imperative (Id.: 53–4), which allows for a counterfactual construction of normative links between self and other above and beyond any clash among a multiplicity of conceptions of the good that might otherwise divide those who share in common the same socio-political space.

Drawing on the distinction between morality (*Moralität*) and ethics (*Sittlichkeit*) steeped in the philosophies of Kant and Hegel, one may posit "morals" as encompassing universally valid rights, duties, and norms of justice that transcend all conceptions of the good. "Ethics," in contrast, refers, under this approach, to the mores, prudential maxims, and normative standards of a historically grounded community with its own conception of the good.[5] Furthermore, consistent with individualism, the postulation of the equal autonomy of all individuals and reliance on the rule of reason, Kant proposes universally applicable moral norms that are self-imposed. In the Kantian counterfactual construct, every autonomous individual freely assumes the duties flowing from the categorical imperative deduced from the axiom that individuals, being free, equal, and autonomous, ought to treat one another as ends-in-themselves and not as means (Kant 1969: 53–4). It is what is the same in every individual as a moral being that frames the realm of universal rights and duties and that guarantees unity throughout. At the level of

---

[5]   These definitions of "morals" and "ethics" run somewhat counter to the understanding of these terms in Anglo-American philosophy. Nevertheless, the definitions in question are particularly useful in the present context, not only in terms of the discussion centering on Kant and Hegel, but also in terms of theories propounded by Rawls and Habermas.

Kantian morals, therefore, individuals, rights, duties, and criteria of justice com-
mensurate with the conception of persons as ends-in-themselves transcend all
competing conceptions of the good and remain, in principle, neutral as between
all of the latter.[6]

Pursuant to Kant's theory, there is unity at the level of the right and plurality at
that of the good. But given the priority of the right over the good, there ought to be
also a significant measure of unity within the arena reserved for intersubjective dealings regarding the good, to the extent that the right is meant to restrict the bounds
within which pursuit of the good can proceed legitimately. On closer examination,
however, Kant's categorical imperative renders plurality incompatible with morals,
and morals impossible as patently inconsistent with any intersubjective dealings in
which real interests and conflicting conceptions of the good are at play. If the self
must treat all others *only* as ends-in-themselves, then all market exchanges, employment relations, professional services, and the like would be immoral because they
require treating the other, at least in part, as means. It would thus make no difference whether an employment contract were fair or unfair, humane or exploitative,
for both employer and employee must per force relate to one another in some significant way as means. As Hegel has emphasized, Kant's morals are ultimately purely
formal and empty (Hegel 1952: Para. 135,135A), and that is because to achieve unity,
each individual must be shorn of all attributes and of all individuality. Accordingly,
Kantian morals reduces self and other to equivalent, and hence interchangeable,
purely abstract egos. And as such, the pursuit of unity in a realm of ends ruled
by universal duties ultimately boils down to solipsistic self-effacement and self-
constraint.[7]

The conclusion that Kant's theory leads to the radical and revolutionary proposition that morals are both necessary to ground the normatively requisite unity and
impossible in the real world imparts a very important negative lesson for the search
for a normative bridge between unity and plurality. There can be no perfect or
purely transcendent unity. At the same time, morals cannot be derived legitimately
from any single contested conception of the good, or from any particular culturally
grounded vision of ethics.

---

[6] Neutrality-in-principle, does not necessarily entail neutrality-in-fact. This might be for largely trivial
    reasons, as in a case in which some of those involved were to pick the categorical imperative as the
    overriding principle of their own conception of the good. In that case, we would seem to have, at
    most, a semantic quibble. Is the categorical imperative good because it is right? Or is it right because
    it looms as equally good for all? In other cases, however, there may be conceptions of the good that
    happen to fare better than others when subjected to the regime of rights and duties stemming from
    the categorical imperative. In the latter cases, formal impartiality may be preserved, but not substan-
    tive neutrality. This issue will be further explored in the course of the following discussion.
[7] It is noteworthy in this connection that Kant himself places pragmatism ahead of morals when it
    comes to evaluating law (Kant 1970: 118–19).

1.2.1. *Adapting Kant: The Pure Social Contract Proceduralist Approach*

One could remain consistent with the negative lesson deriving from Kant's theory, and yet remain in the deontological monistic camp, by embracing a procedural conception of morals. Such a procedural approach seems to present important advantages: It does not set the realm of unity above and beyond that of plurality; it does not seem to require the ego to shed its interests or conception of the good; and it presumably allows for fair substantive results, which would permit (re)integrating morals within the realm of the possible.

The procedural approach in question is that put forth by modern social contract theory, or more precisely by one of the two principal versions of it, namely *pure* social contract theory. The latter, which is to be distinguished from *derivative* social contract theory (Rosenfeld 1985: 857), holds in essence that given fair bargaining conditions, just and legitimate norms and institutions are those that are the product of a freely entered into, mutually agreed upon, pact among all those who will be subjected to the norms and institutions in question. In pure social contract theory, it is the contractual procedure and the fact of agreement that bestow normative validity. In derivative social contract theory, in contrast, the ultimate source of normative validity is not contractual, relegating the contractual device to a heuristic function. Of the four major modern social contract theorists, Hobbes and Rousseau are exponents of pure social contract theory, whereas Locke and Kant are advocates of derivative social contract theory (Id.), For Kant as we have seen, what makes norms binding is their universality, and hence in his invocation, the social contract, is largely rhetorical. Since every rational person should recognize universal norms as valid and binding, it follows that all rational persons would agree to be bound by such norms based on the dictates of reason (Gough 1957: 18).

For pure social contract theory, the relevant contract is supposed to operate in a way that is analogous to that in which contracts of exchange do in an economic market pursuant to modern contract law. The paradigmatic legal contract is one of exchange between two individuals, each with different interests and aims who must find common ground to advance their respective aims. If they reach a contractual agreement, then the terms of their contract embody their joint will in relation to the exchange at stake. That joint will differs, however, from the initial respective wills of the two (then) would-be contractors who set out to bargain for an exchange. A buyer wishes to pay the least possible for the good he covets while the seller seeks to charge as much as possible for it. As a consequence of fair bargaining between the two, the buyer will end up paying more than initially hoped for but less than what would have prompted him to walk away from the transaction; and, the seller will get less than initially sought, but more than what would have caused her to refuse to sell. In this setting, the contract provides unity and protects plurality, but only in a somewhat restricted and redirected manner. Significantly, the unity embodied in the contract terms is parasitic on there being a plurality of interests among would-be contractors, and, conversely, the plurality that results from the consummation of the relevant contractual transaction is reprocessed through the unity embodied in the relevant contractual terms.

The social contract under pure social contract theory is supposed to operate analogously, the main differences being that it is a contract among all individuals who find themselves within the same polity – be it a city-state, a Westphalian nation-state, a supra-national entity such as the EU, or even an eventual global republic – and that the subject matter of that contract is norms and institutions rather than goods. In both cases, the contract device affords procedural means to reconcile unity and plurality "from within," and the *fact* of agreement becomes the source of justice, legitimacy, and normative validity. Through market contracts, individuals acquire as many as possible of the material goods they covet in the pursuit of their conception of the good under the best possible terms they can bargain for with equally situated individuals seeking exchanges to further their own conception of the good. Through the social contract, on the other hand, individuals agree to be bound by the norms and institutions that would lend support to the pursuit of their conception of the good as best as possible under the best possible terms they can bargain for with similarly situated individuals who have a similar design and who are within the same polity.

There is a crucial dis-analogy between a legally binding contract and one associated with pure social contract theory insofar as the former involves an actual factual agreement among the contractors whereas the latter does not (Rosenfeld 1998a: 294). Pure social contract theory draws its procedural legitimacy from the *making* of the relevant contract, yet that crucial event turns out to be counterfactual. The social contractors envisaged by Hobbes do not actually conclude an agreement, but are imagined to produce one counterfactually given their stark choice between living in a state of war and finding peace and security in organized civil society (Hobbes 1973: 64–5; 1978: 184). Moreover, if that were not problematic enough, there is no equivalent to Adam Smith's "invisible hand" or to the relationship between use value and exchange value, which ultimately renders arbitrary what is produced (albeit counterfactually) through deployment of the social contract procedure. For Hobbes, so great is the fear of the war of all against all that the social contract results in voluntary submission to an absolute monarch (Hobbes 1978: 189–90). For Rousseau, on the other hand, the focus is so much centered on self-government that individuals must greatly limit, if not abandon, their private pursuits to partake in the political implementation of the general will, which he characterizes as the sum of differences between all the individual wills, or as the "agreement of all interests" which "is produced by opposition to that of each" (Rousseau 1947: 26 & n.2). More generally, given different conceptions of background conditions, actual interests and conceptions of the good represented, and the relative strength of each of the represented groups involved, any resulting agreement would be either purely contingent or arbitrary. Suppose a group that shares Hobbes's vision tries to reach an agreement with a group that subscribes to Rousseau's. Is there any reason to believe that either group would convince the other, or that some midpoint could be found between those who seek security above all and those who consider self-government paramount? And, even supposing an agreement, is there any reason to believe that the resulting institutional agreement could be regarded plausibly as equally fair to both groups?

Pure social contract theory does bring unity and plurality within the same plane, but even when it gives them both determinate content within a purely procedural framework, it fails to yield, except perhaps by pure happenstance, institutions that all social contractors would or should accept as just, legitimate or normatively valid. One possible way to overcome this difficulty while staying within the bounds of proceduralist contractarian deontological monism is to combine Kantian universalism with contractarianism. This is what Rawls sets out to achieve in his *A Theory of Justice* (Rawls 1971), and Habermas, in his discourse theoretical proceduralism, which though it exceeds the bounds of contractarianism (Rosenfeld 1998a: 33), also combines Kant with consensus-based legitimation.

1.2.2. *Rawls's Kantian Contractarianism in* A Theory of Justice

Both Rawls and Habermas incorporate Kantian universalism as the source for the normative validation of the requisite pole of unity, but purport to make it of this world by refusing to sever morals from interests. Rawls's contractarianism, based on a hypothetical social contract which contractors conclude behind "a veil of ignorance" (Rawls 1971: 11) allows for interests to be factored in, but holds back from its hypothetical contractors *which* particular interests they may actually have (Id.: 12). Habermas, for his part, though he embraces Kant's universalism and split between morals and ethics, parts company with Kant by allowing consideration of all interests in the communicative process designed to determine the validity of norms (Habermas 1990: 195, 203–4).

Rawls places his hypothetical contractors in an original position behind a veil of ignorance to overcome the moral arbitrariness of Hobbesian contractarianism. In contrast to Hobbes's contractors who seek the most advantageous terms to best further their own arbitrary will, Rawls's contractors seek to agree on mutually acceptable principles of justice (Rawls 1971: 11–12). The veil of ignorance is supposed to preclude bargaining power advantages for any of the contractors. As Rawls specifies, none of the contractors "knows … his class position or social status … his fortune in the distribution of natural assets and abilities … [his] conception [ ] of the good or [his] special psychological propensities" (Id.: 12). Based on this, it is clear that each contractor is severed from his own interests, but not from interests in general, as Rawls attributes to each contractor an attitude of prudence and risk averseness in regard to what remains hidden behind the veil of ignorance. Rawls postulates that his contractors will embrace the "maximin rule," according to which each alternative will be considered from the standpoint of those who would be the worst off under it, and the maximin rule will compel the choice of the alternative in which the worst off are better off than would the worst off be in all other alternatives (Id.: 152–3). Consistent with all this, the contractors are led to settle on the following two principles of justice. The first principle, which is lexically prior to the second, is that all should be entitled to equal liberty (Id.: 60). The second principle, known as the "difference principle," in turn, postulates that inequalities in wealth and social status are only justified if they improve the lot of the worst off, and if they maintain fair equality of opportunity regarding access to positions of wealth and power (Id.: 302).

I have extensively examined the shortcomings stemming from Rawls's contractarian approach elsewhere (Rosenfeld 1991: 233–7; 1998: 126–8). For present purposes, I will only focus briefly on three problems that highlight Rawls's unwitting sacrifice of plurality in A *Theory of Justice* in his efforts to safeguard Kantian unity by fitting it within a contractarian framework. First, by putting on the veil of ignorance, Rawls's hypothetical contractors are reduced to abstract egos that are completely uprooted from any social, cultural, or ideological setting. The only thing they know about diversity or plurality is that it exists, but they do not know in what it consists, or how it would affect them. From this standpoint, there seems to be no significant difference between Rawls's and Kant's conceptions of the abstract ego.

Second, there is an important difference in how Rawls and Kant arrive at unity and universality, and that difference creates serious additional problems for Rawls. Unlike Kant, who casts unity as transcendent and otherworldly, Rawls is intent on situating unity within the bounds of the immanent world in which intersubjective dealings actually take place. Rawls does this by taking actual individuals and peeling off layer by layer what makes them different from others until he arrives at the abstract egos behind the veil of ignorance that are ready to agree on commonly shared principles of justice for their polity. The process of abstraction involved, however, is not neutral and it ends up favoring certain perspectives and certain conceptions of the good over others. Is the abstract ego that emerges at the end of the process of abstraction a man or a woman? Even assuming that one could imagine an individual without any sex identity whatsoever, there are gender-based differences that may not be transcended, forcing a choice, albeit an unconscious one, between a masculinist or feminist perspective. Some feminists have claimed that he social contract itself is full of bias as it establishes a "fraternal patriarchy" through which men rule over women (Pateman 1988: 2, 108). But even if one believes that

Rawlsian contractarianism in itself is not gender biased, the hypothetical contractors on which it relies cannot be genderless. And that means that the relevant process of abstraction cannot avoid preferring one gender-based perspective over others while projecting an image of gender-based neutrality. Moreover, the same goes for race, ethnicity, religion, culture and ideology to the extent that these raise identity-based issues.[8]

Finally, the third problem stems from Rawls's reliance on the maximin rule, which far from being neutral introduces two key biases that several actual, as opposed to hypothetical, social contractors would object to. First, risk averseness is hardly universally shared and many would-be contractors could well have conceptions of the good or plans of life according to which taking greater risks to achieve loftier aims would be normatively compelling. These normative perspectives would be excluded ex ante from the search for principles of justice. Second, maximin works in contexts in which quantification is relevant, but not in most others. Maximin is thus geared to social and economic policy as the difference principle attests. But what about would-be contractors for whom economic justice is of relatively minor concern as they focus above all on non-quantifiable concerns? For example, an individual who believes that the sanctity of life is absolute and that life begins at conception may well consider equal respect for all life as the paramount moral duty and the most important requirement of justice. For such an individual maximin is of little use, for even if as a prudential matter she would prefer a polity with fewer abortions over one with more, she could not agree to any principle of justice that would condone even one abortion as morally defensible.

It may be objected that an anti-abortion absolutist would not have concerns with Rawls's second principle of justice, but rather with the interpretation of equal liberty under his first principle. Even if this objection were valid, it would remain problematic for Rawls, by underscoring fundamental difficulties with his first principle of justice. Either equal liberty means the same for all, including those who hold abortion rights to be an essential component of women's equality and the anti-abortionists, or it may be open to so many different interpretations as to defy any meaningful agreement. In the former case, plurality would have to be suppressed; in the latter, unity dissipated. Finally, even if the links between maximin and the difference principle were considered plausible beyond the socio-economic sphere, it seems much more ill adapted to the needs and designs of those who place identity politics issues far above socio-economic well-being. Accordingly, at the very least, maximin and the

---

[8] For example, ideally race-based differences ought not factor in the determination of principles of justice, and one can imagine an abstract ego without any determinate skin pigmentation. But in a country like the United States with slavery and massive racial injustice in its past, is not ignoring different perspectives relating to racism and racial politics more likely to lead to injustice than properly factoring them in? For a more extended discussion of this point, see Rosenfeld 1991: 236–8.

difference principle fail the test of neutrality with respect to competing conceptions of the good, by blending much better with some of them than with others.

1.2.3. *Habermas's Dialogical Kantian Proceduralism*

In the last analysis, Rawls's contractarian proceduralism is purely derivative, and his principles of justice the product of a monological rather than a dialogical process. This conclusion is consistent with Habermas's assessment of Rawls's theory (Habermas 1990: 66). Habermas proposes to overcome both Kant's and Rawls's monological approaches and to allow all interests full access in the determination of valid moral and legal norms.[9] Kant's and Rawls's approaches are monological because the abstract egos they postulate as being all identical and interchangeable, any one of them is fully equipped to discover universal morality or fair principles of justice. Habermas overcomes this suppression of plurality by allowing every interest as is to be brought to the table without any filter or censorship (Id.: 122). Moreover, Habermas replaces contractarian proceduralism with discursive proceduralism. Everyone concerned can bring his or her full interests, aspirations, and concerns to bear in a counterfactual dialogue under ideal-speech conditions, which provides every participant an equal opportunity to be heard, with a view to achieving a reasoned consensus. In the case of determining legal validity, Habermas postulates a dialogue among strangers resulting in the adoption of norms that would qualify at once as self-imposed and universalizable, thus reconciling democracy and rights (Habermas 1996: 459–60).

I have extensively examined elsewhere Habermas's discourse theory of morals and law, noted its successes in overcoming certain of the previously mentioned problems with the theories of Kant and Rawls, and assessed its key shortcomings in its endeavors to reconcile unity and plurality (Rosenfeld 1998: ch. 5). Moreover, I will further address some of these issues in my discussion of Habermas's analysis of the challenges posed by global terrorism in Chapter 9. For the moment, therefore, I will limit myself to two brief observations. First, the requirement that laws be justified as self-imposed – meaning that those who are subjected to a law would have voted for its adoption, providing only that they adhere to a fair and principled approach to all intersubjective matters – does seem fit to fully accommodate pluralism-in-fact. The problem, however, is that whether all those subjected to a law would agree to consider it as self-imposed is, at best, purely contingent and dependent on the actual competing conceptions of the good at play, and, at worse, simply inconceivable. Absolute opponents of abortion and those who consider a right to it indispensable

---

[9] For Habermas's own account of the principal differences between his discourse theory of normative validity and Kant's moral theory, see Habermas 1990: 195, 203–4.

could thus never agree that any law on the subject should be deemed self-imposed by all those subjected to it.

Second, the dialogical process geared to universalization cannot ultimately stand the test of neutrality among all relevant conceptions of the good. Thus, metaphysical conceptions of the good, including religious ones, would effectively be excluded from the dialogue even if formally welcome to participate. This is because Habermas's conception of universalizability, as he readily acknowledges, entails acceptability of arguments that appeal to reason, but not those that appeal to faith. Furthermore, Habermas's dialogical proceduralism seems biased even as among non-metaphysical conceptions of the good. For example, the proceduralism in question is strongly oriented toward rights and justice, which are contested by some feminists as being male-oriented concerns that tend to drown their own aspiration to replace "the hierarchy of rights with a web of relationships" based above all on care and concern (Gilligan 1982: 57).[10]

In the end, none of the deontological or proceduralist theories discussed earlier successfully manage to properly reconcile unity and plurality. Kant's categorical imperative is certainly neutral, but it defies all practical implementation. Hobbesian contractarian proceduralism certainly includes all plurality ex ante but produces outcomes that are arbitrary and contingent. Rawls and Habermas, on the other hand, although to different extents, both exclude significant amounts of plurality and rely on procedures that yield rights and criteria of justice that fail ex ante to be neutral among all relevant competing conceptions of the good.

1.3. TELEOLOGICAL MONISM: THE UTILITARIAN ALTERNATIVE

Teleological or consequentialist normative theory need not be monistic as will become clear from the account of comprehensive pluralism provided in Section 1.7, but it does offer a monistic alternative to deontological theory that does not present the kinds of problems for the accommodation of plurality that the latter does. Teleological theories determine normative validity in terms of the consequences of actions, and monistic ones, in terms of their impact on advancing or realizing a universally applicable common conception of the good. Teleological theory does not place a wedge between the realm of rights and that of the good, and is thus poised to avoid the kind of suppression and distortion of plurality that deontological theory is bound to provoke. Teleological theory places the good above the right, and monistic teleological theory, a single integrated conception of the good above all else.

---

[10] For a more detailed account of the feminist case against Habermas's proceduralism, see Rosenfeld 1998: 138–44.

The most prominent monistic teleological normative theory consistent with modern individualism and the project of the Enlightenment is utilitarianism. Its most prominent classical exponents, Jeremy Bentham and John Stuart Mill, postulate pursuit of the greatest happiness of the greatest possible number of persons as *the* good and as the normative criterion for the evaluation of the consequences of all actions (Bentham 1970; Mill 1962). In other words, an action is good if it results in a net increase in happiness. Although utilitarianism is focused on the common good of humanity as a whole, it by no means loses sight of the individual. For utilitarianism, the common good is not a whole greater than the sum of its parts, but rather a mere aggregate of individual interests. As Mill states, "Each person's happiness is a good to that person, and the general happiness, therefore a good to the aggregate of all persons" (Mill 1962: 288–9). Similarly, Bentham emphasizes that it is "vain to talk of the interests of community, without understanding what is the interest of the individual" (Bentham 1970: 12). Moreover, both Bentham and Mill consider individuals to be fundamentally selfish (Pitkin 1967: 201–2).

As long as individuals know what would make them happy, and as long as one can count on a common denominator permitting to measure and compare amounts of happiness, utilitarianism would appear to foster both unity and plurality in a way that neither distorts nor suppresses them. Every individual's conception and measure of her own happiness is supposed to be taken as is, without filter, distortion, or suppression. Furthermore, individual happiness and the common good are presumably aligned so long as increases in an individual's happiness are not outweighed by a net decrease in the aggregate happiness of all other individuals. If an action or policy were to increase the happiness of everyone, then there would be a perfect harmony between unity and plurality. On the other hand, if the increase in one's happiness resulted in a net decrease in aggregate happiness, then the individual's interests would appear at odds with the common good,[11] but utilitarianism would still seem to provide the best possible blending of unity and plurality consistent with equal liberty for all individual happiness seekers. Finally, utilitarianism's concern for individuals to the exclusion of groups as such need not pose serious problems so long as individuals remain free to pursue greater happiness through the formation of groups and through participation in them with other like-minded individuals.

For all its apparent virtues in the context of reconciling unity and plurality, utilitarianism has long been under fierce attack for failing to account for differences among persons (Rawls 1971: 27). As one critic puts it, the main concern of utilitarianism is "to aggregate experiences of satisfaction or utility, no matter *whose* experiences they

---

[11] This may not be the case if the focus is on the individual's long-term or overall interests as opposed to her immediate ones. Indeed, it seems quite plausible that in the long run, the utilitarian common good will protect the individual who loses in happiness in the short run, by insuring against dramatic decreases in individual happiness due to the preferences or actions of others.

are: thus it is committed to 'atomism' applied to the individual person and need be no 'respecter of person' in its computation of utilities and disutilities" (Lukes 1973: 48). In other words, utilitarianism emphasizes unmediated feelings of happiness and unhappiness, pleasure and pain, and discrete units of utility and disutility, without regard for the individuality of each person and of her concern for her identity as a meaning endowed and endowing being with genuine normative concerns. If Kantian deontology yields a completely detached abstract ego, utilitarian consequentialism disaggregates all plurality into raw interests and feelings unconnected to their owner's sense of herself as a purposive unified self. Ironically, therefore, by tackling plurality-in-fact in its most immediate and spontaneous manifestations, utilitarianism ends up obliterating all genuine diversity as that requires the self to possess the means to perceive herself as being distinct from her raw feelings and desires as much as being different from the other.

Even if one objects to the preceding criticism of utilitarianism for lacking respect for individual personhood as being overly harsh, it is difficult to escape the conclusion that utilitarianism cannot satisfactorily account for the requisite nexus between unity and plurality. For example, it seems most unlikely that one could come up with appropriate means to quantify and measure pleasure and pain, happiness and unhappiness, and utility and disutility.[12] Can one devise units of pain or pleasure? Are these to be subjective or objective? And even if one could, should pain caused by jealousy and envy be allowed to offset the pleasure caused by reward for hard work?

In the end, neither the monistic deontological approach nor its teleological counterpart can satisfactorily reconcile unity and plurality. The time has now come to inquire whether, and how, pluralism might provide a better alternative. There are different conceptions of pluralism, but what distinguishes them all is that they start from the many rather than from the one.

1.4. THE ALLURE AND LIMITATIONS OF VALUE PLURALISM

For Isaiah Berlin, monism is both unpersuasive, as it defies experience, and dangerous, as it has been invoked throughout history to subjugate large numbers of persons in the name of a purportedly all encompassing single overarching ideal, including nationalism, fascism, and Marxism (Berlin 1997: 20–48). From an empirical standpoint, according to Berlin, human beings are guided in their intersubjective relationships by a plurality of values that can be neither logically ranked

---

[12] "Utility" and "disutility" may be quantifiable and comparable if understood in terms of "efficiency" and "inefficiency" as would be "maximizing utilities" if it were understood in terms of "maximizing wealth." But these terms are not necessarily equivalent. Maximizing wealth may not lead to maximizing pleasure or happiness and vice versa (Rosenfeld 1998: 166 n. 33).

nor fully harmonized into a coherent whole (Berlin 2002: 12). Moreover, although value pluralism may make many uneasy by dampening hopes of finding unity or harmony in the normative universe, it does have a major salutary effect, which might well result in considerable decreases in human cruelty and oppression. As Berlin puts it,

> If pluralism is a valid view, and respect between systems of values which are not necessarily hostile to each other is possible, then toleration and liberal consequences follow, as they do not either from monism (only one set of values is true, all the others are false) or from relativism (my values are mine, yours are yours, and if we clash, too bad, neither of us can claim to be right) (Id.: 13).

As an empiricist and historian of ideas, Berlin does not provide a systematic philosophical account of value pluralism, but he has kindled a value pluralist movement in contemporary moral philosophy that has enlisted a broad range of prominent thinkers, including William Galston, Stuart Hampshire, Thomas Nagel, Martha Nussbaum, Joseph Raz, Charles Taylor, and Bernard Williams (Galston 2009: 803). These and other theorists provide a wide range of differing accounts of value pluralism and of its implications for moral and political philosophy. Given the present focus, however, I will limit my discussion to a brief examination of value pluralism and of its possible implications for the relationship between pluralism-in-fact and normative pluralism, by concentrating on salient aspects of Berlin's account, and in particular on his description of value pluralism in the context of the history of ideas as it evolved from the times of the French Enlightenment.

Value pluralism in Berlin's account emerges out of what may be characterized as mid-level theory. By empirically observing a person who endeavors to act in conformity with worthy moral values, one is bound to notice that such person will inevitably act over time pursuant to several such values, and that she will not be able to convincingly place such values within a hierarchy or coherent whole. For example, within the broad confines of liberalism, both liberty and equality constitute important moral and political values. However, the pursuit of one often results in frustration of the other. Great liberty may frustrate or limit achieving material equality or social welfare and vice versa. For Berlin, we are better-off accepting and living with the fact that liberty pursuits cannot be ultimately harmonized with equality pursuits, that some will be more inclined towards one or the other, and that the same person may switch her priorities back and forth over time. Furthermore, for Berlin, living with this plurality is far better for all than trying to subordinate one value to another, or fashioning an all encompassing unifying theory, as for example Marx did, and then seek to impose it on everyone (Berlin 1970: 167–9).

Although Berlin asserts that values vary both among different cultures and within any one of them, he insists, as we have seen, that his value pluralism does not veer into relativism. Berlin assets that "there is a world of objective values" by which he means "those ends that men pursue for their own sakes, to which other things are means" (Berlin 2002: 11). There are, therefore, according to Berlin, many different forms of life, ends, moral principles, and values associated with these, "but not infinitely many" (Id.).

Berlin's assertion that there are but a limited number of objective values raises a key question: by what criterion can we determine whether a value that we hold dear, and that we recognize is in competition with others, is actually an objective one? The answer to this question should reveal what binds Berlin's value pluralism together and whether, from the standpoint of deep level theory, Berlin is ultimately a pluralist. If the criterion in question is coherent and consistent, then it would endow Berlin's value pluralism with the unity it needs to ensure its remaining distinguishable from relativism. Moreover, depending on the criterion involved, it should be possible to determine whether or not Berlin is, in the last analysis, a deep level theory pluralist.

Before looking further into Berlin's own views relating to the question posed earlier, it should be stressed that there would be nothing inconsistent or contradictory with being a deep level theory monist while at the same time embracing Berlin's value pluralism from the standpoint of middle level theory. Thus, for example, a liberal committed to individualism, equal liberty for all, and adherence to the rule of reason would be ultimately be monistic at the deepest level, and would, for all essential purposes, agree at that level with Kant, Rawls, and John Stuart Mill. Unlike the latter who are monistic all the way up and all the way down – though they may leave room for limited pluralism that remains cabined within their monistic approach, as in the case in which a plurality of conceptions of the good is deemed legitimate so long as it remains consistent with the priority of the right over the good – the value pluralist in our example is not monistic all the way through. Whereas libertarian liberalism primes liberty over equality and egalitarian liberalism posits equality as prior to liberty, value pluralist liberalism prizes both liberty and equality, but seeks neither to place them in a hierarchy nor to reconcile their demands in the realm of normative interaction. By the same token, however, value pluralist liberalism unequivocally rejects slavery or a widespread ban on religious expression. Berlin himself is not all that clear about his criterion for discerning objective values or about his deep level commitments. He does unambiguously embrace liberalism (Id.: 47–8), and his preference for negative liberty over positive liberty (Berlin 1970: 171) is in line with commitment to liberal individualism and with rejection of deep level alternatives such as Rousseauian republicanism or Marxist class-based liberation. Be that as it may, from the standpoint of the potential of placing plurality above unity, it is Berlin's illustrative excursions into intellectual history that loom as most promising.

Modern monism is rooted in the Enlightenment, and, as it emerges in Berlin's account, it displays distinct Janus-face-like characteristics. The monism in question is above all the product of the eighteenth-century French *Philosophes* who were convinced that through use of a methodology akin to that of Newtonian physics, which had brought rational order and unity to nature, one could achieve similar results in the realms of morals and politics (Berlin 2001: 1). The *Philosophes* replaced Christian revelation with reason and projected that the deployment of the latter "would sweep away irrational and oppressive legal systems and economic policies ... would rescue men from political and moral injustice and misery and set them on the path of wisdom, happiness and virtue" (Id.: 2).

In his explorations into the history of ideas following the revolutionary conception of normative theory launched by the *Philosophes*, Berlin concentrates on, and sides with, critics of the French Enlightenment who reject the analogy between the unity of the realm of nature and that of morals (Id.; Berlin 2000). Prominent among these, in Berlin's account, is Vico, an eighteenth-century Italian thinker, who accepted the new scientific approach as applied to nature, but rejected its appropriateness for application to human interaction (Berlin 2000: 41–2). In Berlin's words, according to Vico,

> we judge human activity in terms of purposes, motives, acts of will, decisions, doubts, hesitations, thoughts, hopes, fears, desires, and so forth; these are among the ways in which we distinguish human beings from the rest of nature. (Id.: 42)

Moreover, for Vico, human nature is not fixed, but evolves through history and accordingly the law, morals, and politics of one epoch are not likely to be suitable for another (Id.: 106–7).

By conceiving human nature and natural law as uniform and unchanging, the Enlightenment moralists paved the way for an oppressive monism bound to frustrate the rich and manifold potential for human self-expression and flourishing. When Berlin focuses on the contrast between this kind of Enlightenment monism and pluralists such as Vico, it is clear where his sympathies lie. Berlin is too subtle and nuanced an historian of ideas, however, not to also note that Enlightenment monism was engaged in a historical battle with other monisms as well as with pluralism. One of these battles is retrospective and is, as already noted, against Christian revelation; the other is prospective against one of the main currents of anti-Enlightenment ideology grounded in excessive expressions of romanticism, and leading to, among others, xenophobic nationalism and fascism (Berlin 2001: 17–24).

In his recounting of both these struggles against other forms of monism, Berlin's sympathies emerge as clearly aligned on the side of Enlightenment rationalism, and hence the French Enlightenment's Janus-face characteristic in Berlin's narrative. Though monistic, the Enlightenment approach is obviously preferable to the kind of religious authoritarianism that it fought to replace, and to the dangerous irratio-nalist ideologies that were spread in reaction to it. At the same time, Enlightenment monism in morals looms as patently inferior to value pluralism grounded in reason and objectivity.

How might one reconcile unity and plurality in connection with Berlin's value pluralism as situated in the historical context briefly evoked previously? Perhaps, the best clue to what might qualify as a correct answer to this question is to be found in the views of Montesquieu as sympathetically summarized by Berlin (Id.: 130–61). Montesquieu's case is particularly telling because he was a contemporary of Voltaire and of the Encyclopedists, and because he was like the latter committed to the rule of reason, yet contrary to the spirit of the French Enlightenment, he believed that societies differ not only in relation to means but also to the ends that they each set to pursue. As a consequence, for Montesquieu, laws should be adapted to the particular social, economic, political, and ideological conditions that prevail in the actual polity for which they are meant. Just as the clothing suited for a cold climate is not fit for a warm one, the laws tailored for a country with certain physical conditions and mores would be unsuited for another country with very different characteristics and mores.

One might think that Montesquieu is at bottom a moral relativist, but Berlin assures us that he is not, that he is instead a pluralist (Id.: 143, 157). On the one hand, Montesquieu believes that law should be relative to the particular mores of the society concerned; on the other hand, he conceives justice, as Berlin puts it, to be "a transcendent eternal standard" (Id.: 155). Berlin goes on to observe that

> There is a kind of continuous dialectic in all Montesquieu's writings between abso-lute values which seem to correspond to the permanent interests of men as such, and those which depend upon time and place in a concrete situation (Id.: 157)

which lead him to conclude that the contradiction inherent in Montesquieu's views remains unresolved (Id.).

From the standpoint of the relationship between unity and plurality, there seem to be two possible different implications that could be drawn from Montesquieu's theory. The first is that there is an inconsistency within the normative universe as conceived by Montesquieu much like the one noted earlier in the context of the dichotomy between Adam Smith's prescriptions for the morals of the mar-ket and those for morals outside the market.[13] The second possible implication is that Montesquieu is, contrary to Berlin's assertion (Id.), ultimately, at the deepest level, a monist. At the level of legitimate laws for a particular polity, pluralism is called for; in relation to whether these laws are just, however, there is only one universal standard.

---

[13] *See supra*, at 26.

I think the second alternative is much more convincing in the case of Montesquieu and also in that of Berlin himself. Otherwise, neither of the two could avoid ending up as a deep level relativist or as someone who purely arbitrarily sets limits to the scope of legitimate value pluralism. If I am right, at the deepest level, value pluralists are still monists though they be monists that are more open to, and more sympathetic toward, pluralism. Value pluralists may shift the focus to pluralism but they still, perhaps unwittingly, ultimately give priority to unity over plurality. To overcome the seemingly unavoidable fall into either monism or relativism that this conclusion entails requires, as I will argue in what follows, recasting the relationship between unity and plurality in terms of an ongoing dialectic.

1.5. THE HEGELIAN DIMENSION OF COMPREHENSIVE PLURALISM

Comprehensive pluralism is conceived and intended as being pluralistic all the way up and all the way down, placing plurality ahead of unity, but nonetheless reserving an indispensable role for the latter. Comprehensive pluralism concurs with two of Berlin's insights, namely that pluralism is good, preferable to monism because it is less likely to result in all manner of tyranny be it in the realm of ideas, of morals, or of politics; and, that pluralism does not, and should not, give unconditional normative imprimatur to the full panoply of existing conceptions of the good or to all asserted values. Comprehensive pluralism goes much farther, however, than does Berlin's value pluralism in implanting the normative foundations of pluralism deeper and more systematically. Moreover, the difference between the two is not merely a matter of abstract theory, but also leads to practical consequences as evinced by the fact that comprehensive pluralism does not establish any inbuilt preference for liberalism, individualism, or negative liberty as does Berlin.

As already mentioned in the Introduction, comprehensive pluralism was originally predicated on the proposition that in the presence of pluralism-in-fact, pluralism-as-norm provides the best means to the good. Upon further consideration, a strong argument can be mounted in favor of the broader claim that pluralism-as-norm is best in all circumstances, regardless of the presence of pluralism-in-fact. The minimum conditions for the prescription of pluralism-as-norm to make sense are satisfied so long as a *potential for pluralism* is present. Moreover, it suffices that there be one self and one other for there to be such a potential, given that the very notions of selfhood and otherness entail a minimum of difference and of plurality. Accordingly, even in the most homogeneous of polities, with no toleration for deviation from official ideology and policy, there is bound to be some potential for pluralism as not all individual perspectives would be exactly the same, and as the polity in question could not be hermetically sealed from any change of perspective over time.

The allure of pluralism in terms of pursuit of the good is essentially threefold: It promotes enrichment of the self, a superior normative aesthetics, and the greatest possible mutual accommodation among proponents of different perspectives and conceptions of the good. These three goods, moreover, are complementary and mutually reinforcing. I have already argued at length elsewhere about the superiority of comprehensive pluralism for purposes of fostering mutual accommodation (Rosenfeld 1998: 213–24). Suffice it here, therefore, to return briefly to the core of the argument. Comprehensive pluralism considers all perspectives and conceptions of the good on their own terms and commands that empathy be deployed toward each of these to approximate as much as possible an understanding and appreciation of each of the contending perspectives from the "internal point of view" of its proponents. This allows comprehensive pluralism to grasp the uniqueness of the other and of the differences that make it other than the self far better than any of the monistic theories previously discussed. Indeed, as we have seen, Kant and Rawls treat persons as having perspectives but separate them from their particular perspectives in the course of devising moral norms and principles of justice for them. Habermas, on the other had, accounts for some perspectives but excludes others ex ante, while utilitarianism largely suppresses or ignores actual perspectives by accounting for feelings with scarce concerns for the identity of their owners. Furthermore, because of its greater openness and sensitivity to different perspectives, comprehensive pluralism clearly seems better suited than its rivals to furnish preferable normative standards to polities that are pluralistic-in-fact.

The remaining two goods identified, self-enrichment and the aesthetic of the normative, are the ones that most strongly lend support to the conviction that comprehensive pluralism should extend to all polities, not just those that are pluralistic-in-fact. As will be discussed shortly, Hegel has emphatically underscored, in his famous account of the struggle for recognition between the lord and the bondsman (Hegel 1977: paras. 178–96), that the self can only be defined in terms of the other, or, in other words, that selfhood only makes sense in relation to, and, as set against, the other. At the most abstract level, the Hegelian self cannot conceive itself as such before it realizes that the other is also a self, but that it itself is a self that is other than the other. That means that the self defines itself not only in terms of differences from, but also of similarities to, the other. Moving beyond the image of the atomistic individual portrayed in certain liberal visions, in Hegel's account, the concrete individual becomes who she is as a distinct self, by processing the rich diversity she encounters in dealing with other selves – beginning with the imprint made by her family and immediate community in childhood – in order to incorporate, modify, and adapt some of this diversity and to differentiate and distance herself from the remainder in order to fashion her own self-identity. Also, this process of self-identification is a dynamic and continuous one, starting in childhood and evolving throughout life.

This conception of the formation and evolution of self-identity is equally applicable to individual persons and to all purposive collective units capable of projecting a self-identity, such as nations, religions, cultures, ideologies, non-governmental organizations, transnational groupings including the likes of human rights activists and environmentalists. Moreover, individual identities are inextricably tied to group identities. Groups just like other individuals offer poles of identification and of differentiation while providing another layer and dimension of self-identification. The "I" cannot subsist in isolation and must thus be integrated into one "we" or several of them. The "I" does not thereby fully merge into the "we" but commits her allegiance to it while remaining to some degree differentiated from it. One can, for example, identify with one's nation and fully merge into the national "we" when the nation is threatened in war. At some other time, however, without forswearing one's national allegiance, one can, as a matter of individual conscience, object to national policy and even oppose it with the hope of eventually prompting a change.

At present, self-identities tend to be complex, varied, and plural. Think, for instance, of a German woman who is a Catholic and a feminist. She is German as opposed to French or Italian, but with the French and the Italian, and as contrasted to Americans and Chinese, she is a citizen of the European Union and is afforded protection under the ECHR. She is a Catholic as opposed to a Protestant, the other dominant religion in Germany, and as opposed to a Jew or a Muslim who belong to minority religions within her country. She is also a committed feminist, which sets her apart from those who embrace ideologies that incorporate or condone male dominance.

Although the woman in question has all these group allegiances, she is herself more than the sum of these (and of the many other allegiances that any flesh and blood person is bound to have), if for no other reason that she processes and combines these in her own unique way. Furthermore, these group allegiances combine and interrelate in dynamic ways, sometimes being in relative harmony, and sometimes in downright tension. Thus, this woman may strongly feel German as opposed to French in the context of a dispute between the two nations regarding EU policy. On another occasion, she may feel above all European, as she asserts that Europeans are morally and constitutionally superior to Americans for having abolished the death penalty whereas the latter have not. In another facet of her life, her feminism may come in conflict with her commitment to Catholicism because of the Church's stance against women priests. In short, this woman has a plurality of evolving, interacting, and shifting allegiances to different "we" groups with whom she identifies. Her own sense of self depends on how she manages, negotiates, and integrates all the group affiliations in play. And that entails not only finding harmony among a plurality of group affiliations but also learning to live with, and making room within one's self-identity for, a fair amount of dissonance, as for example, feminism and the Catholic Church's policy seem at present impossible fully to reconcile.

Consistent with these observations, the claim that a pluralist vision leads to self-enrichment boils down to the following. Because self-identify is constructed and adjusted throughout one's lifetime; and since it inescapably involves reprocessing and incorporating elements originating in the other; a pluralist openness and endeavor to empathize with what is cast as worthy from the other's perspective allows for greater choice, enhanced options, and better opportunities for orchestrating a more satisfactory and more rewarding path to self-realization and self-fulfillment. Anti-pluralistic stances militate against those self-enriching potentials whereas non-pluralistic ones are only likely to open avenues to partial fulfillment.

The pluralist aesthetic of the normative stands as a corollary to pluralist self-enrichment. The individual benefits from the availability of a plurality of sources from which she can draw for purposes of constructing her self-identity, and humanity is enriched by the spread of a large panoply of diverse conceptions of the good. Just as the arts seem bound to be benefited by the coexistence of a multiplicity of varied aesthetic approaches and styles, so too the normative universe would appear to gain from the development of manifold diverse conceptions of the good. Thus, different religions and different secular ideologies can each in its own way contribute to mapping out multiple constructive paths to intersubjective cooperation and individual self-realization. Some religions may emphasize the importance of charity; others, that of self-reliance; some may encourage our hopes; others quell our fears; some religions may provide comfort by evoking the beauties of an afterlife; others may insist that the good must be sought exclusively on this earth, and so on. Similarly, secular ideologies may offer worthy alternatives for doing good to others and to ourselves with an urgency and sobriety that may not equally motivate some of those who feel comfortable entrusting their fate to a divine or transcendent presence.

It bears emphasizing that the pluralistic aesthetic of the normative is not meant to undermine anyone's commitment to his own conception of the good or belief in the truth of his religion or secular outlook. It is not the aim of the pluralistic aesthetic to relativize everyone's convictions and propagate self-doubt, but to encourage recasting the differences that separate the others from the self in ways that promote better understanding and mutual accommodation. Instead of treating those who adhere to religions other than mine as enemies of the truth, the aesthetic approach counsels that I learn to focus on the latter as persons who seek the same type of spiritual goods and avenues to fulfillment as I do. This does not require me to give up my truth or to accept "their" truth as being equivalent to mine; it only requires that I accept that even if they are in error, they are still seeking the truth in good faith rather than denigrating it as its enemies.

Comprehensive pluralism is pluralist all the way down inasmuch as it requires that prima facie and ex ante there be equal room around the table for all conceptions of the good embraced by one person or more within the relevant polity – and for some matters, such as adherence to universal human rights standards, the relevant polity is the world at large. Put in another way, ex ante all conceptions of the good should be accepted on their own terms as their proponents conceive them from their own internal viewpoint.[14]

It may be reasonably objected that giving a place at the same table to a conception of the good centered on pacifism and helping the needy and to Nazism and proponents of global terrorism, even if only for a brief moment, is both absurd and dangerous. From the standpoint of comprehensive pluralism, however, all perspectives should be given an opportunity to be heard, and everyone should be afforded a view of every perspective, even the most frightful ones, "from the inside." In part, this is justified because most conceptions of the good, including some of the most monstrous ones, may in part address legitimate needs and aspirations – and may even provide certain ways for dealing with these that may be in themselves widely acceptable – even if for the most part, they set to propagate unspeakable evils. In part also, giving an opportunity to be heard to the most pernicious conceptions of the good should make it possible to better understand them so as a to combat them more efficiently and to provide viable alternatives means for addressing the genuine needs and aspirations that may have been highjacked and forcibly led into completely unacceptable directions.

Comprehensive pluralism is at the same time pluralistic all the way up. It seeks to maximize peaceful coexistence among the greatest possible number of conceptions of the good while maintaining a reciprocal equilibrium between self and other. Where that reciprocal equilibrium may be struck depends on the particular self and other involved, and on their actual respective conceptions of the good. Thus, for example, if the conception of the good of the other requires destruction of the self, then pluralism calls for the requisite equilibrium to be pursued thorough restraint of the other. That restraint, moreover, would have to extend all the way up. In other words, the search for a reciprocal equilibrium must extend to all arenas of intersubjective interaction, and it unleashes an unending continuous search as every pursuit

---

[14] This raises a difficult question regarding what should count as a genuine conception of the good. Is the mere assertion by a thief that his stealing constitutes the good for him sufficient to cast that position as a conception of good? The answer would seem to be in the negative in as much as the assertion in question sounds more like an excuse, a whim, or an act of defiance than a principled expression of one's normative vision and values. Thus, though some line drawing problems may be inevitable, there seem to be workable criteria available for deciding what should count as a conception of the good. Accordingly, mere rationalization for being a thief would not count, but Nazism and Stalinism, as monstrous, abhorrent and pernicious as they have proven to be, would.

of the self, even if totally non-belligerent, impinges on any other with whom the self interacts and vice versa. Accordingly, the norms that comprehensive pluralism deploys to foster the requisite reciprocal equilibrium between self and other must be systematically applied to all intersubjective dealings.

I tried to capture comprehensive pluralism's concurrent process of inclusion all the way down and of constraint all the way up in terms of a dialectic comprised of two different *logical* moments. The first, or negative, one calls for equalization of all conceptions of the good. Historically, in all typical polities, certain actual conceptions of the good are institutionally, traditionally, or culturally given preference over others. In its negative moment, comprehensive pluralism counterfactually levels all hierarchy and places all the conceptions of the good on the same footing. In its second, or positive, moment, in contrast, comprehensive pluralism imposes its normative constraints on all (now) equalized conceptions of the good to aim at the requisite reciprocal equilibrium, which could well result in exclusion of some conceptions, partial inclusion of others, and nearly full inclusion of yet others. Moreover, the criterion for inclusion is *compatibility*, as opposed to *consistency* with the constraints emanating from comprehensive pluralism, – the norms associated with all competing conceptions of the good being referred to as "first-order norms," and those identified with comprehensive pluralism as "second-order norms."

There is but little question that taken separately, the negative moment of the preceding dialectic appears to veer toward relativism, whereas the positive moment seems strongly to tend toward monism. Consistent with this, critics such as Michelman have suggested that, in the end, comprehensive pluralism either results in monism or in relativism (Michelman 2000: 1962–70). In order to be in a better position to counter these criticisms, it is necessary to clarify the sense in which comprehensive pluralism and the dialectic between the negative and positive moments that it launches are the product of a Hegelian vision and approach. Indeed, such a clarification is crucial, particularly in view of how discredited some of Hegel's ideas have become, and how even some of his most sympathetic exponents, such as Charles Taylor, have concluded that his grandiose synthesis has become obsolete (Taylor 1975: 537–8).[15]

Whereas Hegel's idea of inexorable historical progress culminating in the triumph of Absolute Spirit can be readily discarded, his insight that every generation is embedded in a concrete historical setting confronting particular conflicts and contradictions seems as valid today as it ever was. So is his dialectical approach,

---

[15] Most notably, as Taylor observes, the complete overlap of reason and reality in Absolute Spirit – the crowning culmination of Hegel's system – seems highly implausible today. Taylor 1975: 547, 551. But see Zizek 1989: 6 ("[F]ar from being a story of [the] progressive overcoming [of antagonism], dialectics is for Hegel a systematic notation of the failure of all such attempts").

which essentially seeks to resolve contradictions through reconciliation of the part with the whole – with the part only becoming understandable in terms of its place within the whole, and, conversely, the whole only susceptible to being adequately grasped in terms of the full panoply of determinate relationships that bind together its various constituent parts.[16] As applied to the intersubjective arena in which relationships center around law, ethics, and politics, moreover, the dialectical approach focuses on various antagonistic positions considered as partial and seeks to overcome existing conflicts and contradictions. The dialectical approach accomplishes this by mediating between the various partial perspectives and a suitable overall perspective meant to transcend all its partial counterparts, not by repudiating the latter, but rather by recasting each perspective in terms of its more comprehensive outlook, and then incorporating them into an integrated and cohesive whole. As will be more fully discussed later, each of these partial perspectives figures as one facet of a multifaceted theoretical construct.

In Hegel's view, the dialectical process of incorporating parts into a whole that transcends them implies both a cancellation and a preservation of the parts involved. Hegel refers to this process as *Aufhebung*. In his own words:

> What transcends (*Aufheben*) itself does not thereby become [n]othing.... It... retains the determinateness whence it started. To transcend (*Aufheben*) has this double meaning, that it signifies to keep or to preserve and also to make to cease, to finish.... Thus, what is transcended is also preserved; it has only lost its immediacy and is not on that account annihilated. (Hegel 1999: 119–20)

In the context of Hegel's system, the unfolding of the dialectic results in a progression not only from part to whole but also from less differentiated wholes to ever more differentiated wholes, culminating in a fully differentiated whole. This process is made possible because the whole that results from the resolution of the conflict among its parts becomes itself a part in the new conflict, which erupts upon reaching the next higher stage of the dialectic. This process is then repeated until the culmination of the dialectic at the end of history, when the fully differentiated whole is to become completely intelligible.

Comprehensive pluralism, however, makes no assumptions concerning historical progress or the possibility of reaching higher stages of ever more encompassing integration. In spite of this agnosticism, comprehensive pluralism remains firmly within the Hegelian camp as it strives to cope with the conflicts it encounters through deployment of a dialectical approach moving from part to whole.

---

[16] As Hegel states, "The whole is a stable equilibrium of all the parts, and each part is … at home in this whole … because it is itself in this equilibrium with the whole" (Hegel 1977: Para. 277); see also Hyppolite 1946: 322 (explaining that, for Hegel, "the Truth is the Whole and … each of its moments only acquires meaning in relation to its place in the overall dialectic") (author's translation).

Specifically, confronted with plurality and with competing conceptions of the good that are, at least in part, mutually incompatible, comprehensive pluralism strives for reconciliation beyond the current standoff. And given constraints imposed by its agnosticism, comprehensive pluralism must pursue reconciliation counterfactually, through postulation of an imagined resolution of existing conflicts into a larger whole. Such imagined resolution, moreover, needs to conform to the strict requirements of dialectical logic (which is not a formal logic, but rather one built on negation and confrontation as a means of progressing from the part to the whole[17]) and thus cannot be merely arbitrary or fanciful. Finally, even if the conflicts targeted by comprehensive pluralism proved impossible to resolve, their imagined resolution consistent with dialectical logic would still remain important, as it would provide a critical (counterfactual) perspective from which to gauge the failures of the status quo.

There is another crucial point of convergence between comprehensive pluralism and Hegel's philosophy: They both agree on the centrality of reciprocal recognition between self and other in the context of all normatively oriented relationships. To be sure, reciprocal recognition is also key for certain liberal theorists such as Habermas and Rawls, and undoubtedly has certain Hegelian roots for them. But, as we have seen, for Habermas and Rawls, the normative implications associated with the need for genuine reciprocal recognition turn out to be Kantian rather than Hegelian in nature.

For Hegel, all moral, ethical, and legal relationships are premised on previous acceptance of reciprocal recognition.[18] Moreover, reciprocal recognition for Hegel is the result of a struggle that he details, most notably through the celebrated dialectic between lord and bondsman (Hegel 1977: paras. 178–96). For present purposes, what is most important about this struggle is that the antagonists are transformed through a series of dialectical reverses. Thus, the lord seeks recognition without having to recognize the bondsman as another self, and therefore endeavors to become the master by enslaving the bondsman. But by forcing the bondsman to work for him, the lord becomes dependent on the labor of the bondsman, and accordingly the relationship becomes transformed. As a consequence of this dialectical reversal, in the words of Hyppolite, the slave becomes the master of the master, while the master becomes the slave of the slave (Hyppolite 1946: 166). Furthermore, this reversal makes it plain that the desired recognition, which led the lord to subordinate the bondsman, cannot be attained so long as the antagonists remain unequal. To resolve

---

[17] For a more extended summary of the principal features of dialectical logic, see Rosenfeld 1989: 1207–9.

[18] *See* Hegel 1952: para. 51A (noting that property rights entail recognition by others); and Id. para. 71R ("Contract presupposes that the parties entering it recognize each other as persons and property owners.").

the struggle for recognition, another dialectical reversal must take place, in order to put the antagonists in a position to grant each other mutual recognition as equals.

Just as reciprocal recognition emerges as the culmination of a dialectic process for Hegel, so, too, it does for comprehensive pluralism. Indeed, settings in which pluralism-in-fact prevails are characterized by a struggle among competing, and at least to some degree incompatible, conceptions of the good. So long as each actor remains entrenched within her conception of the good, one can only envisage keeping the competition among antagonistic conceptions of the good under control through subordination of some of these conceptions to others. To overcome this predicament and advance toward reciprocal recognition, it is necessary to embark on a dialectical course capable of defusing antagonisms among rival conceptions of the good by recombining them as parts of a yet to be fully articulated, more inclusive whole. Ideally, in this new whole the underlying conceptions of the good will not fade, but rather become better integrated within a more encompassing perspective.

In sum, for both Hegel and comprehensive pluralism, reciprocal recognition is the result of a dialectical process. Moreover, to adequately grasp the full import of such reciprocal recognition, it is as crucial to take proper account of the various phases of the dialectic as it is to appreciate the product emanating from that process. For liberal theory, such as that of Habermas or Rawls, on the other hand, reciprocal recognition is largely axiomatic, given the presupposition that all persons are inherently equal. In contrast, for comprehensive pluralism, keeping in mind the difference between reciprocal recognition *as process* as opposed to *as product* is indispensable for purposes of capturing its dialectics of recognition and its seemingly relativistic facets.

With the Hegelian dialectics of reciprocal recognition in mind, it is now possible to offer a systematic refutation of the claim that comprehensive pluralism must either collapse into monism or into relativism. Unlike a non-dialectical pluralism, such as Berlin's value pluralism, that cannot stand on its own, comprehensive pluralism can remain pluralistic through and through by emerging as a distinct whole from the struggle between its (partial) monistic moment and its (partial) relativistic moment. It is the *process* set in motion by the dialectic, which seeks to reconcile the clash between the first-order norms unleashed in that dialectic's first negative moment in ways that prove *compatible* (even if inconsistent) with the second-order norms activated in the positive moment of that dialectic. Moreover, it is the very process that channels the ongoing tension between monistic and pluralistic tensions toward a truly pluralistic resolution. The *product* of that process, in turn, is only pluralistic when taken retrospectively as a Hegelian whole that has transcended a prior contradiction. Viewed prospectively, however, the product in question will be transformed inevitably into one of the sides to a new conflict setting a new contradiction.

And that transformation will require continuing the pluralist process with the aim of generating new pluralistic products.

Because comprehensive pluralism forswears any design to follow a Hegelian path to anything resembling an Absolute Spirit, it is impossible to apprehend the particulars of its dialectical process and product beyond the actual socio-political context in which it happens to unfold. A clash between Catholics and Protestants will necessarily be concretized through a different conflict among different sets of first-order norms than a clash between Christians and Muslims, or between Serbs and Croats, or between Marxists and capitalists. By the same token, a clash between all the above will present comprehensive pluralism with quite a different challenge than would any conflict confined to any one of the aforementioned pairs.

Similarly, *which* second-order norms will have to be called upon to constrain conceptions of the good at war with one another; and *how* these second-order norms should channel the conflicting first-order norms toward a suitable reciprocal equilibrium; will also depend on the particulars of the actual cultures and norms at play. It certainly stands to reason that certain norms that play a key role in liberal approaches, such as tolerance, liberty, equality, and dignity should also figure prominently among the second-order norms activated by comprehensive pluralism's dialectic. It would be a serious mistake, however, to assume that these norms would end up being of a cloth with their liberal counterparts. Actually, the norms in question are likely to differ in their definition and scope even within the confines of pluralism as they must be constantly adapted to the actual first-order norms in conflict that they must confront. A fortiori, appearances of similarities with liberal counterparts may be, more often than not, deceiving as will be made plain through examination of certain concrete examples in the chapters that follow.

1.6. FROM THE MODERN TO THE POST-MODERN AND FROM HOMOGENEOUS TO HETEROGENEOUS SOCIETIES

A key feature that sets comprehensive pluralism apart from liberal theories, such as those of Rawls and Habermas, is its commitment to the priority of the good over the right. I will detail this commitment in the next section but will first address in this section two important related background matters that will allow me to place the claim that comprehensive pluralism is a teleological theory in its proper context. The two matters in question are: first, the relation of the modern to the post-modern, not in its epistemological dimension alluded to earlier[19] but as it emerges from the *participant* perspective of those who experience the prevalent normative order within their polity and, second, the dichotomy between homogeneous and heterogeneous

---

[19] See supra, at 7–8.

societies – and not that between pluralistic-in-fact and non-pluralistic ones – also from the participant perspective of the political actors within them.

To place the following discussion in its proper setting, it is useful to start by mentioning three criticisms of comprehensive pluralism that I seek to refute in this section and the next. The first criticism made by Habermas is that "comprehensive pluralism is not substantive theory, but rather proceduralism in substantive garb" (Habermas 1998a: 405). Elaborating on this criticism, one could claim that the two-pronged dialectic launched by comprehensive pluralism boils down to a purely procedural approach. The first negative moment can be viewed as but a procedure to automatically put all competing conceptions of the good on an equal footing; the second, positive moment, as subjection of all now equalized conceptions of the good to the set bundle of normative constraints mandated by the second-order norms (which though labeled as goods, actually function as rights and correlative duties). Thus, comprehensive pluralism would rely on a proceduralism predicated on equalization and opening the space for a maximum of ordered plurality through subjection to rights-like norms, as contrasted to Habermas's proceduralism based on open and fair communication combined with universalizability.

The second criticism consists in questioning the soundness of the distinction between the modern and the post-modern in relation to political actors (Arato 2000: 1931; Michelman 2000: 1947–9), and in maintaining further that if post-modernism has in fact displaced modernism, then comprehensive pluralism is bound to collapse into relativism (Michelman 2000: 1959).

The third criticism, in turn, uses the contrast between homogeneous and heterogeneous to question the soundness of comprehensive pluralism's normative claim that pluralism-in-fact calls for pluralism-as-norm. Indeed, as these critics see it, there can well be a plurality of interests in a society, and yet its political actors might well agree on common principles for all (Id.: 1947). With this in mind, I will now attempt to clarify my conception of the distinction between the modern and the post-modern and that between homogeneous and heterogeneous societies.

1.6.1. *The Modern versus the Post-Modern*

As Michelman points out, the distinction I draw between modern and post-modern societies is an "ideal-typical" one (Id.: 1949). A modern society is thus one in which social cohesion – albeit a tenuous one – is perceived as possible through the maintenance of procedural safeguards, notwithstanding widely diverging conceptions of the good. A post-modern society, on the other hand, is one in which no apparent common ground – procedural or substantive – can emerge above the clash between conceptions of the good, and in which any social order is bound to be considered by significant segments of the population as arbitrary, coercive, and unjust. Consistent

with this, whether a society is modern or post-modern is above all a matter of perception within the relevant society – that is, a matter of self-consciousness. In other
words, insofar as it is relevant here, the divide between modern and post-modern
must be gauged from the internal standpoint of participants rather than from the
external standpoint of observers.

In view of the second criticism, two further points relating to the distinction
between the modern and the post-modern must be briefly addressed. First, the conclusion that a particular society was modern at some point in its history need not be
questioned solely because subsequently observers can give a cogent account of it in
post-modern terms. For example, if participants within a society perceived certain
procedural safeguards within their society as neutral among prevailing conceptions
of the good, that society would properly be characterized as modern, even if outside
observers could persuasively demonstrate that what was believed by participants to
be neutral was in fact biased in favor of certain prevailing conceptions of the good
as against others.

Second, the fact that a modern society requires rallying around certain procedural safeguards, perceived as transcending the clash among competing conceptions
of the good, does not necessarily imply that there must be a consensus over which
safeguards should be prevalent. Moreover, the fact in question does not require limiting the relevant procedural safeguards to ones that are purely procedural – or, in
other words, entirely devoid of any substantive content. For example, a society would
not cease being modern simply because there was a disagreement over whether fairness and greater social cohesion would best be secured through increased liberty
or through greater equality. Similarly, a society's modernity would not be altered
depending on whether the procedural safeguards of its basic institutions depended
on formal liberty and equality or on a more substantively grounded conception of
the two.[20]

---

[20] Admittedly, the use of "procedural" in the present context is rather broad, and at times can even
be misleading. It is certainly not limited to a "pure" or "mere" procedure, such as the flipping of a
coin to adjudicate a dispute. Beyond that, the distinction between "procedural" or "process based"
and "substantive" is a highly contested one in both constitutional theory, compare, for example, Ely
1980 (arguing that the fundamental rights protected by the Bill of Rights of the U.S. Constitution
are essentially process based), with Tribe 1980: 1063 (arguing that the Bill of Rights guarantees substantive rights above all), and in political philosophy (Rosenfeld 1998a :291). Thus, for example, Rawls's
"justice as fairness," which he characterizes as procedural (Rawls 1971: 120), could just as plausibly be
considered as being more substantive than procedural (Rosenfeld 1998a). Strictly speaking, the key
distinction is not between "substantive" and "procedural," but between "neutral" as between competing conceptions of the good and "biased" as between these competing conceptions. Accordingly, if
justice depends on contract or democracy it ought to be viewed mainly as procedural, whereas if it
depends on enforcement of natural rights it should be considered primarily substantive. However, if
contract, democracy, and natural rights were equally neutral as between competing conceptions of
the good, then they would all loom as equally suitable for purposes of modern justice. In short, within
the perspective of modern societies, if a procedural standpoint is just it must be deemed neutral, and

These last two points can be usefully illustrated by means of a brief reference to the *Lochner* case, which recognized a constitutional "substantive due process" right to freedom of contract.[21] To better appreciate this illustration, moreover, let us set aside questions peculiar to American constitutional jurisprudence – such as those dealing with Framers' intent issues – and focus instead on the more general question concerning the need for constitutional protection of freedom of contract as a requirement of justice for a modern society. *Lochner* was a 5–4 decision striking down a New York law prohibiting the employment of bakery employees in excess of ten hours per day or sixty hours per week on the ground that it violated the fundamental right to freedom of contract embedded in the federal Constitution. From a modern perspective, this decision can be regarded as just, provided freedom of contract is deemed neutral as between competing conceptions of the good, and fundamental to maintaining a requisite degree of social cohesion in the face of widely diverse aims and interests.

For the dissenting Justices, in contrast, freedom of contract was not essential to basic constitutional justice, but rather the cornerstone of a particular economic vision which a large part of the population did not share. In Justice Holmes's famous words:

> The 14th Amendment does not enact Mr. Herbert Spencer's social statics … [A] constitution is not intended to embody a particular economic theory, whether of paternalism and the organic relation of the citizen to the state or of laissez faire.[22]

Notwithstanding this conclusion, Holmes did not reject the proposition that liberty as enshrined in the Fourteenth Amendment can rise above partisan politics and become integrated as a pillar of constitutional justice. As he puts it:

> I think that the word liberty in the 14th Amendment is perverted when it is held to prevent the natural outcome of a dominant opinion, unless it can be said that a rational and fair man would admit that the statute proposed would infringe fundamental principles as they have been understood by the traditions of our people and our law.[23]

Significantly, Holmes did not reject the possibility of fundamental principles that are neutral as between the diverse conceptions of the good embraced by Americans. He merely disagreed with the Court's majority concerning which principles ought to count as truly neutral in the requisite sense. Therefore, both the majority Justices

---

if a neutral standpoint is just, then it must either be procedural or the functional equivalent of a procedural standard.

[21] *Lochner* v. *New York, 198 U.S. 45 (1905)*.

[22] Id. at 75.

[23] Id. at 76.

and their dissenting brethren in *Lochner* held constitutional views entirely consistent with a modern outlook.

From a post-modern perspective, however, all positions articulated in *Lochner* fail the neutrality test and are ultimately reducible to partisan expressions inextricably linked to highly contestable as well as actually contested conceptions of the good. Indeed, even if laissez-faire, or any other economic regime, could be proven to lead to maximization of wealth, it would still fail the previously described test of neutrality. This is because wealth maximization is not a priority for all conceptions of the good and may even plausibly be considered a serious threat to certain fundamental values and objectives linked to certain conceptions of the good. On the other hand, from a post-modern perspective, neither rationality nor fairness nor any single set of traditions is ever likely to rise above divisions over the good in a country as diverse as the United States. Accordingly, from a post-modern perspective, Justice Holmes's position in *Lochner*, in the end, is as partisan and as tied to particular conceptions of the good as that of the majority Justices.

Acceptance of the post-modern perspective has an important consequence – namely, that the meaning of norms can only be grasped from within the conception(s) of the good from which they issue. Accordingly, no norm transcends particular conceptions of the good, and anyone who becomes aware of this must concede that the norms that he or she embraces cannot be legitimately cast as neutral or universally valid. This does not mean that one should weaken one's commitment to one's conception of the good or to the norms derived from it, but it does mean that one has no right to be confident that one's conception of the good and the norms associated with it would be good or right for others committed to different conceptions of the good. Furthermore, inasmuch as no such confidence is warranted, everyone should become more open to coexistence among a plurality of conceptions of the good.

Acceptance of the proposition that what is good for me is not necessarily good for others is the point of departure of the search for justice within the framework of comprehensive pluralism. Leaving aside, for the moment, whether justice falls within the domain of the good or within that of the right, which will be discussed in Section 1.7, the challenge confronting justice consists in finding a fair halfway point between self and other. Justice cannot fully meet that challenge, however, for that would require total reconciliation of all identities and differences and of the universal, the particular, the singular, and the plural. Under those circumstances, the best that can be hoped for is to inch closer to justice without ever achieving it, through deployment of a dialectic between a disassembling process to ferret out all differences that separate the self from the other and as reassembling or reconstructive process designed to locate knots of identity that would sustain common links between them.

Viewed as two distinct moments within the same dialectic, the disassembling process focuses on differences between self and other, whereas the reconstructive one concentrates on the identities between the two. From the standpoint of justice, approaching full integration of all identities and differences within a larger whole arising from resolution of the struggle between self and other appears impossible, but achieving certain levels of integration seems quite plausible – at least from a critical counterfactual perspective. And, among plausible levels of imperfect integration, some will undoubtedly be more satisfactory than others. Thus, for example, regardless of the particular identities and differences most at stake in a given struggle between self and other, an attempted resolution of that struggle, which takes into account that the other has his or her own perspective, would, in all likelihood, be less just than one that seeks to accommodate the other in terms of the perspective the other has actually embraced.[24] In short, although all relevant identities and differences cannot be fully or definitely reconciled, and although justice can never be realized, the search for justice remains imperative, and some plausible resolutions of actual conflicts less unjust than others.

Within the ambit of comprehensive pluralism, the preceding conception of justice assumes that self and other, each from his or her own perspective, prefer some accommodation with one another to complete lack of contact. Moreover, this conception of justice also assumes that, in spite of unbridgeable differences, self and other share enough in common that dialogue between them and search for mutual accommodation (even if ultimately unsuccessful) are neither altogether impossible nor utterly futile. That said, however, comprehensive pluralism does not rely on the existence of any common perspective linking self to other, and it emphatically rejects the possibility of "the view from nowhere" (Nagel 1986). Even though self and other may both seek fair means of mutual accommodation, each of them can only do so from the standpoint of his or her own perspective.[25] Accordingly, the impossibility of full justice from the standpoint of comprehensive pluralism stems from the impossibility of at once preserving and transcending the respective perspectives of self and other.

---

[24] The former kind of justice corresponds to what I call "justice as mere reciprocity," while the latter kind corresponds to what I call "justice as reversible reciprocity" (Rosenfeld 1998: 249–50).

[25] This last statement is not inconsistent with the commitment to justice as reversible reciprocity, see supra note – 24, which requires that the self seek to understand the claims of the other from the perspective of the other. While the latter requirement obligates the self to take into account what it would be like to be in the skin of the other, this can only be done through imagination and projection, which necessarily remain connected to the self's perspective. For example, I can imagine and empathize with another's pain – but only through an act of imagination based on recollection of my own pain, as I cannot literally feel any other person's pain.

1.6.2. *The Contrast Between Homogeneous and Heterogeneous Societies*

Critics of comprehensive pluralism challenge the claim that pluralism-in-fact necessarily makes for a heterogeneous society. Thus, Michelman questions my assertion that the crisis in constitutional interpretation experienced in the United States is only typical of a heterogeneous society and argues that the crisis in question also can be cogently understood in all its relevant respects as that of homogeneous society (Michelman 2000: 1950–1). In this connection, the crucial issue for Michelman is whether principles can maintain their identities under differing sets of applications. If they can, then, in Michelman's view, even though Americans may disagree vehemently on particular applications of certain constitutional rights, such as those to the free exercise of religion or to equal protection, it would nonetheless be fair to conclude that they widely agree on the broad principles on which these rights are founded (Id.: 1950).

To deal with these issues, it is imperative to keep in mind that the distinction between homogeneous and heterogeneous societies, which is based on the distinction between self and other, is relational, fluid, and contextual, rather than fixed or pertaining to essence. As already noted, the relationship between self and other is in some contexts one between individuals, and in others one among groups. Moreover, a single individual may belong to different selves confronting different others as illustrated earlier in the example of the German Catholic feminist woman. Furthermore, what distinguishes a homogeneous society from a heterogeneous one is that in the former intersubjective dealings are intra-communal, whereas in the latter they are to a very significant degree inter-communal. In other words, in a homogeneous society, there is a strong sense at the group level that the entire society constitutes a single self – albeit that at the individual level most relationships remain best characterized as being between self and other. Conversely, in a heterogeneous society collective dealings, which are societywide – and most likely those that involve different groups without being societywide – are definitely structured as confrontations between self and other.[26]

Given these criteria, it seems fair to conclude that most, if not all, contemporary constitutional democracies – including the United States – are sufficiently heterogeneous that societywide dealings within any of them cannot be cogently regarded as being in all relevant respects intra-communal. Furthermore, inasmuch as modern

---

[26] Given the contextual nature of the relationship between self and other, societies can span the entire spectrum from completely homogeneous to extremely heterogeneous, with most being partly homogeneous and partly heterogeneous. For our purposes, it suffices to characterize a society as heterogeneous if it divides into self and other over important issues likely to have a significant impact on the realization or maintenance of social cohesion.

societies are heterogeneous,[27] the difference between modern and post modern heterogeneous societies can be summarized as follows: In both modern and post-modern heterogeneous societies, societywide dealings are inter-communal, but in modern settings the relevant inter-communal norms are deemed fair and neutral among competing, purely intra-communal conceptions of the good.[28] In contrast, post-modern societies would deny the very possibility of finding fair and neutral inter-communal norms to mediate among those who adhere to different conceptions of the good.

Determining whether particular dealings within a heterogeneous society are best characterized as intra-communal rather than inter-communal is not always easy. This is because the nature of the relations involved is not fixed but rather depends on contextual factors that can only be properly assessed in terms of the totality of relevant circumstances in play. Moreover, the appearances surrounding such relations can often be deceiving. In particular, generalized professions of commitment to the same abstract principles may, in certain cases, conceal irreconcilable differences in perspective, which would ultimately undermine any genuine attempt to cast the conflicts involved as intra-communal.

Inter-communal relations can result from encounters among alien cultures, such as liberal Western culture and illiberal non-Western culture, or from a profound split within a particular culture, such as that between fundamentalist Protestants and liberals in the United States or between religious and secular Jews in Israel. It may not always be easy to pinpoint when splits within a culture are serious enough to transform relations within that culture from intra-communal to inter-communal ones. More specifically, in some cases, consensus – or apparent consensus – on broad abstract principles, combined with sharp disagreement on application of such principles, may fall within the ambit of intra-communal relationships; in others, such combinations definitely play out in the context of inter-communal relationships. For example, both partisans and foes of abortion may concur that respect for human dignity is a paramount value. However, to the extent that abortion foes consider abortion to be murder and defenders of the right to abortion consider it essential to a women's dignity, dealings between the two camps would clearly have to be characterized as inter-communal. Moreover, although Michelman's example relating to adherence to the principle of equality may not be as clear, it is certainly plausible that the dispute between supporters of the majority opinion and those of the dissent

---

[27] Even though I believe that all modern societies are pluralistic-in-fact, and hence heterogeneous, the argument I pursue here depends only on acceptance that some modern societies are heterogeneous.

[28] This does not necessarily mean that all relevant actors would agree on which particular norms would guarantee fairness and neutrality, but it does imply that they would all agree that it is possible to find some such norms.

in *Plessey* v. *Ferguson*[29] is better characterized as an inter-communal rather than an intra-communal disagreement. Similarly, some of the vehemence among professed supporters of equality over affirmative action suggest inter-communal rather than intra-communal feuds.[30] In such cases, ideals such as human dignity or equality mean such different things to different people that they share little in common other than their names.

1.7. COMPREHENSIVE PLURALISM AND THE PRIORITY OF THE GOOD OVER THE RIGHT

Along the lines of the criticism by Habermas cited previously, Michelman claims that comprehensive pluralism advances a position that, in the end, is much like that elaborated by Rawls in *Political Liberalism*. Michelman's claim depends heavily on the distinction he draws between the "right" and the "good." As Michelman puts it, the right "asks what ought to be done" whereas the good "asks what is of value to a person, group or society" (Id.: 1962). Furthermore, Michelman asserts that even if there were unanimous agreement on the good, questions concerning the right would still be inevitable in relation to issues of aggregation or distribution (Id.).

One may quibble with Michelman's last assertion, for it seems entirely plausible to have a sufficiently elaborated theory of the good, which could quite naturally subsume issues of aggregation and distribution. To take Michelman's own example of a society in which there is universal agreement that glory is the ultimate good for all humankind, it does not necessarily follow, as he claims, that determination of how much glory for whom would have to be a question of the right. Indeed, the theory of the good based on glory could be elaborated to the point that it would prescribe how much glory for whom would best approximate the ultimate good. Moreover, under those circumstances, any person's claim to glory would not be a claim of right but rather one predicated on the conviction that satisfaction of such claim would contribute to realization of the good.

In the context of a homogeneous society operating pursuant to a single, unanimously shared conception of good, there would arguably be no need for the right. Be that as it may, in the context of heterogeneous modern societies, there is an inescapable need for both the good and the right. And this squarely raises the question of priority between the two.

---

[29] 163 U.S. 537 (1896). In *Plessy*, the majority held that "separate but equal" was consistent with equal protection and intimated that racial segregation was in the public good. The dissent deemed state-required segregation unconstitutional and pernicious, given its tendency to perpetuate the notion that African Americans are inherently inferior to whites.

[30] *See* Rosenfeld, 1989 (discussing the irreconcilable visions of race relations and affirmative action espoused, respectively, by Justice O'Connor and Justice Marshall).

The key to the split between the right and the good in modern societies is found in the pluralization or fragmentation of the good. This is most obvious in the case of pluralist societies with a multiplicity of competing conceptions of the good. In such societies, inter-communal dealings among the various different groups raise issues of distribution that fall within the domain of the right – at least in the sense that, to be fairly resolved, the distribution questions at issue must be considered above and beyond the competing conceptions of the good that divide the polity. Furthermore, the split between the right and the good would also remain important even in a society that shared a single conception of the good at the collective level, but that allowed each individual, to a significant extent, to pursue his or her own good consistent with that conception.

In any setting in which there is a multiplicity of conceptions of the good or a fragmentation of the good, there seems to be a need for coexistence between the right and the good. Moreover, inasmuch as the right can ascend above the conflict among conceptions of the good or the competition among individuals who seek to reach their own perceived good – or, in other words, inasmuch as the right can secure neutrality in relation to the conflict or competition in question – the right ought to receive priority over the good. Conversely, so long as the problems resulting from pluralization and fragmentation of the good can best be dealt with terms of a more encompassing conception of the good, the good ought to receive priority over the right.

Comprehensive pluralism emerges in the context of clashes among competing conceptions of good which do not lead to any fair or neutral resolution under any plausible conception of the right as having priority over the good. Indeed, although it shares with Habermas and Rawls the goal of fostering reciprocity among self and other, comprehensive pluralism parts company with them precisely because, as already pointed out, the reciprocity they promote from the standpoint of the priority of the right inherently favors certain conceptions of the good over others. Thus, the key question confronting comprehensive pluralism is: How can the normative impasse, stemming from the inability to overcome the clash among competing conceptions of the good by appealing to inter-communal norms predicated on the priority of the right, be adequately resolved?

The answer provided by comprehensive pluralism is that the only way out of the normative impasse in question is through counterfactual imagination of a community of communities, which would incorporate the various conceptions of the good associated with the different existing communities dialectically into a more broadly encompassing conception of the good. Moreover, consistent with its Hegelian underpinnings, comprehensive pluralism regards this community of communities as a whole seeking to incorporate the conceptions of the good emanating from the various existing communities that are its parts. To be sure, this projected community of communities remains ultimately counterfactual and retains the quality of a work in progress. Also, it incorporates existing conceptions of good not on their own terms, but as reconceived from its more encompassing perspective.

Although mediation between the norms of the community of communities (second-order norms) and the norms of the individual community (first-order norms) requires reliance on the right, comprehensive pluralism clearly depends on the priority of the good over the right. Actually, structurally speaking, comprehensive pluralism shares much in common with a certain plausible version of utilitarianism. Utilitarianism as discussed in Section 1.3 can be conceived as resolving all normative questions by reference to the good, thus dispensing altogether with the right. However, another plausible conception of utilitarianism could stipulate that the individual is the best judge of what is good for her, and thus to the extent that the individual good figures in the determination of the greatest good for the greatest number, it would make sense to carve out some rights to allow each individual some space to discover and pursue what is good for her. In this conception of utilitarianism, the good is still prior to the right, but the latter plays a significant role that contributes to the overall good. In such a utilitarian vision, the individual good figures in the collective good and requires the right for its protection. Similarly, in the context of comprehensive pluralism, the good targeted through vindication of second-order norms depends on protection of first-order norms, which requires a certain degree of reliance on the right. Furthermore, in the utilitarian ethos, questions about proper limitations on the pursuits motivated by the good of the individual or about proper constraints on rights must be resolved in terms of the overall collective good (i.e., the greatest good for the greatest number). Likewise, in the normative universe carved out by comprehensive pluralism, limits on the vindication of first-order norms and proper delimitation of the domain of the right must be made in terms of the vision of the good projected by the totality of second-order norms. In sum, like utilitarianism, comprehensive pluralism is a teleological rather than a deontological theory. The crucial distinction between the two, however, is that they prescribe sharply different conceptions of the good. Whereas utilitarianism is concerned with maximizing utilities, comprehensive pluralism embraces a vision of the good predicated on the greatest possible accommodation of diverse conceptions of the good consistent with promotion of a reciprocal equilibrium between self and other.

Consistent with this, when properly viewed in its full dialectic dimensions, comprehensive pluralism is both substantive and non-neutral. It does not rely on agreement, consensus, or universalizability. It seems to carve out the largest possible space for the concurrent pursuit of the maximum possible number of perspectives and conceptions of the good. But in the course of this pursuit, comprehensive pluralism requires different prices of admission for different conceptions of the good, trampling heavily on some of them while imposing slight burdens on others. Comprehensive pluralism's good (as embodied in its second-order norms) is parasitic on all other conceptions of the good, for without even the potential of a conflict

among first-order norms gauged from different perspectives, comprehensive pluralism would become meaningless. So long as conflicts among competing conceptions
of the good are prevalent, however, comprehensive pluralism sets out to be as inclusive as one could imagine and ends up standing against all of the conceptions of the
good that vie for admission. In sum, comprehensive pluralism's ideal is a community of communities, but consistent with its Hegelian heritage, it can only integrate
the communities it seeks to preserve by forcing upon the latter uneven burdens and
limitations in the name of the greater good of which they are intended to become
an integral part.

1.8. COMPREHENSIVE PLURALISM AND RAWLS'S POLITICAL LIBERALISM

Upon realizing that his conception of justice as fairness embodied in the two principles of justice articulated in *A Theory of Justice* did not properly account for the
plurality of comprehensive views present in typical contemporary societies, Rawls
set out to remedy this problem by shifting his focus from comprehensive to political
justice in *Political Liberalism* (Rawls 1993: 59–60). By thus retreating and confining
the quest for justice of the basic structure of society and of its constitutional essentials to the political sphere, *Political Liberalism* grounds justice on an "overlapping
consensus" (Id.: 15) that allows for full inclusion of a plurality of comprehensive
views[31] that differ on morals and ethics so long as these views come within the sweep
of what he calls "reasonable pluralism" (Id.: 64). Moreover, Rawls continued to
work till the end of his life on making his conception of political justice ever more
inclusive of a wider range of plurality. Accordingly, the last version of Rawls's theory,
first published in 1997 was, according to him, capable of accommodating all major
Western religions, Catholicism, Protestantism, Judaism and Islam,[32] only excluding
fundamentalism (Rawls 2005: 438).[33]

---

[31] Rawls's conception of a "comprehensive view 'is in essence the equivalent of what I would characterize a "comprehensive conception of the good." As I understand it, a comprehensive conception of
the good is systematic and accounts for the entirety of the normative universe. From the standpoint
of comprehensive pluralism, in contrast, a conception of the good need not be comprehensive to
be entitled to as much consideration and inclusion as its comprehensive counterparts. For example,
those who join together to run a worldwide NGO to promote environmentalist goals presumably
do not have a common position on religion or personal morality. They are thus unlike the Catholic
religion which is comprehensive in its normative vision.

[32] This does not imply that the latest version of Rawls's theory could not also include Eastern religions
such as Buddhism or Hinduism, only that Rawls was not sufficiently familiar with them to opine on
the matter.

[33] Rawls's last version of his position was first published in 1997 in the *Chicago Law Review* (Rawls 1997)
and then reprinted posthumously in an expanded edition of *Political Liberalism* (Rawls 2005). All
references in this book are made to the latter source.

It certainly seems that Rawls's last revised conception of political justice, overlapping consensus, and reasonable pluralism shares much in common with comprehensive pluralism. Michelman asserts that, in the end, there are no relevant differences between the two (Michelman 2000: 1959). And, admittedly, when viewed in the broadest terms there seems to be a remarkable analogy between Rawls's overlapping consensus and comprehensive pluralism. Within Rawls's sphere of political justice, the same set of norms is applicable to everyone; beyond that sphere, a large plurality of norms can coexist legitimately without threatening the justice or fairness of basic institutions. Similarly, comprehensive pluralism seems to divide into a core and a periphery, with commonly shared second-order norms operative at the core, and diverse first-order norms competing at the periphery.

Upon closer examination, however, and particularly if one does not lose sight of comprehensive pluralism's Hegelian underpinnings, the analogy between Rawls's overlapping consensus and comprehensive pluralism breaks down. In the first place, as will be briefly considered later, Rawls's last conception of overlapping consensus is far less pluralistic than he claims. In the second place, Rawls's deontological conception, even if he had taken it farther than he did at the end of his life (or if someone else now ventured along that path) could never be as encompassing of plurality as a teleological theory, such as comprehensive pluralism, which places fostering pluralism as extensively as possible as the top priority within the realm of the good. As I will seek to prove, the differences between Rawls's overlapping consensus and comprehensive pluralism far outweigh the similarities between them, both from the standpoint of theory and from that of practice.

Rawls's last revision of his theory does not go as far as he claims primarily because to be included within the realm of "reasonable pluralism," a comprehensive view must consent to being bound by justice as fairness or a close equivalent within the political sphere. Rawls does not veer an iota from his allegiance to the priority of the right over the good, but he does depart from his requirement in the initial version of *Political Liberalism* that comprehensive views worthy of inclusion must adhere to justice as fairness. They can deviate, but the margin that Rawls allows for that is quite narrow.

As he specifies,

> Political liberalism … does not try to fix public reason once and for all in the form of one favored political conception of justice. That would not be a sensible approach. For instance, political liberalism also admits Habermas's discourse conception of legitimacy … as well as Catholic views of the common good and solidarity when they are expressed in terms of political values. (Rawls 2005: 451–2)

As we have already indicated, shifting from Rawls's conception of justice to Habermas's may alter the final configuration of inclusions and exclusions, but does not change much in terms of imposing on all conceptions of the good involved a right that is biased *ex ante* against some of them.[34] Moreover, presumably the Catholic values that Rawls has in mind are those that relate to social solidarity and to concern for the welfare of the poor, which can easily be incorporated within the precincts of the liberal vision, unlike, for instance, the Catholic stance on abortion or homosexuality.

Rawls's move from A *Theory of Justice* to *Political Liberalism* does make for accommodation of greater plurality. Those comprehensive views that cannot accept liberalism at the comprehensive level but can live with it if it is confined to the domain of the political can indeed find room within the revised Rawlsian normative universe. And, significantly the dichotomy between the moral and the political that this type of accommodation entails seems to fit quite naturally with Christianity's split between the realm of God and that of Caesar, but not with Judaism or Islam where no such split is recognized (Wallace 2009: 26–33).

Does Rawls's additional move to incorporate theories of political justice other than justice as fairness further expand plurality beyond opening the door to those like Habermas who are already firmly implanted in the liberal camp? The answer is most likely in the negative as it is hard to imagine that those whose comprehensive views are in conflict with liberal political justice (of whatever stripe) would willingly consent to be bound by it.

Take the example of equality between the sexes. It is undoubtedly fundamental to justice as fairness, to Habermas's discourse theory of justice and, at least in principle, to all contemporary conceptions of liberalism.[35] Moreover, equality between the sexes is a matter of political justice, which must be incorporated in the liberal polity's basic structure and in its constitutional essentials. It is most unlikely, however, that several non-fundamentalist branches or denominations of Christianity, Judaism and Islam would agree to be bound in the realm of politics to any liberal conception of gender-based equality. One need only consider a few examples, such as Jewish divorce law as interpreted by Orthodox Judaism (Esther Rosenfeld 1995) or property or inheritance law under the Shariah (Radford 2000), to realize that these deny basic equality rights to women under any conception of liberalism. Furthermore, since neither Judaism nor Islam draws any firm lines between the religious, the moral, and the political, there would be no reason for them to agree to be bound by liberal political justice, except if necessary to their survival as members of

---

[34] See supra, at 32–33, 35.
[35] This is true even in light of feminist critique of liberalism, such as those mentioned earlier. See supra, at 35. In other words, liberalism postulates equality between the sexes but may fall short either in successfully discarding certain remnants of illiberalism or in embracing polices that can successfully translate equality in theory into equality in practice, or it may even fall short on both counts. Be that as it may, all versions of liberalism require that all accept that men and women are inherently equal.

minority religions in liberal polities. But in that case, the accord involved would be in the nature of a "modus vivendi," and not of an "overlapping consensus." Finally, substantial arguments can be mounted in support of the claim that many existing non-fundamentalist interpretations of Christianity and the practical consequences that follow from these would also run afoul the minimum requirements of liberal equality between the sexes or relating to sexual orientation (Fineman 2004: 131).

Consistent with these observations, Rawls's claim that Christianity, Judaism, and Islam can find room within his reasonable pluralism is highly exaggerated, if not downright misleading. It would be more accurate to assert that certain branches or denominations of these religions, such as Reform Judaism and mainstream American Protestantism or Anglicanism, all of which have already incorporated essential liberal tenets within their normative visions, would willingly subscribe to a Rawlsian overlapping consensus. But that would not be because Rawls's expanded conception of liberal political justice, but because these religious conceptions have already internalized key liberal values. In this respect, it is quite noteworthy that Rawls refers to an early version of Islam that supposedly interpreted Shariah as providing for equality between men and women, but which has not been prevalent for most of Islam's history, as lending support to his conclusion (Rawls 2005: 461, n. 46). Unfortunately for Rawls, the very consideration of this example leads most naturally precisely to the contrary conclusion that, for the most part, contemporary Islam cannot be included within reasonable pluralism.

Let us now turn briefly to the second main reason identified earlier why the apparent analogy between comprehensive pluralism and an overlapping consensus does not hold, for the most part, under close scrutiny. In a word, as already stressed in the course of the previous analysis, there is an unbridgeable gap between Rawls's deontological approach and the brand of dialectically grounded teleological position espoused by comprehensive pluralism. This is vividly illustrated by the case of fundamentalist religion that Rawls concludes cannot be included within the ambit of reasonable pluralism. Comprehensive pluralism, in contrast, is inclusive ex ante and accommodating ex post of fundamentalist religion – especially if it is non-belligerent – as it commands that efforts be made to "feel" and understand such religion from "within" and to provide, to the extent possible, consistent with the requirement of reciprocal equilibrium for the satisfaction of its needs and the realization of its aspirations. Also, at the same time, comprehensive pluralism remains indifferent concerning whether fundamentalist religion would freely accept under any circumstances to live by the requirements flowing from a set of second-order norms. As a matter of fact, comprehensive pluralism fully justifies imposing *its* conception of the good, as embodied in its second-order norms, on everyone, including proponents of religious fundamentalism. In the end, this is but another way of expressing comprehensive pluralism's core imperative in the pursuit of it own conception of the good, namely, its goal of establishing the community of communities. To encapsulate it in a slogan: "include, understand and accommodate the *inconsistent*, but impose on, and fight against, the *incompatible*."

Even conceding that comprehensive pluralism differs from an overlapping consensus in the ways detailed previously, a Rawlsian may still insist that comprehensive pluralism amounts to a comprehensive view in Rawlsian terms, and that it satisfies the criteria of "reasonable pluralism." Consistent with this, moreover, whatever relevant differences there may be between comprehensive pluralism and justice as fairness or any of the other conceptions deemed legitimate by Rawls would lie beyond the realm of political justice.

Notwithstanding the palpable appeal of the preceding argument, comprehensive pluralism ultimately fails to satisfy the Rawlsian requirements regarding "reasonable pluralism," for both philosophical and practical reasons. From a philosophical standpoint, even in the absence of any practical differences, the mere fact that comprehensive pluralism prescribes the priority of the good over the right in the realm of political justice suffices to disqualify comprehensive pluralism from inclusion in the requisite Rawlsian overlapping consensus. Indeed, unless one can prove the existence of a fixed coincidence between the good prescribed by comprehensive pluralism and the right circumscribed by justice as fairness or its alternatives recognized by Rawls, it is always possible that comprehensive pluralism will legitimate institutional arrangements that are incompatible with the dictates of any of the theories of the right sanctioned by Rawls. In this sense, comprehensive pluralism is no different from other teleological theories, such as utilitarianism. Accordingly, just as the implementation of criteria of justice acceptable to Rawls would not always be consistent with maximizing utilities – and even if they were, this would be impossible to ascertain ex ante – so, too, it would not always be consistent with the good as dialectically articulated in accordance with the normative guidelines imposed by comprehensive pluralism.

From a practical standpoint, on the other hand, comprehensive pluralism parts company with justice as fairness, along with all other liberal theories of justice, insofar as it does not privilege individual-regarding claims over group-regarding ones. Although the issue of whether a particular group-regarding claim would prevail over a competing individual-regarding claim is always context-specific within comprehensive pluralism, as will be more fully addressed in Chapter 3, there are certainly significant cases in which group concerns would be entitled to priority. This would occur when the centrality of the relevant group right in relation to that group's conception of the good was palpably greater than the centrality of the competing individual right in relation to that individual's conception of the good. Thus, comprehensive pluralism would require a comparative weighing of the competing claims in terms of the respective perspectives on the good involved, in ways that seem altogether incompatible with the lexical priority of the right over the good prescribed by Rawls.

Because what comprehensive pluralism prescribes in specific cases is very much context dependent, further specification of its functioning and potential is best postponed till consideration of the particular issues that will be addressed in the following chapters. Before proceeding, however, there is one point that warrants further clarification. The assertion that comprehensive pluralism is ultimately agnostic among individual-regarding goods and rights, on the one hand, and their group-regarding counterparts, on the other, and that, under certain circumstances, it would give priority to group-regarding goods over individual ones may appear to repudiate individualism which is not only inextricably linked to pluralism, but also key to the passage from the Middle Ages to the modern period.[36] If the group can prevail over the individual, does that foreshadow a return to an earlier age where the individual could only fit as a part of a larger collective whole?

Comprehensive pluralism does treat the individual as the equal to the group and not as its subordinate. The individual is an autonomous self, who has a perspective and a conception of the good, and so is a group that engages in the pursuit of normative ends. Moreover, the actual conception of the good of every individual is entitled ex ante to the same consideration as that of every other individual or group with the characteristics mentioned earlier. Comprehensive pluralism does not look backward; it looks forward, but forward in a dialectical way. In the struggle for differentiation from the Middle Ages, it became normatively imperative to put the individual ahead of the group. Given the shortcomings of liberal individualism that have emerged over time as discussed previously, however, it is now necessary to place the individual and the group on an equal normative footing. Indeed, in this increasingly concurrently globalized and balkanized world, the individual can seemingly best pursue self-realization through the group and against it – or, more precisely through and against a plurality of groups from which and through which that individual develops a distinct sense of self by weaving together elements drawn respectively from poles of identity and from poles of differentiation.

---

[36] See supra, at 24.

2

Equality and the Dialectic Between
Identity and Difference

Equality is of paramount concern for both liberalism and pluralism; it plays a central role in mapping out the relationship between the self and the other as made manifest in Hegel's account of the struggle between the lord and the bondsman discussed in Chapter 1, and it figures prominently in all modern and post-modern conceptions of justice. Equality must properly account for identity and difference – or, more precisely, identities and differences – between self and other. As underscored by the key role of the abstract ego in theories such as those of Kant and Rawls, liberal individualism is well poised to focus on identity, but, as will be discussed in this chapter, it has had persistent trouble coping with difference. This difficulty becomes more acute in the face of equality claims arising in the context of identity politics.

In what follows, I will compare the liberal and pluralist approaches to equality and argue that the latter is better suited for purposes of approximating justice between self and other. In this chapter, I tackle equality in general. In Chapter 3, I will address the question of minority group rights in terms of the dialectic between identity and difference as it plays out in relation to the determination of what is encompassed by human rights.

Modern equality, which emerged from the Enlightenment's repudiation of feudalism, has had a vexing and persistent problem with difference. Feudalism was built upon status-based differences, which divided society into inherently unequal classes of people: noblemen, clergymen, commoners, and serfs. The legacy of the Enlightenment and of the core precept of political liberalism, in contrast, is, consistent with the preceding discussion, that all human beings are equal because they all share a common identity as autonomous agents with a capacity for moral choice. Consistent with this, equality has been largely correlated to identity and inequality to difference.

Unlike in feudalism, where status-based inequality is a given, in liberalism, equality is the norm, and inequality can only be justified on the basis of the existence of relevant differences. Thus, within a liberal framework, for example, men and women are inherently equal, but differences between the sexes may be invoked in efforts to justify casting women as legal or political unequals.[1] Historically, moreover, embrace of the principle of equality has not resulted in a rapid or even spread of political or legal equality within the polity. Indeed, in many democracies women were denied the franchise for a long time *because* of real or constructed differences between the sexes, while African Americans in the United States were first enslaved and then treated as free but inferior citizens *because* of racial differences.[2] Furthermore, to the extent that over time legal and political equality have actually achieved greater conformity with the principle of equality, this has been largely due to stress on identities at the expense of differences. Thus, for example, it is now accepted that women and men, and blacks and whites, ought to be treated equally in the realms of politics and employment. This is associated with the belief that gender-based differences and race-based ones have no relevance to suitability for political participation or, in most cases, in relation to qualifications for employment.[3] In short, it seems that once the liberal principle of equality is in place, the actual achievement of equality in various realms such as those of law and politics depends on an evolving shift of focus from differences to identities.

In this context, more recent demands for equality based on identity politics, which call for equality taking account of differences rather than in spite of them, to give full expression to such differences rather than underemphasizing them or restraining them, have been troubling and perplexing for political liberals. For example, underneath a claim for equal treatment of all religions (i.e., a claim that from a legal and political standpoint all religions ought to be treated identically in spite of their differences) may lurk a demand for recognition and acceptance of treatment of women as subordinate in accordance with religious doctrine. In other words, if you take seriously that all religions qua religions are identical in the sense that they deserve equal recognition and protection under the law, then you must tolerate or even actively protect the subordination of women to the extent that it derives from an essential precept of one of the active religions within the polity.

How should liberalism handle such identity-based claims for difference? By creating exceptions to generally applicable laws? By promoting group-based autonomy

---

[1]   See, for example, *Bradwell* v. *Illinois*, 83 U.S. 130 (1873) (barring women from admission to the bar and from practicing law upheld based, in part, on belief of women's greater suitability for raising children in the family home).

[2]   See, for example, the infamous decision in *Dred Scott* v. *Sanford*, 60 U.S.393 (1857) (slavery argued to be justified based on purported differences between the white and black races), and *Plessy* v. *Ferguson*, 163 U.S. 537 (1896) (racial segregation in public accommodations held not to violate constitutional equality rights because of supposed differences among the races).

[3]   In some small numbers of cases, differences in sex may still be relevant in the realm of employment. For instance, it does not seem inconsistent with legal equality that only women be eligible to play the leading female role in a movie.

and self-government even at the risk of balkanizing the polity? Or, on the contrary, by rejecting such demands for recognition of differences and by reinforcing equality as identity?

Building upon the idea that liberalism requires establishing a single-status community that must aim at self-realization through law, politics, and social relations, Jeremy Waldron advocates responding to claims based on cultural difference by allowing a place for them in the political marketplace of ideas (Waldron 2007). In essence, what Waldron proposes is that claims to legal or institutional recognition and accommodation of cultural difference be given a fair hearing in the lawmaking process. If an open-minded majority decides to provide accommodation, all the better. If not, that means that the clash between liberalism and the particular cultural difference involved is irreconcilable and that equality-as-identity must trump attempts to institutionalize equality-as-difference (Id.: 155).

Commitment to equal status on the basis of having the same capacity for moral choice – a commitment that pluralism and Waldron share – does not entail, however, adherence to equality-as-identity *above* equality-as-difference or require as limited an incorporation of cultural difference as Waldron proposes. If the modern conception of equality is understood dialectically, then commitment to equal status leads eventually beyond liberalism to pluralism and beyond the monolithic nation-state to more elastic and more diverse multi-layered interconnected arenas of collective autonomy and self-government. Moreover, within the pluralist perspective and beyond the conception of the polity as a unitary and indivisible nation-state, it becomes apparent that Waldron's conception of equal status leads him to shortchange cultural difference.

To lay out the argument in support of this position, Section 2.1 provides a brief account of the dialectic of equality as a succession of attempts to better reconcile identity and difference. Section 2.3 indicates why, when placed in proper historical perspective, commitment to equal status eventually calls for transition from liberalism to pluralism. Section 2.3 takes a closer look at the dynamic between identity and difference, and Section 2.4 inquires into the relationship between equal status and divisibility of the polity. Section 2.5 assesses cultural differences in the context of pluralism and of the dialectic of equality, and Section 2.6 considers what legal and institutional framework may be best suited to achieve accommodation of cultural differences.

2.1. THE DIALECTIC OF EQUALITY: A THREE-STAGE PROGRESSION

Going back to Aristotle, justice and equality require treating equals equally and unequals unequally (Aristotle 1980: bk. v), or, in other words, treating everyone proportionately. Treating equals unequally or unequals equally is disproportionate as is treating unequals more unequally than they are unequal. The criterion of proportionality, however, does not tell us who is equal to whom, or what makes one equal or unequal to another. To be able to answer these questions, it is necessary to have a baseline as well as indicia of identity and of difference, and these vary depending on one's substantive normative criteria. Thus, in a multi-status feudal society, one's very being makes one the equal of some and the unequal of others. In a single-status society, in contrast, all human beings as such are equals and, by and large, can only become unequals by virtue of what they do or suffer. In a feudal society thus, inequality is the baseline (e.g., the serf is unequal to the lord from birth till death because of who each of them is), whereas in a modern single-status society, equality is the baseline. In a feudal society, one can be treated unequally because of who one is, whereas in a single-status society, one cannot.

Since in liberal single-status societies all humans are considered inherently equal, unequal treatment can only be justified on account of differences between those involved. For example, dispensing free medicine to the sick but not the remainder of the citizenry is justified in terms of differences regarding health and well-being. More generally, proportional treatment, sometimes requiring equal treatment, sometimes unequal, depends on identities and differences with respect to what those involved do or suffer. Moreover, it is clear that not all identities or differences are relevant in the circumstances involved (e.g., race, sex, or eye color differences are irrelevant in the context of dispensing free medicines to cure the sick), but which identities and which differences ought to be taken into account in given circumstances is often a source of disagreement (e.g., libertarians do not believe that differences in wealth justify redistribution through taxation and welfare payments whereas egalitarians do).

Ideally, single-status societies with equality as the baseline could achieve justice, equality, and proportionality by properly accounting for all *relevant* identities and differences and by disregarding all identities and differences that are irrelevant. This task is fraught with great difficulty not only because of disagreements over the relevance of particular identities or differences but also because even among those who may be in general agreement concerning such relevance, an identity or difference relevant in one context may be irrelevant in another. For example, there is widespread agreement that religious differences should be irrelevant in the allocation of competitive positions in the liberal professions. However, many who share this latter view would undoubtedly also agree that religious differences ought to matter where accommodation of religion is appropriate (e.g., facilitating observance of a religiously mandated day of rest would require freeing Muslims on Friday, Jews on Saturday, and Christians on Sunday).

In spite of these inevitable disagreements and difficulties, if the origin of modern single-status equality is placed in its historical context, and if its conceptual deployment is understood in terms of the dialectic that animates it, one can obtain sufficient insights to determine how cultural difference ought to be treated. Indeed, single-status equality was set against multiple status hierarchy with inequality as the baseline. The most dramatic historical confrontation between the two, moreover, was the one that occurred during the French Revolution. The revolutionaries leveled all feudal hierarchies and institutionalized a new order based on equal citizenship. In principle and in the abstract, equal citizenship was meant to provide the glue for the single-status society and to extend it to all individuals within the polity. In practice, however, the concept of equal citizenship had to perform two separate tasks. Looking backward, it stood for negation of the absolute monarch and of feudal privilege; projected forward, on the other hand, equal citizenship was supposed to stand for affirmation of the political equality of all (adult) persons belonging to the polity. Significantly, the French Revolution led to achievement of equal citizenship's negative mission, but not of its affirmative one. It abolished feudal privilege, but it did not extend its benefits to all adults, as, for example, women were not granted the franchise.[4]

It is this discrepancy between concept and practice that sets off the dialectic of equality in modern single-status societies. Those who benefit from the discrepancy are drawn into a struggle with those who suffer from it and seek to overcome it. Moreover, depending on whether one is a beneficiary of a discrepancy or a victim of it, one is more likely to stress identity or difference. Thus, when men alone had the franchise they could only justify the status quo, consistent with baseline equality, by pointing to differences (real or constructed) between the sexes, such as that women's responsibilities at the family home left them no time to become informed about political issues and thus they could not exercise the franchise responsibly. Conversely, women under those circumstances could only combat the status quo by denying the differences claimed by men and by stressing identities between the sexes.[5] Accordingly, in the struggles traceable to discrepancies between concept and practice, above and beyond the particular identities and differences that may be relevant, there is a more general tendency to stress identity at the expense of difference or vice versa. Moreover, the general tendency will give direction to the dialectic and hopefully furnish sufficient guidance to deal in a principled manner with the problem of cultural difference. Finally, the need to adhere to a tendency that

---

[4] In fact, women were not accorded the right to vote in France until 1944. See http://www.justice. gouv.fr/actualites/60ansvotefemmes.htm. Similarly, in the United States, notwithstanding the 1776 Declaration of Independence's famous dictum that "All men are created equal" (meaning "all humans") women did not obtain the right to vote till 1920. See U.S. Const. Amend. XIX.

[5] I use "men" and "women'" here as shorthand for "advocates to restrict political rights to men" and "advocates to extend such rights to women," respectively. It is of course obvious that some men fall in the latter category, and some women in the former.

overly stresses identity or difference in order to overcome a discrepancy skews the optimal balance between identity and difference for those engaged in the struggle regarding that discrepancy. This skewing, in turn, may lead to new discrepancies or exacerbate existing ones. As we shall now see, the adverse effects of the skewing in question leads to new struggles that give shape to the evolving dialectic of equality.

Looking at the trajectory of claims since the institution of modern baseline equality, one can discern a dialectical process that has unfolded in three distinct stages. These stages can be characterized respectively as (1) difference as inequality, (2) equality as identity, and (3) equality as difference. These stages represent above all a logical progression, and although in their broad outlines they have succeeded one another over time, there is no inevitable historical progress. As a matter of fact, there are unavoidable setbacks, reversals, and inconsistencies and time lags among various particular domains of equality. Overall, however, the dialectic operates through shifts in predominance alternating between identity and difference. Moreover, whereas there may be a fairly constant conflict concerning the relevance of particular identities or differences, the predominance of identity or difference at a given stage of the dialectic imposes a certain order on the realm of particular identities and differences in play, and orients the clashes among them towards certain paths to resolution to the exclusion of other such paths.

To illustrate how this three-stage dialectic unfolds, I shall focus on the evolving struggle regarding equality between the sexes, which includes, but is not limited to, issues of gender-based equality. This example is particularly useful not only because few would deny that some differences between the sexes ought to count while others ought not, but also because, as will be more fully explored in Chapter 3, claims for recognition of cultural difference frequently seem to clash with *adherence* to women's equality rights.[6]

The subordination of women to men was prevalent during feudalism and congruent with feudalism's status-based stratification, but not necessarily entailed by it. On the other hand, upon the toppling of feudalism and the institution of a single-status society, commitment to baseline equality called for elimination of the subordination of women. Even though this was entailed by the concept upon which the single-status society was founded, it was resisted as a practical matter, lest the changes brought by the overthrow of feudalism became too radical or too disruptive to permit a successful transition into a post-feudal order. Consistent with this, a contradiction arose between baseline equality as a general precept and the continuing subordination of women as a matter of practice. In an attempt to overcome this contradiction

---

[6] See, for example, *Santa Clara Pueblo v. Martinez*, 436 U.S. 49 (1978) (Pueblo Tribe patriarchal institutional order privileges inheritance rules that clash with woman member's fundamental equality rights under U.S. law).

and to remain faithful to baseline equality, focus was brought to bear on plausible differences between the sexes, which might justify unequal treatment. Specifically, there developed an overemphasis on real and constructed differences between the sexes, including physical and psychological differences as well as those stemming from differentiated gender-based social roles. Thus, pursuant to these perspectives, women were in principle equal to men, but in practice they were perceived as physically weaker, psychologically less stable, and socially as best suited for the role of wife and mother in the home.[7] In sum, in stage 1 equality, women are nominally the equals of men, but with emphasis on the above mentioned differences, they are persistently portrayed as deserving unequal treatment.

To overcome the disadvantages they experience, in stage 1, it is not enough for women to insist on the principle of baseline equality. Instead, they must counter the overemphasis on difference with a concerted effort to shift attention to identity. Focusing on identity is meant to take away from assertions of difference which have come to connote inferiority and hence to lend apparent justification to continuing subordination. In short, in stage 2, women can demand equal treatment by claiming that for all relevant purposes they are essentially similar to men.

For example, in the 1970s, feminists in the United States fought against gender-based discrimination in employment by stressing identities over differences. Employers had sought to justify discrimination against women on the grounds that the latter were less reliable than men because more apt to leave employment in a few years to start a family and raise children. To counter that perception, many women actually chose to postpone or forgo having children to demonstrate that they were no different than men in the context of employment. What feminists were then advocating, which eventually met with widespread success, was equality as identity.

Passage to stage 2 equality overcomes the contradictions of stage 1, but comes at a price. The shift of focus from difference to identity requires suppression of, or downplaying, certain differences, and that may give rise to new forms of inequality. Thus, for example, to gain equality in employment, certain women may have had to suppress their desire to raise children, thus postponing or abandoning an important part of what they saw as essential to their self-fulfillment in order not to lose the chance to enjoy the satisfaction they sought to derive from a professional career. To the extent that men do not confront such a choice, the pursuit of equality as identity causes women to confront a new form of inequality.[8]

---

[7] See *Bradwell* v. *Illinois*, supra note 1, which draws on some of these beliefs to justify banning women from practicing law.

[8] See Minow 1987 (arguing that U.S. Supreme Court sex discrimination jurisprudence posits men's experience as the "norm" against which women are measured).

Another consequence of the shift to stage 2 equality is an increase in the level of abstraction suited to the comparisons needed to entrench equality as identity. To justify inequalities in stage 1, real and constructed differences had to be exaggerated and de-contextualized to make them appear as so particular and concrete that they could not be explained away within a larger framework. For its part, the struggle to overcome stage 1 equality and to reach equality as identity required opposing de-contextualized concrete differences through overemphasis on identities. Such emphasis depended on de-contextualizing identities by casting similarities at higher levels of abstraction. For example, to counter the argument that women can be treated differently than men *because* of concrete physical differences between the sexes,[9] one could ascend to the highest level of abstraction and claim that ultimately men and women are identical since they all are human beings. The latter argument is not likely to be effective because it is so abstract that it does not engage claims of difference made from the standpoint of stage 1 equality. A somewhat less abstract argument, however, could be made which would sufficiently address the claims of difference made by an antagonist without abandoning a perspective within which identity remains predominant. For example, the claim that women make less desirable employees because after they are trained they are likely to leave to bear and raise children can be countered by the claim that women are as capable as men to excel in their jobs and that all employees, men and women alike, are subjected to unforeseen circumstances, such as sickness and desire for a career change, which may end up being detrimental to the interests of employers. The most effective strategy against stage 1 arguments, therefore, is to increase the levels of abstraction no more than necessary to neutralize existing advantages based on uses of difference to maintain inequalities, or to portray equality as identity as a more attractive alternative.[10] In any event, what is crucial in the context of the transition to stage 2 equality is that

[9] See, for example, *Michael M. v. Sonoma County Superior Court*, 450 U.S. 464 (1981) (punishing underage male but not underage female for consensual sex held constitutional on account of fact that only females risk pregnancy. Dissenting opinion argued that invocation of the physical difference in question masked the real reason for differential treatment, which was the biased belief that sixteen-year-old females were incapable of consenting to sexual relations).

[10] A good example is provided in the now invalidated decision in *Bowers v. Hardwick*, 478 U.S. 186 (1986) overruled in *Lawrence v. Texas*, 539 U.S. 558 (2003). The majority in *Bowers* held that it was constitutional to criminalize consensual sodomy among same-sex adult partners even if opposite sex sodomy was legal. The Court's majority in this 5–4 decision focused on differences between homosexuals and heterosexuals and invoked a history or moral and legal condemnation of homosexuality going back to Judeo-Christian scriptures and extending throughout the history of the common law. The dissenters, in contrast, emphasized that all adults should be left alone to choose adult partners for consensual intimate sexual relations regardless of whether the couplings involved are homosexuals or heterosexual. For the dissenters, therefore, because homosexual sex satisfies the same needs for those who engage in it as does heterosexual sex for those whose choice it is, it ought to be a constitutionally protected privacy right, not a criminal act.

to counter the de-contextualized concreteness of differences it is necessary to press de-contextualized identities at a sufficient level of abstraction to allow for a persuasive case in favor of equal treatment and against entrenched inequalities set in place by the deployment of stage 1 equality.

Equality as identity requires suppressing differences. Moreover, as the preceding example of women who have to conform to rules designed for men in order to be accepted as equals in the workplace indicates, often achieving identity demands greater sacrifices from some classes of people than from other classes, hence creating a new inequality. But even aside from that, by requiring that all individuals repress or restrain differences, stage 2 equality frustrates expression of differences and significantly limits the potential for individual self-fulfillment.

Stage 3 equality seeks to overcome both these inequalities and these frustrations by encompassing differences rather than rejecting them. There is no question of reverting to stage 1 treatment of difference as a badge of inferiority (or superiority). Instead, equality is meant to be recast so as to treat every one equally according to the needs and aspirations of each, regardless of whether these stem from similarities or differences among the members of society. Thus, for example, consistent with stage 3 equality, the workplace would accommodate women's desire to both work and have children by allowing for generous leaves, flexible work hours, daycare, and the like. Similarly, in the context of stage 3 equality, a woman's right to have an abortion can be defended as deriving from equality between the sexes. Indeed, without a right to abortion, a woman would not have the same control over her body as does a man (Ginsburg 1985). More generally, equality as difference seeks to re-contextualize identity and difference and to strike a proper balance between them by fostering as much diversity as possible without shattering the unity necessary to preserve identity. The point is to realize that the other not only is like myself in that we both have moral capacity and a perspective of our own, but also has a perspective that is different than mine. In stage 2 equality, it is sufficient to treat the other as the owner of a perspective; in contrast, in stage 3 the perspective of the other must be taken into full account.

The pursuit of equality as difference confronts two serious problems. One is the danger of falling back into stage 1. The other is that given the actual differences present in a given society, that society cannot strike a working balance between unity and diversity or cannot accommodate some differences without suppressing others.

From a *dialectical* standpoint, there is no danger that an attempted transition to stage 3 equality would backfire resulting into a retreat to stage 1. Dialectically, stage 3 resolves the conflicts of the preceding stages and strikes the proper balance between identity and difference by reframing and recasting their relationship. From the standpoint of internalization of the normative and institutional implications of the dialectic of equality in real historical time, however, it is all too possible that some with a purely superficial adherence to stage 2 equality would regard emphasis on suppressed differences as a license to revert to their use for purposes of fostering inequality. Therefore, there may be cases in which it would be logical, but perhaps not politically advisable, to ask for transition to equality as difference.

The dialectic of equality does not by itself provide a solution to the second problem. To determine whether apparent impossibilities relating to striking a minimum balance between unity and diversity or to simultaneously satisfying seemingly mutually exclusive differences can be overcome, it is necessary to turn to more comprehensive theories that place equality in a broader context. Both liberalism and pluralism appear particularly attractive because they endorse the single-status society, the proposition that all humans have and equal moral capacity, and equality as the baseline.

2.2. FROM LIBERALISM TO PLURALISM

Equality is central to both liberalism and pluralism and they each provide criteria of justice, a coherent normative perspective, and institutional guidance for dealing with conflicting demands regarding equality. Liberalism places equality within an individualistic framework where the pursuit of individual self-realization within the ambit of just institutions is paramount. Pluralism, on the other hand, and particularly "comprehensive pluralism," as we have seen, focuses more on equality among the diverse identities variously embraced by different individuals or groups within a pluralistic society, than on equality among individuals as mere possessors of an identity. What is paramount for pluralism is not individualism, but promotion of mutual respect and mutual accommodation among as many proponents of competing conceptions of the good as possible. As we will now see, liberalism goes hand in hand with equality as identity, and pluralism with equality as difference. Hence, I will argue that pluralism is superior to liberalism from the standpoint of equality, and will indicate how, in any event, pluralism is better suited to accommodate cultural difference than is liberalism.

Historically, liberalism has played a crucial role in the evolution toward equality. Liberalism in all its versions posits individual equality above all hierarchy and stands for some conception of equality as identity.[11] By positing equal individual autonomy and an equal opportunity for individual pursuit of self-realization[12] as paramount,

---

[11] It is noteworthy in this respect that a nineteenth-century liberal like John Stuart Mill was a champion for stage 2 equality for women (Mill 1869).

[12] While agreeing on these general propositions, liberals disagree on what is needed to secure such equal opportunity. For some, it is purely formal equal rights, see, for example, Nozick 1974; for others, it also includes material rights that call for some measure of wealth redistribution, see, for example, Rawls 1971. These differences, however, have no impact on the contrast between liberalism and pluralism.

libcrals lcavc virtually no room for anti-individualistic views or conceptions of the good. It allows for some limited tolerance of non-individualistic views, but is ill-suited to accommodate non-individualistic difference, in general, and collectively based cultural difference, in particular. In short, liberalism is suited to accommodate individual-regarding differences, but not group-regarding ones.[13]

By privileging individual-regarding differences over group-regarding ones, liberalism allows for subordination or disregard of the latter whenever they conflict with the former. On the other hand, as we have seen with respect to conflicts and incompatibilities among individual-regarding differences, liberalism purports to provide neutral rules or standards – to sort out the difficulties, and if needed, to separate the differences that can be accommodated from those that cannot. Moreover, liberalism seems to work best when two institutional devices work smoothly and are accepted as equitable and legitimate. These are the separation between the public sphere and the private sphere and an open and accessible forum for democratic debate and lawmaking.

The divide between the private sphere and the public sphere allows for space for individual-regarding differences and non-threatening (to liberalism) group-regarding ones buttressed by constitutional protections (e.g., property, privacy, freedom of expression, freedom of assembly) without threatening the unity of the liberal polity. The private sphere thus becomes the realm of (limited) difference, and the public sphere that of unity and equality as identity. So long as the public sphere remains very restricted and the private sphere sharply separated from it, liberalism can accommodate a great deal of difference. In more recent times, with the advent of the welfare state and the pervasive expansion of public education, however, the spread and importance of the public sphere has not only greatly increased, but also the boundaries between the two spheres have become increasingly blurred. Under these latter circumstances, liberalism's stress on individualism and equality as identity must become much more aggressive in an effort to ward off balkanization of the public sphere or seriously risk being taken over by proponents of anti-liberal ideologies.[14]

[13] Whereas some collective rights can be recast as individual rights – for example, the practice of some religions can be safeguarded either through collective rights belonging to the religion as an organized self-governing entity or through individual rights to freedom of expression, freedom of religion, and freedom of assembly – others cannot – for example, language rights can only be meaningful as groups rights, and the same is true for indigenous tribes functioning as self-contained religious and cultural units under sacred ancestral rules of kinship.

[14] The need to reinforce liberal unity and identity does not necessitate foregoing all difference or all stage 3 equality. For example, abortion rights based on equality as difference considerations seem entirely compatible with liberal individualism. Moreover, even a fair amount of cultural difference may be tolerated, although there may be disagreements concerning specific differences from one setting to another. Thus, two liberal polities, France and the United States, treat girls seeking to wear the Muslim veil to public school very differently. The French prohibit it (see French Law 2004–228 of

The forum for democratic debate and lawmaking, on the other hand, provides a procedure that is arguably neutral for settling conflicts among competing differences that do not qualify for constitutional protection. After full debate on how to prioritize competing differences, disagreements are settled by majority vote. As previously mentioned, Waldron suggests submitting cultural difference to a somewhat idealized version of this democratic process. This democratic process, however, can only strike losers as fair and legitimate if there is enough unity and identity within the polity so as to avoid a permanent "we" versus "they" division in which the "they" are always in the minority[15] and hence perennial losers. Accordingly, within a unified polity with strong liberal values and a firm commitment to equality as identity, the democratic process may be optimal as a means to settle policy differences as all participants within the process are likely to be winners some days on some issues and losers on other days on other issues. A cultural minority, and particularly one that adheres to illiberal values, in contrast, seems bound to be permanently relegated to a loser status within such a democracy.

Comprehensive pluralism is inherently more open to equality as difference than is liberalism. This is because pluralism does not privilege the individual over the group (or vice versa) and therefore does not impose individualism as the norm. Also, pluralism is inherently more open to difference than is liberalism, making it prima facie more hospitable toward non-mainstream perspectives.

Pluralism's rejection of liberalism's inextricable attachment to individualism does not entail repudiation of the individual's capacity for moral choice as providing the equality baseline for single-status societies. What pluralism does reject, however, is liberalism's bias for individualist choices and objectives and its privileging individual pursuits over collective ones. In theory at least, every individual should be free to choose the conception of the good that suits her the best,[16] and such conception may as well be an individualist one as a community-based one. For example, one person may seek self-fulfillment through adhesion to a monastic order in which individuals agree to be bound by strict communal norms.

Upon closer inspection, liberal individualism is as dependent on collective institutions and commitments as communal-based ideologies consistent with

---

March 15, 2004), whereas the Americans permit it (see, e.g., Muslim Girl in Oklahoma Public School OK'd to Wear Headscarf, *Dallas Morning News*, Nov. 12, 2004). There are many possible explanations for this discrepancy. One is that whereas the Americans regard wearing the veil as an expression of individuality, the French regard it as an assertion of an anti-liberal (and anti-republican) collective identity.

[15] Cf. Ely 1980 (arguing, largely based on the example of race relations in the United States, that permanent "we"/"they" politics distorts democracy and calls for judicial intervention to protect discriminated against minorities).

[16] In practice, such choice is bound to be limited by historical, cultural, educational, and various other circumstances.

pluralism are on the integrity of the individual. Indeed, a liberal-individualistic polity is not made up of mutually independent monads who interact by accident. Such polity is instead dependent on a shared collective vision and collective institutions, such as strong institutional protection of fundamental individual rights, of contractual rights, and of a culture that promotes individual self-reliance and self-fulfillment. For its part, pluralism though indifferent as between individualist and communal-based ideology, can only accommodate communally bound groupings to the extent that they afford basic respect to individual integrity. At a minimum, such groups should grant a right of exit to those individuals who disagree fundamentally with the group's aims or who feel oppressed within it. At best, such groups would afford each of their members a voice in shaping and carrying out communal affairs.

As discussed in Chapter 1, from comprehensive pluralism's standpoint, all conceptions of the good with one or a multitude of proponents within a society are prima facie entitled to equal acceptance. If such acceptance could be actually realized – or, in other words, if the negative moment of comprehensive pluralism were not complemented by its positive counterpart – this would result in complete and unrestricted realization of stage 3 equality. In no pluralistic society, however, is that ever possible as some conceptions of the good may seek elimination or suppression of others, or even were that not the case, as deployment of the projects derived from one conception would inevitably bump up against the projects deriving from other such conceptions.

Although pluralism cannot reach its ultimate goal of providing equal accommodation to all competing conceptions of the good, it can strive to approximate that goal as much as possible. This can be done by systematically implementing a process that comprises three distinct operations: a critical one, a constructive one, and a comparative one. The critical and the constructive operations are those, respectively, carried out by comprehensive pluralism's negative and positive moments. The comparative operation, on the other hand, is essential for purposes of giving each conception of the good, insofar as it is consistent with comprehensive pluralism its due, by ensuring that claims issuing from such a conception are considered from the latter's perspective (i.e., in terms of its centrality or importance regarding achievement of the aims of the conception to which it is linked) and not simply weighted directly against competing claims originating in rival conceptions.

This comparative operation is needed to deal with competing claims issuing from rival conceptions of the good that have secured a place in the pluralist polity. From a pluralist standpoint, competing claims issuing, respectively, from different conceptions of the good are not necessarily on the same plane. To the extent that pluralism seeks to promote fulfillment of conceptions of the good rather than mere satisfaction of claims, the relative place of a claim within the conception from which it issues is important for purposes of establishing priorities among competing claims. For example, if a claim ranks among the highest within the conception from which it is issued, such that its frustration or denial would impact on the core of that conception's integrity, then it ought to rank higher than a competing claim that is more peripheral to the core aims of the particular conception of the good from which it issues.

Giving priority to competing or conflicting claims according to their hierarchical position within the perspective within which they originate promotes realization of equality as difference. If the highest need from perspective A is X, whereas that from perspective B is Y, then granting X to proponents of A and Y to proponents of B would amount to treating them equally in function of their different needs. Full stage 3 equality cannot be achieved, however, for two principal reasons. First, a fully accurate comparison of the relative importance of claims issuing from different perspectives would require complete empathy for, and comprehension of, each perspective involved, which is impossible as an "outsider" can never assume the exact same position as an "insider." And, second, the second-order norms of comprehensive pluralism have a different impact on diverse conceptions of the good and on particular claims, such that higher-ranking claims from one conception may bump against second-order norms, whereas similar ranking claims from another may not.

Notwithstanding the impossibility of full and accurate comparison, limiting assertions of cultural difference to a fair hearing in the political marketplace, as suggested by Waldron, seems clearly insufficient. As much as possible, an effort must be made to understand the other from the latter's perspective, and this can be done by implementation of the principle of "justice as reversible reciprocity."[17] Consistent with this principle, all conflicts must be considered from each of the perspectives involved – and one must as much as possible successively take the place of a proponent of each of the contending conceptions of the good until one grasps the conflict in question from all the perspectives involved – to ensure the greatest possible consideration for relevant differences.

The inevitable bumping against the restrictions imposed by pluralism's second-order norms, on the other hand, serves as a point of convergence toward a common identity that circumscribes the realm of differences entitled to full recognition. As full identity is too abstract to be workable, pure difference makes comparison and hence equality impossible. Ultimately, it is the tension between the imperfect identity derived from pluralism's second-order norms and the inevitably constrained differences mediated by such norms, which determines the closest possible approximation to equality as difference.

---

[17] For a more extended discussion of this principle, see Rosenfeld 1998: 245–50.

2.3. THE DYNAMIC BETWEEN IDENTITY AND DIFFERENCE

Pluralism as does liberalism and other comprehensive perspectives anchors the relationship between identity and difference. That relationship, moreover, is not only
contextual but also dynamic. Identity connotes "sameness" as in A is identical to A,
and it also connotes "selfhood," a complex relationship of identification above, or in
spite of, difference. For example, I conceive of myself as the same continuous and
unique self in spite of all the changes I have experienced since childhood, adoles-
cence, early adulthood, and so on. Those who share a strong nationalistic bond with
their fellow countrymen do so above and beyond manifold differences concerning
social class, religious affiliation, family status, political ideology, and the like.

Difference also has a double connotation. On the one hand, it connotes "dis-
similarity," and in this sense it is the opposite of identity-as-sameness. On the other
hand, difference connotes "differentiation" in the sense of establishing a distinction between a multiplicity of units that are, in important respects, similar to one
another, such as one "self" is to another "self." For example, in some societies, each
individual constitutes a separate self and is similar to all other individuals qua separate self, yet what makes each individual a *separate* self is that he or she is differentiated from other selves, by beliefs, actions, voluntary affiliations, and so on. In
contrast, in other societies, the concept of the individual self is repressed or subordinated to a concept of collective self, such as that of a religious community. In the
latter context, moreover, the relevant differentiations are not among individuals but
among distinct religious communities.

Which links of identification are constitutive of selfhood and which uncou-
plings through differentiation yield alterity depends in part on context, in part on
the dynamics between identity and difference, and in part on the place that the
dynamic in question comes to occupy within the dialectic of equality. Consistent
with this, a particular difference may be relevant in one context but not in another.
For example, differences between Catholics and Protestants play little if any role
in defining the contemporary national political identity of certain countries with
significant Catholic and Protestant populations such as Germany or the United
States,[18] but they certainly have played a key role in the recent politics of Northern
Ireland.

From a dynamic standpoint, identities and differences evolve both in relation to
one another and in relation to their own adaptation to context and to the dialectic of
equality. Thus, in the context of individualism, such as that associated with liberalism, the predominant identities and differences are individual-regarding rather than

---

[18]   This is not to say that Catholicism or Protestantism may not have such a role. In that case, however,
the influence in question – say, the Protestant influence on capitalism as envisaged by Weber (Weber
1930) – would prima facie at least have a similar impact on both Catholics and Protestants.

group-regarding. The self is the individual and others are other individuals. Both identification and differentiation are predominantly considered from the standpoint of the individual. For example, cultural difference or religious difference is not that important in itself, but it counts mainly as a marker of differentiation among individuals. From a practical standpoint, cultural difference should not obscure the inherent similarly of all individuals, while at the same time individual expression of cultural difference should be permitted as a means for individuals to lay down a marker of differentiation. In short, in an individualist setting, the optimal is neither too much cultural difference such that it could upset the bond of identity among individuals nor too little such that it would unduly hamper differentiation among individuals.

In contrast, in a setting in which group-regarding identities and differences are predominant, cultural or religious difference may be paramount. This is so because for a group to cohere it must rally around a culture or a religion. Similarly, to be differentiated from other groups, a group may have to identify with a culture or religion that is other than that which characterizes other groups. Accordingly, the kind of accommodation of cultural difference that is adequate for an individualist setting seems bound to remain highly insufficient for a group-regarding setting.

We have seen that the dialectic of equality results in a greater pull toward identity or toward difference, depending on the particular stage in which it finds itself. Furthermore, because the dialectic in question was set off against the multi-status nature of feudal society, it is logical that it called for focus on individual-regarding identities and differences rather than group-regarding ones in its first two stages. Stage 1 equality, with its concern with mitigation of the full impact of the shift from multi-status to single-status society, individualized differences that are primarily group-regarding to link differentiation to inequality. Thus, for example, gender-based differences that pertain or are attributed to men as a group as opposed to women as a group are individualized to emphasize that an individual woman (e.g., Myra Bradwell, the nineteenth-century trained lawyer who was denied admission to the Illinois bar[19]) can be differentiated from individual men for in spite of similarities (e.g., equal capacity for practicing law) there are more important differences (e.g., women's greater frailty and their role as wives and mothers make it undesirable for them to be working outside the home) that justify unequal treatment (e.g., men but not women are allowed to practice law). Conversely, stage 2 equality, with its focus on equality as identity, promoted even further individualization, by downplaying differentiation through ascension to higher levels of abstraction. Thus, for example, to gain parity in a workplace designed for the needs and aspirations of men, women qua individuals must detach themselves from individualized group-regarding

[19] See *Bradwell v. Illinois*, supra, note 1.

characteristics such as the capacity for childrearing and the (social) responsibility for childbearing. Consistent with this, a woman who would want admission on an equal footing to the male-dominated realm of employment would have to argue as follows: "Even through as a woman I may be primed to bear and raise children, as an individual I choose to forgo (or postpone) childbearing and childrearing and therefore am entitled to the same employment as an individual man who is as qualified as I am because, as a consequence of my choice, there is no relevant difference between me and a similarly qualified man in the context of employment."

Stage 3 equality, as we have seen, involves a revalorization of difference, this time for purposes of reconciling differentiation with equality rather than tying it to inequality. Whereas in the context of individual-regarding differences, the move from equality-as-identity to equality-as-difference seems fairly straightforward – in spite of the danger of regression to equation of difference to inequality – the incorporation of group-regarding differences in the transition to stage 3 equality seems much more problematic. On the one hand, full equality as difference cannot be achieved (or even approximated) without recognition and attempted accommodation of group-regarding differences such as cultural differences. On the other hand, vindication of group-regarding differences requires some reduction in emphasis on individual differences. In order to obtain accommodation for my culture, particularly if it runs counter to mainstream culture and to individualism, I must downplay the individual strains, which the need for cultural conformity may force upon me. More generally, to the extent that group-regarding cultural differences run counter to individual-regarding identities (e.g., a culture that requires what, at least from an individualist standpoint, appears to be subordination of women) accommodation of group-regarding differences may eventually result in reinstatement of a multi-status society in a polity which aspires to stage 3 equality.

Individualism and liberalism, which seems particularly well suited to stage 2 equality, require that group-related differences be transformed into individual-regarding differences or filtered down to something equivalent to the latter. Pluralism, in contrast, is set, at least in principle, to accommodate group-regarding differences and bets that such accommodation will further the transition to stage 3 equality without seriously risking a fall back into a multi-status society. Analysis of whether such bet is realistic and whether extending acceptable differentiation to group-related assertions of collective identity is consistent within the ambit of pluralism's second-order norms is essential, but will be postponed until Section 2.5. This is, in order to get a better grasp of the dynamics between identity and difference through consideration of a concrete example, which will be discussed next. Furthermore, it is also crucial to consider how group-related difference may be accommodated in a non-hierarchical society through adjustment in the institutional design of the single-status polity, which will be the focus of Section 2.4.

One concrete example that well illustrates the dynamic between identity and diffe-rence in the context of contemporary Western democracies is that of the struggle for equality waged in relation to differences between homosexuals and heterosexuals. In stage 1 equality, the homosexual can be cast as different and as such treated as an inferior. Consistent with this, discrimination against homosexuals could be justified on two different counts, one relating to sexual practices and the other to non-sexual relations within society. Homosexual sex can be criminalized, whereas heterosexual sex is not in either of two ways: one is by affording legal validity to practices that are exclusively heterosexual, such as genital intercourse among opposite sex partners; the other is by legalizing the same practice, such as sodomy, if engaged in by an opposite sex couple, and penalizing it if it occurs between same sex partners. In the first of these two forms of differentiation, heterosexual sex becomes the norm and homosexual sex, the exception, with the consequence that passage to stage 2 equal-ity as identity does not apparently pave the way for equal treatment of heterosexual and homosexual sex. In the second form of differentiation, however, it becomes easy for homosexuals to demand de-criminalization of homosexual's sodomy since it involves the same sexual practices as those that are entirely legal if performed among heterosexuals.

Discrimination against homosexuals with respect to non-sexual relations, such as employment, housing, and places of worship, on the other hand, seem to be status-related or at least group-regarding as involving a distinct lifestyle that is subject to disapproval or even condemnation by the heterosexual majority.[20] Reaction against such discrimination, in turn, can either be individualized or conducted mainly at a group-regarding level. As individualized, it can be cast in an analogous way to reac-tions against discrimination on the basis of race. Just as race is irrelevant for purposes of employment so too is the fact that a would-be employee engages in homosexual sex within the privacy of his own home. From a group-regarding lifestyle standpoint, on the other hand, homosexual culture is as entitled to accommodation as hetero-sexual culture, and homosexuals cannot enjoy equality as difference unless their minority culture can be afforded sufficient protection to co-exist on an equivalent footing with its heterosexual counterpart.

Though brief and schematic, the foregoing description affords an insight into the complexities confronting any attempt to achieve equality for homosexuals. To the extent that homosexual sex is different than heterosexual sex, it is not clear whether stage 2 or only stage 3 equality can bring about equality for homosexuals. If state 2 were to, sexual relations would have to be conceived at a high level of

---

[20] Cf. *Romer v. Evans*, 517 U.S. 620 (1996) (state of Colorado constitutional provision forbidding adop-tion of antidiscrimination laws prohibiting discrimination against homosexuals to protect *inter alia* religious freedom of those whose religion prohibits dealing with homosexuals held to violate federal constitutional equal protection rights).

abstraction as, for example, the natural outlet for intimate relations between consenting adults. But at such a high level of abstraction, it may be impossible to distinguish in any systematic way between heterosexual and homosexual sex, on the one hand, and incest, on the other. Furthermore, if equality for homosexuals seems only achievable in the context of stage 3 equality, it can either be justified in individual-regarding terms – homosexual sex is to homosexuals what heterosexual sex is to heterosexuals – or in group-regarding terms – gay culture is as deserving of recognition as is straight culture.

In the end, which of the plausible paths referred to earlier will be most likely to lead to the achievement of equality for homosexuals is likely to depend in part on historical contextual factors, in part on the prevailing interplay between identity and difference, and in part on the actual moment in the dialectic of equality. The possible permutations may seem extensive in the abstract, but they are likely to diminish dramatically once the relevant factors are teased out after choosing between liberalism and pluralism.

2.4. SINGLE-STATUS SOCIETY AND THE FEDERALIZATION OF DIFFERENCE

A functioning pluralist polity requires establishing a level of common identification making it possible for the polity to operate as a unit; progressive erasure of all correlation of difference with inequality through the spread of stage 2 equality; and accommodation of cultural difference through recourse to stage 3 equality. Even if the spread of stage 2 equality were unproblematic, accommodation of cultural difference may be fraught with difficulties not only in terms of the passage of from equality-as-identity to equality-as-difference but also because it may threaten the unity of the polity. This is clearly illustrated by the example of a cohesive cultural minority that subordinates women (at least from the vantage point of majority perceptions) within the ambit of its collective life. To the extent that the women members of this cultural minority willingly assume their differentiated role within their cultural group, there seems to be no reason consistent with pluralism to deny the group stage 3 equality or full membership in the polity. Nevertheless, recognizing the legitimacy of the cultural minority in question may unhinge the equilibrium reached between men and women through implementation of stage 2 equality and create a fear of regression to stage 1 equality and to the subordination of all women with whom it had been associated. Moreover, in certain cases, such fear may threaten a relatively fragile polity-wide identity tied to the majority culture and to commitment to stage 2 equality among the sexes.

The liberal response to this problem would be to reject the cultural minority's group regarding equality-as-difference claims. From the pluralist standpoint, however, such claims should only be rejected if incompatible with second-order norms, which they need not be.[21] But even if they are not, the most important cultural minority claims may clash with the most important cultural majority claims. One option in such a case would be to federalize the polity comprising the preceding majority and minority and to make room for greater group-related autonomy and self-determination for both, provided that the unity of the polity – now the federation as opposed to the federated entities – is preserved or reconstituted.

Federalization is easiest to accomplish where each diverse cultural group occupies a distinct contiguous territory within the polity. For example, where language functions as a paramount cultural marker and different languages predominate in different regions, as in the case in Switzerland where cantons are either French-, German-, Italian-, or (in part) Romanch-speaking, then language-based federalization seems best suited to reconcile the aspirations of each linguistic community with that of others and with that of the unity of the polity as a whole. Furthermore, with respect to some cultural markers, such as religion, though not others, it is possible to "federalize" on a non-territorial basis. This is what is done through the "millet" system which originated in the Ottoman Empire and according to which each religious community is given autonomy and governance rights over its own membership.

Federalization is available within the nation-state, but by now it has been institutionalized beyond. Supra-national association, such as that achieved within the ambit of the EU makes for additional and novel ways of coordinating poles of identity and poles of difference. This allows, for example, for tensions between sub-national units and national ones to be eased through supra-national dealings. Thus, tensions between Cataluña and Spain or Scotland and the United Kingdom may be reduced by affording sub-national units a voice in EU bodies. More generally, there are many instances of transnational and even global (e.g., the UN, the WTO, the ICC) association as well as possibilities of peaceful disengagement through pacted secessions such as that which transformed the former Czechoslovakia into the Czech Republic and Slovakia. Accordingly, the need of common identification of all single-status societies need not be fulfilled within the strictures of the nation-state. Likewise, the opportunities for dealing with conflicting group-regarding agendas through federalization have multiplied well beyond the traditional outlets. This means that there is significant room for accommodating group-regarding equality as difference, including cultural difference, before even having to subject competing claims to the requirements of justice as reversible reciprocity.

---

[21] Women's subordination may be non-coercive, the internal dynamic of the group may leave it open to change, and there may be realistic opportunities for individual exit for those who find group norms oppressive.

2.5. ACCOMMODATING CULTURAL DIFFERENCE WITHIN PLURALISM AND THE DIALECTIC OF EQUALITY

The preceding discussion revealed that stage 3 equality requires accommodation of cultural difference and that pluralism grants room to some cultural difference but not all. A culturally differentiated group shares a conception of the good that is distinct from those promoted by others within the polity. If that conception is incompatible with an ordering of the polity pursuant to pluralism's second-order norms, then the cultural difference it promotes is not entitled to acceptance or toleration. On the other hand, if the conception of the good that defines a particular instance of cultural differentiation is in basic harmony with pluralist norms, then its integration within the polity should be welcome and uneventful.

The more difficult problem, already mentioned in Section 2.3, is whether cultural difference predicated on group-related identities that seem inegalitarian though not incompatible with implementation of second-order norms can genuinely be accommodated consistent with pluralism and transition to stage 3 equality. Take, for example, the case of a culture that appears to give women a subordinate role, but that does not seek to prevent dissidents (including women) from leaving the group or to proselytize outside the group. The argument against granting such group recognition and some measure of self-determination is essentially twofold: (1) The group provides a bad example that may inspire some to attempt to reverse liberal gains that led to the implantation of equality as identity; and, (2) most women born into the group and fed its ideology may not fully appreciate their state of subordination or, even if they do, may be too trapped or inhibited to leave the group. On the other hand, the arguments in favor of extending stage 3 equality to the group in question are also essentially twofold: (1) What appears as subordination from one perspective may not be subordination from another, and suppression of what does not conform to the views of the majority may ultimately prove inegalitarian; and (2) if one seeks to deny recognition to group-regarding differences that seem unpalatable to a progressive liberal majority, one may well block transition to stage 3 equality and frustrate the deployment of pluralism.

In theory at least, each case involving apparent subordination could be settled through application of the principle of justice as reversible reciprocity. That would allow women belonging to a group that allegedly subordinates them to consider their status from the perspective of outsiders, critics, and so on, as compared to their own, and to decide whether, when aware of all available options, they would continue with their own group or opt out. Although it is impossible in practice to fully experience the world from the perspective of another, it certainly seems plausible that women living within a culture that others consider defective from the standpoint of gender-based equality would nonetheless choose to remain within that culture even if they could fully intuit all the benefits and drawbacks of all available alternatives.[22]

Turning to the two objections listed earlier, we see that the claim that a culture that appears to subordinate women provides a bad example only seems troubling in the context of a society that has not yet firmly implanted stage 2 equality. In one that has, if anything, it is the minority culture that seems non-egalitarian that would appear more vulnerable to intolerance. In any event, if inter-group channels of communication are open, and if the minority culture though benefiting from a fair amount of autonomy cannot avoid openness to other groups and to institutionalized pluralist norms, then it may be subject to pressure for inner reform. This is exemplified by the movements within several religious communities that bar women from the ministry for change opening the way to greater gender-based equality.

With respect to the second objection – that those subordinated may not be fully aware of their status – beyond what has already been said, it should be pointed out that the risk of misperception is not one-sided. Indeed, the outsider's risk of misperceiving unfamiliar mores as causing subordination may be equivalent to the insider's risk of misjudging to what extent her role within her culture may conform with some acceptable conception of equality. Furthermore, if on account of the dangers of misperception one were to fall back on liberalism and stage 2 equality, one would not only sacrifice the diversity of a multi-cultural polity but also possibly unwittingly restrict the reach of stage 2 equality in difficult or borderline cases such as that concerning homosexuals. Indeed, as we have seen, it is not clear whether promotion of acceptance of gay lifestyles can be encompassed within the ambit of stage 2 equality or whether it is dependent on initiating a transition to stage 3 equality. By rejecting the latter, one may actually constrain full realization of the former.

Overall, it seems that the advantages of pluralism and initiating a transition to stage 3 equality far outweigh the possible disadvantages considered earlier. This is consistent with what has been argued throughout: Cultural difference, pluralism, and movement to stage 3 equality are better suited to promote an optimal reconciliation between identity and difference than are, under current circumstances, liberalism and stage 2 equality.

---

[22] There are cases where the trade-offs are quite familiar as when Orthodox Jewish or Muslim women, who work side by side with secular women, can compare notes, and nonetheless consciously determine that for them secularism would be a less desirable alternative. Of course, these women cannot shed their background, history, upbringing, family, etc., and thus their conclusions could not, strictly speaking, satisfy the test imposed by justice as reversible reciprocity.

2.6. DESIGNING A LEGAL AND INSTITUTIONAL FRAMEWORK TO ACCOMMODATE CULTURAL DIFFERENCE

As discussed in Section 2.4, federalization provides an important institutional tool for purposes of accommodating cultural difference. Federalization, however, is neither always possible nor always desirable. It is not possible where there is no way to disentangle one culture from another and it is not desirable where it leads unnecessarily at once to further balkanization and to a markedly more abstract and detached realm of common identification. Accordingly, room must be left for accommodation of cultural difference within the very same legal, political, and institutional precincts reserved for majority or dominant cultures. In short, the single-status society must be up to a point a single-space polity.

Waldron's suggestion that cultural difference be given a voice in parliamentary democracy coupled with his suggestion that exceptions from laws and common practices be available for non-mainstream cultures (Waldron 2007: 154–155) divides the common space of the polity into areas of inclusion and areas of separation. Inclusion in a political arena in which cultural difference is virtually assured to be a loser, however, far from vindicating equality as difference, either fosters equality as identity – all can equally propose legislation and all are equally bound by majority backed legislation – or, in the end, deepens alienation – having a voice that is never heeded may be as frustrating as being deprived of one. On the other hand, separation from majorities through series of exceptions that draw attention to the non-conforming nature of proponents of non-mainstream cultures leads to mere toleration of difference rather than to progress toward equality as difference.

Ideally, as already suggested, conflicting claims made from different perspectives should be submitted to the criterion of justice as reversible reciprocity. But since institutional deployment of this criterion is not feasible, it is necessary to turn to the legal, political, and institutional tools that may be used to best approximate justice as reversible reciprocity. For cultural difference (to the extent it is compatible with pluralism) to be treated as something as valuable as mainstream ideology (as equality as difference requires), it is necessary to place its highest priorities on the same plane as those of much more widely shared perspectives. This can be done, in turn, by placing the highest priorities of all acceptable conceptions of the good within the realm of constitutional protections while relegating lower priorities to the give and take of everyday parliamentary democracy.

No sharp distinction can be drawn between what ought to be protected by the constitution and what ought to be exposed to ordinary democratic politics. Moreover, where to draw the boundary will likely always be a matter of dispute. Nevertheless, it seems clear that claims likely to directly impact the identity of the claimant ought to be subject to constitutional regulation, whereas claims related to benefits and burdens that do not directly impinge on identity concerns should be left to democratic politics.

In the end, the legal and institutional setting best fit to orient a polity toward pluralist equality as difference resembles its typical liberal counterpart. There are, however, important differences. A pluralist constitution must afford group-equality rights as well as individual ones and must strike a balance between group-regarding equality rights and the individual-regarding equality rights of dissenters within a constitutionally protected group. The most important difference, though, does not concern institutions, but attitude. For liberals, cultural difference is like an outsider who must be accorded the hospitality owed foreign visitors. For the pluralist, in contrast, cultural difference is like an insider who is so intrinsically linked to the rest that he or she need not fear being different.

3

Human Rights and the Clash Between Universalism and Relativism

The Case of Minority Group Rights

Liberalism's difficulty with difference in relation to equality is exacerbated in the context of group-based equality, and in particular in situations in which individual-regarding equality considerations come into conflict with group-regarding ones. This can be illustrated by reference to the following purely formal example. Suppose there are 200 units of a good available for distribution and two groups, A and B, respectively comprised of 100 and 50 members. In that scenario, an equal distribution to each group would lead to individual-regarding inequality as individual members of B would each receive two units whereas individual members of A would each acquire one unit. Conversely, if distribution is made through the groups but on an individual-regarding equality basis, then A and B will be awarded unequal quantities of the goods under distribution. Furthermore, because of liberalism's commitment to individualism, in case of conflict[1] individual-regarding equality would always trump group-regarding equality. For communitarianism, on the other hand, group-regarding equality would always prevail over individual-regarding equality when the two could not be readily reconciled.

In both cases, there would thus be a strong bias for identity at the expense of difference; in the case of liberal equality because of the built-in preference for identity discussed in Chapter 2; in that of communitarian equality because of refusal to accommodate any individual-based (or subgroup-based) deviations that would adversely impact on group identity. These biases, moreover, would be greatly magnified for minority groups. This is obvious in the case of communitarianism deployed on a national scale. For example, if a minority group language is different than the national one and the latter is deemed essential to the preservation of national identity, then the minority language will undoubtedly be subjected to unequal

---

[1] There are, of course, several situations in which there is no conflict between individual-regarding and group-regarding objectives. Thus, if the entire population within a country speaks the same language, the individual's right to be educated in her own language and the relevant corresponding group right would be thoroughly consistent with one another and mutually reinforcing.

treatment resulting in linguistic difference being widely suppressed, or, at least, significantly constrained. On the other hand, the bias in question may be less obvious though equally operative in the case of liberal individualism. Logically, it would seem that since liberalism is biased against all group-regarding concerns, minority groups should fare no worse than majority ones. Upon further consideration, however, it becomes apparent that once one moves away from purely abstract egos in the Kantian mold, liberal individualism cannot be deployed within a polity without some, at least implicit, attachment to group identity. Even if it strictly adheres to the priority of individual-regarding concerns over collective ones, a liberal individualist political unit requires a common language and common institutions in order to function. French individualism, for example, has French as its common language and secular institutions that are more compatible with Catholicism, the country's majority religion (Troper 2009) than with Islam, the religion of a significant minority of French citizens. Accordingly, a Muslim student who would wish to express her individual "difference" within a French state school by wearing the Islamic veil, but is prohibited by law from doing so, is disadvantaged in comparison to her Catholic fellow students who may legally express their religious allegiance by wearing a small cross on a chain around their necks (Mancini 2009). Moreover, whereas French *laicite* steeped in republicanism may be excessively restrictive of difference from the standpoint of the needs of liberal individualism, even as seemingly innocuous a policy as choosing Sunday as the national day of rest in a country with a large Christian majority can significantly disadvantage Jewish or Muslim citizens.[2]

Comprehensive pluralism is, in principle, better suited than liberalism to do justice to minority group equality claims based to a large extent on difference. This follows from its commitment to afford priority to perspectives and conceptions of the good over the individual or the group as such. A minority group perspective is thus prima facie entitled to the same consideration as individual or majority group perspectives. In the first negative moment of comprehensive pluralism's dialectic, all conceptions of the good are entitled to equal acceptance regardless of whether they belong to a single individual, a minority group, or a majority one. Moreover, whereas it is true that in the second positive moment of the dialectic in question, not all conceptions of the good fare equally, minority group ones are still likely to fare better than they would under liberal individualism or communitarianism.

Regarding the two principal constraints imposed by comprehensive pluralism in its positive moment, namely compatibility with second-order norms and conformity with the tenets of justice as reversible reciprocity, minority group conceptions of the

---

[2] Cf. *Braunfeld* v. *Brown*, 366 U.S. 599 (1962) (Freedom of religion rights do not extend to allowing Orthodox Jews who must close business on Saturday in accordance with the commands of his religion to open business on Sunday in order to be able to remain competitive).

good as such should be at no disadvantage. Indeed, whether, and to what extent, a conception of the good should be afforded institutional support depends on its par-ticular content and not on whom it counts as its proponent or how many of these there are. Similarly, the nature or number of proponents play no role in the crucial initial determinations that need to be undertaken under justice as reversible reci-procity. When two (or more) conceptions of the good compatible with comprehen-sive pluralism clash so that pursuit of one of them frustrates pursuit of the other, as already mentioned, justice as reversible reciprocity requires ranking the first-order norms and values involved in order of importance in relation to the particular con-ception of the good with which they are linked. Based upon such ranking, what is most important to the conception in question ought to be given priority over what is less important from the perspective of the competing conception. For example, if a mountain is considered sacred under the most important precepts of a particular religion, and should accordingly remain inviolate, then objections by proponents of that religion to proposed construction of recreational facilities on that mountain by individuals or a group for whom such facilities loom as desirable, but not essential to their way of life, should be heeded, and the construction should be prohibited according to justice as reversible reciprocity.[3] Needless to say, whether or not the religion in question is a minority or majority one and whether those wishing recre-ational facilities on the sacred mountain represent most or a few among the remain-ing members of the polity, the result should be the same.

Pursuant to justice as reversible reciprocity, numbers matter primarily as tie-breakers in conflicts among first-order norms belonging to competing conceptions of the good, in cases in which the norms involved are of equal rank within the respective conceptions of the good involved. In such cases, no legitimate hierarchy can be invoked, and thus it makes sense to accord priority to majority objectives over minority ones.[4] In sum then, all things being equal, there are still disadvantages in

---

3   Cf. *Lyng v. Northwest Indian Cemetery Protective Association*, 485 U.S. 439 (1988).
4   Although in theory a single individual's most crucial first-order norms under his purely unique con-ception of the good ought to have priority over what occupies the next level of importance for the entire remainder of the polity, practical considerations may militate against such a result. If only one person, all of a sudden, declares that a mountain is sacred, considerations of credibility and propor-tionality would militate against thwarting the recreational goals of the rest of the population. On the other hand, if a minority religion is firmly entrenched, and its precepts historically settled, then cred-ibility concerns would seem less justified, and proportionality solely based on the number of propo-nents and opponents, unwarranted. In the latter case, however, numbers could still matter indirectly. If a mountain that is sacred to a small minority is an important and difficult to replace source of food to many, then comprehensive pluralism's principles of justice would command according priority to food production on the mountain concerned. Furthermore, if the religion that proclaims the moun-tain in the dispute to be sacred considers exploitation of the latter's soil much more offensive than all other uses, then allowing the proposed recreational facilities may have such a relatively minimal impact on the irresolvable underlying conflict – assuming it is not hoisted as a symbol of the prevailing clash of identities – as to warrant justification on proportionality grounds.

being a minority group that seeks adequate means to express its differences under comprehensive pluralism, but these are far fewer in scope and extent than those prevalent under liberalism, republicanism, or communitarianism.

There is one big apparent obstacle to minority group rights, particularly those that are tied to illiberal ideologies, which also poses a daunting theoretical challenge to comprehensive pluralism. That is the deployment of universal human rights. From a theoretical standpoint, if universal human rights are *truly* universal, then they would seem to call for monism and that would prevent comprehensive pluralism from reaching all the way down. From a practical perspective, on the other hand, to the extent that human rights closely intertwine with a liberal conception of universalism, they would inevitably suppress or severely limit all differences emanating from non-liberal sources.

Consistent with these observations, in order properly to assess whether and how comprehensive pluralism can better promote minority group equality through greater inclusion of difference as a practical as well as theoretical matter, it is first necessary to take a closer look at the claim to universalism made on behalf of international human rights. This will be the subject of Section 3.1. Following that, to better grasp the practical dynamic between individual rights, and majority as well as minority group rights in the context of a pluralist normative agenda, Section 3.2 will concentrate on the difficult problems raised in the context of constitutional protection of minority group rights. Section 3.3 will focus on the additional difficulties faced by liberal individualist constitutionalism through review of the minimal protection afforded minority group rights under the U.S. Constitution. Section 3.4 will seek to demonstrate how a constitutional jurisprudence normatively anchored in comprehensive pluralism would be better suited to do justice to group-based differences, in general, and to minority group rights, in particular. Finally, Section 3.5 will address the connection between constitutional rights and human rights that are similar in content, such as basic liberty or equality rights, with a view to buttressing the claim that from a practical standpoint, and in particular from that of their best possible deployment, the universalist aspirations of human rights do not undermine the preferability of a pluralist approach to implementation of the latter.

3.1. HUMAN RIGHTS AND THE CONFRONTATION BETWEEN UNIVERSALISM, PARTICULARISM, AND RELATIVISM

General concepts are often best understood in terms of what they stand against. Universal human rights, as forged by the 1948 United Nations Universal Declaration of Human Rights, can thus be viewed as truly universal both in scope and content. Set against the genocidal horrors of the Third Reich, the Universal Declaration was grounded in the firm conviction that all humans, by the simple virtue of being human, are equally entitled to the most basic fundamental rights. Emerging from the smoldering ashes of the Nazi legacy, the Universal Declaration was aimed at securing a minimum of human dignity for every person on earth.

Over sixty years after the Universal Declaration, however, it is much more diffi-cult to tell what human rights can now be said to stand against. To be sure, even so many years after the proclamation of the Universal Declaration, torture, murder, and genocide still claim far too many victims.[5] Increasingly, however, human rights norms have been attacked by those who believe the current standards comprom-ise expressions of national, ethnic, cultural, and religious diversity.[6] Stated strongly, the charge is that current human rights rhetoric and policy impose Western liberal ideology and values on those who strongly identify with, and voluntarily embrace, significantly incompatible traditions and value systems.

There is a much discussed question concerning whether human rights are truly universal or whether they are culturally dependent, an issue that has become ever more intense and urgent since the recent revival of nationalism and ethnic politics in the aftermath of the downfall of the Soviet Empire (Kymlicka 1995: 1). Moreover, the problems raised by minority group rights cast an even sharper focus on the issue. These problems typically involve a confrontation between collective claims, steeped in an ideology or tradition that runs counter to central tenets of the relevant majority mores or culture, and individual claims, couched in terms of fundamental constitutional rights that are largely equivalent in content to basic civil and polit-ical human rights. Also, inasmuch as claims to minority group rights often arise in the context of constitutional disputes, they are more highly prone than human rights claims to being judicially resolved through application of established legal standards.[7]

The following analysis leads to the conclusion that the opposition between a universalist conception of human rights and its cultural relativist counterpart is altogether miscast. First, there is no single vision of universalism, but many differ-ent ones. Second, the opposite of universalism is not relativism, but particularism.

---

5   See, for example, Elaine Scolino, Abuses by Serbs the Worst since Nazi Era, Report Says, *N. Y. Times*, Jan. 20, 1993, at A8 (U.S. Government comparing Serb atrocities in Bosnia to Nazi conduct); Marlise Simons, Rwandan Rebel Handed Over to Court, *N.Y. Times*, Jan. 26, 2011, at A6 (terror campaign against civilians in the Democratic Republic of Congo); Marlise Simons, Former Liberian President Boycotts War Crimes Trial for Second Day, *N.Y. Times*, Feb. 9, 2011 (discussing atrocities during the civil war in Sierra Leone).

6   See, for example, Farer & Gaer 1993: 240, 294–5 (reporting beliefs of certain political leaders that many of the civil and political rights enumerated in the Universal Declaration and other sacred texts are "provincial products of the West's singular historical experience and the liberal ideology stemming there from.").

7   This is not to imply that legal/constitutional standards are apolitical or that human rights disputes are merely political. Rather, the point is that law and established constitutional standards tend to imply a greater degree of political consensus than is likely in transnational human rights controversies.

Furthermore, the conflict between universalism and relativism tends to be exacerbated by liberal perspectives as well as by confrontations between liberals and communitarians. As I will argue later in this chapter, these difficulties can be largely avoided by sticking to pluralism and to its conception of the conflict between cultures as dynamic and somewhat fluid. Although clashes between universalism and particularism seem inevitable, these clashes often tend to be more partial and more local than expected. Also, in an increasingly interdependent world, there may well be greater opportunities for convergences than are readily apparent.

Before further discussion of minority group rights, however, it is necessary to briefly look into the relationship between universalism, relativism, and particularism.

The stereotypical image conjured by invocation of the contrast between universalism and particularism is that of the dichotomy between Western liberal individualism and non-Western forms of communalism, not to say tribalism. On the one hand, we have the liberal individual who is committed to constitutional democracy; on the other, the tightly knit non-Western community, with its sometimes peculiar if not (from a Western perspective) downright repulsive rituals, such as, for example, female circumcision. Needless to say, however, this image proves largely false. Indeed, strictly speaking, though Western liberal individualism may be universalist in its aspirations, it is in the end as much a particular ideology and value system as any of its non-Western communal counterparts.

As already discussed, Western liberal individualism is by no means the only ideology that is universalist in its aspirations as so is Marxist collectivism.[8] Other visions, in contrast, such as that embraced by Judaism, for example, are not universalist in aspiration but espouse certain norms, which they postulate as being universal in scope.[9] From a philosophical standpoint, therefore, the key distinction is between norms that are universally embraced or justified, and norms that are particular, either because they are adopted in certain, but not all, cultures, or because they cannot be justified across all cultures. Moreover, it is important to distinguish between factual claims to universality and normative claims to it. For example, many different societies may practice some forms of torture with the consequence that from a factual standpoint it would be false to claim that there exists a universal repudiation of torture. Nonetheless, it could still be consistent to claim that torture is morally wrong universally, and that those societies that practice or condone it ought to be morally condemned.

---

[8]   See supra, at Introduction.

[9]   The Jewish religion is the religion of a single people and thus does not seek to spread all its precepts to other people. Some of the norms it embraces are meant to be particular to it, whereas others purport to be universal in scope. For example, it considers that most, but not all, of the Ten Commandments are applicable to other peoples. Accordingly, the Fourth Commandment to observe the Sabbath applies only to Jews. See generally Stone 1991.

In view of these observations, it seems more accurate to speak of universalisms and particularisms in the plural rather than in the singular. Emphasizing the plural, moreover, is helpful in dispelling the temptation to equate particularism with relativism. Indeed, a set practice of values may be particular in nature and scope without thereby becoming merely relative. Imagine, for example, that there is universal agreement that monotheistic religion is the highest moral good, but that different ways of worshiping the same God are equally praiseworthy. Under this conception, Christianity, Islam, and Judaism are three particular religions, but the value-systems and practices which each of them promotes are by no means merely relative. Instead, they are three different and particular expressions of the same ultimate universal moral truth.

Because the relation between what is particular and what is relative is multifaceted and complex,[10] I shall confine relativism to the situation in which a normative claim can only be ultimately justified in terms of a contested conception of the good. In other words, when a normative claim can only be justified in terms of some among several competing conceptions of the good, then the justification for such claim will be deemed relativist in nature. In all other cases, though the justification of a normative claim may be dependent on particular facts or norms, the justification in question will be deemed to be particularist rather than relativist.

Before proceeding to an examination of the problem of collective minority rights, it is necessary to focus briefly on one further distinction. Values that are universal in both aspiration and scope may, on close scrutiny, prove much more particular or even much more relativist than initially contemplated. Take the presumably universal prohibition against murder as an illustration. Not only do all societies proscribe murder, but there also appears to be unanimity in favor of treating murder as universally – that is, regardless of culture or of historical circumstances – wrong. Once we move from the general concept of murder to the somewhat less abstract issue of what ought to count as murder, however, the operative consensus seems prone to unravel even within the confines of a single polity. To refer again to one striking example, in the United States, some consider abortion to be murder and the premeditated killing of physicians who perform abortions to be justified homicide (Moore 1997: 269). Others, just as unequivocally, regard the latter as murder while maintaining that abortion in no way involves homicide.[11] Moreover, it is unclear from this example

---

[10] For example, it may be that one owes a moral duty to one's fellow under conditions of drought that one does not owe otherwise. Although it is proper in that case to state that the duty involved is relative to the presence of certain conditions, it does not follow at all that the morality involved is "relativist" in nature. Indeed, the operative moral norm in question may be the universal one that one must assist one's fellow in times of difficulty, but not when everyone is equally capable of fending for him/herself.

[11] This is the view of pro-choice organizations such as the National Abortion Federation. See Sam Howe Verhovek, Anti-Abortion Site on Web Has Ignited Free Speech Debate, N.Y. *Times*, Jan 13, 1999, at A14.

whether there exists a consensus on murder in general, with disagreements regarding certain particulars in determinate circumstances, or, whether beneath a seemingly universal consensus, there lurks an actual relativism derived from an insoluble conflict among irreconcilable clashing conceptions of the good.

A similar tension is manifest in the context of claims for collective minority rights within the bounds of a constitutional democracy. At the highest levels of abstraction, all concerned are likely to agree that liberty and equality rank among the paramount values deserving of vigilant pursuit. As discussions become more concrete, however, proponents and opponents of group rights are likely to be divided both in terms of their perception of the proper relationship between liberty and equality and in terms of their respective conception of these terms.[12] With this caveat in mind, let us now take a closer look at the rights of minorities.

3.2. THE CONSTITUTIONAL PROTECTION OF MINORITIES AND THE CONFLICT BETWEEN INDIVIDUAL AND GROUP RIGHTS

Providing adequate constitutional protection to minorities is highly problematic. This is in large part due to the apparent impossibility for any workable constitutional regime to reconcile the clashing individual and collective interests implicated in most types of relationships between majority and minority. Minority rights can be conceived either as individual rights or as collective rights pertaining to the group as a whole. Likewise, constitutional rights of minorities may be framed as individual rights, affording each member of a minority the same rights enjoyed by every other individual within the polity, or as group rights, granting certain powers and immunities to the group as a whole. Although to a significant extent group rights may be recast as individual ones and vice versa, there remains a crucial core of irreducible individual and group rights. In particular, a constitutional regime based on individual rights looms as inadequate for purposes of protecting group autonomy, self-government, and survival; conversely, a constitutional regime that relies on group rights appears incapable of affording sufficient protection to minorities within a minority or to non-conforming or dissident individuals within the protected group. To put the conflict in the strongest terms, it appears impossible for any constitutional regime to guarantee at once a minority group's survival and the most fundamental rights of an individual dissident within that group.

---

[12] For example, even though there is a wide-ranging consensus in the United States concerning constitutional equality at the highest levels of abstraction, see Rosenfeld 1991a: 588 (equal protection requires upholding the equal worth, dignity, and respect of every individual, regardless of race or ethnic origin), bitter contentiousness often mars consideration of constitutional equality in more concrete terms as vividly illustrated by the Supreme Court's bitterly divided affirmative action jurisprudence (Rosenfeld 1991: 163–215).

Even though it may be impossible to fully resolve this conflict, different options are available to manage the clash between the individual and the group. I will argue that the best among them is that based on the principles of comprehensive pluralism. Before pursuing this alternative any further, however, it is imperative to take a closer look at the claim that minorities ought to be granted group rights. Indeed, as not all minorities are equally situated, it is not clear whether group rights ought to be granted or denied across the board, or whether they are appropriate in certain particular circumstances. For example, a culturally homogeneous, tightly knit, self-governing community that has become incorporated into a vast multinational state through conquest may have much more compelling group interests than a loosely connected ethnic minority made up of immigrants who voluntarily left their native country to seek a better future for their family in a new adoptive country (Kymlicka 1995a: 11–33). Consistent with this, I will briefly discuss relevant differences among various types of groups, and explore the extent to which individual rights can be legitimately recast as group rights and vice versa.

Even if we only focus on North America, we find a wide variety among diverse groups. Thus, in the United States there are significant differences between national minorities, such as Native Americans and Puerto Ricans; racial minorities gathered together through forced immigration and subjected to slavery, such as African Americans; and ethnic minorities resulting from voluntary immigration, such as Irish Americans or Italian Americans.[13] Likewise, in Canada, the Aboriginal community has different problems and aspirations than the Quebecois (Id.: 12–13). Moreover, various countries have different attitudes and ideals regarding the relationship between majority and minority groups within their borders. Thus, the American assimilationist ideal of the "melting pot" can be contrasted with the Canadian objective of greater diversity through adherence to the model of the "ethnic mosaic" (Id.: 14).[14]

It is obvious that the differences noted earlier among groups and ideologies matter when devising an optimal constitutional regime for a particular polity. Furthermore, depending on the circumstances, these differences may be properly accounted for through apportionment of powers of self-determination or through allocation of suitable fundamental rights. For example, as already mentioned, where a minority group is concentrated within a compact territory, a federal system with extensive regional autonomy may afford the best means for the minority

---

[13] Even among the latter groups, there may be significant differences. For example, unlike Irish or Italian Americans who are now well established and unlikely to be subject to palpable discrimination, recent immigrants from Central or South America often experience much discrimination and poverty (Kymlicka 1995a: 10–24).

[14] Kymlicka argues that this contrast is misleading to the extent that Canada's actual commitment is not to a genuine diversity of cultures but rather to the maintenance of two dominant cultures (Id.: 14).

in question to realize its group aspirations. On the other hand, in the context of a widely dispersed ethnic minority immigrant group found within a polity with a strong "melting pot" ideology, effective protection of fundamental individual rights might well be paramount.

Collective autonomy through regional apportionment of the powers of sovereignty is often in conflict with the nation-state's responsibility to provide universal protection of fundamental individual rights. Conversely, it stands to reason that granting broad autonomy to a minority group whose culture is to a large degree inimical to the ideology of universal individual rights would weaken the protection of individual liberties within the group.

Conflicts between group autonomy and individual rights may be eased to the extent that individual rights may be recast as group rights and vice versa.[15] Moreover, in many cases, such a recasting is entirely possible. For example, as already mentioned, an individual right to freedom of worship and of association looms as the functional equivalent of a group right to worship according to the precepts of its commonly shared religion. It may be objected that though there may be functional equivalence in theory it does not necessarily follow that such equivalence would prevail in practice. Thus, a group right to freedom of religion might end up favoring established religions to the detriment of the formation of new sects and may thus leave the individual with fewer choices. Even if that is true, however, so long as the individual may choose among many religions and is in no way penalized for refusing to join any religious group, a satisfactory degree of functional equivalence could be maintained both in theory and in practice.

In certain other cases, recasting may lead to functional equivalence in theory but not in practice. Take, for instance, the right to be educated in one's own native language. Whether this right is cast as a group right belonging to a linguistic community or as an individual right extending to all members of that community makes little difference from a theoretical standpoint. On the other hand, to the extent that the state must provide for education in every citizen's native language, an individual right might be so impractical and costly as to make it virtually impossible to implement. In contrast, a group right extended to sizable groups may leave out only small scattered groups and a certain number of individuals, but it would in all likelihood be quite manageable in practice.

---

[15] Philosophers are in disagreement about the conceptual soundness of the notion of group or collective rights. Some have argued that, when properly analyzed, all rights tend ultimately to be, at bottom, individual (Hartney 1995: 202). Nonetheless, at least from a legal and political standpoint, it seems undeniable both that there can be group rights and that such rights are distinct from individual rights. Thus, if the Quebecois had an absolute right of self-government within their province, that would clearly *function* as a group right, and it could obviously be exercised in ways that would trample on the individual rights granted by the federal government to all Canadian individuals.

More generally, a distinction must be drawn between negative and positive rights – with "negative rights" being loosely defined as those that protect against state interference and "positive rights" as those that entail state help or subsidy. By and large, negative rights that may be cast either as individual or collective are likely to be functionally equivalent in practice if they are in theory. In contrast, positive rights susceptible of being thus recast are much less likely to be functionally equivalent in practice even if they are in theory. Accordingly, negative freedom of worship rights, be they individual or group rights, are very likely to be functionally equivalent in both theory and in practice. However, when such rights are positive they are less likely to be functionally equivalent in practice. Government subsidy of religion through building places of worship, financing religious education, and so on seems much more likely to boost the collective aims of organized religions than expending similar amounts through direct distribution among individual citizens, regardless of religious affiliation.

Notwithstanding these nuances, cases that allow for recasting are much less likely to present insurmountable constitutional dilemmas than cases in which recasting is altogether impossible or meaningless. For example, language rights understood in terms of the cultural heritage of a group may well be ultimately incompatible with any individual language rights. Where the heritage in question is threatened, and the group's language in danger of extinction, it may become necessary to impose an obligation on individuals belonging to the group to learn and communicate in the group's language. But in such a case, the very survival of the group's rights seemingly necessitates suppression of individual freedom and autonomy rights. In general, as already mentioned, when group survival clashes with individual autonomy, then group rights foster coercion of the individual, and individual rights threaten the viability and integrity of the group.

In spite of inevitable clashes, some may argue that individual rights ought to ultimately prevail over group rights because either individual exits would leave the group as such largely unaffected, or, if a mass exodus from the group occurred, the group would have no plausible claim to collective rights. In short, either the group can persevere in spite of individual defections, or such defections will result in what is tantamount to voluntary dissolution of the group.

Upon closer scrutiny, this argument falls short for at least two reasons. First, even though it is true that once a group completely dissolves, there remains no ground for group rights, group survival may require a critical mass of members. If the group is about to fall below that critical mass, then the remaining group members are in danger of suffering great harm and arguably in need of group rights. Second in a contemporary pluralistic society, clashes between the individual and her own group are unlikely to be exclusively over the individual's right to exit. Instead, some members may also avail themselves of claims to individual rights to change the group from within. For example, some women may seek to gain acceptance to the clergy of their own religion even though that clergy has been traditionally open only to men. In such a case, rather than accepting the status quo or leaving their religious congregation, the women in question may well press for changes from within, and in the eyes of many of their co-religionists threaten the integrity and viability of their commonly shared religion.

Because it is impossible to recast all individual rights as group rights and vice versa, a constitutional treatment of minorities that relies exclusively on one of these two kinds of rights is bound to be seriously flawed. What is required, therefore, is a constitutional regime that cogently apportions the domain of minority rights among individual and group rights. My contention is that the best available alternative is that carved out by comprehensive pluralism. Before pursuing this argument any further, however, it is useful to briefly examine how the constitutional treatment of minorities has actually fared in a diverse polity that encompasses many different types of minorities, such as the United States.

3.3. MINORITY RIGHTS UNDER THE U.S. CONSTITUTION

A survey of the constitutional landscape in the United States reveals an overwhelmingly, if not exclusively liberal, individualistic approach to minority rights. Although in the history and politics of the U.S. relations among different racial, ethnic, and religious groups have occupied a very prominent position, American constitutional jurisprudence has largely abstracted the individual from his collective setting. Indeed, even where group affiliation looms as most relevant, as in the unhappy and often violent history of race relations, such group affiliation has often been systematically suppressed or subordinated. Thus, the Equal Protection Clause of the U.S. Constitution, which was adopted in the aftermath of the Civil War, has been interpreted traditionally as recognizing the individual and not the group as the one afforded constitutional equality rights.[16]. Also, because of either adherence to liberal principles or focus on the individual to the detriment of the group, American constitutional jurisprudence has given group concerns short shrift in the areas of fundamental rights.

One may seek to justify America's downplaying of group concerns in terms of the country's embrace of the melting pot ideology. Such an attempt at justification seems inadequate, however, given the United States' long history of discrimination against a sizable portion of its individual inhabitants based on their group affiliations.[17] As a matter of fact, the principal defect of American constitutional

---

[16] See *Shelley* v. *Kramer*, 334 U.S. 1, 22–3 (1948).

[17] Even after the abolition of slavery based on race, the United States endured a long period of racial apartheid – a situation given constitutional approval in the Supreme Court's decision in

treatment of minorities and other groups that have endured discrimination and
sought legal redress has been largely to ignore or downplay injuries stemming from
group affiliation. Typically, victims of racism or sexism suffer individual harms as a
consequence of attacks or oppressive practices directed against the relevant racial
or gender group. Because of their race or gender, and regardless of all their other
attributes or accomplishments, individuals have been denied opportunities or benefits available to others. Yet, when these individuals seek redress, their claims are
rejected on the grounds that their asserted injury has not been sufficiently individualized. For example, in *Richmond v. J. A. Croson*, the Supreme Court struck
down as unconstitutional an affirmative action plan requiring a municipality to set
aside for minority-owned businesses a certain percentage of its public contracts
for construction as a remedy for persistent racial discrimination in the construction industry.[18] Fifty percent of the population of the municipality in question was
African American, but they comprised less than one percent of those engaged in the
construction industry. Nevertheless, the Court struck down the affirmative action
plan, partly on the ground that there was no proof that its intended beneficiaries had
suffered individually. Moreover, the Court's majority refused to accept the almost
complete absence of African Americans in construction in the face of an undisputed
history of racism in that industry as sufficient proof of individually experienced racial
discrimination. Implausibly, the Court's majority speculated that the lack of African
Americans in construction might be due to their choice in pursuing other employment avenues.[19]

The preceding example reveals not only that American constitutional jurisprudence, by and large, ignores group rights and group harms, but also that it severely
limits individual rights by ignoring individual interests deriving from group affiliation. The disparity in treatment between the latter interests and those that are
apparently severable from particular group affiliations emerges sharply in the contrast between the treatment of individual and group defamation. American constitutional jurisprudence as developed by the Supreme Court has established that
freedom of speech does not extend to defamation.[20] At an earlier time, moreover,

---

Plessy v. Ferguson, 163 U.S. 537 (1896) (upholding laws requiring separate accommodations for blacks
and whites as constitutional). Similarly, for a long time, discrimination against women because of
their gender was commonplace and deemed constitutional. See, for example, *Bradwell v. State of
Illinois*, 83 U.S. 130 (1873) (holding that a state may constitutionally bar a fully qualified individual
from practicing law on the sole ground that she is a woman).

[18] 488 U.S. 469 (1989).

[19] Id., at 501–3. Even if that assumption had been warranted, it is quite remarkable that the Court's
majority refused to admit any link between that choice and the fact that the construction industry
had rightfully earned a notorious reputation for being hostile to African Americans (Rosenfeld 1989a:
1764).

[20] See, for example, *New York Times v. Sullivan*, 376 U.S. 254 (1964) (holding that a public official may
recover damages in a libel action if he proves actual malice); *Gertz v. Welch*, 418 U.S. 323 (1974)

this limitation extended to group defamation as well as to defamation of an individual.[21] But in more recent years, group defamation has for all practical purposes become constitutionally protected speech.[22]

One may seek to justify the disparate constitutional treatment of individual and group defamation by insisting that injuries in the case of individuals tend to be more serious than those involved when a group as a whole is targeted. A public declaration falsely accusing an individual of being dishonest is more injurious, according to this view, than labeling an entire ethnic or religious group as dishonest. Moreover, the principal reasons for this discrepancy are that individual slander is usually much more believable than group slander and that even if it happens to be widely believed, group defamation has a much more diffuse effect on individual members of the defamed group than individual defamation baa on its lone victim.

Upon closer scrutiny, however, these justifications prove unpersuasive. Although it is true that few would literally believe that all members of a given ethnic group are in fact dishonest, sustained group defamation may convince the general population that members of the targeted group are likely – and certainly more likely than fellow citizens who do not belong to the group – to be dishonest. This can result in pervasive employment, social, and political discrimination against members of the targeted group, thus producing individual injuries on account of group affiliation. These injuries seem to be no less acute than those suffered by an individual denied employment, socially ostracized, or politically excluded as a consequence of being a victim of individual defamation. In short, by abstracting the individual from his or her group in the context of defamation, American free speech jurisprudence denies individual protection to certain victims of group defamation who are, for all relevant purposes, equally situated with others who are accorded such individual protection.[23]

Even though group affiliation may be abstracted or submerged, it cannot be eradicated because it plays an important role in the life of every citizen. Accordingly, constitutional jurisprudence cannot simply ignore group affiliation, but must incorporate it – albeit implicitly – in the course of its development and application.

(holding that defamatory information published by a newspaper or broadcaster about an individual who is neither a public figure nor a public official is not constitutionally protected).

[21] See *Beauharnais. v. Illinois*, 343 U.S. 250 (1952) (holding that racist and anti-Semitic invective uttered by white supremacists does not amount to constitutionally protected speech).

[22] See, for example, *R.A.V. v. City of St Paul, Minnesota*, 505 U.S. 377 (1992) (holding that state law outlawing hate speech on the basis. of race. creed, color, religion, or gender is unconstitutional); *Collins v. Smith*, 578 F.2d 1197 (7th Cir. 1978), *cert. den*, 439 U.S. 916 (1978) (holding that Neo-Nazi march in military uniform with swastika and anti-Semitic propaganda in a Jewish neighborhood comprised of numerous holocaust survivors is protected speech).

[23] Unlike the United States, Canada has upheld criminalization of group defamation. See *Regina v. Keegstra*, 3 S.C.R. 697 (1990) (holding that criminalization of anti-Semitic hate propaganda is constitutional).

By relegating group affiliation to the background, American constitutional jurisprudence has sometimes carved out individual rights in ways that promote discrimination against individuals who belong to certain minority groups. A prime example of this phenomenon is found in the context of the scope of exemptions from generally applicable laws on the grounds that compliance with such laws infringes on the free exercise of religion.[24] Thus, in *Employment Division v Smith*, the Supreme Court held that an individual member of a Native American religion could not obtain an exemption from a generally applicable criminal law prohibiting the use of peyote, even though the exemption was sought exclusively for ritual use in the course of religious worship.[25] This decision would not be remarkable, at least from the standpoint of the present inquiry, if it were not for the fact that similar exemptions had been granted to Catholics and Jews for the ritual use of wine during the Prohibition – the era in which the U.S. Constitution enshrined a general prohibition against the consumption of alcoholic beverages throughout the United States.[26] Although the denial of a peyote exemption was court ordered whereas the grant of an alcohol exemption was enshrined in constitutional text, it is nonetheless striking that the individual right to freely exercise one's religion fluctuates depending on whether one belongs to a mainstream religious group such as Catholics or Jews or to a much more marginal group such as Native Americans.

Notwithstanding the United States' constitutional aversion to group rights, there are a handful of Supreme Court decisions that can be fairly characterized as protective of the group rather than the individual (Johnston 1995: 185). Two such decisions are *Wisconsin v. Yoder*,[27] and *Santa Clara Pueblo v. Martinez*.[28] These decisions are truly exceptional, and their placement of group concerns ahead of individual ones may be purely contingent, but, as I will discuss in this section, their consequences illustrate the drawbacks stemming from protecting the group at the expense of the individual.

In *Yoder*, parents belonging to the tightly knit, traditional Amish community sought an exemption from the state's compulsory education requirement for their children over the age of fourteen. The Amish are a small religious community that is economically self-sufficient, and they live in certain rural areas apart from the rest of society. Their claim for an exemption was predicated on their freedom to freely exercise their religion and was pursued to maintain control over the socialization of their young – an issue that they considered essential to preserving their communal way of

[24] Freedom of religion is guaranteed by the "Free Exercise" Clause of the First Amendment to the U.S. Constitution.
[25] 494 U.S. 872 (1990).
[26] Id.
[27] 406 U.S. 205 (1972).
[28] 436 U.S. 49 (1978).

life (Johnston 1995: 185). In deciding that the requested exemption was constitutionally permissible, the Supreme Court stressed that the Amish were a self-contained,
self-sufficient, and law-abiding group and that, therefore, the grant of the requested
exemption would not burden the state or the remainder of its citizens.[29]

As a small isolated group, the Amish have little interaction with others and pose
no threat to other groups. Because of their distinct dress and simple farming lifestyles, the Amish are mainly viewed by their fellow citizens as a quaint and pictur-
esque remnant of a bygone era. Nevertheless, as emphasized by one of the Justices
who concurred in the Court's decision, deferring to the Amish community without
inquiring whether the adolescent about to be taken out of school agrees with his
or her parents is troubling.[30] Indeed, once out of school and lacking the level of
education attained by the rest of the population, the Amish adolescent is effectively
deprived of the opportunity to leave the confines of the group to become integrated
into the mainstream of society should he or she prefer to do so. In other words, the
decision in *Yoder* does vindicate a group right – albeit that the group in question is
completely peripheral and poses no threat whatsoever to the lifestyles of others – but
it does so by approving of the subordination of individual members to the collective
destiny of the group.

In the *Martinez* case, on the other hand, the Supreme Court considered Native
Americans, the only kind of group that has historically been accorded group rights
in the United States.[31] Although the treatment of Native Americans has often been
dismal in American history (Clinton 1993: 77), they have been entitled to significant collective autonomy and broad powers of self-government.[32] Thus, consistent
with self-government rights, Native American tribal councils have traditionally been
exempt from compliance with the Bill of Rights of the American Constitution and
from judicial review of their internal decisions.[33]

Against this background and in the face of strong opposition from Native American
groups, the U.S. Congress passed the Indian Civil Rights Act in 1968.[34] In *Martinez*,
a woman member of the Pueblo Tribe invoked the Act to challenge tribal kinship
rules as discriminatory against women. Specifically, these kinship rules refused certain rights to Pueblo women married to nonmembers, while allowing Pueblo men
who had nonmember wives to retain the rights in question.

[29] See generally *Yoder*, 406 U.S. 205.
[30] Id. at 237 (Stewart, J., concurring).
[31] See *Martinez*, 436 U.S. 49.
[32] See, for example, *Oklahoma Tax Commission v. Citizen Bank Potawatomi Indian Tribe of Oklahoma*,
      498 U.S. 505, 509 (1991) ("Indian Tribes are 'domestic dependent nations' that exercise inherent sov-
      ereign authority over their members and territories").
[33] See *Martinez*, 436 U.S. at 55–6.
[34] 25 U.S.C. §§ 1301–1303 (1968).

The Pueblo claimed that its patrilineal kinship rules were essential to the group's identity, integrity, and continued viability, and Martinez claimed that such rules deprived her of her fundamental freedom regarding marital choice and relationship to her children. The *Martinez* case thus represents a prime example of the clash between group survival and an individual member's most fundamental rights. Accordingly, it is hardly surprising that the lower federal courts split, with the trial court upholding the tribe's group right at the expense of the individual,[35] and the Court of Appeals reversing in favor of the individual against the group.[36] Finally, the Supreme Court avoided siding with either of the lower courts, by ruling that the federal courts lacked jurisdiction to resolve the kind of dispute involved in *Martinez*. Although it thus managed not to rule on the merits, the Supreme Court's jurisdictional decision nevertheless amounted to a choice between the individual and the group. Indeed, the Court's refusal of jurisdiction amounted to deference to tribal sovereignty and therefore indirectly to a vindication of group rights at the expense of those of the individual (Johnston 1995: 185).

From the standpoint of American constitutional jurisprudence, *Yoder* and *Martinez* are exceptional in their implicit recognition of group rights. These cases, however, do not represent a significant departure from liberal individualism. First, the groups involved are peripheral and so far removed from the mainstream as to remain beyond the pressures of the melting pot. Second, there was no actual conflict between parent and child in *Yoder*, and there has been a tradition of self-government among Native American tribes in sharp contrast to all other groups in the United States.

If *Yoder* and *Martinez* had been decided in the context of a polity that, unlike that of the United States, afforded strong protection to group rights, these cases might figure as prime examples of a communitarian constitutional jurisprudence.[37] Indeed, both of these cases give priority to the community over both the individual and society's general welfare as envisioned by the democratic state (Id.: 187). Moreover, inasmuch as these cases uphold the priority of the community even when it clashes with fundamental interests of the individual and important state welfare objectives,

---

[35] *Martinez v. Santa Clara Pueblo*, 402 F. Supp. 5 (D.N.M. 1975).
[36] *Martinez v. Santa Clara Pueblo*, 540 F. 1039 (10th Cir. 1976).
[37] Actually, the district court opinion in *Martinez* emerges as squarely communitarian. Though it espoused a balancing approach, the district court concluded that tribal group survival, self-determination, and preservation of cultural identity clearly outweighed any individual interest against very substantial sex discrimination regarding such fundamental issues as relationship to one's children, property and inheritance rights, and even membership in one's community. See *Martinez*, 402 F. Supp. at 18–19. Needless to say, had any of the fifty states treated any woman within its jurisdiction in a similar way, that conduct would unquestionably have been struck down as unconstitutional under the Equal Protection Clause. See *U.S. v. Virginia*. 518 U.S. 515 (1996).

they illustrate the main shortcoming of a communitarian approach. That shortcoming consists of a tendency to undervalue individual interests and autonomy as well as social goods that are inter-communal rather than intra-communal in scope.

3.4. COMPREHENSIVE PLURALISM, THE CONSTITUTION, AND GROUP RIGHTS

The preceding glimpse into American constitutional jurisprudence provides a brief illustration of the respective drawbacks of a liberal and a communitarian approach to the constitutional rights of minorities. The liberal approach is generally inimical to group rights and tends to disfavor individual rights predicated on group affiliation. In other words, it tends to prefer individual rights that promote identity over individual rights that protect or foster difference. Conversely, the communitarian approach is well suited to optimize communal rights but only at the expense of the individual and society as a whole.[38]

In contrast to liberalism and communitarianism, comprehensive pluralism is capable of striking a principled balance between the interests of the individual, the group, and society taken as a whole. Indeed, even though it may be impossible to fully resolve these conflicts, the different options available to manage clashes between the individual, the group, and society are hardly equivalent. And, this is, as already noted, because unlike its principal rivals, comprehensive pluralism regards individual and group concerns as intrinsically and normatively equivalent.

Even if one concedes that pluralistic solutions are likely to be more equitable as between the individual and the group, one may still object that liberal or communitarian solutions are quite adequate inasmuch as liberalism does not foreclose protecting groups, and communitarianism does not prevent taking the individual into account. Thus, Will Kymlicka has articulated a liberal defense of group rights, relying on a distinction between "external protections" and "internal restrictions" (Kymlicka 1995a: 7). According to Kymlicka, a minority group as such ought to be protected from external intervention or coercion coming from the larger society, but should have no right to impose internal restrictions on its individual members in order to safeguard cultural purity or group solidarity (Id.: 34–48).

Kymlicka's liberal conception of group rights does afford minorities important protections in the context of inter-group or inter-communal relationships. In particular, such rights provide a shield against involuntary entry into a melting

---

[38] A communitarian approach could also be used to optimize protection of the collective interests of society as a whole. In that case, the group interests of the nation-state would be promoted at the expense of the individual and minority groups within the polity.

pot and a weapon against polities, such as France, which seek to rid the political space of all entities other than individuals or the nation as a unified whole. Kymlicka's conception of group rights, however, does nothing to bolster the group in intra-group or intra-communal conflicts. In short, although Kymlicka's liberalism seems particularly attractive to the extent that it does not reduce the group to a mere aggregate of individuals, it ultimately cannot escape the fate of all liberalism: In conflicts between group survival and individual autonomy, the latter must prevail.

Although some versions of communitarianism may leave significant room for the pursuit of individual interests, in the end communitarianism is as much a prisoner of its monistic moorings as is liberalism. In intra-communal conflicts that pit group survival against individual autonomy, communitarianism, like liberalism, cannot avoid taking sides. The only difference between the two is that whereas liberalism necessarily sides with the individual, communitarianism must always decide in favor of the group. Just as liberalism is wedded to individualism, so too is communitarianism to collectivism.

Although because of its inherent indifference as between the individual and the group the pluralist approach looms as the best available alternative, it is still far from perfect. First, its weighing of different conceptions of the good, though principled, is bound to remain imprecise. Second, the results it produces may be the best possible under the circumstances, but they will hardly be definitive, and in some cases might even fail to yield a workable equilibrium between individual and group concerns. Simply stated, comprehensive pluralism provides the best alternative among imperfect options.

A constitutional jurisprudence emanating from comprehensive pluralism would have to concentrate on two separate inquiries when dealing with issues relating to minorities. First, such constitutional jurisprudence would have to scrutinize all proposals and claims to ensure conformity with the second-order norms put forth by comprehensive pluralism. Thus, whether in the context of devising constitutional norms or in that of adjudicating constitutional claims, a comprehensively pluralistic jurisprudence would have to apply suitable principles deriving from its second-order norms. Second, the jurisprudence in question would have to develop means to conduct "inter-perspectival" and "intra-perspectival" comparisons for purposes of settling disputes among proponents of different conceptions of the good. The conceptions should be compatible (at least to the extent relevant in the case of the dispute at hand) with the constitutional principles that give expression to second-order norms. In other words, a comprehensively pluralistic constitutional jurisprudence must devise means properly to assess the relative weight to be attributed to an individual claim of autonomy in relation to a similar group claim, as well as means to compare, in terms of the dictates of second-order norms, the demands of a group (as viewed from within its own conception of the good) as against those of other groups or of society at large (as viewed from within their own respective conception of the good).

These requirements, which combine application of principles and weighing of claims in accordance with their relative importance to the claimant, raise a number of practical issues that remain beyond the scope of the present inquiry. Accordingly, I shall focus on the broad contours of these requirements and consider them in the light of an actual minority rights case decided by the Canadian Supreme Court, with a view to suggesting how these requirements may be implemented in the context of an actual constitutional regime.

Compliance with second-order norms may be broadly equated with promotion of mutual respect between self and other, tolerance, concern for the autonomy of self and other, and for the integrity of all conceptions of the good (to the extent that the latter are not inimical to the integrity of other such conceptions), and also the aim of fostering coexistence among as wide as possible an array of different conceptions of the good. These prescriptions, moreover, ought to be used in all cases involving regulation of inter-communal dealings. For intra-communal dealings or relations between an individual and his or her own group that may fairly be categorized as being intra-communal in nature,[39] however, direct or unmediated application of the foregoing norms would not always be appropriate. In other words, the inter-communal implementation of comprehensive pluralism's second-order norms does not necessarily require an across-the-board compliance with such norms in the context of intra-communal dealings. In fact, the wholesale subjection of all intra-communal dealings to the dictates of second-order norms would threaten to completely undermine comprehensive pluralism as it would eventually eviscerate all first-order norms, thus destroying the very possibility of a coexistence among a large number of diverse conceptions of the good.

Maintenance of the tension between first- and second-order norms is essential to the successful deployment of comprehensive pluralism. Within the framework of constitutional jurisprudence, moreover, this tension can be nurtured through a juxtaposition of standards. This makes for a predominance of second-order norms applicable to inter-communal matters with precepts that allow for primacy of first-order norms when it comes to intra-communal matters. As already mentioned, second-order norms ought to inform constitutional principles applicable to inter-communal dealings or society as a whole, but a preference ought to be instituted for those

[39] In general terms, the relation between an individual who identifies with his or her group and has every intention to remain an active member of it, but who seeks to foster change or reform from within, should be deemed an intra-communal one. On the other hand, the relation between a group and a dissident member who rejects *some* of the essential tenets of group identity would qualify as an inter-communal relation.

implementations of such principles that allow for the greatest possible accommodation toward first-order norms. On the other hand, constitutional precepts ought to leave intra-communal dealings to be conducted in accordance with first-order norms except to the extent that this would pose a threat to the prescribed constitutional treatment of inter-communal relations. Thus, for example, it ought to be constitutionally permissible for the state to impose a requirement that communally run schools teach a course in civics and civic tolerance if the state could demonstrate that in the absence of such a course the members of the community involved would be more likely than not to refuse to abide by established inter-communal constitutional norms.

Consistent with the preceding observations, minority groups would receive considerable "external protection" under a constitutional regime fashioned according to the prescriptions of comprehensive pluralism. On the other hand, when a group seeks to enforce "internal restrictions" (Id.) against its members, inter-communal issues arise, and constitutional norms largely dependent on second-order norms ought to prevail. Unlike under a liberal regime such as that advocated by Kymlicka (1995a: 34–48), however, a constitutional regime deriving from comprehensive pluralism does not necessarily require that the individual prevail over the group. In that case, although second-order norms would be predominant, properly fashioned constitutional norms would require that both the individual's and the group's respective (first-order) perspective be seriously taken into account as a precondition to settling the dispute at hand. In other words, pursuant to comprehensive pluralism, it would not suffice to apply second-order norms *directly* in order to resolve the dispute. Instead, it would first be necessary to understand the respective claims in the context of the first-order norms, which give them support, in order to be in a position to devise a solution that allows for as much free adherence to first-order norms as possible for each of the parties involved.

Also, unlike the liberalism endorsed by Kymlicka, as already specified, consistent with justice as reversible reciprocity comprehensive pluralism requires an inter-perspectival assessment of the respective claims of the individual and the group for the purpose of establishing, if possible, an order of priority that might facilitate resolution of the conflict. Indeed, not all claims occupy a similar position *within* the very conception of the good from which they emerge. Some claims are likely to be central while others are likely to be more peripheral. Thus, in case of a conflict between a group and one of its individual members, the importance of the claim of each within the conception of the good from which it emanates ought to be assessed for purposes of determining how central or peripheral each claim is from within the perspective of its claimant. In some cases, such determination ought to be conclusive for the disposition of the controversy. For example, if in a case that pits a group claim pertaining to its survival against a claim deriving from the right to individual autonomy, satisfaction of the group claim were less central to its survival than satisfaction of the individual claim to the latter's autonomy, then the individual claim ought to prevail over the collective one.

The kind of inter-perspectival comparison from *within* each of the perspectives described previously may be sufficient to decide some, but not all, cases. Indeed, whereas for practical purposes it may be in some cases sufficient to submit conflicts between the individual and her group to a process of inter-perspectival comparison, in principle that process must be supplemented by an evaluation of all the claims involved from the standpoint of the relevant dictates prescribed by second-order norms. In many cases, therefore, the right constitutional outcome will depend on both a proper inter-perspectival comparison and a proper assessment of the antagonistic claims involved from the standpoint of standards deriving from second-order norms. Assume, for example, that a group demanded the right to put to death an individual member who had blasphemed against that group's religion. Even if the requisite inter-perspectival comparison revealed that upholding respect for the group's religion were essential for the group's continued survival and that the utterance of the blasphemous statement was an act to which the individual in question attached a low level of importance within his or her own perspective, the group's request would have to be denied on the grounds that it would be violative of fundamental principles deriving from second-order norms.[40] Indeed, in that case the relative importance of the act at the center of the controversy respectively for the group and the individual would be clearly outweighed by the fact that the remedy proposed by the group would be much more repugnant from the standpoint of comprehensive pluralism than would the individual's act that gave rise to the controversy.

It may be objected that this outlined approach, which is consistent with comprehensive pluralism and may be attractive in theory, is nonetheless unsuited for constitutional adjudication in practice. Moreover, underlying this objection is the belief that there is no reliable or judicially manageable way to conduct the requisite inter-perspectival comparison. In reply, however, one may point out that even though the comparisons in question may not be that precise and even though they may not furnish a clear-cut result in every case, they are nonetheless quite comparable to many of the kinds of analyses that are routinely used in constitutional adjudication.[41]

---

[40] This is not to say that the group may not legitimately prevail against the individual, under the circumstances, should the group's request be more compatible with what is required by second-order norms. For example, had Salman Rushdie been living within a tightly knit Muslim community and had he declared that the sole purpose of his *Satanic Verses* was to offend that community and that he considered that work to be of little literary value, then his expulsion from that religious community might not have been necessarily violative of his fundamental rights within a constitutional order governed by comprehensive pluralism. For a nuanced analysis of the constitutional implications or the actual Rushdie affair from a multi-cultural perspective, see Slaughter, 1993: 153.

[41] For example, neither in the United States nor in Canada are constitutional rights absolute. In both countries such rights are limited in accordance with certain important needs of society as a whole

In order to buttress this latter claim, I briefly refer to the Canadian case of *Regina* v. *Adams*. The case involves the constitutional adjudication of a claim to aboriginal rights by that country's Supreme Court.[42] In *Adams*, a member of the Mohawk Tribe, who was convicted under a Quebec ordinance prohibiting fishing without a license in certain inland waterways, claimed that he was entitled to an exemption from that ordinance on account of his aboriginal rights under the Canadian Constitution.[43] The Canadian Supreme Court upheld the aboriginal right and reversed the conviction. In part, the Court based its decision on a comparison of the need to fish from an aboriginal perspective with the need to curb fishing from the standpoint of the state. Thus, whereas the Mohawks had traditionally fished for food, which was true in this case, the state's regulation through licensing had been for the purpose of protecting sport-fishing rather than to promote ecological concern.[44] Accordingly, the claim within the perspective of the Mohawk was superior to that within the perspective of the state, thus justifying giving priority to the aboriginal right over that carved out by the state for its majority population.

Even though the *Adams* case may not be particularly difficult from the standpoint of inter-perspectival comparison, it proves that such comparisons are not inherently impossible or unmanageable. Accordingly, a constitutional regime fashioned to suit the requirements of comprehensive pluralism seems highly desirable because it is more flexible and nuanced than its liberal and communitarian counterparts. Indeed, without losing sight of its many imperfections, the constitutional treatment of minority rights according to the precepts of comprehensive pluralism offers the best available means to tackle conflicts between the individual, the group, and society as a whole. With this in mind, let us now examine how comprehensive pluralism might contribute to bridging the gap between universalism and relativism in the context of human rights.

---

that are not always susceptible to being precisely measured. For the United States, see, for example, *Planned Parenthood of Southeastern Pennsylvania* v. *Casey*, 5 U.S. 833 (1992) (restrictions on abortion where state advances a compelling interest or where it imposes a burden that is not undue are constitutional); *Roe* v. *Wade*, 410 U.S. 113 (1973); *Brandenburg* v. *Ohio* 395 U.S. 444 (1969) (freedom of speech rights do not extend to utterances that pose a "clear and present danger" to society or that tend to incite rather than merely advocate violence); *Griswold* v. *Connecticut*, 381 U.S. 479 (1965) (privacy rights must yield where the state interposes a conflicting interest that is compelling); and *Schenk* v. *United States*, 249 U.S. 47 (1919). For Canada, see Article 1 of the 1982 constitution, which provides that "*The Canadian Charter of Rights and Freedoms* guarantees the rights and freedoms set out in it subject only to such reasonable limits described by law as can be demonstrably justified in a free and democratic society."

[42] 3 S.C.R. 101 (1996).
[43] Can. Const. (Constitution Act, 1982) Sec. 35(1).
[44] 3 S.C.R. 133 (1996).

3.5. COMPREHENSIVE PLURALISM AND THE NEXUS BETWEEN HUMAN RIGHTS AND CONSTITUTIONAL RIGHTS

Consistent with the preceding analysis of minority group rights, the challenge against the universality of human rights can be profitably likened to claims that implementation of individually oriented constitutional rights (virtually identical in content to particular human rights promoted by the International Covenant on Civil and Political Rights or by the ECHR) would be destructive of the very survival or cultural integrity of the objecting group. Moreover, as between the different kinds of groups identified earlier, it is the culturally homogeneous, tightly knit community incorporated involuntarily as a distinct minority within the polity where the majority embraces a profoundly incompatible conception of the good that presents the most formidable challenge to the normative claim that (at least certain) fundamental individual-regarding human rights ought to be universal in scope.[45] It is true that on an international scale, such a group may not have the status of a minority within a larger hostile polity, but rather that of an independent self-governing state. Nevertheless, the claim of such a state may be in all relevant respects equivalent to that of the previously mentioned minority group if the state in question is subjected to strong economic, political, or cultural pressures from more powerful states or supra-national organizations that promote ideologies that it finds both unacceptable and threatening.

As the degree and kind of plurality involved in any clash between majority and minority groups is likely to vary from one setting to the next (i.e., which clusters of first-order norms compete for predominance, and the ways and extent that they clash with one another are bound to vary depending on the makeup of the polity involved), comprehensive pluralism is poised to lead to solutions that are context-specific and thus particular. For example, accommodating aboriginal group interests and cultural and linguistic differences such as those that divide English-speaking from French-speaking Canadians seems likely to require different measures than those called for to mediate between religious fundamentalists, feminists, and gay-rights advocates. At least prima facie, therefore comprehensive pluralism seems much more likely to promote particularism rather than either universalism or relativism.

---

[45] As an example of such human rights, one may cite Article 19 of the Universal Declaration of Human Rights, which provides: "Everyone has the right to freedom of opinion and expression; this right includes freedom to hold opinions without interference and to seek, receive and impart information and ideas through any media and regardless of frontiers." Universal Declaration of Human Rights, Dec. 10, 1948, G.A. Rea. 217A, U.N. GAOR, 3d Sess., U.N. Doc A/810 (1948).

Suppose, moreover, that a homogeneous society where women are made strictly dependent on, and subordinate to, men but where women seem fully to accept their fate and to be integrated into their culture objected to compliance with Article 19 on the grounds that receipt of Western feminist views would cause social upheaval and undermine the very survival of the prevailing culture.

This can be illustrated by reference to the purely counterfactual limiting case of the homogeneous polity hostile to all individually oriented rights. Comprehensive pluralism does not justify subjecting such a polity to the imposition of individually oriented human rights. Although comprehensive pluralism grants priority to second-order norms over first-order norms, such priority only comes into play in the context of an actual or potential conflict among first-order norms. As already mentioned, second-order norms are called upon to regulate all relations, with even the most minimal inter-communal component, but not to rule over *purely* intra-communal ones (in the context of fully homogeneous groups).[46] Moreover, unless this division of labor between first- and second-order norms is preserved, comprehensive pluralism would end up destroying the very plurality of conceptions of the good that it needs for its survival. Once again, the example of tolerance, which is the cornerstone of the second-order norms associated with comprehensive pluralism, is illustrative. Indeed, tolerance, although crucial to the viability of a heterogeneous polity, seems entirely superfluous in the limiting case of a completely homogeneous society that has no dealings with any of its neighbors.

This last conclusion may seem counterintuitive, and, more generally, it may be objectionable that respect for the integrity of the beliefs and practices of even the most homogeneous group cannot be seriously meant to be without limits. What if such a group, for example, regularly engages in the murder, torture, or mutilation of some of its own members in the course of performing institutionalized rituals? Does comprehensive pluralism deny that some acts are so heinous that no human being regardless of his or her circumstances ought to be universally protected against them?[47]

At the risk of being accused of paying too much attention to what may appear as a mere philosophical technicality, a consistent proponent of comprehensive pluralism must insist that, strictly speaking, a completely homogeneous group without any potential for internal dissent need not practice tolerance or refrain from any purely intra-communal act no matter how repulsive to outsiders. As we shall see, from a practical standpoint, comprehensive pluralism condemns all forms of human degradation just as vehemently as any of its monistic rivals. Nonetheless, comprehensive pluralism's refusal to condemn certain purely internal practices is not merely

---

[46] This latter qualification is crucial because from the standpoint of comprehensive pluralism, internal dissent by a single member of an otherwise strictly homogeneous polity must be viewed, strictly speaking as involving inter-communal rather than purely intra-communal dealings. Thus, for example, whereas the conflict in the *Martinez* case discussed above erupted within a distinct Native American community, the fact that the woman involved was advancing equality claims derived from the larger culture transformed the dispute into an inter-communal clash.

[47] Cf. Perry 1998: ch. 3 (arguing that even if one accepts moral pluralism and cultural relativism, some evils are so pernicious regardless of circumstances that every human being ought to have a right to protection against them by virtue of the simple fact of being human).

of theoretical interest as it has palpable repercussions for cases in which the optimal resolution of a clash between collective ideology and individual-regarding rights is far from obvious.

That tolerance is superfluous in the context of a completely homogeneous and fully self-contained and self-sufficient group is easy to grasp. Because such a group is completely absorbed in its communal affairs and has absolutely no dealings with any outsiders, it is difficult to see the purpose of insisting that members of the group develop a sense of tolerance toward views that are only held by people with whom they will never come into contact. Needless to add, no actual organized society could even come close to being as homogeneous and as isolated as the group envisioned earlier. Since no such organized group exists, and no actual group is ever likely to evolve in that fashion, no living group whether predominantly homogeneous or heterogeneous is therefore exempt from practicing tolerance consistent with the precepts of comprehensive pluralism.

It is only by keeping in mind that the completely homogeneous, self-contained group is merely a counterfactual ideal designed to provide a useful baseline that the claim that no purely internal act, no matter how repulsive, can be cogently repudiated on normative grounds by a proponent of comprehensive pluralism. To illustrate this point, let us consider the particularly revolting example of excruciatingly painful prolonged torture leading to death. Now, for a group to remain completely homogeneous as understood here, all members of the group must agree on a commonly held conception of the good, on the normative validity of practices consistent with such common ideology, and on the impossibility of any future deviation or dissent from the conception or practices involved. Consistent with this, a practice of torture within such a homogeneous group must be assumed to be equally fully voluntarily accepted by both the torturer and the victim. And if this seems too absurd to be conceivable, consider the case of a tightly knit, religious community where every member fervently believes that to be chosen to be tortured unto death is to be considered the highest honor on earth as well as a guarantee of eternal bliss in the afterlife. In such a case, no matter how horrendous, comprehensive pluralism does not allow for intervention.

Moreover, so long as a religious community, such as that in the example is counterfactually conceivable – in the same way as a perfect economic market is *logically* conceivable, but *practically* impossible – comprehensive pluralism does not justify, strictly speaking, a universal human right against torture.[48]

---

[48] It may be argued that so long as the victim of torture knows he or she has a right against it, the fact that such victim in effect waived such right does not affect its universality. This argument is not persuasive, however, inasmuch as all rights imply correlative duties and as not all voluntary waivers of a right result in an exemption from the correlative duty. For example, the consent of the victim does not furnish an excuse for murder. Similarly, if the human right against torture is deemed truly

Before further pursuing the full theoretical implications of this last conclusion, it bears emphasizing that its practical consequences are far less drastic than might at first be thought. Indeed, comprehensive pluralism mandates full condemnation of all systematic human rights violations that occurred since the proclamation of the 1948 declaration, such as genocide, ethnic cleansing, or torture and murder of political enemies. All these cases involve inter-communal dealings in settings that are all to varying degrees heterogeneous. Moreover, even in the context of fairly homogeneous polities, one ought to view with great suspicion any proclaimed consensual acceptance of subordination, pain, or violence. Accordingly, comprehensive pluralism is entirely consistent with a strong presumption against such acceptance, particularly when it is expressed by, or on behalf of, the weak or the powerless.

The theoretical implications of comprehensive pluralism's rejection of strict universalism become clear in the context of less extreme but nonetheless difficult and troubling situations. Of particular current concern are many situations involving the subordination of women or the voluntary acceptance of practices considered cruel and inhuman in the West, such as female circumcision.[49] Consider, for example, a situation in which, in spite of presumptions to the contrary, it becomes clear that women have fully endorsed a communal life that by Western standards relegates them to a subordinate position. Suppose further, that the women in question not only voluntarily embrace female circumcision, but also sincerely believe that its prohibition would lead to the destruction of a way of life they cherish and fully endorse.[50] Under such circumstances, provided no coercion is involved, and provided the women to the contested practice are fully adult and treated as genuine members (albeit not equal members by Western standards) of their community, comprehensive pluralism does not justify upsetting communal bonds for purposes of implementing fundamental individually oriented equality rights.[51]

---

universal, the consent of the victim would not exempt from responsibility those charged with the correlative duty.

[49] The literature on both the human rights of women and female circumcision is vast. For a good feminist account of the clash between women's equality and cultural and religious group rights, see Raday 2003. Regarding female circumcision, see generally Brennan 1989.

[50] Cf. Perry 1998: 74 ("In the view of ... many of the mothers who persist in subjecting their often willing daughters to the practice, female circumcision is morally proper – even, for the girl subjected to the practice, ennobling.").

[51] In this respect, comprehensive pluralism is somewhat inconsistent with some current international human rights norms. Indeed, both the Convention on the Elimination of Violence Against Women (CEDAW) and the U.N. Sub-Commission for the Prevention of Discrimination and the Protection of Minorities take the position that female circumcision amounts to a violation of human rights (Breitung 1996: 683, 691). Notwithstanding this discrepancy, a proponent of comprehensive pluralism would wholeheartedly support condemnation of female circumcision in any setting in which the women involved are not full adults or see themselves less as full partners than as victims of this traditional communal practice.

It must be emphasized that if comprehensive pluralism does not justify combating female circumcision in certain settings, it is not because it occasionally lapses into relativism, but rather because loyalty to its own principles require it. In other words, if female circumcision is tolerable in some other community, it is not because it is good for "them" but not for "us." It is because, on balance, given the particular circumstances of that other community, prohibiting female circumcision would be a greater affront to that community's integrity and to its members' dignity than would allowing the practice to continue. Conversely, within our own community, integrity and dignity militate in favor of prohibiting rather than permitting female circumcision. From the standpoint of comprehensive pluralism, dignified membership and the integrity of a commonly shared way of life are values that ought to be constantly promoted but that take different forms depending on the particular context in which they are embedded.

Based on the preceding analysis, consistent with comprehensive pluralism, human rights are neither strictly universal nor purely particular. Rather, they ought to be shaped by a dynamic and evolving tension caused by a simultaneous pull toward the universal and toward the particular. For example, all humans, or at least all born humans, are entitled to membership in their community, country, and humanity at large. Moreover, all humans are entitled to be treated with dignity. The actual attributes of membership or dignity, however, will tend to depend on the particular circumstances involved. Similarly, although the same basic human rights may be honored in many, if not most, polities, the actual contours of such rights are likely to vary from one setting to the next. As we saw earlier, although both the United States and Canada protect freedom of speech, there are significant differences in scope between their respective approaches. From the standpoint of comprehensive pluralism, these differences may well be warranted if they properly account for different needs and aspirations between the two societies. If this is true, not only are the differences in question justified, but any attempt to eradicate them would undermine rather than bolster freedom of speech.

I have thus far focused on the counterfactual case of the purely homogeneous self-contained group because it affords a better insight into the baseline that sets comprehensive pluralism apart from its principal rivals. From a practical standpoint, however, all contemporary polities are heterogeneous (or at least potentially so) as are various minorities within such polities and obviously as is the concert of nations that interact on a global scale. Accordingly, consistent with the precepts of comprehensive pluralism, second-order norms should play a far more important role within actual societies and groups than they would in the context of an idealized group conceived as fully homogeneous. For one thing, tolerance, which could be largely dispensed within the latter setting, must be promoted as a fundamental value in any heterogeneous setting. In addition, heterogeneity is bound to generate pressure for change from within. Returning to the example of women, as their plight to overcome the manifold burdens of subordination is widespread, both increased awareness of such plight and mobilization to overcome it become increasingly likely to spill over from one culture to another and from polity to polity. As intercultural bonds between women multiply, the intra-cultural struggle to improve their fate is intensified. A telling example of this phenomenon is the outlawing of female circumcision by the Senegalese parliament pursuant to a campaign by Senegalese women.[52]

In the last analysis, while the tension between the pull toward the universal and that toward the particular is unlikely to ever cease, there is currently an unmistakable tendency toward both greater convergence among communities and greater divergence within communities (Rosenfeld 2010: ch. 8) We should applaud the determination of Senegalese women to put an end to female circumcision; however, this does not justify eradicating other cultural differences of which we disapprove inasmuch as these contribute to individual dignity and communal integrity (or as their eradication would threaten such dignity or integrity) in a particular cultural setting. From the standpoint of comprehensive pluralism, therefore, human rights still stand against the failure to treat all humans as human. But they also stand against imposing one particular vision of what being human normatively entails on those who do not share that vision.

The preceding analysis confirms that the deployment of universal human rights as interpreted through a pluralist ethos does not call for any return to monism in order to avoid any logical or performative contradiction. The multiplication of spheres of convergence – as commonalities are emphasized in transnational and global arenas – set against the proliferation of spheres of divergence in national and sub-national arenas – as large waves of migration lead to increased confrontations among different cultures – provides a particularly well-suited context for a conception of international human rights and of traditional constitutional rights that conforms to the normative precepts of comprehensive pluralism and to its dialectical dynamic. In other words, the need for greater external nodes of convergence and greater internal nodes of divergence (Rosenfeld 2008: 438) calls for poles of identity that range from the local to the global to interact with, and constantly adjust to, poles of differentiation that originate in separate and distinct groups and that eventually penetrate within a broad range of increasingly heterogeneous communities. Under these circumstances, human rights should be open to plural interpretations and constitutionally guaranteed fundamental rights to interpretations that overlap more with human rights ones and with those of similar rights under other constitutions.

---

[52] See Barbara Crossette, Senegal Bans Cutting of Genitals of Girls, *N.Y. Times*, Jan. 18, 1999, at A10.

This is already in place to an important extent in the European region subject to the ECHR. Indeed, the ECtHR has officially endorsed a plurality of interpretations of the same ECHR right through deployment of its "margin of appreciation" standard of review, according to which different national interpretations of the same ECHR right are legitimate so long as they fall within a range that is deemed acceptable by the ECtHR (Rosenfeld 2010: 256–8). At the same time, constitutional courts within countries subject to the ECHR have moved toward greater convergence of their respective constitutional jurisprudences through conscious attempts at achieving greater congruence with the relevant jurisprudence of the ECtHR (Id.).

In the end, a pluralist conception of universal human rights and of constitutional fundamental rights is entirely plausible. Accordingly, international human rights can be universal in the previously described pluralist sense and yet remain fully compatible with comprehensive pluralism all the way up and all the way down. Moreover, the pluralist approach to human rights and constitutional rights outlined here leaves ample room for the vindication of group-based equality rights grounded in difference, including those advanced by minority groups. And, whereas such minority group equality rights must constantly compete for vindication against other individual and group equality rights and must constantly remain open to adjustments, the preceding discussion illustrates how they are prone to fare much better under comprehensive pluralism than under either liberalism or communitarianism.

PART II

E Pluribus Unum?

4

Spinoza's Dialectic and the Paradoxes of Tolerance

Can Unity Be Willed out of Necessity?

For comprehensive pluralism to be truly pluralistic all the way up and all the way down, it must successfully harmonize the one and the many. Monism starts from the one and subordinates the many to it, unduly suppressing the differences that animate the distinct plurality of the many. Relativism, for its part, starts from the many, but altogether denies any possibility of inter-communal or transcommunal unity. Comprehensive pluralism, in contrast, as we have seen, does provide the means to reconcile the one and the many, by starting with a full accounting of the entire spectrum of plurality of the many and then confronting the latter with the need to accommodate imperatives deriving from its second-order norms. Accordingly, comprehensive pluralism seems best suited to harmonize unity and plurality, but thus far the focus has been on the highest levels of abstraction, leaving open whether and how such harmonization could be put into practice in concrete sets of circumstances.

The aim of the chapters in Part II of the book is to examine particular attempts to arrive at unity starting out of plurality and to reconcile the two in concrete sets of circumstances. Each of the three chapters in this part treats a concrete challenge that is different from those broached in the other chapters, but together they illustrate both the potential and the pitfalls in the quest for extracting unity out of plurality and for finding ways to harmonize the two. This chapter is devoted to Spinoza's theory of tolerance; Chapter 5, to the search for constitutional unity amidst religious plurality; and Chapter 6, to Dworkin's search for interpretive unity amidst the clash of interpretations that is typical when dealing with hard cases. Admittedly, both Spinoza and Dworkin are monists, but, as we shall see, they both truly confront plurality in their respective pursuits of tolerance and interpretive unity, and they both take such plurality seriously.

4.1. SPINOZA AND TOLERANCE: PARADOXES
AND CONTRADICTIONS

Spinoza advanced extensive and systematic arguments in support of tolerance,[1] and his treatment of the subject is particularly relevant today both because he justifies tolerance on grounds other than skepticism or moral relativism and because he argued for it at a time in which democracy was seeking to establish a firm footing amidst vehement religious conflicts (Balibar 1998: 16–24).[2] Moreover, Spinoza was deeply affected personally by religious intolerance both as a Jew in a Christian world[3] and as an outcast from the Amsterdam Jewish community that excommunicated him in 1656 (Yovel 1989: 3–14). Thus Spinoza, the ardent proponent of tolerance on prudential grounds (Rosenthal 2001: 537) and of tolerance as a private and public virtue (Id.: 538) was well acquainted with the effects of both inter-communal and intra-communal intolerance.

Yet Spinoza's arguments for tolerance, particularly when considered in light of his entire system of philosophy, are quite puzzling. For example, why does Spinoza, the vehement critic of religious superstition in the name of reason, preach religious tolerance?[4] And, given that he equates reason with truth and reality (Spinoza 1955: pt. 2)[5] and virtue with acting according to reason, why does he demand tolerance for all ideas?[6] More generally, Spinoza's pantheism, driven by the all-encompassing *Deus sive natura*, equates God with nature in an indivisible totality, leaving no room for legitimate deviation or fragmentation. In other words, either pantheism is a smokescreen for a radical form of atheism, squarely at odds with religion and superstition, in which case tolerance of what is false, disruptive, and all too often leads to violence does not seem particularly rational. Or, pantheism is the true religion, whose adoption and implementation is hampered because of the deep rootedness

---

[1] Tolerance is a central theme of Spinoza's *Theological–Political Treatise* (*TTP*) (Spinoza 1951) and figures prominently in other works, such as his *Ethics* (Spinoza 1955). See Rosenthal 2001.

[2] As Balibar specifies, "[t]he TTP is pervaded by a sense of urgency. There is an urgent need to reform philosophy so as to eliminate, from within, theological prejudice" (Balibar 1998: 23).

[3] See Yovel 1989: 12–13 (discussing the effects of burnings at the stake in Spain under the Inquisition of relatives of members of the Amsterdam Jewish community).

[4] See, for example, Spinoza 1951: 189 ("[B]etween faith or theology, and philosophy, there is no connection, nor affinity.... Philosophy has no end in view save truth: faith ... looks for nothing but obedience and piety."). Spinoza also emphasized: "I know how deeply rooted are the prejudices embraced under the name of religion, I am aware that in the mind of the masses superstition ... [leads] to praise or blame by impulse rather than reason." Id., 11.

[5] In Spinoza's view, "It is in the nature of reason to perceive things truly ... namely ... as they are in themselves – that is .... not as contingent but as necessary.... Reason perceives this necessity of things ... truly – that is ... as it is in itself. But ... this necessity of things is the very necessity of the eternal nature of God; therefore, it is in the nature of reason to regard things under this form of eternity (Spinoza 1955: 116–17).

[6] See Spinoza 1955: 211 ("To act virtuously is to act in obedience with reason").

of superstition and false religion, hence logically requiring intolerance rather than tolerance of the latter.

It has been suggested that Spinoza's arguments for toleration may, in the end, be more Augustinian than liberal (Poscher 2003). Augustine, like Spinoza, maintains that there is a single truth, though for Augustine it is revealed through faith, whereas for Spinoza it is discovered through reason. For Augustine, intolerance in pursuit of the unity of the Christian Church is a virtue, and tolerance is only defensible when, due to political weakness, preservation of the Church requires accommodation for, rather than confrontation with, its enemies (Id.: pt. 1). This is a purely prudential justification of tolerance, borne out of weakness. So too, it is argued, Spinoza's view may amount to a prudential counsel for tolerance in cases where the possessor of truth is too weak to win an outright confrontation against the enemies of truth, specifically in cases where a sovereign seeking to maintain the State's stability by suppressing the views expressed by the masses would be more likely to undermine truth than to promote it (Id.: 722).[7] Consistent with this, it is arguable that Spinoza's defense of tolerance ultimately rests on a contradiction, or rather a series of contradictions. The first apparent contradiction is within Spinoza's philosophy: reason, truth, and virtue are inextricably linked, universal, and accessible to the human mind, yet falsity, superstition, and prejudice must be tolerated. This contradiction is all the more glaring given that Spinoza, unlike many contemporary defenders of extensive free speech rights, believes that words alone, even if not followed by actions, can cause significant harms (Spinoza 1951: 258).

A second apparent contradiction stems from Spinoza's conflation of epistemology, ontology, morals and politics. This conflation produces the apparent preclusion of a critical perspective that would allow for reconciliation without contradiction of the duty to conform to the truth and the prudential counsel for toleration of falsity. This can be illustrated through a comparison with Kant. Kant maintains a clear distinction between the realm of morals governed by the categorical imperative and the realm of politics subjected to a prudential or utilitarian standard (Kant 1970: 118–19). The categorical imperative requires treating persons exclusively as ends,

---

7   A non-Spinozist may object that this argument as it relates to the political realm need not be consistent with the same arguments in the context of religion (Augustine) or epistemology (Spinoza). It may be politic for a holder of religious truth or a possessor of rational truth to countenance purveyors of falsity who cannot be effectively silenced. Yet that would not change anything regarding the ultimate religious or epistemological truth. In the political realm, however, where the goal is to promote the common good within the polity, tolerance of falsity (at least to a certain extent) may be more conductive to the common good than its suppression. This is, for example, the position of pragmatic defenders of extensive free speech rights in the United States, such as Justice Oliver Wendell Holmes. See Rosenfeld 1998: 181 for a discussion of Holmes's pragmatic approach. For Spinoza, however, there is no ultimate divide between epistemology, morals, and politics: all three culminate in the rational pursuit of the truth.

and thus circumscribes a moral universe of absolute rights and duties. Politics, however, cannot be conducted in strict conformity with the categorical imperative because pursuit of any plausible political agenda requires treating persons, at least in part, as means. By keeping the two realms separate, Kant endows the moral realm with a critical dimension. The moral realm of ends provides a critical ideal against which we can assess the realm of politics. Since there is nothing comparable in Spinoza's case, it is difficult to reconcile the moral command to pursue the truth with toleration of falsity for what may amount to purely tactical reasons.

A third apparent contradiction emerges through a juxtaposition of Spinoza's philosophy with his personal predicament. Spinoza's philosophy is radical in its fundamental critique of traditional religion, its rejection of widely held notions of free will,[8] its equation of liberty with acceptance of necessity (Spinoza 1955: pt. I, 46), and its implacable refusal to give in to any appeal to transcendence.[9] Because of these radical views, Spinoza was justified in fearing the wrath and intolerance of his contemporaries. It is therefore not surprising that he published the *TTP* anonymously (Balibar 1998: 1) and that he refrained from publishing his *Ethics* during his lifetime (Id.: 76). Spinoza the man thus depended on tolerance to promote his philosophy, albeit that his quest for such tolerance would end up being anonymous and posthumous. That philosophy, however, were it to become dominant, would not seem to logically leave room for tolerance of those who defy the truth or who reject virtue.

These contradictions, as well as many others within or surrounding Spinoza's works, take on an altogether different meaning when grasped dialectically. Spinoza is one of the great dialectical thinkers, and an acknowledged precursor to the two most influential proponents of dialectics: Hegel and Marx.[10] If Spinoza's dialectic has been less influential than that of Hegel or Marx, it is because they both elaborated a dynamic dialectic, whereas his seems static by comparison. Indeed, both Hegel's and Marx's dialectics highlight an inexorable path of human progress through history, whereas Spinoza's seems geared to understanding and living with things as they are in the present. In short, Hegel and Marx offer visions for overcoming contradictions whereas Spinoza focuses on how best to live with our inevitable contradictions.

---

[8] See Yovel 1989: vol. 2, 4 (for Spinoza, free will is a "metaphysical illusion").

[9] See Yovel 1989: vol. 2, 27 (explaining that the immanence of God and hence nature is key to Spinoza's entire system).

[10] There is no consensus that Spinoza is a dialectical philosopher; some have characterized his philosophy as non-dialectical. These include Hegel and Yovel. See Yovel 1989: vol. 2, 27–50. Others, however, insist that Spinoza is a dialectical philosopher. See, for example, Macherey 1979: 259. It is beyond the scope of this chapter to go into this issue in any depth. For present purposes, suffice it to stipulate that Spinoza is a dialectical thinker to the extent that he seeks to resolve contradictions, borne out of the clash of conflicting perspectives, by aiming for non-reductionist resolutions from the standpoint of a more encompassing perspective.

Just as Spinoza's philosophy must be understood dialectically, so too must we understand the paradoxes of tolerance. Tolerance leads inevitably to contradictions. In particular Spinoza's defense of tolerance in the context of certainty about the truth seems altogether counterintuitive from a philosophical standpoint, even if justifiable prudentially. Even from a practical standpoint, tolerance leads to contradiction. This point is well illustrated by Karl Popper's paradox of tolerance (Popper 1966: vol. 1, 265–6 n. 4). According to Popper, tolerance of the intolerant is ultimately self-contradictory because it eventually leads to the abolition of tolerance by the intolerant. For example, the Nazis and their extremist intolerant ideology were allowed to participate in the democratic process of the Weimar Republic; they acceded to power legitimately, and then proceeded to ruthlessly and systematically uproot and destroy all that was not in conformity with Nazi dogma. Popper, accordingly, advocates intolerance of the intolerant (Id.). But does that ultimately undermine tolerance? Does it reduce it to acceptance of minor variations among the converted?[11]

If both Spinoza and tolerance are understood dialectically, then Spinoza's views on tolerance point the way to a cogent conception and defense of tolerance for present-day proponents of pluralism. To be sure, Spinoza was not an advocate of pluralism. My contention, rather, is that a certain plausible reading of Spinoza allows for further elaborations of his insights in a pluralistic direction. In other words, Spinoza's prescriptions for living with our contradictions can be adapted to shed further light on why it might be best to accept, and even celebrate, the existence of a multiplicity of conceptions of the good rather than trying to eradicate or minimize differences to forge a common path to the good. In short, if Spinoza, the most rigorous proponent of unity among monists, can be understood as a cogent defender of the moral worth of plurality, then there are grounds to hope that a workable harmony between the one and the many may be within reach.

The return to Spinoza may seem anachronistic. Some have argued that we are living in a post-dialectical age and at the end of history (Fukuyama 1992). Furthermore, even if the dialectic is as relevant today as it ever was, why return to Spinoza given that Hegel and Marx clearly seem to have perfected the dialectic found in Spinoza and to have better adapted it to the needs of modern society?

Section 4.2 attempts to justify the partial return to Spinoza. In Section 4.3, Spinoza's arguments for tolerance are situated in the context of his dialectic. Finally, Section 4.4 assesses the dialectics of tolerance in the context of contemporary liberal democracies and indicates how Spinoza's dialectic and views on tolerance can be adapted to frame a cogent dialectical justification of tolerance in the context of comprehensive pluralism.

---

[11] This issue arises vividly in the debates concerning the constitutionality of laws that criminalize hate speech. For a comparative analysis, see Rosenfeld 2003.

4.2. FROM MARX AND HEGEL TO SPINOZA

A return to Spinoza's dialectic raises an important threshold question: Why set aside the considerable contributions to the dialectical approach developed by Hegel and Marx in favor of the seemingly less advanced dialectic propounded by Spinoza?

Spinoza figures prominently in the philosophies of both Hegel and Marx (Yovel 1989: vol. 2, 28, 78). All three deal with negation and contradictory perspectives from a broader, more comprehensive perspective. All three regard the conflicting perspectives generating paradoxes and contradictions as partial and offer solutions that emerge from the standpoint of a totality that casts the initial perspectives as partial and one-sided, that reintegrates them into a systematic comprehensive whole, and that does so in a way that is dialectical rather than reductionist (i.e., that properly accounts for the initial contradictions rather than minimizing them or glossing over them).

Hegel and Marx part company with Spinoza, however, in that their dialectic is progressive and unfolds through history, whereas his is set in the present and is seemingly timeless. Indeed, for Hegel and Marx, the dialectic progresses through history in a sequence of evermore encompassing stages, culminating in an all comprehensive stage in which all contradictions are finally resolved – for Hegel, the stage of Absolute Spirit;[12] for Marx, the establishment of a fully emancipated communist society putting a definite end to human alienation (Marx 1964: 155). For Spinoza, by contrast, the dialectic does not proceed through a progressive historical process, but through rational comprehension from the standpoint of the world (*Deus sive natura*) conceived as a unified whole. In short, whereas the respective dialectics of Hegel and Marx are inextricably tied to a trajectory of human progress through history, Spinoza's dialectic is predicated on understanding the vicissitudes of our current predicament from the vantage of the most comprehensive perspective possible.

If Spinoza's dialectic is more appealing today than Hegel's or Marx's, it must be, at least in part, because it lacks Hegel's idealism (Yovel 1999: vol. 2, 42) and Marx's utopianism (Id.: 92–3). Before pursuing this any further, however, it is first necessary to focus briefly on what Hegel and Marx found objectionable in Spinoza's philosophy in order to understand how their dialectic may have "improved" on Spinoza's systematic approach. Moreover, since the approach and methodology of Hegel's and Marx's dialectics differ from Spinoza's in similar ways, I shall concentrate on Hegel's critique of Spinoza.

Hegel raised two major related objections to Spinoza. First, Spinoza fails to conceive of substance as subject (Hegel 1999: 536–7), and, second, although Spinoza postulates that determination is negation, he fails to realize that the full and final

---

¹² See supra, at Chapter 1.

realization of substance as subject depends on taking a further dialectical step consisting in the negation of the negation (Id.: 538). Summarizing the essentials of this critique for present purposes, Hegel's conclusion that substance is also subject follows from his dialectic of the subject. In the first moment of that dialectic, the subject establishes an immediate identity with itself. That identity, however, is a purely abstract one as it casts the subject as being other than the other (Hegel 1977: para. 18), without drawing any link between the subject and its manifold determinations. That first self-identity, being partial and one-sided, is led by the dialectic through negation to the realization that what constitutes the subject is its multiple particular determinations. Accordingly, in a second moment, the subject identifies with its concrete determinations but perceives these as part of the world, or as beyond the control of the subject, thus becoming alienated from itself (Id.). In the second moment, therefore, the subject conceives itself as other than itself. It is only in the third moment of the dialectic, through negation of the negation, that the subject realizes that its concrete determinations are its own, and that substance and subject become fully reconciled as the subject becomes conscious of itself as subject and substance (Id.). Moreover, in Hegel's system, this dialectic unfolds within each stage of history and throughout history as a whole. Thus, at each historical stage, the subject gains a partial grasp of itself as substance, partial in the sense of being circumscribed by the zeitgeist of the historical epoch in question. At the final stage, at the end of history, the subject achieves a final comprehensive consciousness of itself as substance within the ambit of Absolute Spirit.[13]

Hegel's critique of Spinoza thus boils down to the charge that the latter fails to account for the fact that human beings have an active hand in molding the destiny of their society in every historical epoch, by striving to cope with that epoch's contradictions from the standpoint of the horizon of possible resolutions framed by the (partial) perspective of the times. Moreover, consistent with his belief in the inexorable march of historical progress propelled by the dialectic of the subject, Hegel also criticizes Spinoza for failing to realize that historical contradictions, by virtue of their own dynamic, pave the way for human progress through history.[14]

---

[13] See id. See also Rosenfeld 1989: 1204: "In Hegel's system, ontogeny recapitulates philogeny, and the meaning of the whole is produced through integration of the partial meanings yielded by the successive stages of its historical process.... The full truth – or in Hegel's terminology, the subject who is for-itself as it is in-itself – can only be apprehended from the unlimited and unobstructed perspective of the end of history. That full truth, however, is neither independent from the partial truths that precede it, nor intelligible except in relation to them. Instead, the full truth is better envisioned as the reconciliation of the various contradictory partial truths of history from the comprehensive perspective of the subject that has internalized and harmonized the totality of its determinations."

[14] Although Marx replaces Hegel's idealism with a materialism that bears many affinities with Spinoza, Marx's critique of Spinoza parallels that of Hegel: For Marx, human beings shape history through transformation of nature as a consequence of their economic activity, and historical progress

It should now be clear why Spinoza's "failure" to conceive of substance as subject or to account for the negation of the negation may make his dialectic more appealing for contemporary audiences than Hegel's or Marx's. Indeed, as already noted, the notion of history's inexorable progress sounds hollow today, as does the notion that human beings can fully master their historical destiny. Moreover, the conviction shared by Hegel and Marx that historical perspectives become increasingly more comprehensive, in the sense of evolving gradually from the particular to the universal, seems largely misplaced in the present post-Cold War era. So long as the dominant preoccupation in both domestic and world affairs was the struggle between capitalism and communism, the claim that social and political concerns were becoming more universal in nature sounded quite plausible. Today, however, as will be discussed further in Part III, the thrust toward globalization is met with ever-intensifying identity-based local struggles with broader implications, and therefore there seems to be no neat line separating the particular from the universal, let alone any evidence of a systematic progression from the former to the latter.

Even if Spinoza's dialectic seems more attractive than the "improved" dialectic of Hegel and Marx, there still remains the concern, mentioned previously, that Spinoza's seemingly ahistorical, deterministic, and somewhat archaic approach is largely out of step with present-day interests and preoccupations. We may be drawn to Spinoza because of his lack of Hegelian idealism, Marxian utopianism, or belief in the inevitability of historical progress, but should we not be put off by his conception of freedom as recognition of necessity (Spinoza 1955a: 340–1, letter Jan. 28, 1665) and his equation of reason, knowledge *sub specie aeternitatis*, to truth and virtue?

I suggest earlier that these difficulties could be minimized if one reads Spinoza dialectically. With this in mind, it will suffice for present purposes, to stress the following two points. First, Spinoza's emphasis on learning to cope with contradictions as we find them rather than hoping to overcome them by reaching a more advanced stage in the dialectic does not necessarily imply that history does not matter or that the contradictions confronting societies are always the same. It may be that the contradictions that all societies are bound to encounter change from one generation to the next, but absent Hegelian or Marxian notions of historical progress, each generation must cope with its own contradictions without dreaming of transcending them. Second, although Spinoza's central claim is that to know, means to know God, and that God is nature itself, Spinoza's philosophy is nonetheless consistent with his politics, that is, with the particular political problems confronting the Netherlands in the seventeenth century, and with Spinoza's own positions regarding these problems

---

culminates in the resolution of the contradictions of capitalism through the revolution of the proletariat as the universal class culminating in the advent of a truly classless communist society. See Yovel 1989: vol. 1, 78–103.

(Balibar 1998: xxi–xxii, 1–24). In other words, in spite of appearances, Spinoza's conceptual and practical concerns are closely intertwined (Id.: xxi). Thus, his conception of how to deal with contradictions is closely linked to his views on how someone with his political convictions could best approach the conflicts faced by the Dutch polity in which he lived. Nevertheless, as we shall now see, from the standpoint of tolerance, the problems confronting Spinoza's society bear a close affinity to those that currently bedevil our own generation.

4.3. SPINOZA'S DIALECTIC OF TOLERANCE IN POLITICAL CONTEXT

Spinoza's broad-based systematic arguments for tolerance and democracy arose in the context of a Dutch republic that was in a constant state of crisis (Balibar 1998: 16). This crisis was fueled by both external causes, such as foreign wars, and internal ones, principally political and religious strife.[15] Moreover, the political and religious conflicts in question were intertwined. Though in many respects the Dutch crises were similar to those experienced by other seventeenth-century European countries, there were two distinct factors that made the situation in the Netherlands unique. The first was the ascendance of a powerful mercantile class with vast economic power of often-monopolistic proportions that wielded enormous political power and that became increasingly detached from the urban middle class. This new economy led to increasing poverty within the cities, fostering an alliance between the urban and the rural poor that cut across the traditional divide between city and country. The two dominant political forces were the republicans, led by the most powerful mercantile families, and the princes of Orange, who were monarchists backed primarily by the rural aristocracy. The conflict between these two contenders led to three major crises involving violence throughout the seventeenth century.[16] Spinoza identified in part with the powerful leading bourgeois families, and in part – particularly after his excommunication from the Jewish Community – with the middle-class bourgeoisie of Amsterdam.

Second, combined with this unique array of economic and political interests, was a unique religious diversity that exacerbated the conflicts and crises confronting Dutch society. As Balibar specifies:

In the United Provinces, Calvinist reform combined the rejection of "Roman idolatry" with anti-Spanish (and later anti-French) patriotic feeling. Calvinism

---

[15]   This brief summary of the historical circumstances that prevailed in the Netherlands during Spinoza's lifetime is drawn from Balibar's account. See Balibar 1998: 6–24.

[16]   These crises, which took place respectively in 1619, 1650–4, and 1672, included attempts by each of the contenders to consolidate its power to the exclusion of the others, and a popular uprising. See Balibar 1998: 17.

became the official religion of the country but was never its only religion. A significant Catholic minority maintained the right to organize. Similar protection was granted to the prosperous Jewish community in Amsterdam, which was principally of Spanish and Portuguese extraction. But it was the division of Dutch Calvinism itself into two branches that was responsible for overdetermining the nature of social conflict and the identity of the political "parties" through this period. (Id.: 18)

The first of these Calvinist branches was the Remonstrants who believed in free will, considered freedom of conscience indispensable, and thus argued vigorously for tolerance. They regarded salvation as an individual responsibility and accordingly distinguished between "outward religion," giving the State power over external religious manifestations with a view to promoting public order, and "inward religion," which was to remain beyond the reach of the State to allow each individual to follow the dictates of his or her faith. As Balibar emphasizes, this distinction between outward and inward religion opens the way to a "secular" conception of the relation between Church and State (Id.: 19).

The second branch, the Contra-Remonstrants, was made up of orthodox Calvinists. This branch also promoted separation between Church and State and insisted upon double allegiance for the citizenry: allegiance to the State's rulers in temporal matters and to the Church in spiritual matters. Because this branch regarded this dual allegiance as derived from a single unified Christian route to salvation decreed by God, the State was only entitled to obedience from the citizenry so long as it was led by a Christian prince. Thus, though the Church was to remain independent from the State, only the Christian State was legitimate. As Calvinists, the Contra-Remonstrants were set against the absolutism of European monarchs whose powers were inextricably linked to unity between Church and State. Consistent with this, the State was to have no role in the spiritual life of true religion, but it had an obligation to aid in combating false religion, and hence a genuine role in stamping out heresies. In their efforts to combat heresies, the Contra-Remonstrants became an important repressive force in the Netherlands. Nevertheless, they enjoyed great popularity among the mass of rural and urban poor and among the lower middle classes who were by and large Calvinists, and who were inclined to revolt against the bourgeois elite. The bourgeois elite, in turn, were for the most part Remonstrants, whose increasingly opulent lifestyle appeared more hedonistic than genuinely religious. In short, viewed from the standpoint of the intersection of religion and politics, the Remonstrants promoted religious diversity, tolerance, and – at least in the eyes of their opponents – religious laxity combined with an increasing concentration of wealth and power. In contrast, the Contra-Remonstrants pursued religious orthodoxy and intolerance of heresy leading to repressive politics against those cast as irreligious or heretics, combined with a grassroots democratically inspired movement of the impoverished masses against the autocratic rule of the governing elite.

The preceding sketch is highly schematic and barely scratches the surface of the complex interplay between the numerous political and religious factions active in the Netherlands during Spinoza's life. Nonetheless, it suffices for the purpose of situating Spinoza's views on tolerance in the historical context in which they arose.

Given Spinoza's position as a Jew, an outcast from Amsterdam's Jewish community, and a political ally of republicans siding with the Remonstrants, it would seem logical for him to have promoted a typical liberal defense of tolerance. Yet Spinoza's defense of tolerance is not a liberal one. Instead, it arises from a position that bears certain striking similarities with post-liberal and post-modern views that reject any sharp divide between secular and religious viewpoints. On the one hand, Spinoza builds on Descartes's distinction between faith and reason (Descartes 1998) to mount his systematic attack against religious superstition in the *TTP* (Spinoza 1951: 98–9). On the other hand, however, Spinoza does not simply align himself with a philosophy of reason that casts matters of faith as purely irrational or that regards religion as a mere projection of human hope and fear. A philosophy of reason is necessary to unmask the evils produced by theology, but to the extent that such a philosophy thinks that it can do away with faith and religion, it ultimately becomes yet another theology.[17] In other words, for Spinoza, philosophy must not set aside true religion and faith[18] lest it become "an anti-religious discourse" (Id.: 8); rather, it must account for them from the standpoint of reason.[19]

Spinoza's rejection of an unbridgeable gap between faith and reason seems consistent with the religious and post-modern perspectives that regard secular humanism as yet another religion and that will be further discussed in Chapter 5. But there is one key difference: For Spinoza, faith and true religion can apparently be subsumed within the realm of reason, whereas from a post-modern perspective, what purports to belong to the realm of reason (e.g., evolutionary science, secular approaches to morality or politics) seems much like yet another faith. Consistent with this, what divides Spinoza and the proponents of post-modern perspectives seems much more important than what unites them. Indeed, whereas both would reject a liberal approach to tolerance for the same reasons, each would approach tolerance very differently. From a post-modern perspective, either one should be equally tolerant of all faiths, including secular humanism, or intolerant of all faiths that are contrary to one's own. The latter alternative, while logically cogent, seems to lead to the war of all against all, and is thus highly undesirable. The former alternative is much more

---

[17] "The philosopher-scientist who halts his advance once the traditional obstacle to knowledge has been removed may well find himself taken prisoner by another, more subtle, theology. Indeed, was that not what had happened to Descartes and was later to befall Newton?" (Balibar 1998: 7).

[18] "Faith consists in a knowledge of God, without which obedience to Him would be impossible" (Spinoza 1951: 184).

[19] Nothing in "universal religion" is repugnant to reason (Spinoza 1951: 9).

attractive and even appears to approximate the liberal approach, but it should not be confused with it. For example, under the liberal approach, informed by a clear division between reason (science) and faith, it is perfectly legitimate for the State to run public schools that require the study of science and humanistic values. By contrast, from a tolerant post-modern perspective, privileging secular humanism cannot be justified, and since State-sponsored education could not avoid the privileging of certain "faiths" above others, logic would seem to dictate that the State stay out of public education altogether.

Consistent with Spinoza's views, however, there ought not be any tolerance for false religion and for faiths amounting to little more than superstition. Because true faith and religion are in harmony with reason, there would be no good reason to tolerate false religion and superstition, particularly inasmuch as these have inflamed the passions and led to violence and war. Spinoza, nevertheless, advocates tolerance for views that loom as squarely counter to reason. Is he being inconsistent? Or are such views ultimately dialectically reconcilable with reason?

Behind the seeming contradiction behind Spinoza's broad embrace of tolerance, lurks a potentially more fundamental contradiction. In spite of his rejection of the Cartesian divide between faith and reason, Spinoza argues that religion has nothing to do with philosophy: "[T]he Bible leaves reason absolutely free, ... it has nothing in common with philosophy in fact,.... Revelation and Philosophy stand on totally different footings." (Spinoza 1951: 9). Furthermore, he asserts that the purpose of Revelation is to prescribe "obedience to God in singleness of heart, and ... the practice of justice and charity" (Id.). He goes on to make clear that: "[r]evelation has obedience for its sole object, and therefore, in purpose no less than in foundation and in method, stands entirely aloof from ordinary knowledge; each has its separate province, neither can be called the handmaid of the other" (Id.: 9–10).

Has Spinoza merely reintroduced the Cartesian split between faith and reason in a slightly different form? Or, is Spinoza's distinction between Revelation and Philosophy altogether different?

When viewed dialectically and in the context of the *TTP* and the *Ethics*, Spinoza's distinction is completely different from Descartes'. For Spinoza, Revelation differs from philosophy not because it involves a different kind of knowledge, but because it deals with obedience (i.e., what people ought to do) rather than with knowledge (i.e., what the truth about the world is). Just as Spinoza rejects Descartes's dualism – according to which mind and extension are two separate substances – by arguing that mind and extension are but two attributes of the same substance[20] – he rejects the notion that Revelation and reason lead to different kinds of truths.

---

[20] *See* Spinoza 1955: bk. 1, 51 (God is substance); Id.: bk. 2, 83–4 (Props. I and II, arguing that thought and extension are attributes of God).

Keeping in mind that Spinoza identifies God with nature, Revelation and Philosophy provide two distinct routes to the same destination. Revelation directly commands obedience to God, whereas Philosophy allows human beings, through the use of reason, to understand nature and their place in it, and based on that, to realize that what is best for them is to attain their freedom. Since for Spinoza freedom means consciously assuming the course dictated by the necessity of one's nature, and since nature as a whole is the same as God, assuming one's freedom requires the same actions as does obedience to God pursuant to Revelation.

If true religion and philosophy guide human beings toward the same good, false religion built upon exploitation of the masses' superstition leads to oppression and excesses. Spinoza charges that theologians, preying on the fear and superstition of the masses, interpret the Bible to suit their own ambitions with the consequence that "[r]eligion is no longer identified with charity, but with spreading discord and propagating insensate hatred disguised under the name of zeal for the Lord, and eager ardor" (Spinoza 1951: 99). Moreover, this exploitation of passions and superstition is often promoted by theologians, in conjunction with monarchs, for purposes of perpetuating the subordination of ignorant masses (Smith 1997: 33).

To the extent that religion is exploited for purposes of subjugation and oppression, it would seem that intolerance of false religion would be called for. Yet Spinoza remains firm in his advocacy of tolerance. One reason for that may be that tolerance seems useful in combating intolerant autocratic government and repressive power-driven theologians who spread false religion. Thus, the more that tolerance is regarded as a virtue, the more the intolerance of monarchs and their theologians is likely to be perceived as abusive, leading eventually to a loosening of their grip on power. More importantly, however, Spinoza's defense of tolerance is primarily bolstered by his reconceptualization of the divide between faith and reason, and by his conception of human psychology and the source of the State's power and legitimacy.

By recasting the divide between faith and reason in terms of the distinction between revelation and philosophy, Spinoza minimizes the theoretical difficulties (through not the political problems) arising in connection with the clash between religions, and between religious and non-religious perspectives. One possible interpretation of Spinoza's move is that, in effect, it minimizes the importance of religion, thus paving the way for a secular vision driven by reason rising above all religious myths and superstitions.

According to this interpretation, all religions are equally false, but they ought nevertheless be tolerated to the extent that they prescribe obedience to nature (which they call "God"), justice, and charity. In other words, because many people will not follow the path of reason, but may nevertheless be led to what reason commands by following the dictates of their religion, reason requires religious tolerance as a means to its (reason's) own ends. In Spinoza's words:

> [A]s men's habits of mind differ, so that some more readily embrace one form of faith, some another, for what moves one to pray may move another one to scoff, I conclude ... that everyone should be free to choose for himself the foundations of his creed, and that faith should be judged only by its fruits; each would then obey God freely with his whole heart, while nothing would be publicly honored save justice and charity. (Spinoza 1951: 10)

Another plausible interpretation is that all religions which are freed from the distortions of theologians and which lead to the requisite prescriptions are equally valuable and legitimate.[21] Under this interpretation, religion complements reason and fosters supplementary means to the same ends, which would make tolerance part and parcel of this movement toward convergence. In short, either religion contributes to the good in spite of itself, or religions combine with reason, each contributing to the good in its own way.

Pursuant to either of these two interpretations, the State should institute religion to the extent that it commands obedience to God, justice, and charity (Id.: 245). Spinoza refers to this as the "outward observance [ ] of piety" meant to conform to "the public peace and well being" (Id.). In contrast, Spinoza emphasizes that "[i]nward worship of God and piety in itself are within the sphere of everyone's private rights and cannot be alienated" (Id.). In other words, to the extent that religion coincides with the public good, it ought to be imposed by the State because the State is the only source of legitimate power (Id.). Thus, Spinoza insists that both the State and its citizens tolerate every citizen's right to worship (privately) according to the dictates of his or her own faith. To the extent that a citizen's faith leads him or her to obey God and seek justice and charity, it is obvious why it ought to be tolerated. But what if a citizen's faith amounts to false religion? Ought not intolerance toward false religion be justified if it fails to contribute in any palpable way to the common good, or worse, harms the common good by spreading hatred and religious strife?

Spinoza answers in the negative, and for two reasons: (1) One cannot force anyone to change his or her beliefs; and (2) the power and stability of the State ultimately depend on the consent of the governed.

He opposes any attempts to stamp out false beliefs and regards any government attempt to abridge that right as tyrannical (Id.: 257). No matter how powerful

---

[21] Spinoza speaks of "the universal religion" (Spinoza 1951: 186), but his extrapolation of what is valuable in religions comes only from Judaism and Christianity, with greater emphasis on the teachings of Jesus. Whether Spinoza would have drawn from other religions under different circumstances is not clear. The claim here is that Spinoza's idea of drawing common elements from different religions can be extended, at least in principle, beyond Judaism and Christianity.

the State, it cannot force a person to abandon his or her own beliefs (Id.: 258). Therefore, a State bent on stamping out views that it abhors would be bound to achieve "disastrous results" (Id.).

Spinoza also maintains that the best and most natural form of government is democracy (Id.: 207). Once again, Spinoza's assessment is made on the basis of both principle and utility. Democracy is respectful of natural right because it is "most consonant with human liberty" (Id.). Furthermore, as Spinoza conceives it, sovereign power can only effectively impose its will so long as the citizenry accepts it as legitimate (Id.: 205). Tyrants cannot achieve security or stability because the more oppressive their policies, the more unstable their regime and the less likely that the citizenry will willingly heed their edicts or genuinely support their policies. On the other hand, democratic government is most likely to achieve stability and security because it makes every citizen at once the subject and object of sovereign power (Id.: 206).

Considering tolerance from the standpoint of one who is supposed be tolerant of others, Spinoza's argument seems to boil down to a warning that intolerance of false beliefs is futile; intolerance will not do away with false beliefs, and it breeds instability because those whose views are targeted for suppression are unlikely to consent to the powers of the sovereign. Moreover, to the extent that intolerance is the product of fear, superstition, or ambition, being tolerant contributes to the mastery of reason over the passions (Rosenthal 2001: 556). In other words, tolerance promotes the kind of self-restraint that allows for a person's reason to lead to a mastery over his or her own passions. Furthermore, by following reason, a person acts according to his or her own nature. As Spinoza states:

> As reason makes no demands contrary to nature, it demands, that every man should love himself, should seek that which is useful to him – I mean, that which is really useful to him, should desire everything which really brings man to greater perfection …. [V]irtue is nothing else but action in accordance with the laws of one's nature … virtue is to be desired for its own sake (Spinoza 1955: pt. 4, 201).

Accordingly, tolerance is a virtue because it enables the tolerant person to move to greater perfection and to realize the full potential of human nature. In short, tolerance as a virtue plays an important negative role as well as an important positive role. Its negative role is to foster the self-restraint, which is crucial in the quest to control one's passions; its positive role, to aid in the pursuit of greater perfection.

Tolerance's positive role is particularly important because attaining greater perfection is not only an individual matter but also a matter of achieving collective harmony. In Spinoza's words:

> [T]o man there is nothing more useful than man – nothing, I repeat, more excellent for preserving their being can be wished for by men, than that all should so in

all points agree, that the minds and bodies of all should form, as it were, one single mind and one single body, and that all should, with one consent, as far as they are able, endeavor to preserve their being, and all with one consent seek what is useful to them all. (Id.: 201–2)

Thus, to achieve social harmony and a cohesive body politic, self-restraint must be supplemented with restraint vis-à-vis all the members of society; or, to seize on Spinoza's metaphor, what self-restraint can achieve for individual reason, restraints vis-à-vis others can do for unifying the "mind" of the body politic.

From the standpoint of the self, therefore, tolerance becomes a means for reason to achieve mastery over the passions and for attaining the individual's good through promotion of the common good. From the standpoint of the other, on the other hand, tolerance signifies an invitation to join forces with others with diverse views in order to constitute a unified and mutually beneficial ethical community. Thus, by exercising control over one's own passions and learning how to accept others with different passions, the individual can practice tolerance as a private and public virtue and contribute at once to her own good and to the common good.

Spinoza's dialectic recasts the Cartesian split between faith and reason to incorporate the essential universal religious prescriptions disseminated through Revelation within the ethical path carved out by reason. At the same time, Spinoza's dialectic purports to overcome the clash of competing views fueled by diverse passions through a shift in perspectives. Members of a polity marked by vehement clashes among proponents of competing conceptions of the good may be persuaded that the only road to self-preservation consists in vigorous assertions of one's own conception coupled with intolerance toward competing conceptions regarded as threatening, for example the Contra-Remonstrants and their persecution of heretics. Yet as Spinoza was all too aware, such a course often leads to disastrous consequences. Spinoza's proposed alternative, therefore, avoids the two extremes: It promotes neither intolerance of alien conceptions of the good nor abdication of one's own pursuits in deference to those of others. Instead, Spinoza focuses on the fact that underlying the clash of conceptions of the good is the related fact that we are all subjected to different passions that we cannot escape (Id.: 194). Human beings can never achieve complete control over their passions or emotions, but the more they understand them through reason, the better they can cope with them, and the better they will succeed in achieving private and public virtue (Id.: 244–59). In this context, tolerance requires a combination of constraint through reason of one's own passions with acceptance of some of the passions of others that do not comport with one's own or with reason, at least in the sense of resisting any urge to combat them. Thus, though reason cannot do away with the passions, it can bring about a shift in perspective regarding one's own passions as well as those of others, allowing for greater harmony among diverse conceptions of the good through deployment of the virtue of tolerance.

This conception of tolerance as involving a combination of self-constraint and greater openness toward others allows for resolution of one of the vexing paradoxes raised by tolerance. When set in the context of relativism, as we have seen, tolerance is ultimately no more justified than intolerance. Conversely, if it is prescribed notwithstanding certitude about the rightness of one's own views, then tolerance seems, at best, arbitrary. For example, if I am absolutely convinced that women are the equals of men and that anyone who denies this is both wrong and irrational, why tolerate views proclaiming that women are inferior to men? According to Spinoza's view, there is a common denominator – reason – but it cannot supplant all views arising from passions or emotions. Tolerance, therefore, requires both greater acceptance of passions that run counter to our own and greater control over our own passions. Furthermore, inasmuch as Spinoza's view requires a balance between curbing acting pursuant to our own passions and foregoing action against expression by others of passions that we would otherwise combat, it avoids the pitfalls of non-reciprocal tolerance.

Non-reciprocal tolerance is neither a virtue nor a genuine means to greater inclusiveness, but rather an assertion of power against the powerless. Non-reciprocal tolerance involves either extending tolerance as a mere gesture, which may be referred to as "gratuitous tolerance," or, demanding tolerance of oppressive treatment, what Marcuse called "repressive tolerance" (Marcuse 1965: 81). In either case, no genuine tolerance is involved. For example, it is gratuitous tolerance for a prison guard to allow a prisoner to complain about inhuman conditions of confinement if such complaints will never be heard outside the prison, and if prison authorities retain complete control over prison policy and prisoner activity. Repressive tolerance, on the other hand, would be to demand, in the name of freedom of speech, that an oppressed and demeaned powerless racial minority tolerate virulent and sustained propaganda directed against them. In both examples, there is a semblance of tolerance masking what are in substance clearly intolerant actions or policies.[22] By contrast, because of the central role he ascribes to reciprocity, Spinoza's conception makes for a clear distinction between tolerance as a virtue and as a tool for concealing or exacerbating oppression.

Spinoza's conception of tolerance, however, does not appear helpful in connection with Popper's paradox. It is true that, so long as reciprocity is maintained and

[22] One may argue that in the case of racist propaganda and free speech rights, the legal rule is reciprocal though its effects in this particular application are not. Although that may be true in some circumstances, in others the rule's reciprocal structure may amount to little more than a mere formality. Thus, if a racially dominant group controls the government, the media, business, and universities and uses free speech as a means to legitimate the utterance of racist propaganda, the mere fact that members of the racial minority may be free to express racist views about the dominant race on the street or in public parks does not convert the prevailing regime from one of repressive tolerance to one of reciprocal tolerance.

everyone is both tolerant and tolerated, the undermining of tolerance feared by
Popper is unlikely to occur. The difficulty is that Spinoza introduces a sharp dichotomy between those open to philosophy and the superstitious masses who are impervious to philosophical reasoning. Thus, in the preface to the *TTP*, Spinoza makes it
clear that it is futile to expect the masses to shed their superstitions and prejudices.
Accordingly, he addresses his book only to those capable of philosophical reasoning,
thereby excluding the masses, whom he considers incapable of drawing any wisdom
or profit from it (Spinoza 1951: 11). If Spinoza is right on this point, then his conception of tolerance, which in theory allows for reciprocity and mutual self-restraint, in
fact will fail to lead to reciprocity, and will instead lead to a dangerous asymmetry
whereby those led by reason will refrain from fighting to stamp out prejudice while
the prejudiced masses will adhere to no such constraints in their endeavors to stamp
out the rule of reason.

This asymmetry is particularly troubling in view of Spinoza's already mentioned
belief that words can cause as much harm as actions (Id.: 258) and his endorsement
of democracy as the optimal form of government. Spinoza is quite aware of the dangers of mob rule, but downplays them:

> In a democracy, irrational commands are [least] to be feared: for it is almost impos-
> sible that the majority of a people, especially if it be a large one, should agree in an
> irrational design: and, moreover, the basis and aim of a democracy is to avoid the
> desires as irrational, and to bring men as far as possible under the control of reason,
> so that they may live in peace and harmony: if this basis be removed the whole fab-
> ric falls to ruin. (Id.: 206)

This last assessment is unpersuasive so long as the prejudiced mass constitutes a
political majority and remains impervious to the counsel of reason. Moreover, the
political solution to the ever-present potential conflict between tolerance of all ideas
and the adoption of policies favored by the prejudiced masses, which Spinoza suggests, and which parallels his proposed solution to the conflict between theology
and philosophy, is equally unpersuasive. Just as government ought to adopt and
implement the essence of Revelation leaving the rest of what pertains to theology
outside the public square, so too, as Spinoza sees it, the government should enact
policies backed by reason and demand that citizens be loyal in their actions while
leaving them completely free to express their ideas (Id.: 261–5).

Spinoza's failure to adequately address the problem of mass democracy and the
seeming inconsistency in his treatment of the relationship between ideas and actions
certainly presents problems for contemporary readers. This will be addressed later.
Nevertheless, when placed in their proper historical context, these apparent shortcomings are amenable to plausible interpretations that make it possible to regard
Spinoza's theory of tolerance as being, in the last analysis, coherent.

In view of the historical circumstances that he encountered during his lifetime, Spinoza's conception of democracy is more akin to bourgeois democracy than to mass democracy. A democracy of the educated propertied classes could thus be plausibly expected to rule on the basis of reason rather than prejudice or passion. Moreover, Spinoza's plea for virtually limitless freedom of expression, notwithstanding his acknowledgment that words can be as harmful as actions, becomes quite understandable when considered in light of the pervasive censorship and repression imposed by the monarchs of the times with the complicity of their theologians (Balibar 1998).

In the last analysis, Spinoza's dialectic prompts him to award a privileged place to tolerance as an essential tool in coping with contradictions and differences, and in harmonizing the disparate aims fueled by the diverse passions of the various members of the polity. Underlying this vast diversity, there is, for Spinoza, a common essence, and the work of the dialectic is to allow that essence to emerge and impose order amid the prevailing contradictions. Although religion and philosophy constitute two separate discourses sharing nothing in common, they each contribute to discovery of what the common essence of mankind actually prescribes. Within this scheme, tolerance is double faceted: Religious tolerance allows for emergence and institutionalization of the essence of Revelation; tolerance of all views, on the other hand, allows the rule of reason to govern in spite of the persistence of passion and prejudice. So long as a sufficient number can subsume their passions under the rule of reason, and so long as the actions that would result from unbridled passion can be institutionally kept in check, social cohesion is much more likely to be promoted by tolerance than intolerance. Finally, within this conception, it becomes clear that Spinoza's defense of tolerance both as a virtue and as a strategic tool to promote social peace and stability is ultimately coherent. Indeed, both tolerance as a virtue and tolerance as a strategic tool combine to reconcile as best as possible freedom with social peace and stability.

Spinoza proposes to minimize the danger posed by clashing differences and conflicts through a shift in emphasis that highlights what at the very core human beings share in common. What Spinoza's dialectic achieves is to magnify and place greater emphasis on what unifies without seeking to suppress or eradicate differences. Religious wars feed on religious differences and intolerance toward what is different in the other's religion. The liberal response is to relegate religion to the private sphere, thus in effect downgrading all religions. Spinoza, in contrast, does not chase religion away from the public sphere, but instead incorporates its essential common core and grants it official sanction binding on the polity as a whole. Accordingly, it is merely religious differences and not religion itself that are relegated to the private sphere. Significantly, Spinoza's dialectical resolution of the vexing issues raised by religious strife yields a position that is very similar to that promoted by the Remonstrants. By insisting that all the religions that were practiced during his lifetime in the Netherlands share a common core, Spinoza manages to make a compelling case for complete religious tolerance. In particular, he argues that Judaism, though a minority religion, ought to be tolerated because it shares a common core with Christianity. Similarly, Spinoza himself, the Jewish renegade, ought to be tolerated by both Jews and Christians because of his unbinding commitment to the core teaching of Judaism, notwithstanding his rejection of particular glosses imposed by Jewish theologians.

The remaining question, therefore, is whether Spinoza's conception of tolerance elaborated in the context of the particular conflicts and aspirations of his own society can play a useful role in the context of our own conflicts and aspirations. I now turn to this question.

4.4. SPINOZA'S THEORY AND TOLERANCE AND PLURALISM IN A POST-MODERN WORLD

What underlies Spinoza's dialectic of tolerance is a commonly shared core of identity that permeates through the manifold diversity nurtured by religious differences and divergent passions. What makes a viable dialectic of tolerance possible in the context of contemporary comprehensive pluralism, on the other hand, is that the quest to accommodate a wide range of differences and to sustain genuine diversity can only succeed if sufficient points of convergence emerge to sustain the unity of polities that are pluralistic-in-fact. In other words, for Spinoza there is a core of identity that endures in spite of all differences, whereas for comprehensive pluralism, identity emerges as a necessary byproduct of the quest to accommodate as many differences as possible within the same polity. Thus, whereas both Spinoza and the contemporary pluralist appeal to tolerance in order to reconcile identity and difference, pluralists appear to be aiming for the converse of what Spinoza seeks to achieve. Indeed, Spinoza advocates tolerance of difference to bolster identity, whereas the pluralist turns to tolerance to generate the minimum of identity necessary for differences to coexist peacefully in a commonly shared socio-political space (through mutual recognition as equally worthy possessors of their own conceptions of the good).

Even if Spinoza invokes tolerance to achieve the converse of what pluralists seek, his insights remain highly relevant so long as they are placed in their proper dialectical context. Although Spinoza aims for identity and pluralists for difference, they both have to deal dialectically with the conflict between identity and difference. More specifically, they both have to overcome the contradiction between identity and difference by recourse to a new perspective that at the same time recasts the contradiction in question, encompasses it more broadly, and in a significant sense transcends it.[23] Though not a pluralist himself, Spinoza's views on tolerance are highly relevant to present-day pluralists. Furthermore, if relevant differences between Spinoza's historical circumstances and our own are properly kept in perspective, his position has much more affinity with contemporary pluralism than might otherwise appear.

Comprehensive pluralism's second-order norms provide the thread of unity that reason furnishes in the context of Spinoza's theory. In spite of pluralist societies' differences and conflicts, they can maximize freedom, peace, and stability if they mediate their clashing objectives through common adherence to pluralism's second-order norms. Similarly, for Spinoza, religious strife can be overcome through reliance on reason coupled with adherence to the essential dictates of Revelation. Moreover, tolerance occupies a central position among pluralism's second-order norms much as it does in Spinoza's theory. Just as for Spinoza, pluralist tolerance requires a combination of self-restraint and increased openness toward the beliefs of others. Indeed, the pluralist self must somewhat constrain pursuit of her own conception of the good through internalization of comprehensive pluralism's second-order norms. By the same token, these second-order norms require greater acceptance of the other's religion, lifestyle, and ethnic identity as a legitimate component part of the polity's normative universe. Thus, for example, I must curb the pursuit of certain of my religion's proselytizing prescriptions and support institutional protection of religions I consider false in order to meet my obligation to grant genuine recognition to the other's freedom and need to express and follow her own religious convictions.

Comprehensive pluralism's conception of tolerance is also closer to Spinoza's than to the typical liberal one in that it is supported by a mix of moral and prudential concerns. Unlike the liberal conception, that of comprehensive pluralism does not arise out of skepticism, relativism, or a deontological position based on the primacy of the right over the good. For comprehensive pluralism, diversity is a good, and tolerance aimed at consolidating peace and diversity, both a private and public virtue, much as tolerance is in Spinoza's theory. Indeed, each individual should internalize the second-order norms of comprehensive pluralism in order to constrain her own impulse toward intolerance, and society's institutions should be derived from these norms to secure room for the widest possible plurality of conceptions of the good consistent with mutual respect among all citizens. Furthermore, just as it does for Spinoza, tolerance fulfills a contemporary prudential function for comprehensive pluralism. It is most unlikely in polities that are pluralistic-in-fact that proponents

---

[23] This does not mean that it is necessary to eliminate the conflict between identity and difference altogether but, rather, to do away with the particular points of contention that lead to the most immediate impasse, subject to introducing new points of contention issuing from somewhat modified perspectives.

of any conception of the good will succeed in eradicating any rival conception or in subordinating the latter's proponents while preserving any meaningful peace or stability within the polity. Accordingly, even one who is not convinced that pluralism is good may conclude that he may be better able to pursue his own conception of the good by exercising self-constraint and by learning to accept diversity rather than by engaging in a constant and uncertain struggle.

Even though for Spinoza the goal is the unity framed by reason, and for the pluralist, the diversity fostered by difference, they both have to confront the dialectic between identity and difference, to find ways to harmonize unity and plurality and both end up embracing comparable conceptions of tolerance. That said, important differences remain. Perhaps the most noteworthy among these is that whereas Spinoza appears to advocate virtually unlimited tolerance, comprehensive pluralism advocates a tolerance that is clearly bounded by the prescriptions emanating from second-order norms. Thus, whereas Spinoza calls for tolerance of virtually all kinds of religious superstition (at least within the private sphere), comprehensive pluralism prescribes intolerance, in whole or in part, of crusading religions and of non-religious ideologies bent on eradicating competing conceptions of the good. Another major difference concerns the place and role of reason. For Spinoza, reason is the means to truth and to the good, and hence determines the proper role for tolerance and the place for diversity within the morally optimal polity. For pluralism, on the other hand, reason has, at best, a much more modest role. A key assumption of pluralism is that reason plays no useful role in determining the "truth" of competing conceptions of the good. In fact, it is precisely because there is no objective way to assess whether any conception of the good is better than any other, that these conceptions are conceived in terms of their place in their adherents' quest for self-realization rather than as means to the truth. Consistent with this, the role of reason within pluralism is bound to be much more limited than its role within Spinoza's system. In particular, pluralist reason cannot alone set the parameters of legitimate tolerance.

The pluralist notion of tolerance is better suited than Spinoza's is to cope with Popper's paradox of tolerance. In the pluralist conception, tolerance of the intolerant is called for only to the extent that it does not contravene second-order norms. Accordingly, the pluralist must be intolerant of the intolerants' endeavors to undermine the application of second-order norms. Moreover, so long as the pluralist consistently balances tolerance of the views and ways of life of others with intolerance of that which threatens pluralism itself, pluralism can provide a satisfactory solution not only to Popper's paradox, but also to the problem of tolerance in a mass democracy that Spinoza does not address. Spinoza argues for tolerance of all views, notwithstanding his correct insight that when it comes to threats to the social fabric, there is no clear divide between ideas and actions. Whereas Spinoza averts inconsistency by envisaging elite democracy rather than mass democracy, the latter can no longer be avoided today given our own experiences with democratically elected intolerant totalitarian tyrants, as was most notoriously the case with Adolf Hitler. Nevertheless, under a pluralist conception of tolerance, the most extremist passions and prejudices of the masses prone to undermining democracy can be checked through institutional deployment of the prescriptions delimited by second-order norms. Thus, pluralist tolerance differs from Spinoza's, and is better suited to contemporary needs. But arguably the two conceptions are not inconsistent: They provide dialectically analogous solutions to somewhat different conflicts.

The second major difference between contemporary pluralism and Spinoza, regarding the role of reason, seems more difficult to reconcile. Even that difference may not be ultimately as great as it might first seem, provided that relevant historical differences are accounted for dialectically. True, the language of reason, truth, passion, superstition, and Revelation used by Spinoza may strike the contemporary reader as dated. From a contemporary pluralist perspective, the various conceptions of the good embraced by others are not likely to be regarded as the products of superstition or passion, but rather as the result of communal attachments and commitments, and of choices determined in part by what one aspires to become. Thus, for example, a member of a polity that is pluralistic-in-fact is more likely to justify his or her own religious affiliation to one who does not share the same religious convictions in terms of affective bonds grounded in the religious person's ancestry or beliefs, needs and aspirations rather than in terms of an objective truth that ought to be binding on everyone. Accordingly, for the contemporary pluralist, like for Spinoza, one's religion is linked more to one's emotions than to reason, but, unlike Spinoza, the contemporary pluralist does not consider the realm of emotions and of affective bonds within one's religious community as the byproducts of error, weakness, or deficient knowledge.

As for reason itself and its role in a democratic polity, the differences between Spinoza and contemporary pluralists are perhaps best understood in terms of the differences between religious strife in Spinoza's pre-Enlightenment times and conflicts among clashing conceptions of the good in our own times. As already noted, for Spinoza, reason coupled with Revelation of what all Judeo-Christian religions hold in common is the best antidote to the violence bred by virulent religious superstition. Unlike radical Enlightenment secularists, Spinoza does not cast religion aside, but like these secularists he pins much of his hope on reason.[24] In contrast, from a post-modern vantage point, secularism and its reliance on reason to the

---

[24] How secular Spinoza's views ultimately are depends to a significant extent on whether his pantheism is but a disguised atheism. If Spinoza is cast as an atheist, then his reliance on reason is thoroughly secular, and his appeal to an essential core of Revelation purely strategic.

exclusion of faith have failed to produce a viable solution to religious strife, or, more precisely, to the clash among competing conceptions of the good. From a contemporary pluralist standpoint, the principal struggle is not against religions' claims to truth, for such claims have already been significantly undermined by secular Enlightenment policies. Instead, as will be more fully explored in Chapter 5, the key struggle is for maintenance of religious diversity and sustenance of a multiplicity of conceptions of the good given the retreat of secularism as the guarantor of peaceful inter-communal relationships within the public sphere. In short, in the post-modern polity, the struggle is not about (religious) truth, but about identity. Moreover, the aim of comprehensive pluralism's dialectic is to recast the struggling identities so as to make them mutually supportive (or at least mutually compatible) rather than mutually destructive. In this scheme, there is room for reason, but the place for reason is in devising the space within which the recast identities might peacefully coexist, if not mutually reinforce one another, rather than as the source of, and means of devising, a common identity. Comprehensive pluralism does not, therefore, cast away reason; pluralism merely displaces reason because it confronts a conflict that has its origins in the one faced by Spinoza, but that has been transformed as a consequence of the failed adventure of secularism, which will be discussed at greater length in Chapter 5.

In spite of significant differences, there is, in the last analysis, much in common between Spinoza's defense of tolerance and that advanced by comprehensive pluralism. What both Spinoza and comprehensive pluralism share is a similar dialectical approach and a rejection of secularism as the ultimate means to immunize the polity from the evils of religious strife. Whereas pluralism's rejection of secularism as the solution is quite unremarkable to the extent that history has revealed the frailties of the Enlightenment project, Spinoza's refusal to endorse a strict separation between faith and reason is altogether extraordinary, for he anticipates what history would prove centuries after his death. Spinoza's insights regarding tolerance are also quite remarkable in that they serve to highlight the deficiencies of typical liberal defenses of tolerance.

One question that must remain open is whether Spinoza, the seventeenth-century rationalist, would have become a pluralist were he alive today. He certainly argued for tolerance of a plurality of religions and beliefs. But his tolerance of such diversity seems to have been motivated by strategic concerns rather than by a belief that diversity might be a good in itself. It is of course impossible to determine what he would conclude were he confronted with post-modern conflicts. Nevertheless, it is certain that his incisive analysis has much to teach contemporary pluralists who seek to cope with the dilemmas of tolerance, and who seek to harmonize the one and the many without sacrificing either to the other.

5

The Clash Between Deprivatized Religion and Relativized Secularism

The Constitutional Conundrum

At least in theory, liberalism and modernism can reconcile the one and the many in the religiously pluralistic polity by bestowing constitutional primacy on secularism. Consistent with this, constitutional ordering and the public sphere ought to be secular and religion protected so long as it confines its imprint to the private sphere. Post-modernism, however, as already noted, rejects the claim that secularism ought to be entitled to priority in the normative realm.[1] Concurrently, moreover, as already briefly noted,[2] religion has become "deprivatized" (Casanova 1994: 3), by re-emerging in the public sphere and thrusting itself "into the public arena of moral and political contestation" (Id.).

Deprivatized religion combined with relativized secularism poses new and difficult problems for the constitutional handling of the relationship between religion and the state. This is true both in terms of freedom *of* religion and the freedom *from* religion. Indeed, once religious, non-religious, and anti-religious ideologies all stake out claims to the public sphere, it seems inevitable that the advancement of one of the ideologies involved can only be at the expense of others. Freedom of religion may require institutionalizing religion, and conversely, institutional concentration on freedom from religion would most likely prejudice freedom of religion. Furthermore, to the extent that religions within a polity are mutually antagonistic,

---

[1] A distinction must be drawn between secularism as a normative perspective and as associated with contemporary approaches and practices relating to scientific and empirical inquiry. Whereas the factual and ideological dimensions of secularism are well suited to go hand in hand, acceptance of the former does not logically require embrace of the latter. For example, one may fully accept as an established medical fact that a patient who happens to be a Jehovah's Witness will die without a blood transfusion, and at the same time maintain that the fact in question does not militate in favor of a secular conception of the good as against the conception of the good embraced by the Jehovah's Witness religion, which prohibits blood transfusions. For present purposes, post-modernism will be understood as rejecting the primacy of secularism in the realm of norms, but not in that of facts. As we shall see, some contemporary religious ideologies also reject, at least in part, secularism in the realm of facts. See at 177–178, infra.

[2] See supra, at Introduction.

the institutional advancement of one religion's freedom would have to be to the detriment of the freedom of other religions within the polity. Even leaving aside the already discussed case of a fundamentalist religion that insists on imposing its truth (which it irrevocably posits as *the* truth) on the whole polity and on its entire constitutional and institutional apparatus; and that of "strong" religion that seeks to ensure conformity of the polity's institutions and practices with its norms, precepts, and traditions; there are bound to be vexing conflicts with no apparent satisfactory constitutional solution. For example, the teaching of evolution theory in public schools is prone to offend religious believers committed to creationism just as its prohibition would seriously antagonize secularists (Evans 1960). And even as banal a choice as designation of the official day of weekly rest in a way that conforms with the mores of the majority religion may well result to the detriment of adherents to minority religions. Thus, Sunday closing laws may significantly harm sabbatarian business owners who are committed to honoring their religion's prohibition against working on the day that it sets aside for rest.[3]

Ideally, all ideologies, religious and non-religious alike, ought to be treated equally under applicable constitutional standards. In the context of liberal modernism, secularism anchors the constitutional handling of the relationship between religion and the state, but with the fall of secularism from its liberal pedestal, an alternative is called for in the pursuit of constitutional harmony amidst religious diversity. One seemingly plausible alternative to secularism would be a completely *areligious* perspective that, strictly speaking, neither favored any religion nor privileged secularism, thus remaining completely neutral *as between* all religious and non-religious ideologies affected by the relevant constitutional regime.

The first negative logical moment of comprehensive pluralism is completely areligious in its leveling of all hierarchies and preferences among competing conceptions of the good, but standing alone it does not make for a workable constitutional standard. On the other hand, the second positive logical moment, which legitimates conceptions of the good to the extent that they are compatible with comprehensive pluralism's second-order norms, is not neutral in terms of outcomes as it brands certain religious ideologies as more compatible with the applicable second-order norms than others. Moreover, the second-order norms themselves are not neutral inasmuch as comprehensive pluralism is *a* conception of the good, albeit one that is parasitic on promoting other conceptions of the good, including religious ones. Thus, an antipluralist fundamentalist crusading religion would fare far worse than a widely tolerant and accommodating one, both in terms of the pluralist (positive) process and of the substantive constraints stemming from pluralism's second-order norms.

---

3   *Braunfeld* v. *Brown* 366 U.S. 599 (1962) (mandatory Sunday closing law held not to violate the "Free Exercise" (of religion) rights of an Orthodox Jew who is at a competitive disadvantage because of being compelled by his religion to keep his store closed on the Sabbath).

Taking the putative areligious standard as a counterfactual guidepost, the question becomes whether any constitutional approach to religion can better approximate the counterfactual in question, and, more specifically, whether a pluralist approach would be better suited than any of the existing liberal ones for purposes of harmonizing constitutional unity and religious diversity. With this question in mind, Section 5.1 briefly elaborates the areligious counterfactual and places it in its relevant setting. Section 5.2 canvasses the principal existing models of constitutional treatment of the relationship between religion and the state. Section 5.3 sketches the pluralist approach to the constitutional treatment of the previously mentioned relationship. And, finally Section 5.4 details why the pluralist approach is preferable to its liberal counterpart, and how it may promote unity amidst plurality without being neutral.

5.1. THE SECULAR VERSUS THE "ARELIGIOUS"

There are many conceptions of secularism, and they range from the squarely antireligious to the genuinely welcoming toward religion so long as the Enlightenment-based divide between faith and reason is maintained in the public sphere and as political decisions of constitutional import – however cast – are susceptible of justification under a "public reason" standard (Rawls 2005: 212ff). Even the version of secularism that is most welcoming toward religion, however, is bound to remain inhospitable to some religion-based claims on the public sphere, such as the demand that the teaching of evolution theory in science classes in the public schools be prohibited (Reule 2001) or that the teaching of creationism in those classes be made mandatory (DeWolf 2009: 335). In short, at a minimum, secularism requires that its core precepts be given priority over conflicting precepts, whether or not the latter happen to emanate from religion.

It is clear that from the standpoint of a modern Enlightenment-based ideology, the aforementioned minimum priority to be accorded to secularism is fully justified. But it is equally plain that once secularism is relativized and considered as one (religion-like) ideology among many others, the justification in question evaporates. The areligious ideal, introduced above as a counterfactual, is supposed to replace secularism under post-modern conditions, and to secure constitutional unity and legitimacy amidst religious diversity and the peaceful coexistence between religious and non-religious (including secular) ideologies.

Before exploring how the areligious may be an apt substitute for the secular, it is necessary to briefly explain what is meant by the former term in the present context. As already indicated, "areligious" can be defined negatively as neither in favor of nor against religion. From that, one may infer that "areligious" is the equivalent of "blind to" or "deaf to" religion. That inference may be warranted in certain contexts, but it is not in the present one. Indeed, as understood here, an areligious perspective is one that has no preference as between religion and non-religion and that, at the same time, has full empathy for each conception of the good with which it is confronted. In other words, the areligious counterfactual position is based on a full understanding and complete respect for every existing conception of the good, whether religious or not, as viewed from within, combined with a complete lack of preference among the conceptions that it encounters.

It must also be stressed that, consistent with comprehensive pluralism, the areligious counterfactual position is not a procedural one, but a substantive one. It would be good if all existing conceptions of the good within a polity could be accepted exactly as they envision and understand themselves, that there be absolutely no preference among them, and that a constitutional arrangement designed to ensure promotion of the good as thus defined be deployed.

As substantive, the areligious counterfactual does introduce a bias that is fully intended as contrasted to the unintended biases of procedural approaches, such as Rawls's in *A Theory of Justice*, that purport to be neutral (Rosenfeld 1998: 67). The bias in question militates in favor of accommodation, as opposed to exclusion, of competing religious and non-religious ideologies. Accordingly, if one ideology preaches tolerance of others and another hegemony for itself, then a constitutional regime informed by the areligious counterfactual would unmistakably end up favoring the former over the latter, in contradiction with the areligious counterfactual's ideal of refraining from any preference among competing conceptions of the good.

This latter contradiction must, of course, be interpreted dialectically. The ideal of the areligious counterfactual requires strictly no preference among competing ideologies, but that proves impossible to put into effect to the extent that some ideologies aim at the subjugation or destruction of others. Furthermore, the only way to overcome the contradiction at stake is by actually opposing hegemonic ideologies to the extent that they work against furthering the greatest possible accommodation of the greatest possible number of competing ideologies.

It is important to underscore that the bias in question is neither pro- nor anti-religious. Under the areligious counterfactual, a religion that leaves no space for coexistence with other religions would be disfavored in exactly the same way, as would a militant Marxist ideology leaving no room for religious expression.

Defining the contours of a plausible constitutional approach that is areligious in that it neither inherently favors nor disfavors religion or the non-religious, looms as a daunting task. One may be tempted to anchor an areligious constitutional order on the divide between faith and reason based on the *epistemological* distinction between what falls within the purview of science and what does not. That distinction may be unexceptionable in itself, but it would not follow that a constitutional regime tailored to fit that divide would necessarily qualify as areligious. Indeed, acting in the public sphere in conformity with science may readily qualify as anti-religious from the standpoint of at least some religions. For example, state-mandated vaccination of the entire population to prevent a deadly epidemic would be justified pursuant to universally accepted standards of contemporary medical science and yet at the same time counter to a particular religion's proscription of any medical intervention as being against the will of God. The latter religion need not question the effectiveness of the vaccine as that may be irrelevant in terms of the belief in the divine proscription to which it feels compelled to adhere.

It seems, consistent with the preceding example, that no plausible constitutional approach could be cogently deployed as *inherently* areligious, even as a purely counterfactual matter. This does not mean that the areligious ideal should be abandoned altogether, but it does require that its potential be understood as being relatively modest. Indeed, for a constitutional scheme to count as being areligious, it need not avoid conflict with all religions, but only with those with a presence within the relevant polity. Thus, if a universal state-mandated vaccination policy is introduced in a polity only comprised of religions that would all approve of such policy as life- saving or life- enhancing, then such policy would qualify as areligious within the context of that polity. Under such circumstances, no one within the latter polity would object to the vaccination policy on either religious or non-religious grounds. Similarly, if the public sphere within the polity in question were reserved exclusively for the promotion of public health and the promotion of other political ends equally shared by all existing religious and non- religious ideologies with adherents within that polity, then all political means adopted to further the commonly accepted political ends would comport with a viable counterfactual conception of areligious constitutionalism. Thus, for example, if all religions and non-religious ideologies within a polity concurred on the desirability of the goal of maximizing wealth – even if for different reasons as in the case in which some of the non-religious consider pursuit of that goal an end in itself whereas their religious counterparts deem it a desirable means for purposes of redistribution through charity – then using the public sphere as the locus for deployment of policies designed to promote the maximization of wealth would comport with the implantation of areligious constitutionalism.

The preceding brief discussion provides a fair idea of the optimal conditions for constitutional accommodation of religion and non-religious ideologies. On the other hand, as already noted, some religions seem more inherently compatible than others with areligious constitutionalism as conceived from a pluralist perspective. Specifically, among the three major Western religions, Christianity seems much better suited to both secularism and areligious constitutionalism than Islam or Judaism. This is due, in important part, to Christianity's commitment to the separation between the realm of God and that of Cesar as opposed to Islam's and Judaism's all encompassing approaches requiring that religious rule extend over both the public and the political sphere (Wallace 2009). Because of this key difference, the counterfactual construct pointing to ideal conditions would be better off embracing Christianity rather than its two major Western counterparts in order to yield the best possible approximation of areligious constitutionalism. But that would create a paradox. If the pursuit of areligious constitutionalism leads to a preference for Christianity, would that not undermine the whole project by lifting Christianity above Islam and Judaism?

Based on the preceding analysis, the counterfactual constructed to distill the ideal conditions for an optional constitutional accommodation of secularism and religion does not provide a pristine model that emerges as readily adaptable. Even on the conceptual level, the areligious counterfactual emerges as remarkably tenuous. It provides an ideal of areligious constitutionalism that cannot stand on its own but is dependent on a fortuitous combination of religious and non-religious ideologies being present in the relevant polity. And if that were to happen, it would turn out to be purely contingent. Accordingly, instead of giving shape to the counterfactual universe in which it is designed to operate, areligious constitutionalism looms as entirely dependent on an improbable coincidence resulting in a proper mix of religions and non-religious ideologies. Furthermore, even if areligious constitutionalism does not automatically favor Christianity, it would require limitation, frustration, or even suppression of a sizable number of religious ideologies that happen to be firmly embedded in the daily lives of most contemporary constitutional democracies.

Before inquiring further into how a pluralist understanding of areligious constitutionalism may contribute to the deployment of a meaningful use of the areligious counterfactual, it is now time to focus on how various polities have handled the constitutional relationship between secularism and religion. This focus, moreover, should pave the way to a better grasp of the relevant contrast between liberalism and pluralism that underlies the claim that the latter is preferable in relation to the constitutional treatment of the relationship between religion and the state.

5.2. THE CONSTITUTIONAL TREATMENT OF THE RELATIONSHIP BETWEEN RELIGION AND THE STATE IN COMPARATIVE PERSPECTIVE

To provide even a cursory overview of the current constitutional landscape, it is necessary to address briefly the following three subjects: First, to provide a description of the principal existing models of constitutional regulation of the relationship between religion and the state; second, to compare the functioning of these models in terms of the constitutional jurisprudences which they have respectively generated; and third, to account for important recent historical developments – such as the vast increase in religious pluralism and the large-scale Muslim immigration to Western Europe – that pose vexing challenges to prevailing constitutional arrangements.

5.2.1. *The Constitutional Models*

Under current constitutional practice, there are essentially five different models for managing the relationship between the state and religion. These are (1) the militant secularist model bent on keeping religion completely out of the public sphere (e.g., French and Turkish *laicité*); (2) the agnostic secularist model, which seeks to maintain a neutral stance among religions but does not shy away from favoring religion over atheism and other non-religious perspectives (e.g., this is close to current American constitutional jurisprudence); (3) the confessional secular model, which incorporates elements of the polity's mainstream majority religion, primarily for identitarian purposes, and projects them as part of the polity's constitutional secularism rather than as inextricably linked to the country's main religion (e.g., Italy's or Bavaria's adoption of the crucifix as a secular symbol of national identity); (4) the official religion with institutionalized tolerance for minority religions model (e.g., the United Kingdom, Scandinavian countries, Greece), and (5) the *millet*-based model in which high priority is given to collective self-government by each religious community within the polity (e.g., Israel).

There are significant variants in relation to each of these models. For example, although both fall within model 1, French *laïcité* differs from its Turkish counterpart. Indeed, in France *laïcité* was adopted in a social and political setting that was already significantly secularized (Troper 2009), whereas in Turkey it was imposed by Kemal Attaturk to trigger a shift toward modernism and secularism in a polity where religion was overwhelmingly predominant (Borovali 2009). As a consequence, as evinced by two countries' bans on the Islamic headscarves, French *laïcité* is directed against minority religions while remaining in synchrony with the culture emanating from the majority religion (and those minority religions that are compatible with that culture), whereas Turkish *laïcité* is squarely turned against the country's dominant majority religion (Mancini 2009). Moreover, there is disagreement within the United States where model 2 is in operation whether secularism requires a full "wall of separation" between the state or religion, or whether the state can prefer religion over non-religion so long as it does not single out any religion for preferential treatment (Greenawalt 2009). There can also be significant variants within model 3, the confessional secular model, depending, among other things, on whether the polity at stake has one dominant religion, as in the case in Italy, or whether it has more than one traditionally implanted religion, as is the case in Germany where Catholicism is predominant in some regions and Protestantism, in others. In the context of a single dominant religion, model 3 seems in substance quite close to model 4, which is itself open to a wide range of variants. Indeed, some established religions, such as the Church of England, seem to have little more than a ceremonial presence in the public sphere and may impinge on secularism less than some versions of the separatist approach under model 2 (Id.: 2386–7). In other cases, such as that of Greece, in contrast, the established religion can have a much more dominant role, tending to relegate minority religions close to the status of being merely tolerated. Finally, there are also many conceivable variants in connection with model 5. For instance, currently in Israel, recognized religious communities have a monopoly over marriage and divorce with respect to those whom they deem to be members of their community (Sapir & Statman 2009: 2868–71). One could conceive, and there is much discussion about this in Israel (Id.: 2873–8), of a *millet* system in which a secular civil libertarian alternative is available for those who wish to opt out from the religious community to which they belong.

Even before broaching the constitutional jurisprudence that emerges from these various models, it is quite obvious that all of them are beset by serious shortcomings. Not only do all these models completely fail the areligious ideal, but they also frustrate the aims of the religious or of the non-religious or of minority religions or, in some cases, the aims of all three. Model 1 purports to be neutral toward religion, but the militant brand of secularism promoted by French and Turkish *laïcité* often seem downright hostile to religion. Model 2 may well put the non-religious at a disadvantage, and may also, in spite of its professed neutrality *among* religions, privilege mainstream religion as against "strong" or minority religions (Rosenfeld 1999: 59). Model 3 seems particularly problematic as confessional secularism is likely to be found wanting by most, if not all, religions within the polity and by all those who are genuinely committed toward secularism. Indeed, "confessionalized" secularism is likely to offend both the very religious who would consider their deeply held religious convictions trivialized, and the committed secularists who would feel their position being undermined through saturation of the public space with religious symbols and practices relabeled as secular (Mancini 2009: 2634–5). In addition, Model 3 and Model 4 are bound to disfavor minority religions, thus altogether foreclosing the equal treatment all religions within the polity. Finally, Model 5, based on the *millet* system, not only is prone to disadvantaging secularism as already mentioned, but also to unduly privileging the group over the individual as well as recognized religions and certain denominations within the latter (e.g., in Israel, Orthodox Judaism to the exclusion of Conservative or Reform Judaism).

5.2.2. *Lessons from Constitutional Jurisprudences*

An overview of the constitutional jurisprudences concerning the treatment of religion reveals how fragile and malleable secularism is as a constitutional concept; how difficult it is for minority religions within a polity to secure adequate protection, let alone being treated as equals; how intractable clashes of ideology among religions and among the latter and non-religious ideologies have tended to be; how elusive the search for a proper balance between constitutional rights pertaining to religion and other fundamental rights have proven to be; and how the rhetoric used in the battles over the constitutional treatment of religion has been stretched to the point that key doctrinal distinctions become almost completely blurred.

The fragility of secularism as a constitutional marker can be boiled down to the following problems it inevitably confronts: Secularism is not what it appears to be; it is too much for some; and, at the same time, too little for others. In other words, not only is secularism in practice never areligious as it ought to be in theory, but because of its origins, functioning, and the environments in which it is deployed, it can never approximate the areligious ideal, even under the best of possible (as opposed to counterfactual) circumstances. Moreover, secularism has never achieved stability as it has been in a constant tug of war between those who consider it to impinge too much on religion and those others who deem it an insufficient shield against unwarranted encroachments of religion. The former tend to be the religious and the latter the non-religious, atheist or agnostic, but that need not to be the case, as secularism can become a sword or a shield used by one religion against another. It is obvious that if a dominant religion utilizes too much of the public space to the detriment of other religions, then the latter might find it useful to invoke secularism to prevent further encroachments or to regain lost ground. Perhaps less obvious, but also possible is for secularism to be used by a majority religion to fend off a minority one as is arguably the case in France to the extent that *laïcité* is largely compatible with Catholicism and is being used against Islam.[4]

The fragility of secularism is perhaps best illustrated by its trajectory in France. French *laïcité* appears to have the best claim for coming closest to areligious secularism and of coming short, if at all, on the side of anti-religious secularism. Yet, as Michel Troper's conceptual history of the term vividly brings to light, *laïcité* was the product of a particular accommodation between the French Catholic Church and the state (Troper 2009: 2568–9). To be sure, the deployment of *laïcité* in France required some restraints on religion, thus somewhat relativizing Catholicism within the polity. But at the same time, *laïcité* was molded in theory and practice so as to render the public space as compatible as possible with the culture associated with Catholicism, if not with the religion itself. This phenomenon is succinctly captured in the French popular term *Catho-laïque* used often to refer to a Catholicism that

---

4   See Mancini 2009: 2664 (discussing France's policy on the Islamic veil as at once a reinforcement of France's Catholic heritage and an attack against Islam).

has adapted to *laïcité*, but that also connotes the corollary of a *laïcité* that has been fitted for harmonious coexistence with Catholicism.

Even under ideal conditions, for secularism to achieve meaningful neutrality (i.e., to be genuinely areligious), the public sphere must be shrunk to a minimum, becoming almost exclusively the locus for discussions on how best to achieve objectives over which there is unanimous consensus throughout the polity. The ideal neutral secular public square must thus, in effect be, a "naked public square."[5] As Karl-Heinz Ladeur emphasizes in relation to German secularism, however, a naked public square is an unlivable environment, with the consequence that the push for secularism prompts a return of the repressed which takes the form of a hybrid between religion and culture (Ladeur 2009). What this means is that secularism unleashes a process whereby the majority or mainstream religion – or, in the case of Catholic and Protestant Germany, religions – become(s) acculturated while, by the same token, the culture in question incorporates or consolidates the symbols and ways of the world of the religion(s) in question. In Germany, this process is more open than in France as religion is taught as part of the polity's culture in public schools and the state and religion are in other significant ways entangled notwithstanding the country's constitutional commitment to secularism (Mahlmann 2009). In both France and Germany, however, mainstream religion becomes steeped in a culture of secularism, and secularism becomes a viable culture through incorporation and adaptation of elements drawn from mainstream religion. It is, therefore, not surprising that Islam should pose vexing problems in those countries as it neither fits the mainstream religions nor the cultures with which they have become intertwined.[6]

Once one understands the seemingly inescapable alliance between majority or mainstream religion and the particular culture of secularism prevalent in a given polity, it becomes quite clear why minority religions tend to fare poorly in secular constitutional democracies. Moreover, it is not only against Islam, and not only in Europe, that secularism has proven discriminatory against non-mainstream religion. Thus, for example, in the United States, Mormons were refused exemptions from criminal laws against polygamy[7] and adherents to a Native American religion from criminal drug laws that prohibited the sacramental use of peyote.[8] In contrast,

---

[5] See Neuhaus 1984 (providing a critique of the aim of instituting a complete secularized public sphere in the United States).

[6] Some minority religions can be integrated within the mainstream over time by becoming more open to the polity's culture and by in turn making inroads into that culture in the course of a two way dynamic. Thus, Jews who figured as the "other" in nineteenth-century Europe have now joined mainstream religions and been replaced as the "other" by Muslims. See Maleiha Malik, Comment, Muslims Are Now Getting the Same Treatment Jews Had a Century Ago, *The Guardian*, Feb. 2, 2007, at 35.

[7] See *Reynolds v. United States*, 98 U.S. 145 (1878).

[8] See *Employment Division Oregon Dept. of Human Resources v. Smith*, 494 U.S. 872 (1990).

Catholics and Jews were granted exemptions for ritual use of wine at the time that a constitutional prohibition against the consumption of alcoholic beverages was in place.[9]

As repeatedly alluded to in the preceding discussion, ideological clashes among religions and among the latter and secularism abound. Whether those clashes center around the teaching of evolution theory in public schools, or the display of the crucifix, the wearing of the Islamic veil, stem cell research, abortion, euthanasia, same-sex marriage, polygamy, or blasphemy, there seem to be no solutions acceptable to all parties involved. Moreover, though some of these clashes may be definitively resolved pursuant to a counterfactual ideal of secularism, actual versions of secularism vary so significantly and intertwine, respectively, with such diverse array of religious cultures, that agreement even exclusively among secularists often seems impossible to achieve. Furthermore, these kinds of ideological clashes abound even within the confines of individual religions. To cite but one example, interpretations of Islam differ as to whether Muslims in a country in which they constitute a minority ought or ought not interact with secular institutions in the public sphere or with adherents to other Abrahamic religions (March 2009). In sum, all of these profound and divisive ideological clashes seem ultimately intractable. Most of these must eventually be resolved within the ambit of the relevant constitutional jurisprudence. But that often fuels more bitter debate within the polity involved rather than lowering the passions or taking the issue, at least temporarily, off the table.[10]

A further problem is that constitutional rights pertaining to religion often clash with other fundamental rights afforded constitutional protection. The most notorious conflicts are these that pit freedom of religion against the rights of women (Raday 2003), and against free speech rights (Haarscher 2009). As Dieter Grimm points out, doctrinal means have been, and can be, devised to handle the full gamut of constitutional claims relating to religion, including conflicts with other rights (Grimm 2009). In short, constitutional adjudication of such conflicts seem best handled through application of the standard of proportionality and through judicial balancing commonly employed to resolve conflicts among constitutional rights generally (Id.).

Application of the proportionality standard to conflicts of rights involving religion is problematic, however, in ways that are generally not at issue when religion is not at stake. For example, in a conflict between free speech rights and privacy rights, there is generally a background consensus that includes all the parties to the

---

[9] See discussion in Justice Kennedy's concurring opinion in *Board of Education* v. *Grumet*, 512 U.S. 687, 727 (1994). Prohibition was instituted by adoption of the Eighteenth Amendment to the U.S. Constitution in 1919 and was repealed by the Twenty-First Amendment in 1933.

[10] A prime example of this was the aftermath of the U.S. Supreme Court decision in *Roe* v. *Wade*, 410 U.S.113 (1973). See Tribe 1992.

controversy as well as the adjudicator. They all share the premises that impart validity on the secular constitutional order in place and on the particular rights involved
in the dispute. They all agree on the importance of free speech and privacy but
disagree on where to draw the line between them when they happen to be in conflict. When religion rights are at issue, in contrast, often the background consensus
referred to earlier breaks down, with the freedom of religion claimant challenging
the very premises of the secular constitutional order itself.

In a dispute where religion is not involved, proportionality analysis should legitimately assess all claims from the same perspective. But should the same principle
apply when a religious claim is at issue? Or should such claims also be considered
from the internal perspective of the religion involved? Or else, only evaluated from
the secular perspective incorporated in the constitutional order?[11] This problem is
compounded when the religion involved itself has a conception of the very right
that is being invoked against it. Thus, for example, as the various claims made in
relation to the dispute over the Islamic veil amply illustrate, those arguing from
within a religious tradition often oppose their religion's perspective on women's
equality or dignity as against that advanced by liberal constitutionalism.[12] Is the
woman who asserts that she is voluntarily wearing the veil, a victim of gender-based
equality? Or, does the ban she confronts constitute an affront to her dignity and
gender-based bias inasmuch as it assumes that she is not able to decide or fend
for herself?

One further problem contributing to the difficulties posed by claims relating to
religion derives from rhetorical shifts that make it much tougher to get a proper
handle on the constitutional issues actually at stake, and an adequate gauge of the
weight of the competing interests in play. Salient examples of these rhetorical shifts
include the appropriation by proponents of religious worldviews of the rhetoric of
free speech rights or anti-discrimination rights to bolster their freedom of religion
objectives (Haarscher 2009: 2802–10). Free speech rhetoric has been invoked by religious groups to argue for the teaching of creationism and intelligent design alongside
evolution theory in state schools. Use of this rhetoric seeks to displace the nature and
import of the actual claim being made. When donned in free speech garb, the claim
being advanced no longer looms primarily as setting a confrontation between religious truth and secular truth. Instead, it suggests that the State is curtailing the free

---

[11] This last question is only limited to the issue of ascribing a proper weight to the religion-based claim,
     and not to adjudication, proportionality, or the constitutional order itself. In other words, the judges
     must operate from within the existing secular constitutional order but, arguably at least, ought to con-
     sider the importance and weight of the religion-based claim from the internal religious perspective
     from which that claim emanates.
[12] See Rorive 2009 (discussing the European Court of Human Right's failures in using proportionality
     analysis and balancing in various cases on the Islamic veil).

marketplace of ideas by systematically censoring discussion of certain views shared by many within the polity in public fora in which the subject matter upon which these views purport to bear is widely discussed.

In other instances, religious groups have employed the rhetoric of constitutional equality and dignity rights in efforts to curb the free speech rights of those whom they perceive as their religion's enemies. In this connection, critiques of Islam as a religion in a Western European country in which Muslims are a relatively small minority can be cast as being "racist," as amounting to an affront against the "identity" of the Muslim minority, and of "insulting" the latter *because* of its religion. In this way, critiques of religion, which traditionally played a key role in the implantation of Enlightenment-based secularism,[13] are transformed into group defamation based on religious affiliation.

Shifts in rhetoric can also be used by secularists or proponents of a majority religion against a religious minority to curtail the latter's religious freedom. By equating religion with beliefs rather than deeds, one can convey that certain actions or practices prescribed by a religion are not at their core "religious" in nature. If polygamy for the Mormons at the end of the nineteenth century or the use of peyote for Native American religion are regarded as separable from core religious beliefs, they can certainly be ascribed relatively little weight when balanced against societal interests with which they are in conflict. If, on the contrary, the practices are presented as seamlessly intertwined with religious beliefs and as central within the perspective of the religion to which they are linked, then they would immediately seem to warrant being given much greater weight even if in the end they might still be outweighed by pressing societal concerns.

Some of the problems discussed already have beset constitutional jurisprudences, while others have emerged or been aggravated due to significant changes of relatively recent vintage. A brief review of the most important among these is now warranted in order to place both the past and the future of the constitutional treatment of religion in its proper context.

5.2.3. *Recent Historical Changes and New Trends*

Many changes, that may have originated earlier but that have greatly accelerated or become more fully visible in the 1980s, have converged to render the contemporary problems surrounding the relationship between constitutionalism, secularism, and religion seemingly ever more acute. As already mentioned, the 1980s saw a deprivatization of religion in various parts of the world. In addition, by the end of the decade,

---

[13] See Mostefai & Scott 2009: 9 (characterizing Voltaire's famous battle cry, *"Ecraser L'Infâme"* directed against the Catholic Church as the "motto of the French Enlightenment").

the world became witness to the collapse of the Soviet Empire and shortly thereafter to the emergence of concurrent trends toward globalization and balkanization. As will be further examined in Chapters 8 and 9, these trends have set the stage, inter alia, for the emergence of global terrorism predicated on certain brands of fundamentalist religion. Moreover, the trend toward globalization has prompted vast migrations that have led both to significant increases in religious pluralism and diversity in numerous polities and to the arrival of sizable religious minorities – such as Muslims in Western Europe – who find themselves often at profound odds with the secular and religious cultures of their country of immigration.

The significant changes resulting from these historical events and trends are far too numerous and complex to be addressed here in but a most summary fashion. I will therefore focus here on some very general observations that will hopefully shed further light on the conditions surrounding the issues and problems identified previously and on possible avenues toward better future handlings of them.

As already noted, the Cold War period was dominated by the struggle between two superpowers, the United States and the Soviet Union, each committed to ideologies that were sharply at odds over religion. Soviet Marxism promoted atheism, whereas American liberal capitalism was open to, and encouraging toward, religion (Greenawalt 2009: 2383–4). Liberal capitalism is neither inherently religious nor irreligious, but the United States used its favorable views toward religion and its strong protection of religious freedom as a weapon against the Soviet Union.[14] This created a bond between the secular and the religious in America, the secular enlisting religion as an ally in the Cold War, and the religious finding greater government support and encouragement. But notwithstanding this bond, there was little danger of religion capturing the public sphere as both America's secular establishment and its religious communities were united in an existential and a spiritual struggle against their country's Soviet antagonist.

With the fall of the Soviet Empire, the needs for the special alliance between secularism and religion that had been predominant in Cold War America all but disappeared.[15] On the other hand, in post-Soviet Russia and East/Central Europe

[14] In this respect, it is noteworthy that the words "under God" were added to the U.S. Pledge of Allegiance changing the phrase "One nation indivisible" to "One nation indivisible under God" in 1954 during the Eisenhower Administration, sixty-two years after the Pledge was originally written. See *Newtow v. The Congress, et al.*, 292F. 3d. 597,609 (2009) ("[T]he words 'under God' were intended to recognize a 'Supreme Being', at a time when the Government was inveighing against atheistic Communism").

[15] Although the alliance in question was predominant during the Cold War, it was not exclusive as the contested jurisprudence regarding the Religion Clauses attests (Greenawalt 2009). Moreover, the "deprivatization" of religion promoted by Protestant fundamentalists in the United States was already manifest several years before the fall of the Berlin Wall (Casanova 1994: 3). Nevertheless, the thrust of the present account is not affected by these developments. Indeed, by the 1980s tensions with the Soviet Union under Gorbachov had already considerably lessened, thus affording more room to maneuver both to the religious and to the secular.

there was a strong revival of religion in the making in newly emancipated polities. This revival often went hand in hand with a rebirth of nationalism and recourse to ethnic based identity politics. Religion and ethnic origin often combined to spur an identity politics bent on negating the universalist aspirations, and militantly atheist ideology of Soviet Marxism.[16] In short, whereas in the United States religions became emancipated from their *political* subordination during the course of the Cold War, in the area of former Soviet dominance, religion became not only resurgent but often inextricably intertwined with nationalism and ethnic identity.

Globalization, which vastly accelerated in the aftermath of the Cold War, spurs migration as global capitalism calls for global labor. Such migration usually renders the host country more multi-cultural, multi-ethnic, and religiously diverse. As previously indicated, approximating areligious secularism becomes less and less likely as the number of religions in a polity proliferates. Also, the more alien the religion and religious culture of the immigrants to a polity turn out to be, the more problems they are likely to encounter. These problems, in turn, are unlikely to become solved so long as the new religion does not share a common culture with the already established religions within the polity or with the brand of secularism associated with the latter.

Finally, historical change going much farther back, namely to the advent of the welfare state, when combined with the deprivatization of religion, progressively undermines the traditional divide between the public sphere and the private sphere to the point of vitiating most of its use in the context of present-day relationships between religion and the state. On the one hand, the state has become much more omnipresent throughout the contemporary polity. The contemporary state typically provides public education, public health, public funding for medical research, and the apportionment of public benefits, including individual and family welfare and pension benefits, to cite but some of the most obvious examples. At the same time, the contemporary state tends to reach deeper and deeper into what traditionally were deemed purely private relationships. Among other things, private employment relationships as well as most market-based transactions among private parties, and even the most intimate aspects of private family life, such as the relation between spouses and between parents and children (at least when abuse and neglect within the home are at issue) are all, for the most part, subject to state regulation and active intervention.

On the other hand, deprivatized religion tends to increasingly spill over into the public sphere. This is perhaps most obvious under the *millet* system, where religion

---

[16] One of the most salient examples of this amalgam of religion and ethnicity in politics is that of Bosnia, a multi-ethnic republic that had been a part of former Yugoslavia and that became tragically mired in a bloody civil war among ethnic Serbs belonging to Orthodox Christianity, ethnic Croats who were Catholic, and Bosniaks who were Muslims (Mansfield 2003).

monopolizes the regulation of marriage and divorce, but it is also quite present in other contexts. For example, religious institutions are quite active in many polities that are in principle secular in public sphere battles over abortion, euthanasia, stem cell research, same-sex marriage, and multiple other issues of particular interest to religion. Moreover, what is most remarkable in this respect is not so much that they seek to promote and protect the interests of their own religious community within the public arena. It is rather that they seek to subject the entire population of the polity to normative constraints emanating from their own religious tradition, but not shared by many other religious and secular members of the polity. To cite but one obvious example, the Catholic Church has often intervened in the public arena to promote a complete ban on abortion even though abortion may be permissible from the standpoint of certain other religions and from that of the non-religious within the polity. In view of these concurrent trends of greater state intervention in the private sphere combined with the greater active role of religion in the public sphere, one wonders if it still makes sense to center constitutional relationships between religion and the state along the divide between the public and the private spheres.

5.3. A PLURALIST ACCOUNT OF THE CONSTITUTIONAL TREATMENT OF THE RELATIONSHIP BETWEEN RELIGION AND THE STATE

It is clear that the five constitutional models for the treatment of the relationship between religion and of the state are seriously flawed from the standpoint of achieving a satisfactory integration of the one and the many within the polity. Moreover, it also seems plain that the contemporary combination of the relativization of secularism, deprivatization of religion, increased religious and cultural diversity though migration, and profound erosion of the public/private divide exacerbates the shortcomings of the five models and renders approximation of the areligious constitutional ideal apparently evermore elusive. Under such circumstances, can comprehensive pluralism bring us closer to harmonization of the one and the many in spite of its bias in favor of inclusion as against exclusion mentioned earlier? And if, as I will argue, it can, how would that translate in plausible constitutional terms?

As already pointed out, comprehensive pluralism's negative moment fully comports with the areligious counterfactual, but does not of itself yield any workable constitutional standard. In contrast, comprehensive pluralism's positive moment ends up favoring some religions over others, and some versions of secularism over certain religions, and thus seemingly inexorably veers away from the areligious ideal. To be sure, the latter ideal is unattainable and its approximation is dependent on a purely contingent convergence among the existing ideologies within a particular polity. Nevertheless, comprehensive pluralism, conceived dialectically and approaching religion in its full dynamic potential, can arguably yield a constitutional regime that best approximates the areligious ideal *understood dialectically given the actual configuration of existing religious and non-religious conceptions of the good found within the relevant polity*. Moreover, the constitutional regime in question, in its quest to promote the best possible equilibrium between freedom of religion and freedom from religion – both in the sense of freedom from all religion from a secular standpoint and in that of freedom from the religion of the other in the pursuit of one's own religion – can profitably draw, as we shall see, on Spinoza's conception of tolerance based on greater self-restraint in relation to one's own conception of the good and greater acceptance of the conceptions of the good of others.

A pluralist approach to the constitutional treatment of the relationship between religion and the state does not yield any single set of prescriptions and constraints fit for all polities. The approach in question is contextual, relational, and dynamic, and it works through a combination of certain variables – the actual religious and non-religious ideologies that coexist within the relevant polity and how they happen to relate to one another – and certain constants – the prima facie presumption of equal validity of all conceptions of the good, the equal dignity of self and other, and compliance with comprehensive pluralism's second order norms. Moreover, the range of relationships between various conceptions of the good within a given polity is likely to be quite extensive. There are instances of great convergence, such as organized interfaith prayer among Buddhists, Christians, Jews, and Muslims in the United States.[17] These stand in sharp contrast to instances of great divergence such as the teaching at a network of private Islamic schools in the United Kingdom, based on Saudi government-supplied textbooks, that proclaimed that Jews "looked like monkeys and pigs." that prescribed, inter alia, throwing those who had engaged in gay sex off a cliff, and that illustrated where hands and feet should be amputated as punishment for theft in accordance with the Shariah.[18]

Whereas pluralism looks favorably upon convergence, it does not thereby automatically stand against divergence. Pluralism does not seek the deployment of a constitutional regime that would weave together, to the exclusion of others, religious ideologies that have largely internalized the core values of liberalism, such as Anglicanism, mainstream U.S. Protestantism, left-leaning Catholicism, reform Judaism, and certain broadly humanistic interpretations of Islam.[19] Religions that are illiberal but not incompatible with the second-order norms of comprehensive

---

[17] See Peter Applebome, Diverse and Divided, But Praying and Singing Together, *New York Times*, Monday, Nov. 22, 2010, p. A18.

[18] See John F. Burns, Lessons of Hate at Islamic School Network in Britain, *New York Times*, Tuesday, Nov. 23, 2010, p. A8.

[19] See, for example, Arkoun 1994 and 2002 (drawing parallels between the "golden age" of Islam and the Enlightenment).

pluralism should also be afforded constitutional protection, and how much protection would depend on the actual interplay among the competing conceptions of the good at play in the relevant polity. For example, the wearing of the Islamic veil may be regarded as contravening gender-based equality as gauged from liberal secular perspective, but it may be understood very differently from within the perspective of the Muslim woman who opts in favor of it.[20]

Viewed dialectically, a pluralist constitutional regime must strive toward a workable dynamic with sufficient poles of convergence to foster peaceful coexistence and fairness (consistent with applicable pluralist second-order norms) and as many poles of divergence as possible without posing a significant threat to the unity of the whole. Moreover, divergences and differences are as crucial to comprehensive pluralism as are the requisite (constitutional) convergences, for without a multiplicity of paths toward self-expression, self-realization, and self-fulfillment, the normative aspirations of pluralism would be thoroughly thwarted.

To better tap the dynamic between convergences and divergences and to come up with the constitutional regime that would come closer than plausible alternatives to the areligious ideal (while remaining cognizant that it would still fall far short of it), it is useful to reconsider some of the key distinctions that have figured as mainstays in the traditional constitutional approach to the relationship between religion and the state. The first of these distinctions, which as mentioned previously has been thoroughly undermined in recent decades, is that between the private and the public sphere. That distinction no longer seems useful for present purposes, and it may be thus fruitfully replaced by reliance on the oft referred to contrast between *intra*-communal and *inter*-communal relationships. Broadly speaking, all those who share the same religious ideology[21] can be said to belong to a single religious community. Consistent with this, moreover, dealings within a single religious community are "intra-communal," whereas those involving two or more religious communities or a religious and a secular community or those that purport to transcend the bounds of all relevant religious communities are "inter-communal."[22] Finally, it is important to

---

[20] Cf. *Sahin* v. *Turkey*, 44 Eur. H.R. Rep 5 (Grand Chamber 2005) (Tukens, J., dissenting) (Criticizing European Court of Human Rights' majority for upholding Turkey's imposition of ban on wearing the headscarf at the university and noting that prohibiting adult women from choosing to wear the veil may itself be a greater affront to gender-based equality than tolerating the veil) (See also Rorive 2009: 2683–4).

[21] I emphasize "religious ideology" rather than "religion" in order to allow for the characterization of different sects or denominations to be treated as different communities, and for the dealings of a dissident member of a religion with his or her co-religionists to be deemed to be inter-communal if the context warrants.

[22] Although the intra-communal sphere may overlap, and on occasion even completely coincide, with the private sphere, and likewise, the inter-communal sphere with the public sphere, the intra-communal/inter-communal distinction is by no means coextensive with that between private and public. For example, under the *millet* system each religious community is supposed to govern itself in

remember that the distinction between intra-communal and inter-communal is not meant to be understood in an essentialist sense, but rather in a functional and contextual one. Thus, to the extent that an interdenominational group joins forces to combat an external threat, the dealings among the members of the various denominations involved are properly considered intra-communal. But, by the same token, other areas of interaction between the same actors, where they are divided along denominational lines, would be properly considered as inter-communal.

Based on this contrast, inter-communal dealings should be subjected to greater constitutionally sanctioned constraints than genuinely, intra-communal dealings (i.e., those within a group with cohesive internal unity and a strong sense of common identity and solidarity). Accordingly, intra-communal affairs would be, by and large, left alone so long as they would not pose any significant risk of interference with, or harm to, inter-communal dealings or the intra-communal dealings of other groups within the polity, and so long as they did not trample on a certain minimum of state-protected fundamental individual-regarding interests, including the right to exit from the group in question.

This approach would lessen the danger of veering too far in the direction of the naked public square and make more room for a richer communal life among the diverse communities within the polity. In spite of the advantages it presents, however, this approach would by no means afford satisfactory solutions to all the problems associated with the interface between constitutionalism and religion. Even in a polity reconstituted institutionally in terms of the dynamic between inter-communal and intra-communal dealings, the various religious and non-religious communities involved could plausibly remain internally closed and externally hostile, creating an atmosphere more akin to hardening Balkanization than harmonious cooperation and coexistence under the aegis of a common constitutional culture.

In spite of this danger, the fluidity of the relational approach afforded by the dynamic between intra-communal and intra-communal dealings, and the concurrent move away from certain rigid categorical constructs that inhere in the various constitutional models considered previously, should encompass, and perhaps even prompt, greater openness and accommodation both within and among groups within the polity. Religions are not monolithic and are often susceptible of gradual adaptation to changed circumstances. This is illustrated by the different ways in which Islam has dealt with its status as a minority religion in polities dominated by secularism and other religions. As we have seen, these range from virtually total inward withdrawal to significant cooperation with secular groups or with other monotheist

---

internal matters, such as marriage, divorce, and inheritance, with their own legal system and courts. See Kymlicka 1995: 156. Accordingly, in the context of the *millet* system, many matters not confined within the private sphere remain nonetheless purely intra-communal.

religions within the polity (March 2009). By the same token, the non-religious can also adapt to some extent to the ways of the religious without compromising their own ideological commitments (Sapir & Statman 2009).

The attractiveness of framing relationships in terms of the distinction between the intra-communal and the inter-communal is enhanced given that, as illustrated by the example of the German Catholic feminist woman examined earlier,[23] the citizen of a typical contemporary constitutional democracy is bound to become immersed at one in a number of different communities and to have to negotiate conflicts and tensions that arise as a result. As will be remembered concerning the woman of the example in question, on some occasions, her Catholicism may be in tension or conflict with her feminism. Because of that she may decide to live with a certain amount of dissonance and inconsistency or to seek reform from within (e.g., working to achieve changes within the Catholic Church leading to the eventual anointment of women priests) or, feeling alienated from the Church, to become a dissident who nonetheless wishes to remain within her religious community or, also conceivably, to withdraw from one of these two communities because she feels that her commitments to her fellow Catholics and those to her fellow feminists are too incompatible.

What is crucial for our purposes is that this single individual must constantly shift from intra-communal to inter-communal perspectives in the management of her multiple allegiances; that she cannot avoid bringing some of the values she shares with her fellows in one community (e.g., feminist values) into her intra-communal dealings in another community (e.g., her Catholic religious community); and that short of experiencing such a strong sense of incompatibility as would prompt her to quit a group with whom she had strongly identified, she would strive to find ways to juggle her many loyalties and to live with tensions and inconsistencies bound to arise due to her multiple group membership. In short, this woman's difficulties could be mitigated through intermittent compartmentalization (e.g., when praying in Church she would not focus on her frustrations as a feminist) and projection of intra-communal values inter-communally (e.g., bringing her feminist ideals to the table at meetings of her Catholic community group). Moreover, these operations that take place at the individual level can also be carried out at the collective level by various groups of the whole. And, except in cases of clear incompatibility, this dynamic between intra-communal and inter-communal dealings should afford numerous possibilities for peaceful coexistence without coercing sacrifice of core inter-communal differences within a constitutional order among proponents of numerous and diverse religious and secular ideologies.

The dynamic between intra-communal and inter-communal dealing can also be helpful to reconfigure the place of secularism as one among the competing

---

[23] See supra, at Section 1.5.

intra-communal ideologies subjected to constitutional ordering inspired by the areligious ideal. Functionally, the constitutional ordering in question should promote peaceful and productive inter-communal relationships within the polity combined with guaranteeing a maximum of room for intra-communal autonomy consistent with preserving the integrity of the space needed for inter-communal exchanges. Substantively, on the other hand, a pluralist constitutional regime would draw on that which makes possible and facilitates inter-communal coordination and cooperation among religious ideologies, and among the latter and non-religious ones. What would be encompassed within this rubric would vary from one setting to the next, depending on the religions, the non-religious ideologies, the history, and the cultures involved. In any case, incorporation of elements drawn from religion or religious culture would be entirely permissible. The criterion of validity for such elements derived from religion would not depend on how close or removed they may be from religion itself, but on whether they advance or hinder the smooth functioning of the requisite channels of inter-communal exchange.

Within this scheme, secularism and its sources of identity, rooted in the traditional Enlightenment conception of the term, would definitely figure as an intra-communal actor defined by its own separate and distinct ideology. Indeed, in all contemporary constitutional democracies there are significant numbers of citizens who are secular rather than religious, who put science ahead of faith, and who believe that the pursuit of Enlightenment-based liberty and equality for all should trump any claimed divine prescription to the contrary. These "intra-communal" secularists have as much a right to have a place at the inter-communal table, as do the proponents of the various existing religious ideologies.

Secularism's intra-communal identity is self-contained, and one can easily imagine a well-functioning self-enclosed homogeneous secular society cut off from all religion. In actually, however, the gap between secular and non-secular identities may prove far less stark than would initially appear. First, intra-communal secularism must figure in the elaboration of the inter-communal constitutional order to the extent that the secularist ideology is present in the relevant polity. Second, given the tendency to develop plural identities and multi-group memberships, elements of the secularist ideology are bound to slip into the intra-communal precincts of competing ideologies. Thus, some liberal religions are quite compatible with secularism's commitment to Enlightenment-based reason, science and liberty and equality for all. Moreover, some adherents of non-liberal religions may nonetheless embrace certain secular values and cope with the tensions involved through compartmentization. And, third, by the same token, proponents of intra-communal secularism need not shut the door to religion, and may in fact welcome or even practice religion without contradiction so long as they adhere to the primacy of the secular outlook and make religion a matter of personal choice rather than one of collective self-definition at the level of intra-communal interaction.

Given this complex dynamic, it stands to reason that secularism should be in constant interactive flux and that it should be amenable to being used as both sword and shield. It is instructive, in this connection, to consider the example of France. As Pierre Birnbaum explains, Jews and Protestants took the lead in calling for the institutionalization of *laïcité* in France (Birnbaum 2009). Yet, as already mentioned institutionalized French *laïcité* has a distinct Catholic imprint.[24] One plausible explanation for this, consistent with the dynamic conception of secularism advanced here, is that acceptance of the majority religion imprint on secularism was the best achievable compromise for the latter, for the minority religions involved, and for intra-communal secularists.

Taking proper account of the relevant contextual variables and the requisite dialectical logic, it now becomes possible to sketch out the contours of a pluralist constitutional ordering of the relationship between religion, the state, and society. Such constitutional ordering replaces the private–public divide by the distinction between the intra-communal and the inter-communal and does away with the priority of secularism in favor of aspiration toward the ideal of the areligious understood in terms of a concurrent indifference as between all conceptions of the good and complete empathy for each one of them. The latter aspiration, however, is tempered by adherence to the normative prescriptions of comprehensive pluralism, which for present purposes differs primarily from the areligious ideal by virtue of its substantively based preference for pluralist alternatives as against anti-pluralist ones. Furthermore, unlike under the liberal ideal relying on the public–private divide, inter-communal dealings need not always involve state actors, and intra-communal relationships may become at least partially inter-communal as dissidents or would-be reformers in a community cross the line between insider and outsider. Because of this, constitutional ordering (as distinguished from infra-constitutional legal ordering) needs to regulate certain interactions among non-state actors, including some that may arguably qualify as intra-communal ones.

For example, under a *millet* system, such as the one currently in force in Israel, intermarriage between a Christian and a Jew without either converting or committing to educate her children in a religion that is not hers would not be possible under prevailing law. In a pluralist context, the right to marry should be constitutionally guaranteed, and it may be a matter of inter-communal interaction (a person of one community wishing to marry someone from another community or a person becoming an "outsider" within his own community by virtue of seeking to intermarry contrary to his community's rules) or of intra-communal interaction (e.g., to the extent

---

[24]   See supra, at Section 5.2.2.

that all branches of Judaism may be integrated into a single Jewish community, and that a rabbi belonging to Reform Judaism would marry a Jew to a Gentile without seeking to impinge on the religious freedom of the latter, constitutionally requiring legal legitimation of marriage performed by Reform rabbis would amount to constitutionalization of intra-communal affairs).

Before proceeding any further with the pluralist approach to the constitutional regulation of the relationship between religion, the state, and society, it is necessary to deal with a serious objection to pluralism that can be launched from within at least certain religious perspectives. In essence, the objection in question charges pluralism with relativizing religion much as secularism does. Indeed, pluralism may well be less hostile to religion than certain forms of secularism have proven to be, but it nonetheless, in the last analysis, negates the truth of religion, as does secularism. Pluralism subordinates religion and its truth to the postulate that all religions and non-religious ideologies are basically equivalent and interchangeable while at the same time posting its own ideology and its truth as paramount. In short, the objection under consideration is based on the claim that the pursuit of the truth according to pluralism can only proceed at the cost of negating or relativizing the truth of the objecting religion. From within the objecting religion, it possesses *the* truth and the polity ought therefore be (constitutionally) ordered accordingly. Just as does secularism, pluralism militates against such ordering and thus the two of them loom as equivalent when viewed from the objecting religion's internal perspective.

There is, of course, no reply to this objection *from within* the perspective of the objecting religion. Such a religion is inherently anti-pluralistic, and pluralism and anti-pluralism are ultimately but two clashing conceptions of the good. Accordingly, pluralism cannot simply claim to be superior to anti-pluralism. The most pluralism can do is to try to persuade those it addresses that the good life and the good polity are much more likely to emerge if a pluralist rather than an anti-pluralist course is adopted.

This objection against pluralism as a virtually indistinguishable substitute for secularism can be broken down into two separate distinguishable claims. The first is that of a single religion that asserts its truth to be universal, and that therefore deems it legitimate and appropriate to impose its precepts on the polity as a whole, including on the latter's entire (constitutional) ordering or on as much of it as matters from the internal perspective of the religion in question.[25] The second claim, on the other hand, is one made jointly by all religions in the polity against secularism and its imprint on the state and society within that polity. This second claim is strongest in the context of a *laïcité* that is downright anti-religious, but it can

---

[25] For example, a religion may be indifferent as between a monarchy or democratic form of government, a federal or a unitary state, but dead set against abortion, homosexuality, and non-marital sex.

also be leveled against milder forms of secularism or against pluralism perceived as placing secularism and religion on an equal footing, thus thwarting the collectively shared mission of all the religions involved to infuse the polity with religious norms and values jointly deemed superior to those emanating from non-religious or anti-religious perspectives.

The first of these claims, that stemming from a single religion, is easy to refute from both a pragmatic and a pluralist standpoint in the context of any *religiously pluralistic* polity. Even in the complete absence of atheists or agnostics, ceding all inter-communal fora to a dominant religion bent on spreading its truth would most likely signal a return to a pre-modern era characterized by crusades, religious wars, inquisition burnings, and the like. Moreover, even if the religion in question forswore against violence toward infidels and accepted limited tolerance of other religions to the extent that the latter did not contravene its dogmas or prescriptions, it would still seem pragmatically wiser to make greater room for religious diversity. Leaving all religions within the relevant polity enough room to breathe clearly appears to be preferable to leaving all religions other than the dominant one at the mercy of the latter. Needless to stress, the pluralistic reply to this first objection is even stronger than the pragmatic one inasmuch as pluralism considers religious diversity to be preferable to religious uniformity. In short, to pragmatism's negative argument against a hegemonic religion in a religiously diverse polity, pluralism adds an equally strong, or perhaps even stronger, positive argument.

The second claim, that which is made jointly by all religions within the polity against non-religious perspectives, on the other hand, seems, at least initially, much more difficult to refute. In essence, this argument is not one against diversity, but against a modus vivendi that actually thwarts religious diversity. In other words, the claim boils down to the charge that whether pluralism or secularism is involved, in the end they undermine and frustrate all religion hence threatening the diversity introduced by religion as well as the diversity among religions.[26]

This second claim represents a particular instance of a general objection that can be leveled against pluralism. That objection is based on the assertion that comprehensive pluralism lacks adequate means to deal with conceptions of the good that condition self-realization and self-fulfillment on destruction of the other or on eradication of the other's conception of the good.[27] Either pluralism treats such conceptions of the good as all others, in which case it leads to contradictions and to morally repugnant results, or it casts the conceptions of the good in question as unacceptable, thus failing to be pluralistic all the way down.

---

[26] For example, if secularism becomes predominant, all religious truths may become trivialized, making the differences between them appear more anecdotal than existentially important.

[27] I thank my colleague Ekow Yankah for making me aware of the full import of this general objection.

This objection is easily met by the pluralist with respect to conceptions of the good that command elimination of the other but poses a greater challenge, which I will argue later, is nonetheless surmountable, in relation to a demand for elimination of ways of life prescribed by a competing conception of the good. In other words, it is easy for the pluralist to ban the killing of idolaters, but less so to forbid the smashing of the latter's stone or wooden idols.[28]

The prohibition against killing or forcing upon anyone the commandments of one's own conception of the good, no matter how crucial to that conception or how firmly and sincerely adhered to, is central to pluralism's very integrity and consistency. Everyone is actually or potentially a bearer of a conception of the good, either by adhering to an existing one, or by contributing to modifying the latter or to creating new ones. Accordingly, preserving everyone in her capacity as a bearer of a conception of the good is crucial to pluralism, and the failure to do so poses a threat to its survival as the core tenets of a particular conception of the good may prescribe elimination of all those who refuse to adhere to the way of life prescribed by conception of the good but not interfering with the other's personhood or even the other's conscience.[29] On the other hand, it appears that there may be cases where one might justify suppression or curtailment of a conception of the good *on pluralist grounds*. That is obviously true and unproblematic as detailed earlier in the case of a conception of the good that commands killing those who refuse to adhere to it. But what about in other cases, such as that in which a plurality of diverse religions band together against secularism perceived as undermining all religion and hence as frustrating religious diversity? In the latter case, there is no contemplation of killing any proponent of secularism, but only of replacing secularism by a normative order consistent with the common precepts shared by all the relevant religions involved regarding the constitutional ordering and institutional setting in operation within the polity. Accepting, for the sake of argument, the validity of the preceding claim, doesn't the second, positive, logical moment of comprehensive pluralism command limiting the scope of those conceptions of the good that tend to thwart the accommodation of the greatest possible number of competing conceptions susceptible of peaceful coexistence?

The pluralist's answer to the last question is in the negative, based on a crucial distinction between fair competition among diverse conceptions of the good and anti-competitive or destructive conduct by proponents of one conception of the

---

[28] cf. Genesis 11:26–9 (God commanding Abraham to destroy his father's idols).

[29] For example, one may deem secularism pernicious and argue for banning all its manifestations in public and yet nevertheless respect the atheist's freedom of conscience so long as the latter does not speak or act against the accepted ways of life and of behavior common to all religions in their joint endeavors to cast away the evils of secularism.

good against other such conceptions. This can be best understood perhaps by drawing an analogy to the ideal of a free market economy. So long as a competitor runs a rival out of business by offering a better product or by operating more efficiently, the market economy is well served and its aims clearly furthered. However, if a competitor engages in monopolistic practices or destructive competition, such as by intimidating a rival's customers or by destroying the rival's merchandise, then the market economy is thwarted, and if these evils spread, eventually in danger of being totally destroyed. Analogously, fair competition among conceptions of the good, through mutual exposure, open discussion, attempts at persuasion including religious proselytizing (so long as it only addresses adults and is non-intimidating and non-coercive) is deemed a paramount good from the standpoint of comprehensive pluralism. In contrast, seeking to ban or drive away competing conceptions of the good by mobilizing the state or its institutional apparatus against them is inherently anti-pluralist as it artificially and coercively limits the choices open to all.

It may well be that actual fair competition among diverging conceptions of the good on occasion actually results in a diminution in the number of available alternatives. That in itself, however, is no evil from a pluralist standpoint. Pluralism is not concerned about the total number of existing alternatives actually in play in and of itself but rather about every person or group within the polity having all the opportunities she or it deems necessary or helpful for purposes of furthering her or its course toward self-realization and self-fulfillment. Thus, for example, if certain religions of the past, such as those of the Ancient Greeks or of the Aztecs, no longer appeal to anyone within a polity, then, all other things remaining equal, that polity will have experienced a net loss in religious diversity. It would be absurd, however, in light of that to conclude that the polity in question had become less pluralistic from the standpoint of comprehensive pluralism.

Based on the preceding analysis, it becomes clear how a pluralist constitutional order should handle the opposition to secularism advanced jointly by a diverse multiplicity of religions. So long as secularism is constitutionally enshrined as paramount in the context of a liberal enlightenment-based ideology, then the opposition in question may well be justified. If the constitutional endorsement and ensuing competitive disadvantage imposed on the polity's existing religions were actually unfair, then it would actually contravene the pluralist ethos.

Be that as it may, by casting secularism as one conception of the good among many and as being on the same footing as all the rest, including the religious ones, pluralist constitutionalism levels the playing field, and legitimates free competition among various religions and among the latter and secularism. Indeed, under the conditions of pluralist constitutionalism, the atheist and the agnostic perspectives are *prima facie* entitled to the same respect and opportunities as are any of the various religions practiced within the polity.[30] Therefore, once the priority of secularism in the constitutional realm is replaced by the aim to best approximate the areligious ideal, then the competition between secularism and religion seems poised to be fair regardless of whether secularism or religion ends up with more committed adherents over time.

As already alluded to, the particulars of a pluralist constitutional ordering of the relationship among religion, the State, and society is context dependent, and hence there can be no single answer to questions such as whether religion should be taught in state schools, whether religious symbols should be displayed in public spaces, whether a *millet* system with appropriate adjustments to cope with inter-communal personal matters, such as intermarriage, would be optimal, or whether there ought to be a strict separation between religion and the state.

The key overriding guiding principles for structuring a pluralist constitutional regime regarding religion should be modeled on Spinoza's conception of tolerance as combining enhanced self-constraint with greater tolerance for the other, even if one is clearly convinced that what the latter believes and promotes is false. Moreover, as a large number of the religions and non-religious ideologies within the relevant polity may well neither share Spinoza's views or tolerance nor adhere to the precepts of comprehensive pluralism, the means toward self-constraint and toward greater tolerance of the conceptions of the good of others will have to be inscribed in the constitution or in the institutional order that it prescribes.

For example, a dominant religion may seek to spread its prescriptions and symbols throughout the realm of inter-communal dealings within a polity in which significant religious and non-religious minorities would thereby feel alienated and excluded. Thus, a Catholic majority may seek to impose the display of the crucifix in all state schools and the ban of divorce within the polity over the strong objections of proponents of other religions (that permit divorce) and of those who embrace secularism. In such a case, if the constitution were to prohibit the display of religious symbols in state schools and guarantee the right to divorce, then proponents of Catholicism would have to move toward greater self-constraint and wider tolerance.

The Catholics involved may not do this directly or of their own initiative through adjustment of their internal perspective, but rather most likely indirectly, by opting to abide by the constitution as opposed to openly defying it (which they could choose to do, but at the peril of disrupting civil order and peace within the polity).[31]

---

[30] I insist on a "prima facie" rather than a "definitive" entitlement as certain forms of atheism or certain particular religions may end up contravening in whole or part the second-order norms issuing from comprehensive pluralism.

[31] See *Classroom Crucifix Case II*, 93 BVerfGE 1 (1995); *Lautsi v. Italy*, App. No. 30814/06, Eur. Ct. H.R. (2009).

In such a case, the self-constraint would be mediated and the move toward greater tolerance legally compelled, but the result would be constitutionally fostered openness toward increased acceptability and deeper implantation of diversity with significantly diminished risks of subordination.

In contrast, in a polity with no dominant religion and with widespread harmony among proponents of various religious perspectives and their non-religious counterparts, the constitutional handling of religion could be altogether different. Consistent with this the teaching of religion and of non-religious conceptions of the good in state schools as well as the widespread display of the religious symbols of diverse religions alongside secular ones in public places would be entirely warranted within the structures of pluralist constitutionalism.[32]

More generally, to achieve a proper balance between freedom *of* religion and freedom *from* religion (both from *all* religion for secularists and from *the* religion of the *other* to be more free to practice one's *own* religion), pluralist constitutionalism should adapt Spinoza's ethos of tolerance to best fit the prevailing circumstances. This will not only require constitutionally structuring the inter-communal dealings within the polity but also introducing a measure of constitutional reach within the precincts of intra-communal affairs. This, in turn, will at once require greater respect for, and of, religion, as well as some measure of intrusion upon the latter to achieve at least indirectly the requisite levels of self-constraint and acceptance of the other. For example, under appropriate circumstances, a pluralist constitution may provide for state subsidy of religious schools, but in that case it would be proper for the state to require the schools involved to teach pluralist civic tolerance and some meaningfully adjusted version of Spinoza's corresponding ethos. At best, the religions involved will stress those internal interpretive streams that evince greater openness to the other – and all three great Western religions have produced some versions of the latter.[33] But even at worst (from a pluralist standpoint), the religions involved would be free to say that the other remains in profound error, but that he nonetheless must be treated with respect as a human being who is trying (though unsuccessfully) to lead a meaning life. For Spinoza, as discussed in Chapter 4, the possessor of reason must make allowance for even those who are led into error by adherence to mere religious superstition. In contrast, through a dialectical reversal, pluralist constitutionalism calls upon (those who perceive themselves as) holders of the true faith to leave room for those who have fallen into error because they have embraced the wrong faith mistakenly or embraced reason as their faith. In any event, regardless of the particulars, a pluralist constitution will impose some obligations on religions as well as on proponents of secular perspectives in the process of aiming for the best possible equilibrium between freedom of religion and freedom from religion.

---

[32] See Brugger 2003: 450–1.
[33] See Stone 1991; March 2009; Arkoun 1994; Vatican II 1965.

There remains one important question that pluralist constitutionalism must confront, involving the distinction made earlier between secularism as a conception of the good and secularism as it relates to the Enlightenment-based conception of science and the realm of empirical knowledge as being entrusted to the empire of reason rather than to that of faith. Can or should pluralist constitutionalism's acceptance of a relativized secularism in the realm of values extend to the realm of facts? Or, in other words, in light of post-modernism's rejection of any bright-line divide between fact and value, should relativization of secularism as a normative and value-laden perspective extend to that which is comprised within the discourse and practices of scientific discovery and empirical investigation, which have been closely associated since the Enlightenment with the secular approach?

As already pointed out, from the standpoint of comprehensive pluralism, the ignorance or even the negation of established scientific knowledge in the pursuit of one's own conception of truth by an adult in possession of his full capacities is to be fully respected (unless it were to cause great harm to others, such as contributing to the spread of a deadly epidemic). And this, regardless of the consequences, including death, that may befall an adult believer, such as one who would forgo life-saving medical treatment in the pursuit of his faith. Consistent with this, the foregoing questions should be understood here as addressing the narrower concern of whether the pluralist constitution should allow the state to privilege the discourse of science in inter-communal institutions, such as state schools, in spite of that discourse's special links to secularism.

On the surface, state promotion of the "language-game" of science, to put it in Wittgensteinian terms, may appear as amounting to the privileging of one ideological perspective over others. Some believe in evolution theory; others, in creationism. Some believe the earth to be several million years old: others, who interpret biblical accounts literally, that it is less than six thousand years old. And because of this, why not consider the prohibition on teaching evolution theory[34] to be the equivalent to the prohibition on teaching creationism in science classes?[35]

The latter question is the easiest to answer. In a nutshell, the teaching in schools is generally organized and divided in terms of various disciplines, each corresponding to a different language-games. Evolution theory, but not creationism, comes within the language-game of science. Conversely, creationism fits within the language-game of certain religions, whereas evolution theory does not. Because of comprehensive pluralism's concern with making room, whenever possible, for respect of the integrity of diverse conceptions of the good, it ought to promote, and

---

[34] Cf. *The State of Tennessee v. Scopes*, 152 Tenn. 424 (1925).
[35] Cf. *Epperson v. Arkansas*, 393 US 97 (1968); *Edwards v. Aguillard*, 482 US 578 (1987); *Kitzmiller v. Dover Area School Dist.*, 400 F. Supp.2d 707 (2005).

constitutionally back, if necessary, the delimitation of diverse language-games in state school education.[36]

The apparently more difficult question for a pluralist to answer is why give scientific perspectives priority over competing perspectives, including religious ones, with which they happen to be inconsistent. One possible answer, at least for the vast majority of contemporary constitutional democracies, is that the overwhelming majority of the population and of the various conceptions of the good – including religious ones – severally embraced within the polity accept and rely on science. They entrust their health needs to contemporary medicine, their housing and transportation needs to physics, the crops designed to feed them to biology, and so on. Moreover, all this is in spite of the disenchantment of reason and of the evils of its instrumentalization.[37] In short, assuming the claims in favor of science to be as important within the perspectives from which they issue as those against it within the perspectives that lend them support, and assuming that there is no plausible way to reconcile these opposing claims, then favoring the former over the latter is consistent with pluralism's goal to accommodate as many conceptions of the good as much as possible.

There is, however, in addition, another, more powerful pluralist answer. That answer parallels the one advanced earlier to counter any impression that the pursuit of any conception of the good may ever justify killing a person who must be eliminated pursuant to the dictates of the conception in question. Indeed, contemporary science has become indispensable for most persons to secure the essential pre-conditions necessary for purposes of being in position to choose and to pursue a conception of the good. Just as a person must have her life secured before she can seek self-realization and self-fulfillment, so too she must be able to count with existing means to protect her health, subsistence, and shelter. By affording science priority in the context of the language-games of science and empirical inquiry over those who stand ideologically against it, the pluralist constitutional order thus best enables those within the polity to secure the means to pursue the conception of the good of their choice.

5.4. THE PLURALIST CONSTITUTIONAL APPROACH TO RELIGION AS SUPERIOR TO ITS LIBERAL COUNTERPART AND AS MEANS TO UNITY AMIDST DIVERSITY

The pluralist constitutional approach to religion is superior to its liberal counterpart on three principal grounds. First, it is more empathetic toward, and more

---

[36] This latter pluralist ground is independent from any pragmatic pedagogic argument, but it does in practice complement the latter.

[37] See supra, at Introduction.

encompassing of, diverse religious and non-religious world views. Second, it deals better with secularism, by at once properly accounting for its post-modern relativization, while at the same time giving secularism its full due as a particular conception of the good standing in its own right. And third, consistent with its greater openness to, and handling of, group rights discussed at some length in Chapter 3, pluralism emerges as superior to liberalism for purposes of properly dealing with the communal aspects of religion, which happen to be of utmost importance in a vast number of cases.

Beyond the three specific grounds mentioned here, liberalism has most often carved out an awkward relationship to religion that pluralism seems well poised to avoid. Indeed because of its privileging of secularism and individualism, liberal constitutionalism – as exemplified by regimes such as those envisioned by proponents of French *laicitè* and by American partisans of a strict "wall of separation" between religion and the state (Rosenfeld 2009: 2333–4) – seems best suited to confining religion to the private sphere and to reducing all religious claims to claims to individual freedom of belief and of expression. Moreover, to the extent that prevailing sentiment within a relevant polity ill conforms to such a liberal straight jacket, the resulting constitutional jurisprudence tends to be incongruent or inconsistent. This is exemplified by judicial attempts to characterize the crucifix as a cultural symbol consistent with constitutionally mandated secularism (Mancini 2009: 2632–3) and a *crèche* display on municipal property as part of a commercial message meant to entice the citizenry to engage in Christmas shopping rather than as a religious symbol, which the state was constitutionally prohibited to endorse or promote.[38]

The American case concerning the *crèche*, *Lynch* v. *Donnelly*, a 5–4 decision by the U.S. Supreme Court handed down in 1984,[39] is particularly telling in the present context. To conclude that the display of the *crèche* on city-owned property was not violative of the U.S. First Amendment's Establishment Clause, which at a minimum forbids the state from officially preferring one religion over others,[40] the Court's majority had to overcome two daunting doctrinal hurdles. First, it had to find that the display of the *crèche* had a secular purpose and, second, that such display did not amount to an official endorsement of religion by the municipality involved.[41] To overcome the first hurdle, the Court's majority found the municipality's purpose to be secular as it regarded the placement of the *crèche* within a larger Christmas display that included Santa Claus and reindeer near the heart of the municipality's shopping district as an enticement to engage in Christmas shopping and thus

---

[38] See *Lynch v. Donnelly*, 465 U.S. 668 (1984).

[39] Id.

[40] See, for example, Cord 1982: 213–15. Others, however, have argued that the "Establishment Clause" requires a "complete wall of separation" between the state and religion. See, for example, Levy 1986: 188.

[41] 465 U.S., at 679.

inure to the benefit of local merchants.[42] Furthermore, to overcome the second hurdle, the Court's majority reasoned that display of the *crèche* did not endorse (any particular) religion any more than does inscribing the words "In God We Trust" on U.S. coins.[43]

What the Court's majority in *Lynch* ended up doing was to merge the secular and the religious or to subordinate one of the two to the other, with the consequence of causing offence to all but proponents of mainstream religion, who in the United States happen to be Christians prone to embracing a muted version of religion that blends well with principal values associated with liberalism and secularism. It is obvious that atheists and agnostics would feel left out and not taken seriously. But so would non-Christian believers, such as Jews and Muslims. Finally, even deeply committed Christians, for whom the *crèche*, which depicts the nativity, has profound religious significance, would have reason to be offended by having their religion trivialized and its sacred symbols reduced to props used for purposes of boosting retail sales (Rosenfeld 2010: 57–8).[44]

A pluralist constitutional approach, in contrast, could easily avoid all these problems. From a pluralist standpoint, the issue would not be whether the crucifix or the *crèche* could be deemed sufficiently secular or sufficiently assimilable into secular culture. The concern would be, instead, whether or not these religious symbols would be so significantly divisive as to hinder rather than promote the greater self-constraint and greater tolerance required to ensure the greatest possible accommodation of the greatest possible number of religious and non-religious conceptions of the good within the polity. In some settings, the crucifix, the *crèche*, or other dominant religious symbols may emerge as oppressive and exclusionary when officially embraced or endorsed by the state. In other settings, however, they may well have no such connotations and may therefore be promoted by the state without fostering significant divisiveness. More generally, what is crucial from the standpoint of pluralist constitutionalism is that the constitutional architecture and the constitutional jurisprudence of the polity involved be equipped so as to properly distinguish between inclusionary and exclusionary entanglements between the state and religion.

In the last analysis, pluralist constitutionalism can best reconcile the one and the many, in the context of the interface between the state and religion, through the fostering of a productive and mutually reinforcing dynamic between the community of the whole made up of the entire citizenry of the polity and the diverse

---

[42] Id. at 690.

[43] Id. at 676.

[44] In this connection, it is not surprising that some of the strongest advocates of a strict separation between religion and the state in the U.S. have been certain religious leaders. See, for example, *Testimony of J. Brent Walker, General Counsel and Assoc. Dir., Baptist Joint Committee on Public Affairs Before the Senate Committee on the Judiciary*, Federal Document Clearing House, Oct. 25, 1995.

array of particular religious and non-religious communities that apportion among themselves the totality of competing conceptions of the good at play within the polity. The community of the whole must be endowed of a national identity and of a collective imaginary (Anderson 1991: 204–6; Rosenfeld 2010: 262–3) that may incorporate explicit and/or implicit religion-based referrals. In other words, the community of the whole constitutes a self that relates to a wide spectrum of others, ranging from other communities of the whole to particular religious and non-religious communities with which it may partially identify and yet from which it must remain distinct. Much as in the example of the German Catholic feminist woman discussed previously, who as an individual self must at once incorporate her various partial selves and leave room for compartmentalization and a tolerable level of inconsistency and contradiction, the community of the whole must interact with the individual communities it encompasses so as to best secure a workable equilibrium between unity and diversity. Whether and how much religion should figure as part of the glue meant to sustain the unity of a particular community of the whole depends, of course, on the dynamic and dialectic operative in the socio-political and historical context at stake.

6

Dworkin and the One Law Principle

Can Unity Be Imposed Through an Interpretive Turn?

As presented in Chapter 4, Spinoza's conception of tolerance handles the connection between the one and the many by departing from the one and finding traces of it in the many. The one for Spinoza is established through the convergences of reason, truth, and morals, and its imprints can be found most distinctly in true religion, but even to some extent in religion that veers toward superstition. In other words, true religion provides an alternative expression of the unity fashioned by the synthesis of reason, truth, and morals, whereas other religions may be regarded as attempts to approach the unity in question no matter how wide of the mark they may actually end up being. On the other hand, the pluralist constitutional approach to the relation between the state and religion elaborated in Chapter 5 starts from the many and discovers threads of unity that furnish means of fostering peaceful coexistence among the many within the confines of a single polity. Indeed, religions and non-religious ideologies are diverse and divergent, but they are, for relevant constitutional purposes, all on the same plane and all similar in positing paths toward self-fulfillment and self-realization.

In contrast, as will be discussed in this chapter, Ronald Dworkin's famous thesis encapsulated in his steadfast assertion that there is one right answer to hard cases that defy simple logical or clear interpretive resolution starts at once from the one and the many and seeks to forge solid links between them through the deployment of legal hermeneutics. For Dworkin, unity derives from the universal validity of the equal concern and equal respect principle that will be further detailed later in this chapter. As against this, plurality emerges from the multiple competing resolutions that typically emerge in the context of hard cases. For example, to the question of whether there is a constitutional right to an abortion in the United States, many have answered in the affirmative and many others in the negative, and moreover reasons have differed among proponents as well as among opponents of abortion rights.[1]

---

[1] See *Roe v. Wade*, 410 U.S. 113 (1973); *Planned Parenthood of Southeastern Pennsylvania v. Casey*, 5 U.S. 833 (1992); Ginsburg 1985.

As will be argued, Dworkin's thesis and his hermeneutic approach to reconciling the one and the many remain firmly within the liberal camp and are ultimately monistic in nature. Moreover, whether or not one agrees that Dworkin's thesis ultimately falls short on its own terms, it seems quite clear, as we shall see, that it fails from the standpoint of comprehensive pluralism. Nevertheless, Dworkin's approach is important and instructive for purposes of further delimiting the potential scope and limitations of the search for reconciliation of the one and the many.

6.1. DWORKIN'S THESIS AND THE ONE LAW PRINCIPLE

For several decades, Ronald Dworkin has consistently insisted that there is a single right answer for every hard case (Dworkin 1978: ch. 4; 2003: 660–2). He takes this position notwithstanding numerous objections and critiques,[2] and notwithstanding his acknowledgment that pluralistic contemporary constitutional democracies have typically experienced wide-ranging disagreements concerning morals and politics (Dworkin 1978: 123–30). Dworkin's conclusion seems all the more counter-intuitive given that he does not regard legal interpretation as merely mechanical or syllogistic, but rather as hermeneutical and akin to literary interpretation (Dworkin 1986: ch. 7).

It seems at first easy to refute the one-right-answer thesis as vividly illustrated by the example of abortion already briefly alluded to. In a pluralistic democracy with a written constitution containing broadly phased liberty, equality, and privacy rights, but with no explicit reference to abortion, constitutional judges are called upon to decide whether a law criminalizing abortion violates the constitutional rights of women. Suppose further that the polity is deeply divided – some being convinced that abortion amounts to murder, whereas others consider a woman's right to have an abortion as a fundamental component of her constitutional liberty, privacy, and/or equality rights – and that the law banning abortion was adopted with the support of the barest of majorities in the parliament. Under these circumstances, both a ban on abortion (perhaps with the exception of allowing abortions necessary to preserve the life or health of the mother) and extending protection to a woman's decision to abort loom as equally plausible answers to the constitutional question at issue, thus suggesting that Dworkin's one-right-answer thesis is false for at least some hard cases.[3]

When placed in its proper context, however, Dworkin's thesis is not so easily dismissed. Indeed, Dworkin's one-right-answer thesis must be evaluated in light

---

[2]   See, for example, Munzer 1977 and Schlink 2003.

[3]   Inasmuch as constitutional judges *must* decide whether or not the Constitution protects abortion rights, the answer that the Constitution provides no answer to the question at issue cannot be the *right* answer.

of his systematic effort to reconstruct the essential features of complex advanced legal systems, in general, and of the practice of adjudication within such systems, in particular. Moreover, Dworkin's reconstructive endeavor is set against certain particular theories of law and adjudication, principally positivism, legal realism and its successor critical legal theory, and the law and economics approach championed by Richard Posner (Posner 2002) and is *grounded in* a particular political philosophy that is built on the proposition that all persons are entitled to equal concern and respect (Dworkin 1978: 180–3) and that bears a strong affinity to John Rawls's liberal egalitarian position (Rawls 1971). Finally, Dworkin is not content to confine his reconstruction to the realm of abstract theorizing but seeks instead to harmonize abstract principles and concrete practices and to integrate them into a coherent whole. Specifically, even though he likens legal interpretation to literary interpretation, he factors in the differences between constitutional interpretation, statutory interpretation, and common law interpretation, insisting that they are all compatible with the one-right-answer thesis (Dworkin 1978: ch. 4). And this in spite of the fact that statutory interpretation may be sometimes amenable to a deductive or even a syllogistic approach whereas common law interpretation requires an inductive approach that at least prima facie most often yields more than one plausible answer.[4]

By positioning himself against certain theories of law and by embracing a particular political philosophy and moral stance, Dworkin makes it much more difficult to refute his one-right-answer thesis for anyone who shares his liberal egalitarian premises. On the other hand, by turning to hermeneutics and by attempting to account for the full complexity of a common law-based legal system bounded by a written constitution with the force of law such as that of the United States, Dworkin makes proving his thesis much more challenging and elusive. Dworkin is no doubt aware of this challenge, which he has sought to meet through counterfactual reconstruction. Indeed, Dworkin acknowledges that given the complexities involved in seeking to reconcile the constitution, statutes, and relevant norms issued from the common law, ordinary judges may often be unable to discover the right answer, and may thus be relegated to choosing among several other answers over which reasonable judges may disagree. Dworkin rightly insists, however, that this does not mean that there is no right answer, and to prove his point he turns to the heuristic device of imagining a superhuman judge, whom he names Hercules, who is able to grasp all questions of legal interpretation in all their complexity and implications (Dworkin 1986: 239, 264–5). Dworkin's claim is that Hercules can come up with the one right

---

4   See Rosenfeld 2001: 1345 (distinguishing the civil law code paradigm involving deductive and syllogistic interpretation from the open-ended inductive system of common law adjudication based on the reconciliation of a body of relevant precedents).

answer for every hard case. And to prove this, Dworkin engages in a Herculean task of counterfactual reconstruction of his own. The culmination of this task is the reconceptualization of law as a principle-based unified system of regulation consistent with Dworkin's moral and political vision – what we may, in short, refer to as "the one law principle."

Dworkin's thesis amounts, therefore, to the following: If the judge Hercules counterfactually reconstructs laws pursuant to the one law principle, then there is one right answer for every legal question calling for judicial interpretation. In what follows, I will seek to demonstrate that even if one considers Dworkin's thesis in its proper context, shares his convictions concerning the paramouncy of the principle of equal concern and respect for every person, and embraces the virtues of counterfactual reconstruction, one must reject his thesis on pluralist grounds. In other words, if one takes pluralism seriously in both its factual and normative dimensions, then one must reject both the one law principle and the one-right-answer thesis. In short, if, as Dworkin asserts, law cannot be severed from morals or the good, and if there are, as Dworkin acknowledges, different conceptions of the good in complex pluralist societies such as those in the various Western constitutional democracies, then to the extent that interpreting the same law in light of different conceptions of the good (that are consistent with the equal concern and respect principle) leads to different answers in certain hard cases, there cannot be a single right answer in such cases.

To provide a more thorough account of Dworkin's thesis and of its implications for a pluralist handling of the relationship between the one and the many, Section 6.2 places Dworkin's theory in context, by comparing it to rival theories and by examining the critical distinction, he draws between principle and policy. Section 6.3 evaluates the role of counterfactual reconstruction in the context of Dworkin's theory of interpretation. Section 6.4 provides a critical analysis of Dworkin's counterfactual reconstruction of a complex legal system consistent with the one law principle, focusing specifically on his distinction between concept and conception, and on his reliance on the principle of integrity to warrant the legitimacy of judicial interpretation. Finally, Section 6.5 describes the pluralist implications of the equal concern and respect principle and contrasts Dworkin's approach to that of comprehensive pluralism to the quest for reconciliation of the one and the many.

6.2. DWORKIN, HIS RIVALS, AND THE DISTINCTION BETWEEN PRINCIPLE AND POLICY

Dworkin's legal philosophy and one-right-answer thesis arise in response to three principal movements in contemporary jurisprudence: legal positivism; legal realism, its successors critical legal studies, and post modernism; and law and economics.

Legal positivism and legal realism and its progeny reject the proposition that there is a single right answer in hard cases. Law and economics, in contrast, is compatible with the single-right-answer thesis, but is wanting according to Dworkin because it collapses principle into policy (Id.: 155–5, 286–25).

In the broadest terms, legal positivism conceives law as a separate self-enclosed realm that is severable from morals and politics.[5] Consistent with this, the validity of law depends on its pedigree, and thus if parliamentary laws satisfy the operative pedigree requirements, judges must apply such laws faithfully while deciding individual cases. This poses no problems so long as laws can be applied deductively in a syllogistic form, the law figuring as the major premise, the facts as the minor premise, and the judicial decision as the conclusion. But what if the law is unclear or open-ended? Positivists maintain that in those cases judges are given discretion, that they are entitled to act as interstitial legislators to fill gaps left open by legitimately adopted pieces of legislation. In short, for positivists, limited interstitial discretional judicial legislation can satisfy the operative pedigree requirement.

For example, if a law provides that "no vehicles, including automobiles, motorcycles or bicycles, are allowed in public parks," and if a case must resolve whether the law in question prohibits the use of motorized wheelchairs in public parks, then on the positivist view, the judge in that case has the discretion to determine whether or not motorized wheelchairs should be included among the prohibited vehicles. For Dworkin, on the other hand, there is no such discretion as the judge involved must interpret the law in question in accordance with the principle of equal concern and respect. In this case, that principle does provide an answer, namely that for a disabled person to be able to enjoy a public park on a par with non-disabled persons, he may need the use of a motorized wheelchair. Accordingly, the judge should interpret the law under consideration as not prohibiting the use of such wheelchairs.

This example may not amount to a hard case, but the latter should be in principle equally amenable to a resolution leading to one right answer by applying the relevant principles. And whereas in some hard cases, ordinary judges may not be able to ascertain the answer, Hercules will always be able to. Accordingly, the objectivity and solidity of the right answer in hard cases is akin to that of the right answer to a

---

[5] This is but a crude characterization as positivism certainly does not exclude incorporation of moral precepts such as "thou shall not kill" into law. For a nuanced positivist response to Dworkin that indicates how moral precepts may be made part of the content of law from a positivist standpoint, see Raz 1972. Although extended discussion of this issue would take us too far afield, it suffices for present purposes to specify that whereas for Dworkin there is no divide between law and morals, for a positivist law only encompasses those moral precepts that have been explicitly incorporated into it through recognized legitimate forms of lawmaking. Moreover, as positivists conceive of law and morals as different and separate practices, incorporation of a particular moral precept into law means that it will be dealt with according to the strictures of legal practice rather than those of moral practice.

difficult mathematical problem. In both cases human limitations or errors do not detract from the validity of the one right answer.

Leaving aside ontological questions concerning the relationship between law and morals, Dworkin's right answer thesis seems superior to positivist discretion, provided that certain conditions are met. Chief among these are consensus regarding, or proven legitimacy of, the principles invoked in the course of resolving hard cases and the application of the relevant principles that actually lead to a single right answer rather than to a plurality of right answers. If the first of these conditions is not met, then recourse to the principles involved would be merely arbitrary. Alternatively, if the second condition is not met, then recourse to principles would not obviate the need for judicial discretion.

Whether these two conditions are likely to be met in pluralistic contemporary constitutional democracies will be considered in Sections 6.4 and 6.5. For the moment, suffice it to note that if they are met, Dworkin's thesis is superior to that of the positivists, either because it provides a better account of what judges actually do or of what they ought to do. Indeed, if judges actually use what appears to be their discretion to decide hard cases pursuant to moral principles widely shared throughout the polity, then Dworkin's account is more accurate than that of the positivists. If, on the other hand, judges believing they have discretion decided certain hard cases contrary to what the relevant moral principles require, then their decisions are wrong, and Dworkin's theory is clearly better suited than that of the positivists to indicate what judges ought to do.

From the standpoint of legal realism and its progeny, law is inherently indeterminate, allowing for a plurality of interpretations in any particular case, and making every judicial decision ultimately dependent on something extrinsic to the legal material involved. Thus, for critical legal theory, most legal doctrines are sufficiently porous and riddled with exceptions to allow a judge to decide cases according to her political convictions, thus in effect reducing law to politics (Kelman 1981). For example, contract law consists of a series of rules and exceptions leaving enough room for judges to construe the interplay between them so as to reach the politically desired result.[6]

According to the post-modern approach as elaborated by Stanley Fish, on the other hand, law is ultimately reducible to rhetoric (Fish 1994: 152–3, 156). What judges must do, under this approach, is use the materials of legal argumentation to arrive at a decision that appears to be legal rather than moral or political and that appears consistent with prevailing doctrine whether or not it is in fact. In other

---

[6] See Unger 1983: 616–33 (characterizing contemporary American contract doctrine as shaped by a vision encompassing freedom of contract and market values and a countervision based on communitarian values and fairness).

words, what vindicates a judicial decision is the persuasiveness of its rhetoric without regard to its actual consistency with other relevant decisions or to its substantive underpinnings. Needless to say, consistent with Fish's view, there are as many "right" answers to hard cases as the rhetorical skills of judges could fathom.

Dworkin's response to these views is that law is not reducible to politics or mere rhetoric, or even if it sometimes is, it ought not be, and that it is possible for judges to insure that it is not. Specifically, Dworkin's claim against critical legal theory amounts to an assertion that law ought not be reducible to politics, and that it need not be, provided judges decide cases consistent with the principles associated with liberal egalitarian political philosophy. Again, as in Dworkin's arguments against the positivists, the force of his arguments against the critical legal theorists depends, in part, on whether appeal to relevant principles can lead ordinary judges or Hercules to the one right answer. It also depends, in part, on the validity of Dworkin's distinction between principle and policy, which will be explored more fully later. Indeed, for Dworkin law is fundamentally distinct from politics inasmuch as law unfolds in the realm of principle whereas policy does in that of politics. Thus, if the distinction between principle and policy does not hold, then Dworkin's prescription that judges decide cases in conformity with liberal egalitarian principles would amount to no more than a claim that judges decide cases consistent with a particular brand of politics. And that would not contradict the critical legal theorists' contention that law is reducible to politics.

Against post-modern theorists like Fish, Dworkin must demonstrate that legal interpretation is not reducible to mere rhetoric. Examination of Dworkin's theory of interpretation will be postponed until Section 6.3, but for law not to be reducible to rhetoric, there must be a way to establish the right interpretation or the best interpretation. Moreover, since Dworkin is neither a strict textualist (i.e., he does not believe that the meaning of a legal text derives exclusively from the "plain meaning" of the words and phrases contained in it) nor an intentionalist (i.e., he does not believe that the meaning of a text can be established by ascertaining its author's intention), it follows that he must be able to rely on a hermeneutic approach subject to intersubjective verification or approval.

Both in the context of law as politics and in that of law as mere rhetoric, judicial decision-making looms as arbitrary. It is either a mere expression of power requiring no consistency, or an expression of rhetorical power providing a mere appearance of consistency. Dworkin's principle-based approach is meant to counter the notion that judicial decision-making need in any way be arbitrary. Accordingly, Dworkin insists that judicial decision-making faithfully adhere to the principle of integrity that will be addressed in Section 6.4. Because of the complexity of contemporary legal systems, the relevant principles cannot be applied mechanically to the legal texts submitted to judicial interpretation. What is at stake through the hermeneutic binding of principles to legal texts is the unity and coherence of the system of law. Adherence to the principle of integrity is supposed to guide ordinary judges or Hercules toward the right interpretation consistent with such unity and coherence. Therefore, whether or not the principle of integrity imposes significant interpretive constraints on judges is an important factor for the success of Dworkin's hermeneutical undertaking.

According to the law and economics movement lead by Richard Posner, law in general, and judicial interpretations in particular, ought to be geared to maximizing wealth (Posner 2002). Thus, for example, if a common law judge must determine whether a manufacturer ought to be strictly liable for injuries caused by its products, or only liable in cases of negligence, the right answer is the one that would maximize wealth. In this example, this means that the judge should choose the alternative that is most efficient and least costly. If the risk of injury can be borne more economically and efficiently by the manufacturer, then strict liability is the right result. Otherwise, if it would be more efficient to place some of the risk (either because it will lead to greater care or be cheaper to ensure against) on those who may be injured, then the negligence standard would be called for. More generally, at least in principle, recourse to the wealth maximization standard should lead judges to a single right answer consistent with the factual and normative presuppositions of law and economics.[7]

Inasmuch as law and economics allows for a single right answer in hard cases, it seemingly poses a problem for Dworkin's theory. Indeed, even if positivism and legal realism and its progeny are wanting for failing to yield a single right answer, Dworkin's theory seems at best one among many that can remedy that shortcoming. If Posner's theory is as capable as Dworkin's to furnish a single right answer for hard cases, then why chose one over the other? More broadly, if both theories provide a single right answer, but in each case a different one, then the problem of legitimacy that afflicts theories that do not yield a single right answer appears to be replicated at a different level. Not only Posner's and Dworkin's theory lead to a different single right answer but so do, most likely, many others based on different religious, ideological, political, or moral visions. If that is true, then the question becomes whether a judicial choice among the various visions that, respectively, lend support to a different right answer would be any more legitimate than the positivist's discretion, the critical legal theorist's political choice, or the post-modern theorist's rhetorical choice. And prima facie at least, so long as pluralism-in-fact is firmly entrenched and there is no consensus within the polity, all the previously mentioned alternatives would equally seem to lack legitimacy.

---

[7]   But see Rosenfeld 1998: 187 (providing example of two equally efficient legal solutions to the same problem with different consequences from the standpoint of distributive justice). In any event, in a large number of cases, the law and economics approach appears to yield a single answer, and thus for the sake of argument, I will assume that it can in principle do the same for all.

Dworkin seeks to differentiate his theory from Posner's, through reliance on the distinction between principle and policy. As Dworkin specifies, "[a]rguments of principle are arguments intended to establish an individual right; arguments of policy are arguments intended to establish a collective goal" (Dworkin 1978: 90). Furthermore, based on that distinction, which is essentially a formal one (Id.), one may generally conceive of lawmaking as the pursuit of some collective goal through an allocation of certain rights (and correlative duties), and of adjudication as a matter of principle inasmuch as it is focused on interpretation of laws in terms of the specific rights and correlative duties, which they carve out for the parties before the court (and through the force of precedent for similarly situated parties). In short, assuming a common set a political and moral values and a commonly shared set of objectives, policy making will involve pursuing these as collective goals, whereas lawmaking, legal interpretation, and adjudication will consist in turning these into principles and in sorting out the particular individual rights (and duties) that these principles warrant.

Does this distinction between principle and policy sufficiently differentiate Dworkin's theory from Posner's to lend support to the conclusion that even if law and economics leads to a single answer in hard cases that answer is illegitimate because it is based on policy rather than principle? Or, in other words, because it completely subordinates individual rights to collective goals?

The answer could be in the affirmative if Dworkin's theory of principle and rights were Kantian or deontological in nature. Under a Kantian view, based on the priority of the right over the good, the equal concern and respect principle would preclude treating persons merely as means. The goal of wealth maximization pursued by law and economics does appear to put its conception of the good above the right, and it arguably always treats the individual as a means (to the greatest possible collective wealth) rather than as an end in him or herself.

Dworkin, however, does not adhere to a deontological conception of principle or right. Indeed, he declares that a "principle might have to yield to … an urgent policy with which it competes on particular facts" (Id.: 92). Accordingly, far from being lexically prior to goods, rights are to be given a weight that is measured by their "power to withstand … competition" with policy goals (Id.). Dworkin insists that "it follows from the definition of a right that it cannot be outweighed by all social goals" (Id.). What this amounts to is that, in Dworkin's view, a right is not simply reducible to a goal or policy so that it would automatically have to yield to a marginally weightier goal or policy.

This requirement is ultimately very weak. It means that a right can be overridden by important policy considerations, but not by trivial ones. In the absence of any specific quantitative standards, it would seem that consistent adherence to lawmaking and adjudication of legal disputes in the language of principle and in the form of rights would satisfy Dworkin's minimum requirements. Moreover, to the extent that Posner promotes his wealth maximization standard within the framework of common law adjudication, which results in an allocation of rights and duties, there seems to be no reason for it – or for a position that would be in all substantive respects equivalent – not to satisfy Dworkin's minimum requirements. Indeed, Dworkin himself argues that a consequentialist theory such as rule utilitarianism is consistent with principle-based rights (Id.: 95–6).

Unlike act utilitarianism, which requires that every act, including every adjudication, contribute to maximizing utilities, rule utilitarianism maintains that, overall, maximizing utilities is better achieved by adherence to rules even if certain individual applications of such rules do not themselves increase utilities. Thus, whereas in act utilitarianism all principles and rights are ultimately reducible to policy, that is not the case for rule utilitarianism for which the relevant moral criterion is whether particular rules are utility maximizing and not whether every grant of a right pursuant to such rule is. Since law and economics is consequentialist much like utilitarianism – the difference being that the goal of law and economics is to maximize wealth whereas that of utilitarianism is to maximize utilities – both can be promoted through a rule-based approach. As Posner's objective is to have common law judges articulate rules and carve out rights that will promote wealth maximization, his approach is very much in the spirit of rule utilitarianism.

To the extent that law and economics is rule oriented rather than act oriented, it cannot be distinguished sufficiently from Dworkin's theory in terms of the dichotomy between principle and policy. Instead, the two theories differ on substantive grounds: Dworkin is an egalitarian and Posner a libertarian. Therefore, unless libertarianism can be proven to be inconsistent with the equal concern and respect principle – which does not seem prima facie to be the case – then Dworkin's single-right-answer thesis depends for its validity on proof that the egalitarian vision is superior to its libertarian counterpart. Otherwise, both Dworkin's egalitarian answer and Posner's libertarian one would have to count as right answers. Whether in the end, Dworkin makes a successful case for the superiority of his egalitarian vision remains to be seen and cannot be thoroughly considered without further inquiry into Dworkin's reconstructive project and into his hermeneutics.

6.3. COUNTERFACTUAL RECONSTRUCTION AND DWORKIN'S THEORY OF INTERPRETATION

As already mentioned, Dworkin concedes that ordinary judges may sometimes be incapable of coming up with the right answer in hard cases and acknowledges that legal interpretation is neither immediate nor transparent in complex legal systems. These factors need not frustrate the one-right-answer thesis or the one law principle, however, if a persuasive theoretical justification can be provided for them. Dworkin seeks to achieve this by rising above the murky empirical trail left by everyday law and adjudication through counterfactual reconstruction centered around Hercules, the all-seeing and all-knowing superhuman judge and through a hermeneutical approach best suited to reveal the unity and coherence of a system of law as best as possible.

As already indicated, reconstructive theory based on counterfactuals can fill the gap left by empirical analysis and provide a systematic and coherent framework for analysis and evaluation. The use of counterfactuals to demarcate a gap between the reconstructed picture and the prevailing state of affairs is used by Dworkin to differentiate between Hercules and ordinary judges. Moreover, Dworkin's use of counterfactual reconstruction centered around Hercules aims both at perfection and critique of the prevailing state of affairs but is concentrated mainly on perfection, thus largely vindicating the status quo.[8] In other words, Hercules is supposed to illustrate how a perfected version of the system of justice structured like that of the United States could validate Dworkin's one-right-answer thesis and the one law principle. Under this perspective, moreover, an actual system of justice such as that of the United States and ordinary judges operating within that system have the potential of reaching the closest possible approximation to the relevant counterfactual ideal.

Consistent with this analysis, an evaluation of Dworkin's counterfactual reconstruction must revolve around two key questions. First, does the counterfactual reconstruction in which Hercules is the main protagonist mesh with the fundamental premises that underlie Dworkin's project, namely a pluralist society and adherence to the equal concern and respect principle? And, second, assuming an affirmative answer to the first question, does review of actual practices lend support to the best approximation conclusion or does it rather offer a better justification for using Hercules for purposes of a systematic critique of current practices? If the latter, then Dworkin's counterfactual reconstruction would in the end unwittingly buttress the conclusion that there is no single right answer in real-life hard cases or unity and coherence in real-life complex legal systems.

Before tackling these questions, it is necessary briefly to consider Dworkin's theory of interpretation and the place of counterfactual reconstruction within it.

---

[8] More specifically, Dworkin's theory vindicates the quo prevalent in the United States around 1970, at the end of the period of great judicial activism and great expansion of civil rights launched by the Warren Court. This is the status quo based on welfare liberalism that John Rawls's counterfactual reconstruction vindicates in his *A Theory of Justice*. See Habermas 1996: 58 (arguing that Rawls's principles of justice are grounded on the kind of welfare liberalism prevalent in the United States in the 1960s). Dworkin, however, has been a consistent ongoing critic of the U.S. Supreme Court. See, for example, Dworkin 1996: ch. 6.

For Dworkin, interpretation itself is a reconstructive endeavor aimed at grasping that which is interpreted (e.g., an institution or a practice) "in its best light" and then to "restructure it" in terms of the "meaning" that must be imposed on it for it to emerge in its best light (Dworkin 1986: 47). Law, in turn, is a social practice providing for justified uses of "collective power against individual citizens or groups" (Id.. 109). In other words, taken as a whole, law is an interpretive practice designed to determine when and where the use of coercive collective power is justified and to deploy such power consistent with its best possible justification. Ideally, all involved in law as a practice, including constitution makers, legislators, judges, law enforcers, and citizens would engage in the interpretive construction and reconstruction of law to make it the best possible, and hence channel it to its most justified uses.

Since the legitimacy and acceptability of law's coercive power depends on whether it comports with justice and fairness (Id.: 225), law's best interpretation is one that is just and fair. But because there are disagreements over what is fair and just, and because views concerning these change over time, legal interpreters must strive to cast justice and fairness in their best light and to weave a historical narrative that displays the common threads between past and present accounts of these concepts while properly accounting for significant differences.[9]

It is easy to see how the one law principle and the one-right-answer thesis fit in Dworkin's conception of legal interpretation as a reconstructive endeavor designed to reveal the unity and coherence of law in its best possible light, as consistent with justice, fairness, and the equal concern and respect principle. This would be particularly true if counterfactual reconstruction could do away with laws and legal interpretations that could not possibly become integrated within the one law principle. For example, the American Constitution condoned slavery until the adoption of the post-Civil War amendments in the 1860s,[10] and many American states had laws that institutionalized and preserved the institution of slavery. It would therefore have been impossible for someone in 1850 to reconstruct American law as an interpretive practice that comports with the equal concern and respect principle or with any plausible version of a liberal theory of justice or fairness. Counterfactually, however, the American legal system could be *imagined* in 1850 as if it had no constitutional provisions or laws legalizing slavery. But in such case, the counterfactual exercise could only serve a critical function (i.e., to highlight the illegitimacy and injustice of the then prevailing legal regime) but not a perfecting function, for no imaginable

---

[9] In its aim to capture unity and continuity in an evolving process, Dworkinian legal interpretation must be both backward and forward looking. Dworkin distinguishes his theory of legal interpretation from "conventionalism," which is purely backward looking, and from "pragmatism," which is purely forward looking. Id.: 226.

[10] See U.S. Const. Amend. XIII (1865) (making slavery unconstitutional).

interpretation of slavery laws could cast them as instances of justifiable coercion consistent with Dworkin's or any other liberal's fundamental moral premises.

Whereas the example of slavery is a dramatic one that would call on a judge to refuse to enforce the law or to resign rather than contributing to an unjust enterprise,[11] it is much less clear whether counterfactual reconstruction should integrate or do away with laws that do not fit within a liberal egalitarian vision, but that are not inherently immoral. Suppose, for example, that a constitutional amendment had enshrined the U.S. Supreme Court decision in *Lochner* v. *New York*,[12] which held unconstitutional a state law imposing a limit on the number of working hours of certain employees on the grounds that it violated freedom of contract and property rights enshrined in the Due Process Clause.[13] Pursuant to such a constitutional amendment, no minimum wage law or maximum hours law would be constitutional. Now, whereas the legal regime circumscribed by such constitutional amendment would violate the egalitarian conception of equal concern and respect, it would be consistent with its libertarian counterpart (Epstein 1992). Should an egalitarian counterfactual reconstructor ignore the amendment and the legal regime that flows from it? Or should she take them into account and elaborate the best conceivable depiction of law in a system without minimum wage or maximum hours protection?

The answers to these questions are crucial, for depending on them one of two radically different counterfactual exercises would be called for. If the reconstructive exercise is only to include those aspects of an actual legal practice that comports with a unified complete legal system that would best express the moral precepts and objectives of a given vision, then counterfactual reconstruction would yield a purely utopian ideal. Of course, in the context of such an ideal, the one law principle and the one single answer for hard cases (i.e., hard cases in the real world, but not in the ideal world)– would be easy to achieve. They would only depend on how much of the real-world legal system would have to be discarded in the counterfactual reconstruction. Moreover, even if in such ideal context there remained difficult interpretive questions in concrete cases, Hercules would be able to resolve them. In its most extreme form, therefore, this kind of counterfactual reconstruction would be equivalent to a God-given perfect and unified system of law (which in some limited respects may be approximated by some aspects of existing legal systems) interpreted by prophets who are graced with divine understanding. Such a counterfactual reconstruction, however, underscores above all that the unity and coherence it produces is humanly impossible to achieve. Accordingly, it serves as an exclusively

---

[11] See id., at 219. Dworkin indicates that judges in "wicked legal systems" have a moral duty not to enforce unjust laws or may even have a duty to resign.

[12] 198 U.S. 45 (1905).

[13] The *Lochner* doctrine was repudiated during the Depression in the 1930s. See *Nebbia* v. *New York*, 219 U.S. 502 (1934); *West Coast Hotel Co.* v. *Parrish*, 300 U.S. 379 (1937).

critical counterfactual illustrating that the one law principle and the unified and coherent legal system that Dworkin seeks are completely beyond human reach.

If, on the other hand, the counterfactual reconstructor is to take the legal system as she finds it and confine her reconstructive endeavors to unclear or open-ended issues, then it seems highly unlikely that her interpretive work would lead to unity or coherence. For example, filling gaps in a libertarian legal system with egalitarian solutions would result in a system that has neither a libertarian or an egalitarian unity or coherence. Moreover, a counterfactual reconstruction along those lines would presumably highlight above all that there are at least two plausible answers, one libertarian and the other egalitarian, in hard cases.

Dworkin's own position falls somewhat between these two extremes. His approach is best suited for counterfactual reconstruction of the common law. Since the common law develops pursuant to a gradual process of accretion based on accumulation of relevant precedents, and since existing precedents typically confine the range of interpretive choice but rarely predetermine the outcome of any case that is not identical to one already decided, both actual judges and Hercules have a vast amount of room within which to maneuver. For example, judges can privilege certain precedents over others, by according the former greater weight. They can choose among different lines of precedent, and on occasion they can even overrule precedents. Moreover, broadly phrased constitutional provisions, such as the Due Process Clause[14] or the Equal Protection Clause,[15] are remarkably amenable to a common law approach. Thus, for example, the *Lochner* doctrine mentioned earlier was overruled and abandoned by the Supreme Court in the 1930s,[16] and now minimum wage and maximum hours legislation is constitutional in the United States. Finally, even statutes are to some extent amenable to a common law approach as can be illustrated by reference to the earlier example of a law prohibiting the use of vehicles in public parks,[17] In that example, the question was whether a motorized wheelchair came within the prohibition. Assuming that a judge decides that it does not, then that decision would constitute a relevant precedent in a subsequent case dealing with the question of whether an ambulance entering a public park to take a park user who has suffered an injury to the hospital comes within the prohibition.

The common law's open-ended approach makes it highly likely both that there will be more than one plausible answer from which to choose in hard cases and that one such answer will comport with the aims of an egalitarian counterfactual reconstructor. In other words, it is possible, at least in theory, that factually there

[14]   See U.S. Cons. Am. XIV: "No person shall be deprived of life, liberty or property without due process of the laws."

[15]   See U.S. Cons,. Am. XIV: "No State … shall deprive any person of the Equal protection of the laws."

[16]   See supra note 13.

[17]   See supra, at Section 6.2.

are several right answers ("right" according to the conventions of common law practice), but that counterfactually there is only one (from the standpoint of liberal egalitarianism). And, if this is so, then Dworkinian counterfactual reconstruction would have to do much more with perfection of the status quo than with any radical critique of it.

Dworkin's conception of Hercules is consistent with this last conclusion. Dworkin does not endow Hercules with divine or prophetic attributes, but only with enhanced and expanded human capacities that clearly exceed those of any ordinary judge (Dworkin 1986: 265). Accordingly, the contrast between Hercules and an ordinary judge is somewhat analogous to that between a mathematical genius and an ordinary person with mediocre mathematical skills. Hercules, therefore, can discover the right answers and unity and coherence of an existing legal system through a process of rational completion and perfection.

Consistent with these observations, the inquiry concerning whether Dworkin's counterfactual conclusions actually mesh with his premises must be set against the background assumption that the current American legal system and its prevailing practices are by and large compatible with Dworkin's liberal egalitarian vision. To be sure, some laws and some judicial decisions may not be so compatible and are thus fair targets for counterfactual critique. But for the main part, the prevailing constitutional and legal regime should be taken as needing counterfactual perfection, but no counterfactual overhaul. That at least seems to be Dworkin's assumption and it warrants further inquiry in the course of evaluating his theory.

Before turning to that task, there remains one important point relating to Dworkin's theory of interpretation that must be briefly addressed. Dworkin analogizes legal interpretation to literary interpretation. Just as a literary critic ought to strive for the best possible interpretation of a novel, so too a judge should aim to provide (and Hercules will succeed in providing) the best possible interpretation of the law he is called upon to apply (Id.: 50, 228–39). In both cases, the goal is to discover the "best fit," though Dworkin acknowledges that the criteria are different: In literature, the criteria are aesthetic, whereas in law they are found in the realm of political morality (Id.: 239).

This analogy is unfortunate for it is either false or ultimately undermines rather than strengthen Dworkin's thesis about law. There is indeed no general consensus about aesthetics or taste, and there are many competing aesthetic theories, which would undoubtedly yield different and often incompatible "best interpretations" of the same work of art. Marxist aesthetics, for example, is different from psychoanalytic aesthetics, formal aesthetics, or classical aesthetics and is likely to yield a different interpretation of a particular novel than these other theories. Although interpretations from the standpoint of different aesthetics may overlap and be to some extent mutually compatible, they are bound to remain at least in part incongruent or incompatible. Accordingly, the notion of a "best interpretation" only makes sense within the ambit of a particular contestable aesthetic theory.

It may be that law is not analogous, and that a legal system can only be unified and coherent, consistent with the one law principle, and amenable to the one-right-answer thesis, if it is premised on the equal concern and respect principle. In that case Dworkin's counterfactual reconstruction may well provide the "best interpretation" of law. Or it may be that the analogy between art and law does hold and that Dworkin's counterfactual reconstruction is at most compelling for liberal egalitarians, but not for libertarians, contractarians, utilitarians, or any others who subscribe to the equal concern and respect principle. In the latter case, Dworkin's interpretive enterprise seems incompatible with pluralism.

6.4. EVALUATING DWORKIN'S INTERPRETIVE ENTERPRISE: MOVING FROM CONCEPT TO CONCEPTION AND LAW AS INTEGRITY

An important reason for Dworkin's interpretive turn is the need to forge coherent links between past, present, and future. Circumstances change, and it is impossible to preserve the unity or continuity of law without such links. That is why, as we have seen, Dworkin rejects purely backward-looking conventionalism and purely forward-looking pragmatism. Moreover, many links cannot be established and maintained by mechanical applications of the relevant principles. What is needed is the construction of a narrative that endeavors to capture identity and continuity amidst a continuous flow of change. The challenge for someone like Dworkin who seeks to account for the unity and continuity of law in changing times is analogous to that which confronts the individual in the context of Paul Ricoeur's distinction, discussed earlier,[18] between the self as sameness and the self as self-recognition through differences (Ricoeur 1990). Self-recognition, moreover, requires a narrative that integrates the successive periods of a life and the different experiences that have marked each of them into a coherent whole in which a sense of identity rises above all differences. Clearly, this latter process requires interpretive reconstruction much as does Dworkin's project to find unity and coherence in the life of the law.

There is another powerful reason for Dworkin's interpretive enterprise: the rule of law. It is not only that the law invites interpretive reconstruction; it actually requires it. Adherence to the rule of law depends on predictability and fairness. The rule of law demands that citizens be appraised ex ante of the legal obligations for which they will be held accountable. Moreover, the rule of law should endeavor to ensure that laws are fair. Although these two goals – predictability and fairness – are sometimes

---

[18] See supra, at Section 2.3.

in conflict, at the very least the rule of law should strive as best as possible to honor them and to reconcile them. And in order to achieve this, it is necessary to an engage in an interpretive reconstruction that binds together past, present, and future.

One way to resolve conflicts between predictability and fairness is through recourse to principle. If a predictable result is likely to be unfair, then a principled and fair result would be warranted. This would be either because in such a case achieving fairness would be more important than honoring settled expectations, or because a decision consistent with the principle at stake *ought to have been expected* even if it was not actually expected. For example, in its 1954 decision in *Brown* v. *Board of Education*,[19] the U.S. Supreme Court decided that racial segregation in public schools was in violation of constitutional equality rights notwithstanding that, in its 1896 *Plessy* v. *Ferguson* decision,[20] the Court held that state-mandated racial segregation was consistent with constitutional equality. Arguably, by the 1950s it was not morally tenable to insist that constitutional equality and the principle of equal concern and respect were compatible with forced racial segregation. Accordingly, even if *Brown* took people by surprise, they had no right to expect continued adherence to *Plessy*.

It is obvious, in retrospect, that *Brown* and its progeny provide a better interpretation of constitutional equality in the United States than does *Plessy*. Already the dissenting justice in the divided decision in *Plessy* regarded the majority's upholding of mandated racial segregation as morally reprehensible,[21] and today no one would argue that such segregation could be reconciled with the equal concern and respect principle. In short, there is at present a consensus that Brown was rightly decided, and to the extent that such consensus was lacking in 1954, Hercules should have been able to anticipate it, thus boosting Dworkin's interpretative theory.

Brown is no longer a hard case, if it ever was one for anyone who genuinely adhered to the equal concern and respect principle. But what about harder cases, such as those involving affirmative action or minimum welfare rights or minority group rights, over which there is currently considerable public disagreement? Is there a right answer for these latter cases? And will such answer lead to a future consensus? Or, are these cases inherently different, in turn raising serious doubts about Dworkin's theory?

In order to be in a better position to answer these questions, it is first necessary to focus briefly on the distinction that Dworkin draws between "concept" and

[19]   347 U.S. 483 (1954).
[20]   163 U.S. 537 (1896).
[21]   See the celebrated dissenting opinion of Justice Harlan, which included the famous dictum that "Our Constitution is color blind." 163 U.S., at 559.

"conception," and on the interpretive consequences that he draws from his conception of law as "integrity."

Some concepts including many of those such as liberty or equality, which figure prominently in constitutional law, are essentially contested ones (Gallie 1965: 167–8). Contested concepts are characterized by the fact that they find expression in competing conceptions that may be mutually inconsistent. For example, as already noted, the concept of equality encompasses rival conceptions such as the egalitarian conception and the libertarian one. Furthermore, some conceptions of equality promote the principle of equality of opportunity, whereas others rely on the principle of equality of result. In most cases, implementation of one of these principles is inconsistent with implementation of the other. Thus, an equal opportunity to compete for a position would be inconsistent with an equal entitlement to that position.[22]

Dworkin asserts that the American Constitution enshrines the concepts of liberty and equality, among others,[23] but specifies that it does not impose any particular conception of these concepts.[24] Yet judicial interpretation and elaboration of these concepts cannot be carried out, at least in hard cases, without recourse to some particular conception of such concepts. For example, whether affirmative action involving preferential treatment in education or employment comports with constitutional equality depends on whether one adheres to a conception of equality predicated on equal treatment or one that prescribes equality of result.[25] Dworkin acknowledges that there are cases that cannot be decided without resorting to a particular conception of a constitutionalized concept and suggests that Hercules must select the conception that leads to the most "satisfactory elaboration" of the constitutionalized concept at stake (Dworkin 1978: 107).

The combination of Dworkin's assertion that the constitution enshrines certain concepts, but not particular conceptions of these, with his observation that cogent judicial interpretation must at times rely on a particular conception of the constitutionalized concept at stake seems to undermine his one-right-answer thesis. Indeed, as already pointed out, the constitutionality of affirmative action under the Equal Protection Clause of the American Constitution cannot be determined without recourse to some conception or other of equality. Moreover, whereas some

---

[22]   In a purely formal sense, it can be argued that an equal entitlement encompasses an equal opportunity. In most cases, however, proponents of equal opportunity are opposed to adoption of the principle of equal result. For example, equal opportunity proponents may be convinced that equal entitlement would be wasteful, or would undermine self-reliance self-worth or human dignity.

[23]   See, e.g., Dworkin 1986: 382 (the Constitution imposes the "abstract egalitarian principle that people must be treated as equals").

[24]   Id. ("The Constitution cannot be sensibly read as demanding that the nation and every state follow a utilitarian or libertarian or resources-egalitarian or any other particular conception of equality.")

[25]   The conflict between these two conceptions has dominated the U.S. Supreme Court affirmative action cases. See Rosenfeld 1991: Cc. 7.

such conceptions are compatible with the promotion of affirmative action, others are not. Under Dworkin's egalitarian conception of equality, affirmative action is constitutional (Id.: 223–39; Dworkin 1985: ch. 14); under libertarian equality, however, it is not.[26] In other words, under Dworkin's conception of the equal concern and respect principle affirmative action is perfectly legitimate, but under a libertarian conception of that same principle, affirmative action undermines rather than bolsters equality. For Dworkin, the principle in question requires treatment as an equal but not equal treatment. Consistent with this, whereas invidious discrimination against members of oppressed minority groups involves a clear breach of duty to treat all fellow humans as equals, preferential treatment of such minorities for purposes of redressing past wrong, or of ensuring that they enjoy their fair share of society's benefits, does not imply any disregard toward any one else's worth or dignity (Dworkin 1985: 298–303). For the libertarian, in contrast, the principle of equal concern and respect prescribes adherence to the principle of equal opportunity when allocating scarce employment positions or scarce places to study at the university. This means that, in this context at least, treatment as an equal entails equal treatment, and that anyone who is deprived of an equal opportunity to complete – at least so long as he or she bears no individual responsibility for the disadvantages of those designed to benefit from affirmative action – is not genuinely treated as an equal.

The mere fact that a concept may be constitutionalized but that it may not be judicially interpreted or applied without reliance on some among many plausible competing conceptions of it seems to clearly undermine the validity of the one-right-answer thesis. Moreover, this conclusion holds for all contested concepts and not only for the most abstract ones. Thus, for example, the Canadian Constitution specifically provides for affirmative action,[27] in contrast to that of the United States. There are, however, many competing conceptions of the concept of affirmative action even if one assumes that the concept is entirely subsumed under the concept (or under certain conceptions) of equality. There are communitarian and individualistic conceptions, compensatory and distributive conceptions, and so on, that make it inevitable that there will be hard cases in which judges will have to make choices among plausible competing conceptions of affirmative action. More generally, since no constitution for a complex democratic polity can avoid constitutionalizing certain essentially contested concepts, reliance on the distinction between concept and conception undermines rather than lends support to the one-right-answer thesis.

---

[26] Libertarian equality is based on formal equality and the equal treatment principle and thus for the most part rejects all forms of preferential treatment dictated by law or imposed by government. See Rosenfeld, 1991: Ch. 2.

[27] See Canada Constitutional Act of 1982, Sec. 15 (2).

Consistent with Dworkin's systematic counterfactual reconstructive project and with the one law principle, however, the distinction between concept and conception should not be taken in isolation, out of the comprehensive interpretive context in which it is meant to be embedded. Specifically, whereas the distinction between concept and conception may not lead to a single answer in hard cases, it may do so when placed within the ambit of law as integrity. Indeed, the interpretive task of Hercules is not confined to choosing among competing conceptions, but it is much broader. It includes reconciling past, present, and future and weaving them together into a coherent narrative, giving its due to justice, fairness, and due process and reconciling the unity of the legal system taken as a whole with its manifold diversity. What is supposed to guide Hercules in this comprehensive endeavor, in turn, is the principle of integrity, which now warrants a closer look.

An elaborated by Dworkin the principle of integrity is a multifaceted one. It has a positive as well as a negative role, a legislative as well as a judicial dimension (Dworkin 1986: 176), and it can operate at different levels, including more abstract and more concrete ones.[28] In a nutshell, integrity requires consistent adherence to moral principle, and accordingly its negative role in counterfactual reconstruction is obvious: unprincipled, purely political – in the sense of advancing narrow partisan political interests – or deceitful handling of legislative or judicial responsibilities evince a lack of integrity and are ipso facto illegitimate. This negative role, moreover, is an important one in counterfactual reconstruction as critique, providing a principled basis for repudiating certain legislative and judicial outcomes as illegitimate.

The positive role of integrity, however, is much more difficult to grasp. Dworkin asserts that

> We have two principles of political integrity: a legislative principle, which asks lawmakers to try to make the total set of laws morally coherent, and an adjudicative principle, which instructs that the law be seen as coherent in that way, *so far as possible*, (Id.)

We assume that the legislative principle enunciated by Dworkin is transparent enough to provide a workable positive criterion of integrity.[29] But what about integrity as an adjudicative principle that requires interpreting law as morally coherent "so far as possible"? Is that coherent or determinate enough to endow integrity as a positive force with a sufficiently fixed or commonly accepted workable content?

---

[28] Dworkin 1986: 405 (distinguishing between *inclusive* integrity, which requires seeking integrity across all relevant fields, and *pure* integrity, which requires establishing normative coherence from the standpoint of justice).

[29] This assumption is certainly contestable as legislators just as judges operate in a complex ideologically and morally divided universe. For present purposes, however, it will do to accept it as valid in order to focus exclusively on integrity's positive role as an adjudicative principle.

To narrow the inquiry, I will assume that we are dealing with a legal system that generally comports with the equal concern and respect principle broadly understood, but that nonetheless encompasses broad ideological disagreements and a wide array of legislation and adjudications that cannot be reconciled under a single conception of the preceding essentially contested principle. Thus, the legal system in question would not include legalized slavery or apartheid as the American legal system did in the past, but it would include some legislation and adjudications compatible with a libertarian conception of the equal concern and respect principle but not with its egalitarian counterpart, and vice versa. The question then becomes whether Hercules can rise above the conflict among conceptions through positive deployment of the principle of adjudicative integrity.

Dworkin argues that integrity is needed in earthly legal systems because these cannot fully reconcile justice and fairness (Id.: 177–8). In Dworkin's view,

> Justice … is a matter of the right outcome of the political system: the right distribution of goods, opportunities and other resources. Fairness is a matter of the right structure for that system, the system that distributes influence over political decisions in the right way. (Id.: 404)

In other words, in actual polities distributive justice and a fair apportionment of powers do not always mesh. For example, it may be fair to have legislative majorities determine legislative outcomes, but there may be cases where such majorities enact unjust laws. A judge may not simply disregard this, as she should not ignore the tension between law's predictability and its fairness, or procedural due process protections (i.e., "the right procedures for enforcing rules and regulations the system has produced"[Id.: 105]) – even if these sometimes stand in the way of fairness or justice.

In the best of cases, Hercules would rely on the principle of integrity, which requires a principled and judicious attempt to give justice, fairness, due process, precedent, predictability, and justified expectations their due in a coherent reconstruction of law that vindicates the equal concern and respect principle as best as possible. Also, in the best of cases, Hercules would be able to overcome the conflict of conceptions by means of the interpretive work guided by the principle of integrity. Thus, for example, if affirmative action were constitutional under an egalitarian conception of equality, but not under a libertarian one, Hercules would be able to settle on one of these by working through the interpretive implications of the principle of integrity. In that case, moreover, both the one law principle and the one-right-answer thesis would be vindicated by combining reliance on the distinction between concept and conception and on the interpretive work called for by the principle of integrity.

This best of cases, however, cannot be more than an unwarranted leap of faith, even for Hercules, and even in the realm of cogent counterfactual reconstruction.

The reason for this, moreover, is that the principle of integrity as elaborated by Dworkin lacks sufficient positive substantive content to suggest any particular determinate outcome in hard cases. Alternatively, if the principle of integrity is to be understood in procedural terms (i.e., if judges must go through a checklist including testing for consistency and principled readings of precedents and considering all arguments presented on relevant issues of justice, fairness, and due process), it also fails to provide sufficient guidance to settle on a single determinate outcome for hard cases.

The principle of integrity's lack of sufficient substantive positive content becomes apparent if one seeks to reconcile justice and fairness in a hard case. Such reconciliation requires finding the right equilibrium between just outcomes and just or fair institutions when the two conflict. But in order to do so in a hard case, that is a case involving conflicting conceptions of what should count as a just outcome and possibly conflicting conceptions of what constitutes a fair apportionment of institutional power, integrity would have to provide criteria for sorting out substantive divergences concerning just outcomes, fair institutions, and a proper balance between the two. Suppose, for instance that by a bare majority, a legislature enacts a law that requires providing preferential treatment to members of a racial minority in public employment and that a non-minority individual who was denied public employment because of this law sues for a violation of his constitutional equality rights. Suppose further that under a libertarian conception of equality (i.e., under libertarian justice) any preferential treatment would be unjust, but that under an egalitarian conception such preferential treatment would be just so long as it promoted greater equality of result. Suppose finally, that there is a judicial precedent interpreting constitutional equality consistent with the libertarian conception in a non-affirmative action case and that the challenged preferential treatment law would not have been endorsed by a majority within the legislature but for substantial lobbying by civil rights of organizations. How could the principle of integrity guide a judge to a single right answer under these circumstances? Does integrity help resolve the conflict between conceptions? Does it help determine whether the institutional setting was truly fair? Or does it resolve what weight it ought to be given for purposes of determining the right equilibrium between libertarian justice and interest group driven democratic lawmaking? Also, what weight should an egalitarian judge give to a libertarian precedent?

It seems clear that beyond imposing the procedural requirements that a judge be principled, fair, open-minded, morally committed, and diligent, the principle of integrity does not provide guidance in answering any of these questions. Not only would a principled egalitarian judge with integrity likely decide the case differently than a similarly principled libertarian judge, but even a moderate egalitarian might reach a different conclusion than a radical one. Indeed, whereas a moderate egalitarian may with integrity provide significant weight to the libertarian precedent, the radical egalitarian might well feel that it would betray her commitment to justice to adhere to contrary and unpersuasive precedent.

Integrity as elaborated by Dworkin offers neither qualitative norms nor quantitative standards to sort through the conflicting elements pulling in different directions in hard cases. Since integrity cannot settle conflicts among competing conceptions, draw cogent boundaries between justice and fairness, or assign them measurable relative weights, nor can it determine which precedents should be followed when multiple paths are open, or to what extent plausible precedents should be followed, there are bound to be many interpretations rather one for hard cases. Accordingly, the Herculean interpretive enterprise cannot possibly lead to a single "best fit" but rather to several different plausible fits depending on the contested or contestable substantive normative commitments involved. Thus, there may be a best libertarian interpretation of the constitutionality of affirmative action and a different and conflicting best egalitarian interpretation of it. In the last analysis, therefore, the analogy between legal interpretation and aesthetic interpretation does hold as Dworkin asserts. Contrary to Dworkin's analysis, however, there are as many valid legal interpretations as there are different conceptions of justice and of fairness consistent with the equal concern and respect principle, just as they are as many "best" aesthetic interpretations as there are different plausible aesthetic theories.

6.5. CONTRASTING DWORKIN'S THEORY AND PLURALISM IN TERMS OF THE ONE AND THE MANY

The equal concern and respect principle can either be conceived in monistic or pluralistic terms. Libertarian, utilitarian, and egalitarian conceptions of that principle are all monistic in nature. They all approach the equal concern and respect principle from a single unified perspective: libertarianism from that of equal liberty; utilitarianism from that of each person's happiness being ascribed the same value for purposes of the pursuit of the greatest happiness of the greatest number; and egalitarianism from that of an operative standard of material equality, be it equality of resources, equality of result, or equality of satisfaction of every person's basic needs. All these monistic conceptions are encompassed, moreover, within the broader conception of liberal individualism. Now, consistent with the preceding analysis, to the extent that libertarianism and egalitarianism each lead to different answers in hard cases, proponents of liberal individualism cannot secure the one law principle or the one right answer for every hard case. And this holds even for Hercules, since he does not possess any actual or counterfactual means for choosing among the competing conceptions of liberal individualism.

This problem encountered in the context of liberal individualism becomes even more acute in that of a pluralist conception of the equal concern and respect principle. Such a pluralist conception is preferable to its monistic counterparts, including those subsumed under liberal individualism because it allows for a more systematic and more comprehensive realization of the equal concern and respect principle's requirement to treat every person as an equal. Indeed, whereas all versions of liberal individualism treat every person as an equal *in some respect*, pluralism seeks to do so in all respects, including in respect to every person's perspective and conception of the good. This means that not only people but also, at least prima facie, their views should be treated as equal to one another under the equal concern and respect principle. This in turn, would seem to greatly multiply the number of different conceptions in relation to which hard cases may be interpreted, thus rendering Dworkin's one law principle and one-right-answer thesis even more problematic.

Upon closer examination, it becomes apparent that the problem is not so much a quantitative one but rather a qualitative one, or, in other words, not so much a problem regarding the number of competing conceptions of the good within the polity but rather a problem concerning how to reconcile them, or to sort through them, in order to resolve hard cases.

Within the framework of comprehensive pluralism, the interpretive task is both vast and varied. It involves subjecting first-order norms to second-order norms, mediating among competing first-order norms and seeking to enlarge the intersubjective stage to accommodate as many conceptions of the good as much as possible. This interpretive task involves a dynamic process of confrontation between certain constant principles and an array of constantly evolving variables, in search of a fluid and broadly encompassing interplay. This interpretive task, moreover, must be apportioned between morals, law, and politics, envisioned as continuous, overlapping, and yet distinct domains. Finally, this interpretive task, whether applied across domains – to apportion tasks among them in view of current problems or needs – or applied exclusively within the realm of law, must be viewed as dialectical and dialogical rather than as linear. The proper metaphor for this interpretive task, therefore, is not the chain novel but dialogue and conflict mediation geared to accommodation, persuasion, and compromise.

In the last analysis, not only is the spectrum of legitimate positions recognized by comprehensive pluralism much broader than that circumscribed by Dworkin's liberal individualism, but the interpretive endeavors it calls for are much more varied and complex than those contemplated by Dworkin. Although Hercules could certainly carry out certain of these endeavors, such as evaluation of first-order norms from the standpoint of second-order norms, in ways that would lead to a single right answer, this would not be the case, even counterfactually, for others.

Two important examples can be invoked to buttress this last point. The first of these concerns the issue of membership. The overriding concern of comprehensive pluralism is to strive to achieve reconciliation between self and other. For that to be possible, it is necessary to settle questions of membership, and that is not possible in certain hard cases. One such case concerns abortion. For comprehensive pluralism to deploy its second-order norms and to attempt to reconcile first-order norms, it must take into account all the members that belong to its moral universe. The legitimacy of abortion ultimately depends, however, on the question of membership of the unborn fetus in the relevant moral universe. Under some views, the fetus possesses attributes of personhood and hence deserves membership at least for purposes of determining the question of the legitimacy of its elimination. Under other views, membership attaches only at birth, and abortion is consequently a matter that concerns the fundamental rights of women. Comprehensive pluralism depends on a reasonable consensus on membership and hence lacks criteria to resolve the issue in the context of abortion.[30] Accordingly, no judge, whether merely human or Herculean, can arrive at *the* right answer in the case of abortion.

The second example concerns the clash between two sets of first-order norms of equal importance to their respective proponents in cases in which none of these norms contravenes the dictates of second-order norms. This would be the case in a conflict between atheists and believers in God concerning public education in a polity in which neither the constitution non infra-constitutional laws offer clear guidance on the issue. In such a case, not only is there is no right answer, but it is preferable that more than one answer be acknowledged to be legitimate. The reason for this is that from the standpoint of a pluralist ethos, further dialogue and a message of inclusiveness are much more important under such circumstances than a clear-cut decision. To be sure, as a practical matter, a judicial decision may be unavoidable. But the impact of such decision could be softened through publication of dissenting opinions emphasizing the strengths and worthy aspects of the losers' position, and through dissemination of the jurisprudential insight that there are cases that must be decided notwithstanding the fact that there is no one right way to decide them.

In the end, it seems that Dworkin's one-right-answer thesis and his one law principle reconcile the one and the many through various forms of subordination, distortion, and suppression of the many. And, in contrast, it may appear that comprehensive

---

[30] For a more extended discussion of this issue, see Rosenfeld 1998: 269–74. Dworkin argues that since the debate over abortion is at bottom a religious one, the state should stay out of it and allow each person to follow his or her conscience (Dworkin 1993: 164–5). From the standpoint of comprehensive pluralism, Dworkin's solution is question begging since the issue of membership raises a crucial non-religious issue regardless of whether the debate over abortion is a religious one (Rosenfeld 1998: 270–1).

pluralism's interpretive machinery ends up dissolving all that emerges as potentially one into an irretrievable many. Upon closer examination, however, and particularly upon further focus on the two distinct interpretive approaches involved, it should become apparent that comprehensive pluralism does not sacrifice the one to the many much as Dworkin ends up subordinating the many to the one. Indeed, comprehensive pluralism takes plurality as it finds it and processes it through its constant and unified interpretive apparatus delimited by the realm of second-order norms and designed to yield a common currency facilitating comparisons among competing first-order norms. In this context, the relevant unity is located not in the result, but in the process, and it is dynamic and dialectic instead of static. Whereas Dworkin ends up at times forcing unity to foreclose a plurality of results, comprehensive pluralism welcomes such plurality so long as it has gone through its unifying interpretive process and as it is susceptible to going though it each time the dynamic among the currently prevailing many evolves.

The analysis throughout all three chapters of Part II of this book points to the conclusion that pluralism conceived as extending all the way up and all the way down can handle and harmonize the one and the many through a process that is thoroughly dynamic and dialectic. As discussed on the basis of the pluralist approach to the constitutional treatment of the relation between religion and the state, pluralism starts with the many and ends up with the many but uses a unifying process to instill upon the many an aura of coordination and mutual coexistence that was lacking at the start. Moreover, the focus on Spinoza was instructive because, although he was firmly anchored in the one, his dialectic opened the way for greater incorporation of the many. The examination of Dworkin, on the other hand, was illuminative because it underscored the seeming impossibility of reconciling the one and the many on the level of result, thus underscoring the unique importance of process in the present context.

For the pluralist process to play its unifying role, there must be a sufficient degree of openness between self and other. Without a certain measure of mutual tolerance and mutual acceptance, it would seem impossible for the disparate many to become transformed into any kind of harmoniously coexisting plurality. But how much is enough? This last question has become particularly acute in view of recent developments such as the exacerbation of the clash of cultures precipitated by the advent of global terrorism and its aftermath. In Part III, I examine the implications of these developments for the pluralist project.

PART III

Can Pluralism Thrive in Times of Stress?

On Globalization, Terror, and the Clash of Cultures

Rethinking Political Rights in Times of Stress

Can Pluralism Thwart the Progression from Stress to Crisis?

Just as most theories of distributive justice presuppose conditions of moderate scarcity, comprehensive pluralism must count on a certain degree of openness between self and other. Where there is total or near total closure between self and other, as in an imagined fight to the death between global market libertarian capitalists and jihadist religious fundamentalists bent on global terror, there is simply no room for pluralism. Both of the two ideologies at stake in this last example are presumably irreducibly anti-pluralistic, and the war of cultures that they would engender and fuel would leave no room for a pluralist ethos. There may also be little room for pluralism under times of crisis where a polity is confronting a life-threatening emergency, such as a foreign military invasion. In such a case, all those within the attacked polity must close ranks and focus on what they share in common while for the most part ignoring what may differentiate or divide them.

It is obvious that when self and other are bent on mutual elimination, there is no room for pluralism. Furthermore, as already indicated, a pluralist polity cannot countenance religious fundamentalists fixated on forcefully converting or killing the infidel, through crusades, global terrorism, or otherwise.[1] What seems much more puzzling, however, and will be the primary focus of this chapter and of the next two is whether there is room for pluralism, or whether the scope of pluralism must significantly retreat, in the face of an anti-pluralist assault, such as that triggered by global terrorism against those otherwise accustomed to a fair degree of openness between self and other. Significantly in this respect, the September 11, 2001, terrorist attacks on the United States and their aftermath leading to the United States' "war on terror" did not pose an existential threat comparable to that justifiably dreaded in the face of a plausible nuclear confrontation with the Soviet Union during the Cold War. Nevertheless, following the September 11 attacks, the United States set to restrict civil liberties and to narrow the scope of tolerance in the pursuit

---

[1] See supra, at Introduction.

of greater security through, among other things, the adoption of the Patriot Act,[2] the creation of military commissions to circumvent key protections afforded criminal defendants in civilian tribunals,[3] and the deployment of massive surveillance largely without judicial oversight.[4] Similarly, other countries, such as the United Kingdom also adopted extraordinary measures, such as derogating from the protection of certain rights under ECHR.[5]

Whereas the terrorist threat, whether it originates from within or from without the polity, must be fought – and on this point there are no significant differences between liberalism and pluralism – there is a serious question as to whether the pluralist ethos is desirable or achievable in relation to the interplay between identities and differences among those who do not embrace the terrorist cause but who must live with the terrorist threat and the polity-wide mobilization to combat it. To thoroughly explore this latter question, this chapter will concentrate on the proper place and limits of political rights in a constitutional democracy that confronts challenges such as those triggered by the terrorist threat. The choice of political rights seems particularly apt for the purpose at hand, given that self and other must directly negotiate with one another the optimal apportionment of identities and differences in the political arena, and that the prevailing political rights that they can avail themselves of are bound to circumscribe the scope of available options and to pave the way to productive compromises. In Chapters 8 and 9, I will deal with the broader ethical challenges posed by global terrorism, through a critical appraisal of the post-modern account provided by Derrida (Chapter 8) and the modern assessment elaborated by the Habermas (Chapter 9).

7.1. A PLURALIST CONCEPTUAL FRAMEWORK FOR POLITICAL RIGHTS

It is hardly clear which rights should qualify as political, much less which political rights should be deemed indispensable when confronting terrorism or more generally in what can be labeled "times of stress." In a narrow sense, political rights are distinct from civil rights and from social and economic rights. Of the fifty-three articles of the UN's International Covenant on Civil and Political Rights, only two deal strictly speaking with political rights. Article 25 grants citizens an individual right to political participation that boils down to the right to vote and the right to be eligible for elective office. Article 1, in turn, provides a collective right entitling peoples to self-determination, that is to "freely determine their political status and freely pursue

---

2 See *Hamdi v. Rumsfeld*, 542 U.S. 507, 551 (2004).
3 See Yin 2007: 874.
4 See id., at 931–2.
5 See McGoldrick 2004: 409.

their economic, social and cultural development." The collective right seems as broad as the individual right seems narrow, but if one places the latter in its proper context it only remains meaningful so long as it is inextricably linked to a significant bundle of other rights. Indeed, voting and eligibility for public office are valuable above all as means to participate in, direct, or lead the public affairs of one's polity. But to do so meaningfully and effectively, one must be informed and able to assemble with others, organize interest groups and political parties, and possess sufficient resources to make one's voice heard, among others. In short, in the broad sense, political rights encompass a wide array of rights ordinarily categorized as civil rights, such as freedom of expression, association, assembly, equality, privacy, and dignity. Furthermore, if political rights are understood not only as rights of participation but as rights of *effective* participation, then their realization may depend on vindication of some social and economic rights. Indeed, only an educated electorate that is adequately housed and fed can fully and effectively exercise its right to participate in its polity's process of self-determination.

"Times of stress," on the other hand, are neither ordinary times nor times of crisis. In the context of a crisis, be it military, economic, social, or natural, the head of government may be entitled to proclaim exceptional powers and to suspend constitutional rights, including political rights. In an acute crisis, the polity is singularly focused on survival and all other political concerns and objectives recede into the background.[6] In contrast, in ordinary times, the polity can readily absorb the full impact of the give and take of everyday politics, and political rights as well as other constitutional rights ought to be protected to their fullest possible extent.

Times of stress differ from those of crisis primarily in terms of the severity, intensity, and duration of the respective threats involved. The line between the two may be difficult to draw, but a less severe, less intense, and more durable threat is likely to give rise to times of stress, whereas a severe, intense, concentrated threat, of relatively shorter duration, is likely to provoke a crisis. For example, a foreign military invasion or a widespread domestic insurrection is likely to provoke a crisis. On the other hand, the aftermath of the terrorist attacks such as those against New York City on September 11, 2001, or Madrid on March 11, 2004, or London on July 7, 2005, or Mumbai on November 26, 2008, which may involve threats, perceived threats, launching a "war on terror" fought mainly in far away countries, arrest and detention of potential terrorists, but no further comparable terrorist attacks on those countries as of the time of this writing, has produced times of stress rather than times of crisis.[7]

---

[6] The grant and duration of exceptional emergency powers are problematic not in relation to their proper use as a means to combat threats to the life of the polity, but in relation to the potential for abuse in the invocation or prolongation of such powers. See Ackerman 2004.

[7] It is important, for example, to distinguish the long-term aftermath from the immediate impact and short-term consequences of the September 11 attacks. Indeed, the day of the attacks, which resulted in

Should political rights in times of stress fall somewhere between political rights in times of crisis and those in ordinary times? Should political rights in times of stress be the same as those prevalent in ordinary times, but be protected to a lesser extent than the latter? Should there be any special political rights for times of stress?

Cogent answers to these questions depend on an adequate handle on the nature and function of political rights in contemporary constitutional democracies. Given the dichotomy between political rights in the narrow sense and in the broad sense, and given the multiplicity of conceptions of, and the diversity and complexity of configurations of, contemporary constitutional democracies, however, a full analysis of all the plausible alternatives would take us too far afield. To render the task more manageable, therefore, I will tackle political rights from a pluralist perspective and a pluralist conception of contemporary constitutional democracy. Eschewing the distinction between political rights in the narrow or broad sense, I consider those rights – or those aspects or applications of those rights – as political rights that are indispensable for citizens either to run their polity or to benefit from (and/or not be unduly hurt by) the way in which their polity is run. My pluralist conception of contemporary constitutional democracy, on the other hand, is oriented to preserving and fostering pluralism through a constitutional framework that aims at a proper balance between majoritarian and countermajoritarian institutions.

What links the present approach to political rights and to constitutional democracy is a focus on their inherent dynamism and functionality. In this context, the paramount task is to cope with the evolving and shifting tensions between identity and difference – or unity and diversity – that confronts all pluralistic polities. Such polities must constantly strive to cope with conflicts between the need to maintain or promote sufficient unity, on the one hand, and the need to accommodate broad enough diversity to allow for optimal coexistence among adherents of competing conceptions of the good, on the other. Accordingly, political rights are those that relate to the conduct of the affairs of the polity as mediated by a constitutional system that allows for harmonization of key elements of unity and of diversity through a dynamic interplay between majoritarian and countermajoritarian processes and institutions.

To allow for a systematic examination of the nature, role, and place of political rights within a pluralistic conception of constitutional democracy, I will articulate the broad outlines of the conceptual framework within which the inquiry into political rights will be carried out in the remainder of this section. First, I will focus on the theoretical underpinnings of the pluralist conception of constitutional democracy

---

around 3,000 deaths, and subsequent days in which the American nation had to cope with the shock of the sudden and unexpected attacks and with the prospect of the imminence of further such attacks can be characterized fairly as a time of crisis. The long period of disquiet that followed those first few weeks, however, is better described as one of stress than of crisis.

by building on the discussion in Chapter 5 and exploring the proper role of the political in a pluralist polity in which the citizenry both divides and coheres along the cleavage between self and other; I will then situate constitutional democracy within a pluralist perspective and assess the relevance of the distinction between negative and positive political rights as viewed from the said perspective; and, finally, I will further detail he differences between ordinary conditions, times of stress, and times of crisis as they emerge within the confines of the pluralist vision.

The remainder of the chapter will be divided as follows. Section 7.2 will build on the analysis made in Chapter 3, and focus on the three principal approaches to constitutional democracy, namely the liberal, republican, and communitarian approach, each of which justifying a different configuration of, and role for, political rights. Each of these approaches and the political rights it fosters will be compared to the others and critically assessed from a pluralist standpoint. Section 7.3 will explore the nature, function, and derivation of political rights in a pluralist democracy. Emphasis will be placed both on how constitutional democracy itself may imply political rights that are not explicitly constitutionally protected and on the political dimension of protected constitutional rights that are not political in the narrow sense. Finally, Section 7.4 will concentrate on political rights in times of stress through examination of issues arising out of the war on terror, the limits of tolerance, militant democracy, and the prospects of peaceful and constitutionally sanctioned secession.

7.1.1. *Constitutional Framework and Pluralist Politics*

In Aristotle's famous dictum, man (today we would say the human being) is a political animal (Aristotle 1946: I.2. 1253a). Human beings are thus supposed to be immersed in the affairs of their polis and to pursue their well-being and realization of the good through wise and virtuous stewardship of their city-state. In a democracy, moreover, it is all the citizens, rather than one or a few of them that are called upon to determine the political course of their city-state. In other words, in a democracy, citizens must rule for themselves, and in modern parlance, they must possess the rights necessary to permit self-rule without undue impediments or constraints.

What political rights are necessary for successful self-rule depends on whether there is a commonly shared conception of the good or whether citizens within the polity are divided over what constitutes the good. As stressed throughout, in all contemporary constitutional democracies individuals and groups disagree over *the* good. In pluralistic polities, therefore, politics and political rights are concerned not only with implementation of the common good but also with handling conflicts among proponents of competing conceptions of the good. Accordingly, pluralistic polities must determine what good ought to be pursued in the interests of the citizenry as a whole.

From the standpoint of the institutional structure of a pluralist polity, comprehensive pluralism's second-order norms determine the constitutional framework, provide a substantive normative criterion for assessing or designing a working constitutional order, and circumscribe the normative space for constitutional politics. In terms of actual constitutional essentials, pluralist constitutionalism shares much in common with its liberal counterpart: They both require limitation and division of powers, adherence to the rule of law, and protection of fundamental rights (Rosenfeld 1994: 3). The differences between the two, some of which will be addressed in greater detail later, are most apparent when focusing on details or limits. For example, as already examined in Chapter 4, pluralist tolerance is different from liberal tolerance, and hence the scope of pluralist freedom of expression rights is likely to differ from that of its liberal counterpart. Similarity, as discussed in Chapter 3 the mutual relationship between individual and group rights is bound to differ as pluralism does not share liberalism's bias toward individualism.

In the pluralist context, constitutional politics based on the operation of second-order norms on the polity's institutional design and its deployment boil down to two principal tasks: (1) Engaging in constitutional design through application of the relevant second-order norms to the particular circumstances of the polity involved; and (2) determining which subjects ought to be entrusted to the realm of constitutional politics, and which to the realm of ordinary politics.[8] Concerning the first of these two tasks, pluralism's second-order norms do not dictate all constitutional particulars. For example, whether a constitution ought to establish a federal or a unitary republic depends on the actual make-up of the polity in question and on the actual spread of conceptions of the good represented within it. For example, in a polity made up of different religious, linguistic, or ethnic groups, each living within its own discrete geographic area, identity-based federalism may optimize equalization and mutual accommodation of existing conceptions of the good.[9] Sometimes it may be obvious which constitutional institutions would be optimal for all conceptions of

---

[8] The distinction between constitutional and ordinary politics is one drawn by Bruce Ackerman to distinguish between politics motivated by the good of the polity as a whole and politics motivated by narrow self-interests (Ackerman 1991: 12–13, 261–2, 265). In contrast to Ackerman, I use this distinction to underscore the difference between what the second-order norms of comprehensive pluralism require be inscribed in the institutional design of the polity or protected from majoritarian politics and what ought to be left to infra-constitutional political competition subjected to majoritarian decision-making processes. In other words, in my conception, it is the dictates of the second-order norms, not the perceptions and intentions of political actors, that inform the distinction between constitutional and ordinary politics.

[9] "Identity based federalism" is designed to allow for significant autonomy and self-rule for a group with a strong common identity that differs sharply from that of the polity as a whole. In contrast, "distributive federalism" refers to vertical divisions of power designed to empower regional and local majorities

the good concerned, and sometimes it may not be. Particularly in the latter cases, it is important that proponents of competing conceptions of the good be politically empowered to participate in constitution making and in the constitution-amending processes necessary to accommodate, consistent with the relevant second-order norms, changes in the balance of powers among existing conceptions of the good.

Concerning the second of the previously mentioned tasks, on the other hand, which subject should be entrusted to constitutional politics and protection, and which to ordinary majoritarian politics, cannot in many cases be determined from a mere consideration of the dictates of pluralism's second-order norms. Such determinations may depend on the range of conceptions of the good represented within the polity or on choices among a range of plausible interpretations of the implications of the relevant second-order norms. For example, whether linguistic rights should be inscribed in the constitution or left to parliamentary majorities is not self-evident from a pluralist standpoint. The answer may depend on the circumstances. For example, the linguistic claims of Korean immigrants in the United States seem less compelling than those of the French-speaking population in Quebec or the Flemish-speaking population in Belgium.[10] What ought to be included and what excluded from the realm of the constitution is itself a matter of constitutional politics framed by the constraints of the second-order norms of pluralism. Consistent with this, the polity must guarantee political rights of participation in the constitutional politics pursued to settle on which subjects to constitutionalize and which to leave to parliamentary politics.

7.1.2. *Political Rights and the Struggle Between Self and Other*

Comprehensive pluralism calls for political rights relating to constitutional politics and to ordinary politics. Before dwelling any further on whether or how they differ and on what they may actually consist of, however, it is necessary briefly to examine how the realm of political relationships (both constitutional and ordinary) is circumscribed from the standpoint of comprehensive pluralism. In the context of competition among a plurality of distinct conceptions of the good, proponents of the same conception can regard their common beliefs, practices, customs, and objectives as those of a coherent *self* competing against those who do not share these and who with varying degrees of vehemence actually oppose them. The latter, in turn, constitute the *other* that stands against the self identified earlier. Viewed thus, moreover,

---

for certain purposes relating to distribution of societal benefits or burdens though the regional or local groups involved have no identity issues with the polity as a whole. See Dorsen et al., 2010: 385.

[10] Korean speakers enjoy no special linguistic rights under the U.S. Constitution, whereas both English-speaking and French-speaking Canadians have linguistic rights enshrined in their constitution. See Constitution Act of Canada, 1982, Sections 16–23.

political relations are the external relations between a self and another that share a common historical trajectory within a particular geographic space.[11]

Self and other are understood here in a fluid, relational sense. For example, Catholics and Protestants in Northern Ireland relate as self and other; so do French-speaking Quebecois and Anglophone Canadians; Democrats and Republicans, in the United States; and ethnic Hungarians and the rest of the population in Romania. Not only do these examples refer to splits along different divides (respectively, religious, linguistic, ideological, and ethnic) but also the individuals and groups involved can belong at once to different political selves and others and the boundaries between self and other can shift so that former others can become members of the same collective self and vice versa. Thus, for example, individuals who belong, respectively, to the Democratic and Republican Party in the United States are bound to relate as self to other in a presidential election, but they group themselves as a single self in relation to the kind of Islamic fundamentalism that stood behind the attacks of September 11, 2001. For her part, as will be remembered, the Catholic German woman referred to on numerous occasions in the preceding discussion belongs to many intersecting selves confronting an equal number of intersecting others at the levels of country, religion, language, ideology, and so forth.

Relationships of self as against other also occur, as already pointed out, within a single group. Take, for example, the case of Catholic gays. Whereas the Catholic Church rejects homosexuality, it purports to exclude the lifestyle involved, but not the person engaged in it. According to Catholicism, the homosexual is a sinner, but so are all humans, and the Church is compassionate and makes room for eventual repentance and redemption of all sinners. Does that make a Catholic gay an insider or an outsider? It may depend on the degree of alienation experienced by the gay person or group involved. At least some gay Catholics have sought to remain within their religious community and to influence it to becoming more accepting of their lifestyle. Accordingly, some gay Catholics have argued that the Church should accept homosexual sex though it does not lead to procreation just as it recognized the validity of marriage and sex among sterile heterosexual couples (Macedo 1995: 275; Weithman 1997: 238; West 1997: 1328). More generally, self and other and different conceptions of the good need not be impermeable to one another. Issues such as that of women or gay priests in religions where the priesthood traditionally has been the exclusive preserve of heterosexual men have been divisive, and have in certain cases cast the feminists or gays involved as others within their own religious community. In other cases, however, the religion involved has adjusted and accepted

---

[11] Legal relations are also external relations among selves and others, and as such constitute a subset of political relationships. For a discussion of the similarities and differences between legal and political relations, see Rosenfeld, 1998: 76–8.

women or gays as priests. In the latter cases, certain conceptions of the good have evolved, blending with, or incorporating, aspects of other such conceptions.

In spite of the complexity and fluidity of the relationships between self and other, and between conceptions of the good, pluralist political rights can be boiled down to the following. These rights are meant to regulate the external relationships between self and other (or more precisely, others, for although at some level all that is not self is other, in political terms, different others may pose different threats or challenges, e.g., a particular religion may face threats from other religions that are different from the threats from secular ideologies) in such a way as to equalize and accommodate as much as possible the position of self and other within the polity consistent with adherence to the second-order norms of comprehensive pluralism. Because in any complex and diverse society there are many overlapping and shifting selves and others, the political order and political rights must allow for a proper balance between unity and diversity. A polity cannot survive as such within the context of constitutional democracy unless all its constituents can identify at some level as belonging to a single political self. In some sense, all those who belong to the polity must combine into a self that stands against all those who do not belong to it and who, for this purpose, constitute the other. The bond of identity involved at the polity-wide level may be profound and deeply lasting, as in the case of a culturally, ethically, and religiously homogeneous group that has shared the same geographic space over a long period of history. Or, the bond in question may be relatively shallow and fragile, as in the case of a number of disparate groups with different traditions coming together to organize into a single polity for purely external reasons, such as to better be able to defend themselves against a common enemy, or to better compete in global markets.

All individuals and groups within the polity must invest something of themselves into the polity-wide self in order to forge a common identity. At the same time, all those within the polity must protect against allowing the common polity-wide self to unduly threaten or eradicate their more particular identity as a self among others within the polity. Americans who are Catholic, Protestant, Muslim, Jewish, Hindu, or who follow some other religion must reach across religious boundaries to constitute a single political community of citizens of the United States, but each of them will want to do so in a way that does not undermine the life of her religious community within the polity. To best achieve this may require the grant of both positive and negative political rights: positive rights to participate at the constitutional and infra-constitutional level in the politics of the polity as a whole, and negative rights to shield at least certain aspects of communal life and individual life from intergroup politics.

Positive and negative rights are understood here also in relational terms. For example, a religious group may have a negative right against the state requiring that the latter refrain from intervening in that group's internal affairs. At the same time, that group could have a positive right to both organize its institutional life and to impose its norms on its members. Moreover, the arena for the combined negative and positive rights involved here could be a governmental one – if the religious group were large enough and gathered in a geographically contiguous area, it could become a federated unit within a federal polity – or a non-governmental one – in case such group could function as an NGO.[12] Finally, a dissident member of a self-governing governmental or non-governmental group would have a negative right vis à vis that group, which may amount to a right of exit. Moreover, such dissident would also have a positive right of participation in relation to the formation of a new group or to active adhesion to another existing group.

From the standpoint of the dialectic between self and other that animates the politics of the pluralist polity, there is an important distinction between policies that impact on the very identity of self or other and policies that apportion benefits and burdens among the two. In other words, there are policies that threaten the very survival or integrity of a conception of the good and others that merely somewhat advance or hinder the implementation of its societal project without affecting it at its core. Upon close inspection, it becomes apparent that there is no bright line between identity-related policies and benefit/burden-related ones. For example, a complete deprivation of all material resources from an organized religion would threaten its very identity. Indeed, whereas such deprivation would not directly aim at that religion's dogma, beliefs, or worldview, it would make it impossible for the religion in question to carry out basic education and group-worship functions that may be essential to its survival. Consistent with this, whether a benefit deprivation also results in an identity-related deprivation is a matter of degree.

In most cases, however, the distinction is workable. For example, a law that prohibited male circumcision would clearly seem identity-threatening for the Jewish and Muslim communities within the polity, as circumcision constitutes an essential link in the covenant between God and Abraham. On the other hand, the deprivation involved in the *City of Boerne* case decided by the U.S. Supreme Court[13] in no way seems identity-threatening. In that case, a landmark preservation law that prevented Catholic religious authorities from expanding a church building to accommodate an expanding community of the faithful was upheld. While the law

---

[12]   In the case of the NGO, the negative and positive rights involved are arguably non-political. A right to be left alone by government and free to organize a religious community may appear to be a civil rather than a political right. Functionally, however, there seems little difference between self-organization and self-government as a federated entity or as a powerful NGO with virtually complete control over its internal affairs. In both cases, the rights involved are quite different from paradigmatic civil rights, such as the right to own private property.

[13]   *City of Boerne* v. *Flores*, 521 U.S. 507 (1997).

inconvenienced Catholic group worship in the local area, such burden is hardly identity-threatening.

Ideally, identity-related politics should be relegated to the constitutional level, and benefits/burden-related politics to the infra-constitutional one. From a practical standpoint, two difficult issues arise: (1) the already mentioned problem of benefit/burden-related politics that significantly threaten self identity; and (2) identity conflicts between self and other, such as that policies that are identity-reinforcing for self are identity-threatening for other and vice versa. In such a case, conflicts must be resolved according to the dictates of pluralism's second-order norms (at the constitutional level) and in relation to a comparison of the respective hierarchy of values within each self and other. In other words, if the competing identity-related claims of self and other are equally legitimate under the relevant second-order norms, then they should be compared in terms of the hierarchy of norms of each and be resolved in proportion to the relative identity-threat to each. Thus, if the threat to self is clearly greater than that to other, then self should be favored over other, but if the threat to other is greater, then other should be favored over self. Institutional mechanisms of resolution for such identity-related conflicts among competing conceptions of the good must be available within the political sphere. But whether these should operate at the constitutional or infra-constitutional level and what political rights would better serve their purposes are matters that depend on the particular circumstances involved.[14] Because of this, these issues will not be pursued further here. They will be mentioned when appropriate in the course of the following discussion.

7.1.3. *Pluralism and the Distinction Between Ordinary Times, Times of Crisis, and Times of Stress*

The distinction between ordinary times, times of crisis, and times of stress briefly sketched earlier can be further elaborated consistent with the pluralist conception of politics as the ongoing confrontation between self and other. In ordinary times, conflicts between self and other do not threaten the unity of the polity and find resolution, or at least confinement, within the existing constitutional, institutional, and political framework. Thus, in spite of the fact that a number of struggles relating to identity and to the apportionment of benefits and burdens throughout the polity split the citizenry into a multiplicity of selves pitted against numerous others, the common self that binds all citizens to the unity of the polity remains glued together

---

[14] On the theoretical plane, conflicts among equally legitimate claims launched respectively from the standpoint of competing conceptions of the good can be resolved through implementation of the previously mentioned criterion of "justice as reciprocal reversibility," which allows for comparing the intensity of the respective claims and for resolution in terms of their respective centrality. See supra, at 56, 80–81.

and shows no danger of unraveling. For such overall common identity to remain secure, no significant group must feel so alienated or excluded from the political life of the polity as to seriously consider abandoning adhesion to the self that binds together the citizenry as a whole. For all groups concerned firmly to adhere to the indivisibility of the polity, the conception of the good of each must be sufficiently integrated and accommodated within the polity that they can generally accept the resolution of identity and benefit/burden conflicts within the existing constitutional and political order as capable of meeting the requisite minimum degree of justice and fairness. In ordinary times, neither self nor other are fully satisfied with their fate and are likely to struggle continuously to ameliorate their respective position. Neither of them, however, is likely to become so dissatisfied with his or her status or with the existing institutional framework for processing conflicts as to want to withdraw from the polity.

Times of crisis, in contrast, occur when the common identity or the very life of the polity are in imminent peril. The cause of the peril may be external, as in the case of a foreign war, or internal, as in the case of civil war or violent secession. In times of crisis, the conception of the good of self or other is so little integrated or accommodated within the polity that all possible institutional resolutions of the conflict between self and other will strike one or both of them as deeply unsatisfactory and unjust.

As already pointed out, times of stress stand halfway between ordinary times and times of crisis. In times of stress, there is less extensive and less successful accommodation and integration of significantly represented conceptions of the good. Self and other are less likely than in ordinary times to consider institutional process of conflict resolution to be just or fair. The identity or unity of the common self that is supposed to bind together the citizenry is not disintegrating, but it is destabilized and under various pressures. Whereas violent secession creates a crisis, a push for peaceful secession is likely to put the polity under stress. Whereas the threat to overthrow a democratically elected government seems bound to result in a crisis, the increasing popularity of a non-democratic party within a democracy is likely to cause stress. Whereas a conventional war may cause a crisis, terrorism and the war on terror seems more likely to create stress. Indeed, unlike a military invasion, terrorist acts are likely to be sporadic and widespread causing more psychological than physical harm. Having terrorists hidden within the polity's population would undoubtedly be unnerving and can easily lead to reactions and overreactions, undue suppression of fundamental rights or exacerbation of ethnic or racial prejudice such that certain selves and the conceptions of the good they endorse may become increasingly unhinged. At some point erosion of accommodation of certain conceptions of the good may place increasing strain on the working unity of the polity's citizenry.

Further inquiry into the effect of conditions of stress on political rights will be postponed until Section 7.4, in order to focus on the role of political rights in contemporary constitutional democracies.

7.2. LIBERAL, REPUBLICAN, AND COMMUNITARIAN APPROACHES TO CONSTITUTIONAL DEMOCRACY AND POLITICAL RIGHTS

Liberalism, republicanism, and communitarianism are complex comprehensive conceptions, and there are many variants within each of them. It is therefore well beyond the scope of the present undertaking to do justice to their respective views regarding constitutional democracy or political rights, but that is not what is called for here. Instead, I shall approach these comprehensive conceptions from a heuristic standpoint for purposes of sketching out their contrasting approaches to constitutional democracy and politics. These contrasting approaches are rooted in the respective overriding values of each of these comprehensive conceptions, and, as we shall see, bear significant relevance to a pluralistic approach to constitutional democracy and politics. Indeed, though comprehensive pluralism rejects the overriding nature of the paramount values of liberalism, republicanism, and communitarianism, it does have room for them, with some limitations and modifications, within its own dialectical framework.

7.2.1. *Liberalism's, Republicanism's, and Communitarianism's Overriding Values and Pluralism*

As already repeatedly noted, liberalism is individualistic as it primes the individual over the group. Its overriding values are individual liberty and equality, and its principal aim is to optimize the chances of reaching a proper equilibrium between individual autonomy and individual welfare. For libertarians, such equilibrium may be best achieved through extensive liberty and private property rights together with formal equality rights. For welfare-egalitarian liberals, on the other hand, substantive equality and positive welfare rights may be necessary even if they limit negative liberty and property rights. Beyond these differences, however, at a higher level of abstraction, liberalism is pluralistic-in-fact, and its ultimate goal is to promote the best possible conditions for individual self-realization. Consistent with that, moreover, the principal objective of the liberal polity is to promote the most extensive possible equal opportunity for individual *self-realization*.

For republicanism, in contrast, the overriding value is *self-government*. Leaving aside, for the moment, whether republicanism is compatible with pluralism-in-fact, for our purposes the principal difference between the latter and liberalism relates to a shift in the locus of the conflict between self and other. For liberalism, the conflict is between individual selves and individual others with clashing self-interests and life plans. The liberal polity, in turn, is supposed to provide appropriate rules and conditions consistent with respect for individual liberty and equality that make for fair competition between self and other in their respective and in most cases antagonistic quest for self-realization. Republicanism, on the other hand, requires subordination of individual self-realization to deliberative self-government. This emerges clearly in the context of Rousseau's republicanism, in terms of the distinction he draws between the private individual (*bourgeois*) and the public citizen (*citoyen*) (Rousseau 1947: 14–16). For Rousseau, each person is both part of the governed and of the governors, a private individual with particular desires and notions of self-interest and a public citizen obligated to join with fellow citizens to govern the polity according to the dictates of the "general will" (Id.). Within this vision, the conflict between self and other is not a conflict *among* individuals, but rather a conflict *within* each individual. The conflict between self and other is that between the *bourgeois* and the public citizen within each of us, between the private person's self-interested particular will and the public citizen's obligation to govern herself and help govern others by imposing the polity's general will above the clash of particular wills. Whereas the notion of the "general will" advanced by Rousseau remains mysterious – he characterizes it as the sum of differences between all the individual wills or as the "agreement of all interests" that "is produced by opposition to that of each" (Id.: 26 n. 2) – it is clear that self-government must achieve priority over self-realization. Thus, the political self within each of us must prevail over our private self (which for purposes of self-government must be cast as the other or as one other among many others if we take account of the fact that all public citizens are also private persons). In short, civic virtue must prevail over self-interest.

For communitarianism, community is paramount, and *communal solidarity* is the overriding value. For communitarians, moreover, the self is the community and the other is that which lies outside the relevant community. The communities in question may vary in their composition, origin, ideology, and so forth. They may be national, ethnic, or religious communities or primarily socio-political ones, such as communes or kibbutzim. Once again, I leave aside for the moment whether communitarianism is compatible with pluralism. What is essential is that, for communitarianism, the other is always "outside". Most obviously, the "others" are other communities. However, to the extent that an individual within a particular community departs from communal values and objectives, he or she becomes, at least in part, an "other" vis à vis his or her own communal self. In other words, the dissident individual places herself, "outside" her community. Unlike a deficiency in civic virtue in the context of republicanism, which involves some failure to curb or dominate one's *own* self-interest or particular will, dissent from one's community is more like betrayal, as it involves a breach of communal solidarity (and hence implies some kind of loyalty to some "outside" rival community).

It is now time briefly to address whether and to what extent liberalism, republicanism, and communitarianism may be compatible with pluralism. As already noted, liberalism is pluralistic-in-fact. From a normative standpoint, moreover, liberalism is *individualistically* pluralist. As already emphasized, however, liberalism does not recognize or promote group-based pluralism. In other words, in liberalism, groups have no organic collective identity of their own; they become reduced to associations or mere aggregates of individuals. Consistent with this, therefore, from the standpoint of comprehensive pluralism, liberalism is partially pluralistic. Accordingly, liberal constitutional democracy and liberal political rights seem bound to have some relevance in relation to identifying political rights consistent with comprehensive pluralism.

It is by no means as clear that republicanism or communitarianism is compatible with pluralism. Some have even argued that they are not.[15] Moreover, one can easily imagine that republican self-government is incompatible with pursuit of a plurality of interests, (Sunstein 1993: 26–7, 38–9), and that communitarianism requires homogeneity and organic unity.

Nevertheless, neither republicanism nor communitarianism is necessarily incompatible with some degree of pluralism. For republicanism, the question is whether the general will can incorporate, albeit by transforming them, a plurality of particular interests, or, whether, by its very nature, it must stand against all particularity. It is difficult to answer this question with respect to Rousseau given the opacity of his conception of the general will. If the general will is regarded as a universal will that stands against all particularity, then republicanism would be incompatible with pluralism, and self-government would exclude self-realization.[16] Going beyond Rousseau, however, it seems quite plausible to conceive the general will as meant to incorporate as much as possible what is sought by particular wills consistent with maintaining neutrality among particular wills and with maintaining the good of the polity as a whole as paramount. In other words, there is no logical impediment against there being an overlap between the general will and at least part of what is aimed for by some, if not all, particular wills. Consistent with this, republicanism can be compatible with at least some form of limited pluralism.[17] Moreover,

---

[15]   See, for example, Sunstein 1993: 20 (arguing that classical republicanism postulates that civic virtue can only flourish in small, homogeneous, communities); and Sandel 1982: 151 (contrasting the unity of community in a constitutive sense to the plurality associated with Rawlsian liberalism).

[16]   Consistent with this kind of interpretation, it has been suggested that Rousseau was a precursor of totalitarianism. See Masters 1968: 315.

[17]   See Michelman 1988 (elaborating a deliberative republican approach that incorporates pluralism-in-fact).

republicanism would thus be relevant for comprehensive pluralism. Indeed, the work of the general will would seem to bear some analogy to that of pluralism's second-order norms. Even in that case, however, republicanism and comprehensive pluralism would remain fundamentally different. Unlike for republicanism, for comprehensive pluralism civic virtue and self-government may be positive values, but they would never become overriding ones.

At first, communitarianism and communal solidarity seem completely incompatible with pluralism. Whether the glue is ethnic, religious, or ideological, the relevant community is the self and the rest of the world is not only "other" but completely "outside." Other communities are thus alien if not downright the enemy.[18] In this conception, pluralism looms as inherently antagonistic to the overriding values of communal solidarity and group loyalty.

Upon closer inspection, however, even if communitarianism and pluralism remain incompatible from a metaphysical standpoint, they need not be mutually exclusive from a political standpoint. Even if one thinks in purely communal terms, as already noted, one can distinguish between *intra*-communal and *inter*-communal relationships. Assuming, for the moment that intra-communal relations completely preclude pluralism, it does not follow that inter-communal ones must likewise do so. For example, in a polity made up of several distinct ethnic groups, it is quite plausible for each of them to embrace inter-communal pluralism. Thus, each of these groups may become allied with all the others to promote group rights against individual rights, and ethnic-based group autonomy and self-government against universal, polity-wide majoritarianism.

Furthermore, in contemporary polities that are pluralistic-in-fact, communal-based pluralism may extend beyond the realm of constitutional design into that of everyday politics. For example, as already discussed, religions may join hands to combat the forces of secularism within their polity. Moreover, to the extent that the different religions involved remain antagonistic to one another, the religious leaders involved may at once share limited solidarity against secularism, while remaining adversaries on issues of religious dogma and doctrine.

As already noted, in many contemporary pluralistic polities, communities are unlikely to remain impervious to outside views or influences, as it is often difficult neatly to separate intra-communal from inter-communal relationships *within* the same community. As separate communities interact and become open to incorporating certain outside influences, communitarianism becomes adapted to coexistence with some degree of pluralism. Accordingly, some kinds of contemporary communitarianism are relevant to pluralism though the latter rejects the paramouncy of communal solidarity.

---

[18] Cf. Schmitt 1996: 54 (conceiving politics as the struggle between "friends" and "enemies"); Luban 2004.

7.2.2. *Comparing Liberal, Republican, and Communitarian Political Rights*

Actual contemporary constitutional democracies and the political rights they promote are likely to contain liberal, republican, and communitarian elements that coexist side by side.[19] It is useful, however, to distinguish between a liberal, republican, and communitarian paradigm for constitutional democracy and political rights. Not only do these contrasting paradigms provide helpful heuristic tools that facilitate critical appraisal. But also, because each of these paradigms is in its own way partially open to pluralism, a comparison between them can pave the way for the elaboration of an alternative paradigm consistent with the normative dictates of comprehensive pluralism.

Under the liberal paradigm, constitutional democracy and political rights should be devised so as to maximize equal opportunity for individual self-realization; under the republican paradigm, so as to enable the citizens of the polity to resolve its problems and conflicts through self-government and the spread of civic virtue; and, under the communitarian paradigm, so as to reinforce the community or communities involved by promoting and privileging the bonds of communal solidarity.

In the liberal vision, constitutional democracy and political rights are primarily necessary to protect the individual from undue interference with his or her pursuit of self-realization. Within this perspective, political rights would be subordinated to civil rights and constitutionally constrained government kept to a minimum.[20] In a liberal paradise, everyone would be adequately equipped to pursue self-realization, no one would interfere with his neighbor, and government and political rights would be largely superfluous. However, because down on earth there are always actual and potential threats to the unimpeded pursuit of individual self-realization, the state is a necessary presence and politics inevitable.

In the liberal vision, neither the state not politics becomes a vehicle for individual self-realization. The state and politics must be used to prevent or remove

---

[19] See, for example, the Spanish or the Canadian Constitution, which protect core liberal rights, such as freedom of expression and individual equality; self-government (and hence arguably republican) rights through federalism or devolution of powers to "autonomous regions"; and, communitarian rights, such as those granted to Anglophones and Francophones or to indigenous groups under the Canadian Constitution, or those that flow from the increased powers of autonomous regions, such as Catalonia, in Spain. Spanish Constitution, Part VIII, Chapter 3, Self-governing Communities, Sections 143–58; Constitutional Amendment, 1999 (Quebec), Amendment to Constitution Act, 1867 (excludes Quebec from the section relating to the organization of schools in the province (Section 93), thus granting Quebec the sole power to determine the system of education used there).

[20] Cf. Nozick 1974: 26–7, for an argument that the most extensive government that can be justified is the minimal "night-watchman" state limited to affording protection against foreign enemies, providing police protection against physical violence and interference with private property and supplying the institutional support necessary for the enforcement of private contracts.

impediments to the pursuit of individual self-realization, which pursuit itself remains *outside* of politics. Accordingly, the liberal state and liberal politics are supposed to assume an essentially negative role: They must ensure that the individual be (sufficiently) left alone to be able meaningfully to devote him- or herself to the pursuit of self-realization.

What is actually required for the individual to be free of undue impediments in her quest for self-realization depends on which conception of liberalism is at stake. For libertarians, individuals are largely self-sufficient, provided the state protects their fundamental negative rights. This requires a minimal Nozickean state that does not intervene in the economic sphere other than to prevent or punish interference with the free market. In this scenario, moreover, there is very little use for politics, and distinct political rights would be confined to the right to vote, to allow the citizenry to replace those in charge of government who do not carry out satisfactorily the minimal state's night watchman's duties. Consistent with the Lockean metaphor, the state's governors should be viewed as trustees of the citizens (Locke 1960: 375–6), and the latter should be able to replace those who must act on their behalf to secure the space for individual self-realization whenever a majority of the citizenry feels that their "trustees" have let them down.[21]

At the other end of the spectrum, for welfare-egalitarian liberals, the state apparatus must be massive as it is entrusted with an extensive distributive function. The welfare state must ensure that each individual within the polity is guaranteed a level of material well-being that will enable her meaningfully to pursue individual self-realization. Because in a complex contemporary economy, the private sector cannot alone provide sufficient material welfare to all, the government must administer public goods so as to fulfill the basic needs of all.

Whereas the liberal-welfare state is a maximal rather than a minimal state, the former no more than the latter is supposed to be a *political* state. Neither of these states is meant to have a direct role in the pursuit of individual self-realization, which, instead, is supposed to guarantee the requisite preconditions to equality of opportunity in such pursuit. The night watchman state does so by fulfilling a police function; the welfare state, by *administering* as efficiently as possible the distribution of material resources necessary to grant all individuals the requite minimum of

---

[21] The space for government policy choices is highly confined within the libertarian vision, since extensive protection of negative rights combined with prohibition against interference with free markets leave very little to the discretion of governors or of their constituencies. Ideally, there would be no need for voting or voting rights, as the performance of those in charge in government would be amenable to universally accepted criteria of rational determination. In practice, however, there are no universally accepted criteria for evaluating performance in office under evolving conditions. Accordingly, majority rule is introduced as the best available default mechanism, and the political rights it requires – namely, voting, since the other relevant rights, such as freedom of expression and of assembly are already guaranteed civil rights – must be afforded institutional protection.

welfare consistent with an equal opportunity to pursue self-realization.[22] Neither the night watchman state not the welfare state is thus political,[23] and they hence both call for minimal political rights. As already mentioned, the minimal state promotes negative rights and confines the legitimate role of political rights to control over attempts to unduly increase or abuse governmental power. For its part, the liberal-egalitarian welfare state concentrates on welfare entitlements and largely restricts legitimate political rights to maintaining accountability with respect to efficiency and corruption issues relating to the vast state administrative apparatus.[24]

In contrast to the narrow space left to politics by liberalism, in the republican vision all intersubjective dealings – and if one accounts for the Rousseauean struggle between self and other within each individual, all subjective dealings as well – fall within a nearly all-encompassing realm of politics. Paradoxically, if all or nearly all is politics, or within the realm of the political (understood as involving the responsibility to set and to manage the course of the polity), then there may be little left for constitutionalism or political *rights*. In a most extreme Rousseauean universe, with primary emphasis on his dictum that society must "force" all its members to be free (Rousseau 1947: 63–4), and in which civic virtue is interpreted as requiring complete surrender to a general will that stands completely against all private interests, all intersubjective dealings would be within the realm of the political as defined earlier, but civic virtue and all norms related to the political would be *moral* norms, not political ones.

Moral norms regulate internal relationships as opposed to legal and political norms, which, as we have seen, operate with respect to external relationships.[25]

---

[22] Cf. Habermas 1998: 13–25 (distinguishing between a "bourgeois-formal" and a "social-welfare" paradigm of law, the first concerned primarily with negative rights, the second with administration of welfare, which reduces the citizen to being a "client" of the state). In neither of these paradigms can one detect any significant input traceable to politics.

[23] This does not mean, of course, that critiques of either or both of these are not political. Calls for the overhaul of the minimal state on the grounds that it exacerbates disparities in wealth or of the welfare state on the grounds that it fosters passive dependence, for example, are quite obviously political in nature.

[24] Arguably, this latter political function can be exercised through the right to vote for political officials accountable for the proper functioning of the state's administrative apparatus. It is quite plausible, however, to maintain that the integrity of the administrative state is best protected by an impartial judiciary than by elected politicians. In the latter case, the scope of legitimate political rights would be even more modest.

[25] For a more extended discussion of this distinction, see Rosenfeld 1998: 69–75. This distinction is meant to be understood as a relational one and not as one designed to settle substantive content-based issues. The same norm, 'thou shall not kill', for example, may be both a moral and a legal-political one. It is a moral one inasmuch as it is an "internal" prohibition arising from the relationship between God and humans, or out of the basic precepts of secular humanistic morality. On the other hand, it is an "external" prohibition subject to legal sanction to the extent that it is prescribed pursuant to a law enacted by a democratically elected parliament. Some norms are purely "internal," such as "thou shall never lie to a friend" with presumably no external institutional consequences in case of

Accordingly, if civic virtue demands the political involvement of all and requires that each person surrender private needs and interests to the general will, then there is no room for political rights, only for political duties. Moreover, in this scenario virtually no role is left for politics in the conduct of the affairs of the polity: They must be settled according to the all-encompassing morals of civic virtue, which operates primarily through self-denial (of the bourgeois "other" within the public citizen's "self"). Finally, consistent with this, there is little room for either constitutional politics or ordinary politics as the realm of external relations would be completely subordinated to that of internal ones. In other words, there would be no room for politics, only for legal-political reinforcement of the all-encompassing moral norms embodied in civic virtue.

In a more moderate conception of republicanism open to some degree of pluralism, however, democracy and political rights can play a prominent role. If the general will is understood as being capable of incorporating objectives that are in part compatible with a plurality of extant private interests, and if the exercise of civic virtue is viewed as involving comparable measures of morals and politics (i.e., an internal obligation to promote self-rule for the common good combined with an external obligation to negotiate with all other citizens so as to shape the actual definition and pursuit of the public good encompassed within the general will in ways that can accommodate as many different private preferences as possible), then self-government involves political choice as well as moral imperative. Indeed, the need for negotiation and accommodation in the course of the process of endowing the general will with a concrete substantive content calls for both constitutional and ordinary politics. In this conception, although self-realization is subordinated to self-government, the former is not altogether excluded by the latter. Accordingly, to the extent that it is possible to draw on different conceptions of self-realization to shape the course of self-government, the institutional framework guaranteed by constitutional democracy and the protection of political rights can be regarded as playing an indispensable role within this alternative, more moderate republican vision.

Moderate republicanism open to some degree of pluralism requires strong constitutional protection of democratic politics as well as broad ranging political rights and duties. Constitutional protection should extend not only to voting but also to political party formation, organization, and management, as deployment of a multiplicity of political parties becomes imperative for purposes of a well-functioning, politically grounded, self-government drawing on a plurality of views. Moreover, given the priority that republicanism grants to self-government over self-realization, a moderately

transgression. Conversely, other norms are inherently external, such as "thou shalt drive on the right side of the road" (i.e., there is nothing inherently moral or immoral about driving on the right or left side of the road, though it may be derivatively immoral to do so if it is against the law and if it thus unduly endangers the life and safety of others).

republican constitution would have to insist on maintenance of a vigorous, unimpeded democratic process. Finally, with respect to the individual citizen, moderate republican constitutionalism should combine protection of extensive political participation rights with imposition of an obligation to participate in self-government through a legally enforceable duty to vote in periodic elections, for example.[26]

Communitarianism shares with liberalism the pursuit of self-realization, though in the case of communitarianism it is collective self-realization rather than individual. Furthermore, communitarianism shares with republicanism the need for self-government, though for communitarians that need is but a means to better secure communal integrity and solidarity. Thus, how much self-government, and of what kind, depends on many factors, such as whether the community involved is a minority within a multi-ethnic polity or whether it encompasses the totality of the polity by itself. Finally, what kind of constitutional democracy or political rights are called for under a communitarian vision depends on whether a communally monistic or a communally pluralistic collectivity is at involved.

In a communally monistic collectivity, such as a homogeneous ethnocentric nation-state, there may not be a strong need for a vigorous constitutional democracy or for extensive political rights.[27] In a communally pluralistic polity, however, constitutional democracy and political rights, in particular collective ones, are crucial to the maintenance of communal integrity. Where various groups are concentrated in different geographic locations, constitutionally protected identity-based federalism may provide the best means to intra-communal self-determination and harmonious inter-communal coexistence. Where different communities are not neatly separated geographically, on the other hand, other means, such as the *millet* system discussed in Chapter 5, can be used to bolster intra-communal unity and solidarity. Moreover, depending on whether a particular community constitutes a majority or a minority within the polity, the nature of the most important collective rights may vary. For a majority community, political rights of self-determination and self-government would seem paramount; for a minority community, in contrast, collective civil rights would seem most urgent, such as, for example, a collective freedom of religion right which would prevent legislative majorities within the polity from interfering with the intra-communal affairs of the religious minority involved.

---

[26] Some contemporary democracies make voting mandatory and the failure to vote subject to legal sanction, such as the levy of a fine. See, for example, Argentina, Australia, Austria, Belgium, Bolivia, Brazil, Dominican Republic, Egypt, Greece, Guatemala, Honduras, Liechtenstein, Luxembourg, Panama, Philippines, Switzerland (some cantons only), Singapore, Uruguay, and Venezuela.

[27] This observation is consistent with Karl Schmitt's conception of an anti-pluralist ethnocentric constitutionalism the purpose of which was the advancement of the German ethnos and culture and its protection against all "external" enemies, including those within Germany's borders. In Schmitt's view, the collective self-realization of the German ethnos might as well be entrusted to a dictator imbued with the German spirit (Schmitt 1985).

In one respect, communitarianism is like liberalism, and both are unlike republicanism. For republicans, self-government and hence politics – or at least the political – encompass all human endeavors. In contrast, as already mentioned, for liberals, much of individual self-realization is besides or beyond politics. To a significant extent, for communitarians self-realization in the form of the achievement of intra-communal solidarity is, strictly speaking, outside of politics. Thus, fulfillment of the communal life prescribed by a minority religion may well depend on protection of the religious community involved from certain encroachments by majoritarian politics.

Though both liberal individuals and communally oriented groups need protection from external political forces, communally solidaristic groups seemingly more than liberal individuals also require political power to manage their intra-communal life. Thus, within the communitarian vision, communal units must combine freedom *from* external politics and freedom to conduct internal politics to guide intra-communal life and promote communal solidarity. In other words, communal units must at once be protected from external domination and granted power over internal affairs, including the power to stifle individual dissent within the community to the extent that is poses a threat to communal solidarity.

There seems to be a paradox in that protection against external threats posed by more powerful groups or political majorities requires negative rights that are much like liberal rights, whereas the powers required to deal with internal intra-communal threats will inevitably include some that are bound to be highly illiberal. Moreover, beyond the seeming incongruity of demanding liberal rights for oneself while at the same time insisting on illiberal powers over others, there is a further and potentially even more serious contradiction. Viewing the polity as a whole from a communitarian standpoint, communal solidarity should operate at the level of the nation-state as the relevant unit, not at that of ethnic or religious minorities within it. Accordingly, polity-wide relationships would be intra-communal, and all claims by minority groups perceived as threats to solidarity within the nation-state treated as dangerous intra-communal dissent properly subject to suppression. On the other hand, from the standpoint of a minority group involved, relations with the polity as a whole would be clearly inter-communal, and as such would call for negative rights that would allow the minority to defend its collective identity and to promote what it deems to be its legitimate intra-communal solidarity.

There are two complementary ways to minimize this problem: one formal and the other substantive. On the formal level, this problem can be addressed by inserting in the polity's constitution which groups are entitled to communal autonomy, what rights such autonomy entails, and how conflicts among such communal entities or among the latter and the polity as a whole ought to be resolved. Once these questions are constitutionally settled, friction and conflict may be significantly reduced.

On the other hand, by constitutionally enshrining certain forms of group autonomy and groups rights, the polity does not necessarily solve the problem once and for all, but rather shifts the locus of conflicts from the realm of ordinary politics to that of constitutional politics. Such shift may nonetheless be advantageous as constitutional arrangements may be regarded as more authoritative and weighty, and they may be more difficult to change provided amendment criteria are sufficiently onerous. Furthermore, the shift in question is likely to require reinforcement of rights to participate in constitutional politics, including rights of exit, such as rights of secession in case inter-communal consensus breaks down.

On the substantive level, the tension between the pursuit of inter-communal tolerance and that of intra-communal intolerance can be dramatically reduced by embracing communal-based pluralism. Consistent with such pluralism, the polity would comprise a multiplicity of overlapping and intersecting communal groups that would remain fairly open to mutual influence. This, in turn, would make for inter-communal as well as intra-communal solidarity and would allow dissidents within a group either to foster intra-communal changes or to voluntarily leave their own groups and pursue other group affiliations. Moreover, within this vision of communal pluralism, communal solidarity would still remain paramount, but multiple group affiliations requiring varying degrees of communal solidarity would improve the chances of striking a balance between intra-communal and inter-communal commitments. Finally, whereas this kind of pluralistic communitarianism would still require protection of collective rights, including collective self-government rights, it would greatly reduce the need for illiberal treatment of dissidents within one's group.

7.3. PLURALISM AND THE DERIVATION OF POLITICAL RIGHTS

As indicated in the course of the preceding discussion, liberalism, republicanism, and communitarianism are all compatible with varying degrees of limited pluralism. They hence afford a glimpse into what a pluralist regime of political rights might include. To obtain a fuller and more accurate account of the complement of political rights required by comprehensive pluralism, however, it is necessary to shift perspectives. In Section 7.2, I examined perspectives within which pluralism occupied a subordinate position; in what follows, I return to the issues raised there from the perspective of comprehensive pluralism, which posits pluralism as paramount. As we shall see, within a pluralist perspective, there is room for limited liberalism, republicanism, and communitarianism, as all three play a subordinate though indispensable role in the elaboration of pluralist politics and political rights. Furthermore, within a pluralist perspective, the determination of political rights is less categorical than relational and hence is context-dependent.

7.3.1. *Pluralism and Limited Liberalism, Republicanism, and Communitarianism*

Comprehensive pluralism encompasses limited liberalism, republicanism, and communitarianism inasmuch as it recognizes that individual self-realization, self-government, and communal solidarity and communal self-determination have a legitimate place within a pluralist polity.[28] Moreover, liberalism, republicanism, and communitarianism play both a mutually antagonistic and a complementary role when viewed from the dialectical standpoint of comprehensive pluralism. Indeed, the struggle between self and other within a pluralistic perspective is neither a purely individualistic one nor an exclusively communal one, particularly if communities are conceived as homogeneous, self-enclosed, organic units. Self-realization may be *within* or *through* one's community, or even outside of the latter. Whether the self be the individual within a community or a subgroup within a larger group, there is likely to be a conflict between self-realization and group-wide solidarity. Whereas liberalism privileges the individual over the group and communitarianism conversely primes the group over the individual, pluralism favors neither. Instead, pluralism seeks to overcome conflicts involving individual versus group, subgroup versus group, and one group versus another, by subjecting the antagonistic first-order norms competing for vindication to the edicts emanating from second-order norms. Furthermore, within a pluralistic perspective, liberalism and communitarianism are complementary as well as antagonistic inasmuch as the vices of an overly individualistic political order can be mitigated by greater communal emphasis and vice versa.

For its part, republican self-government is not justified for its own sake within a pluralist perspective, but rather for purposes of establishing a political course that maximizes inclusion of competing conceptions of the good consistent with the dictates of second-order norms. This means that every member of the polity – be it an individual or a communal member – must to some degree refrain from the pursuit of self-realization to join with others to manage mutual tensions and to foster mutual accommodation. Unlike republican self-government in its Rousseauean incarnation, pluralist self-government doesn't require suppressing all interests for the common good. It only requires working together to implement mutual restraints that will allow for the proliferation of a plurality of modes of self-realization. Accordingly, whereas pluralist self-government is in tension with individual and communal self-realization, it complements these in the sense that it does not allow either to become dominant or one-sided. Conversely, polity-wide pluralist self-government is not supposed to impose a single society-wide common good, but rather to set the stage for coexistence among a plurality of competing conceptions of good. And consistent

---

[28] This draws upon, and expands on, my discussion of these issues in Rosenfeld 1998: 216–24.

with this, both the pursuit of individual self-realization and of communal solidarity serve to confine the realm of self-government and to place many societal endeavors beyond its reach.

A well-ordered pluralist polity requires sustaining a dynamic tension between liberal, republican, and communitarian tendencies to produce an equilibrium for purposes of accommodating as broad a spectrum of diverse conceptions of the good as possible consistent with adherence to pluralist norms. Approximation of the requisite equilibrium depends on the deployment of an array of political rights, both negative and positive, of certain rights of freedom *from* politics, and on the imposition of certain duties of political participation. Moreover, the nature and scope of the rights and duties in question are predominantly relational and contextual. These rights and duties are relational in the sense that they are the rights of a particular self against a particular other in relation to an identifiable intersubjective domain. For example, as discussed in Chapter 3 an aboriginal minority may have a right to freedom from subjection to the politics of the non-aboriginal majority within the polity in relation to intra-aboriginal affairs and in relation to regulation of aboriginal lands. On the other hand, aboriginal individuals may have different rights and duties vis à vis one another with respect to their intersubjective dealings within the same domain. Also consistent with these sets of relations, from the standpoint of the particular polity involved as a whole, intra-aboriginal affairs are beyond politics, whereas these same affairs are most likely political when considered from within the aboriginal community.[29]

Pluralist political rights are contextual inasmuch as the optimal inclusion of diverse conceptions of the good depends on the nature of the conceptions involved and on the particular circumstances at stake. For example, in a polity comprising several ethnic groups, each living within its own distinct geographic location, federalism and the political rights it entails may be clearly called for. In contrast, if these same ethnic groups were not split along geographical lines, federalism would most likely be of little use in dealing with inter-ethnic group affairs. Moreover, where federalism is not a viable option, the optimal form of political organization and the particular array of political rights that it would require would depend on the actual contending conceptions of the good and on the degree of antagonism among their respective proponents. For example, where ethnic differences are sharp and intense, it might be preferable to discourage ethnic-based political parties and to shape political rights in ways that minimize rather than exacerbate ethnic tensions. On the other hand, where ethnic tensions are not that intense, but where the interests of

---

[29] In theory at least, it would be possible for intra-aboriginal dealings not to be political (i.e., not to involve external relationships), but only moral. This would be the case if all involved acted pursuant to internalized moral or religious imperatives rather than on the basis of political objectives.

certain ethnic minorities tend to get lost in the shuffle, some degree of ethnic-based political representation may well further the aims of pluralism.

7.3.2. *Relational and Contextual Pluralist Political Rights in Action: The Example of Free Speech*

The relational and contextual nature of legitimate political rights within a pluralist perspective not only entails that particular political rights may be appropriate in some contexts but not in others, but also that depending on the particular context involved, the same rights may be political or non-political. A good example of such a right is the right to free speech, which will be examined shortly. Indeed, a functioning democracy is inconceivable in the absence of free speech rights, yet not all conceptions or uses of free speech are in any meaningful sense political.

Certain rights, like the right to vote, are always political and, from the standpoint of pluralism, are indispensable in all contexts. In the presence of pluralism-in-fact, there are bound to be conflicts between proponents of different first-order objectives that cannot be resolved by appeal to second-order norms. At least in some of these cases, reliance on democratic majorities provides the best alternative and call for enforcement of the right to vote.

Other rights, such as the right to privacy with respect to a person's intimate relations are inherently not political though the determination of whether or not to afford them, or to what extent to recognize them, is political. In other words, persons do not usually use their right to choose with whom to engage in an intimate relationship for political purposes. Accordingly, in almost all conceivable circumstances, the right to privacy with respect to intimate associations is a civil right not a political one.

Free speech rights, in contrast, are sometimes political rights, and at other times they are non-political or only incidentally political. Clearly, democracy cannot function without political will-formation or without open and wide-ranging discussion of political alternatives. On the other hand, freedom of artistic expression or freedom to communicate one's feelings may, but need not, be political, and often is not.[30] For example, an abstract painting may neither be intended by the artist who created it nor understood by the viewing public as conveying a political message.[31]

---

[30] See Rosenfeld 2003 (distinguishing four distinct justifications for the free speech: (1) free speech contributes to discovery of the truth; (2) it is a necessary condition of democracy; (3) free self-expression is indispensable for purposes of achieving individual autonomy; and (4) free speech promotes human dignity. Only justification 2 is distinctly political, and the respective domains carved out by each of these justifications vary in scope, with some being more expansive than others though there is a significant amount of overlap among them.

[31] This does not mean that abstract art lacks political significance, or more broadly, that any bright line can be drawn between political and non-political expression.

Consistent with this, moreover, freedom to exhibit abstract art need not be protected speech inasmuch as freedom of speech it construed as a political right. Or, more precisely, abstract art need not be protected under a positive political right, but it may have to be protected by a negative political right (i.e., be protected from intrusions coming from politics at large in order to be free to engage in the politics of art) or as a civil right.

Not only is freedom of speech in a democracy bound to be in part a political right, but also, in certain circumstances, political rights may imply at least a limited free speech right even where such right is afforded no protection as a civil right. This latter case is well illustrated by the Australian High Court's decision in *Australian Capital Television* v. *The Commonwealth of Australia*.[32] Australian law prohibited broadcasting paid political advertisements and otherwise restricted political discussion on the airwaves as elections were nearing. The High Court upheld a challenge against this law notwithstanding that Australia lacks a bill of rights, on the grounds that freedom to propagate and discuss political views prior to an election can be derived from the Australian Constitution's guarantee of a system of representative government. In other words, without freedom to exchange political views, there cannot be genuine representative government and hence a right to free speech is an inextricable part of a more broadly encompassing right to democratic self-government.

More generally, political rights cannot be captured by formal definitions or categorical classifications. Whether a right is political depends on its relation to politics and to the political. Moreover, within the perspective of comprehensive pluralism, all external relationships are directly on indirectly political.[33] Accordingly, a proper carving out of political rights requires submission of first-order pursuits to the constraints imposed by second-order norms supplemented by mutual accommodation of competing objectives equally compatible with second-order norms – through democratic politics, including majoritarian decision making – with a view to maximizing inclusiveness of diverse conceptions of the good. In short, comprehensive pluralism provides a framework for establishing and assessing legitimate political rights, with the actual rights thus identified varying to some degree depending on the particular circumstances involved.

---

[32] 177 C.L.R. 106 (1992).

[33] Legal relationships are also external and yet are distinct from political ones. Legal rights and duties are distinguishable from their political counterparts, but there is a strong connection between law and politics as law can be characterized as frozen or suspended politics. For further discussion, see Rosenfeld 1998 74–83. In a democracy laws are the product of parliamentary politics and are subject to subsequent amendment or repeal through further parliamentary politics. Notwithstanding these strong connections, legal rights and duties remain distinct from their political counterparts even if the former depend for their existence on the latter.

7.4. PLURALIST POLITICAL RIGHTS IN TIMES OF STRESS

As noted in Section 7.1.3, in ordinary times self and other (or more precisely selves and others) disagree and compete with one another, but they reach sufficient accommodation to prevent erosion or fragmentation of the overarching binding self that envelops the polity as a whole. Consistent with that, in ordinary times, citizens can enjoy the full panoply of civil and political rights derived from pluralism's second-order norms and applied to the actual plurality of competing agendas issued from different conceptions of the good and related to different political perspectives.[34] In contrast, in times of crisis, the overarching polity-wide self is threatened with destruction, either from within or from without, and consequently all other objectives may have to be suspended to provide undivided attention to the fight for survival. In an acute crisis, civil and political rights may have to be temporarily suspended. What is more, even from the standpoint of comprehensive pluralism, the pursuit of pluralism may itself have to be provisionally abandoned until the crisis is overcome. This may sound paradoxical, but it remains consistent with the logic of pluralism. Indeed, averting destruction of the space reserved for interaction among a plurality of perspectives must take priority over any actual attempt to foster accommodation within that space.

Times of stress cover the broad spectrum between ordinary times and times of emergency, that is between times where the unity of the polity seems entirely secure and times of struggle devoted to repelling mortal threats posed by an internal or external enemy. Accordingly, it would seem that political rights in times of stress should fall somewhere between the full protection called in ordinary times and the full suspension that may be warranted in an acute crisis.

Upon closer examination, however, it does not necessarily follow that because times of stress are sandwiched between ordinary times and those of crisis that political rights in conditions of stress should be more restricted than those in ordinary times. On the contrary, arguably when the unity of the polity begins to crack but is in no imminent danger of collapse, it would seem better to reinforce rather than weaken political rights. Indeed, when self and other begin to evolve from adversaries committed to cannons of civility and rules of fair play toward downright enemies, pluralist democracy and the political rights that sustain it would seem to need reinforcement not constriction.[35]

---

[34] Different political agendas may be tied to different conceptions of the good (e.g., promoting religion in public schools tied to religious ideologies versus campaigning for secular public education tied to humanistic non-religious perspectives). Different political agendas, however, may also be linked to the same conception of the good when self and other disagree over the best means to the same end. For example, two liberals may differ over whether welfare entitlements promote or stifle individual pursuit of self-realization.

[35] See Mouffe 2004: 70 (distinguishing "agonism" or relation among adversaries from "antagonism" or relation among enemies and arguing that the goal of democratic politics should be to transform antagonism in to agonism).

Whatever the logic behind political rights in times of stress, the shift from ordinary times to times of stress generates its own dialectic that defies the dictates of any straightforward logic. For example, conditions of stress seem to call for militant democracy – that is, a democracy that leaves no room for anti-democratic political parties. Militant democracy, in turn, shrinks the scope of political rights by refusing to extend them to those who seek to use democratic means toward non democratic ends. By the same token, however, militant democracy affords greater rights – or similar rights bearing greater weight – to all political operatives who pursue democratic ends, by eliminating or severely handicapping some of their fiercest competitors. On balance, does militant democracy increase political rights? Does it decrease them? Or, does it change their nature?

To get a better handle on the dialectic at work in shifts from ordinary times to those of stress and from the latter to times of crisis, it is useful to focus on the following exemplary subjects frequently linked to conditions of stress: hate speech and militant democracy, the war on terror, and pacted secession.

7.4.1. *Hate Speech and Militant Democracy*

Hate speech (e.g., expressing highly offensive, insulting and demeaning views regarding certain racial ethnic or religious groups) certainly runs counter to the spirit of pluralism's second-order norms. And, so do anti-democratic political parties bent on using the democratic process to destroy democracy. It does not follow, however, that hate speech and anti-democratic political parties must be banned from the political arena because they contravene pluralist morals. As stressed throughout, inconsistency with second-order norms is not grounds for suspension. Only interference with the *implementation* of second-order norms is. Consistent with this, there may be, from the standpoint of comprehensive pluralism, normative or strategic reasons for tolerating anti-democratic parties or hate speech. For example, an anti-democratic party may provide the means for adherents of a particular religion to pursue their conceptions of the good, which, as long as it did not trample on similar pursuits by proponents of other conceptions, would remain in conformity with pluralist morals. Tolerance of hate speech, on the other hand, may be arguably warranted from a strategic standpoint inasmuch as suppression of such speech might eventually strengthen rather than weaken its proponents.[36]

There are many plausible arguments for and against toleration of hate speech or anti-democratic political parties, but the only relevant ones, for present purposes,

---

[36] This rationale has played a prominent role in the United States' broad tolerance for hate speech. In the United States, hate speech is constitutionally protected so long as it does not incite to violence, whereas in most of the rest of the world, hate speech that incites to racial, ethnic, or religious hatred can be constitutionally banned; see Rosenfeld 2003a.

are those that revolve around the distinction between ordinary times and times of stress. Banning hate speech and insisting on militant democracy seem much more justified in times of stress than in ordinary ones. This is perhaps best illustrated by the different ways in which the United States and Germany treat Neo-Nazi speech. As made manifest by the *Skokie* cases,[37] the United States can afford to tolerate Neo-Nazi propaganda because of its minimal effect on its intended audience or on the affairs of the polity. In contrast, in Germany because of the Nazi past and of the fear that the Nazi monster may one day be reawakened, Neo-Nazi hate speech does loom as a potential threat to the unity and integrity of the polity.[38]

More generally, the distinction between ordinary times and times of stress may account for different responses to Karl Popper's "paradox of tolerance" (Popper 1966 (1): 265–6 n. 4) discussed in Chapter 4. Because tolerance of the intolerant may pave the way for the latter to take power and end tolerance, Popper argues that, to preserve tolerance one must be intolerant of the intolerant. Based on the distinction between ordinary times and those of stress, however, it is plausible to argue that from a strategic standpoint it is preferable to tolerate the intolerant so long as the fabric of the pluralist polity is not threatened.[39] Indeed, in the context of the American *Skokie* cases, for example, the legal struggle over whether or not to permit a march by a small group of Neo-Nazi had a much greater impact than the march itself, which eventually took place with barely any notice (Rosenfeld 2003a: 1538). Under these circumstances, suppression of the march would have had greater negative consequences for the American polity than did the isolated utterance of Nazi propaganda largely ignored by the American public.

In times of stress, however, tolerance of the intolerant may pave the way to times of crisis. For example, had Nazi ideology been ruthlessly suppressed during the 1920s and 1930s, perhaps the Nazis would not have come to power democratically only to destroy tolerance and democracy. In post-World War II Germany, the memory of the Nazi Nightmare and the fear of its possible return create conditions of stress with respect to Nazi propaganda and Neo-Nazi political activity.[40]

---

[37] *Collin* v. *Smith*, 447 F. Supp. 676 (N.D. Ill.), *aff'd*, 578 F.2d 1197 (7th Cir.), cert. denied, 439 U.S. 916 (1978); *Village of Skokie* v. *National Socialist Party*, 69 Ill. 2d 605, 373 N.E. 2d 21 (1978).

[38] See Stein 1986: 279–80; "New German law restricting cyberspace," *New York Times*, July 5, 1997, summary republished by EduCom, July 6, 1997.

[39] There are, of course, other arguments in favor of tolerance of the intolerant. For example, consistent with a Millian belief on the eventual triumph of reason through uninhibited public discourse, refutation of the arguments of the intolerant is much more likely to be successful than attempts at suppression (Mill 1961 ch. 2, 1, 19–32). For present purposes, however, these other arguments need not be addressed.

[40] As this example indicates, conditions of stress may be confined to particular areas of a polity's life, or they may be pervasive throughout all areas within the polity.

Intolerance of the intolerant undoubtedly shrinks the scope of tolerance, and when intolerant political speech is involved, the result is a reduction of the scope of political rights. On the other hand, as the jurisprudence under the German Basic law exemplifies, intolerance of the intolerant may also bolster other rights, including rights with a distinct political dimension (Eberle 1997: 824 n. 115, 833–41). Thus, one reason offered by the German Constitutional Court in justification of its finding intolerance of pro-Nazi expression to be constitutional was that such intolerance was necessary to uphold the dignity of the post-war Jewish population in Germany (Id.: 893). Because of their historical experience, tolerance of Neo-Nazi views in post-war Germany would cause the Jewish community to feel excluded from the communal and political life of the contemporary German polity (Id.).

In short, unlike in the United States, in Germany Neo-Nazi propaganda created conditions of stress by threatening to drive out German Jews from the overarching self that binds the German polity together. To counter this threat, the German Constitutional Court prescribed a reduction in the scope of political speech to reinforce dignity rights indispensable to a sense of belonging to the polity and to meaningful and effective political participation within it.

There are obvious analogies between curbing hate speech and embracing militant democracy (Roach 2004: 171, 183). In an ordinary democracy, all political parties that abide by the rules of the game are allowed to compete for power whatever their ideology. In contrast, in a militant democracy, political parties that pursue anti-democratic ends through democratic means can be constitutionally banned.[41] Furthermore, it is also evident that adherence to militant democracy is likely to be more compelling in times of stress than in ordinary times.

There are also, however, significant disanalogies between the two cases. Pure hate speech (i.e., insulting and demeaning expression against a particular group) possesses no genuine social value and can hence be altogether banned consistent with comprehensive pluralism. If such hate speech is not banned in ordinary times, it is only for purely strategic (political) reasons. In contrast, the anti-democratic agenda of a political party may encompass norms and values entitled to at least partial protection under the dictates of comprehensive pluralism. In addition, upon closer examination, militant democracy taken to its logical extreme seems to rest on an internal contradiction. Ideally, in a democracy, all political views and

---

[41] See Eberle 1997: 825 n. 119 (quoting *Klass Case*, 30 BVerfGE 1, 19–20 (1970), translated in Kommers, 1989: 230 (citation omitted): "Constitutional provisions must not be interpreted in isolation but rather in a manner consistent with the Basic Law's fundamental principles and its system of values.... In the context of this case it is especially significant that the Constitution ... has decided in favor of 'militant democracy' that does not submit to abuse of basic rights or an attack on the liberal order of the state. Enemies of the Constitution must not be allowed to endanger, impair, or destroy the existence of the state while claiming protection of rights granted by the Basic Law."

agendas should be vetted and discussed and eventually submitted to the operative democratic decision-making processes in force within the polity. Moreover,
within this ideal scheme, each political party should project a particular agenda
distinct from all the other agendas issuing from the competing conceptions of the
good vying for vindication within the polity. For each political party to remain true
to its unique agenda, however, it would be necessary for it to curb internal hetero-
doxy or dissent. In other words, to foster optimal inter-party competition and thus
best contribute to the ideal of democracy by giving each political position its own
voice, political parties may have to be internally non-democratic or even internally autocratic.

Aiming thus for representation for all political views implicitly or explicitly
embraced within the polity requires militancy with respect to process – or *process-
based militant democracy*. In contrast, what is customarily referred to as "militant
democracy," which calls for suppression of political parties with anti-democratic
agendas, involves militancy regarding outcomes – or *outcome-based militant democracy*. In either case, militant democracy requires reliance on anti-democratic
devices. Moreover, if one posits that there is bound to be an eventually unavoidable
link between democratic means and ends and between anti-democratic means and
ends, then process-based and outcome-based militant democracy seem to be at log-
ger heads.

Both representation of all views, which calls for process-based militancy, and
exclusion of anti-democratic political parties, which calls for outcome-based militancy, seem much more compelling in times of stress than in ordinary times. Indeed,
in times of stress, various viewpoints are, or seem, threatened with exclusion, and
the unity of the polity is sufficiently frayed to make possible an eventual takeover
by anti-democratic forces. No such pressures are present in ordinary times, which
allows for greater fluidity in the articulation of political positions and for greater
tolerance of political parties with anti-democratic objectives. Accordingly, in ordinary times, neither process-based nor outcome-based militancy loom as necessary or
desirable.

In times of stress, perceived threats to the unity of the polity are likely to be associated not only with anti-democratic political parties, but also with illiberal ones.
Illiberal parties need not be anti-democratic. For example, a religious fundamentalist party that has the support of a majority of the electorate of a polity can remain
essentially democratic both internally and externally, and yet systematically spread
illiberalism. Even from the standpoint of militant democracy, however, illiberal is
not synonymous with anti-democratic, and hence prohibition of illiberal parties in
times of stress would not be justified as suppression of anti-democratic ones would
be. Furthermore, even if suppression of the latter is justified in times of stress, suppression of illiberal parties poses vexing problems that go to the heart of pluralism

and democracy. This is well illustrated by the case of *Refah Partisi* v. *Turkey*.[42] In a divided decision, the European Court of Human Rights held that the dissolution of the Islamic Party Refah, the largest party in Turkey's Parliament, ordered by the Turkish Constitutional Court, was not contrary to the European Convention on Human Rights. The Turkish Court had acted because it found Refah to be a "center of activities" contrary to the principle of secularism enshrined in the Turkish Constitution. Although Refah's means and ends were both democratic in nature, the European Court's majority found that Refah's advocacy of women wearing headscarves in public places and adherence to the Koran would, if successful, lead to an impermissible surrender of the people's democratic rights to religious authorities who, even if backed by large majorities, would implement illiberal policies discriminatory on the basis of sex and of religion. For the European Court's dissenting judges, however, dissolution for mere advocacy of peaceful and legal changes – through constitutional amendment, if necessary – by a political party that is democratic with respect to means and ends and that declares its adherence to the requirement of secularism imposed by the Turkish Constitution, is an unwarranted, overly drastic and disproportionate result.

From the standpoint of pluralism, unlike from that of liberalism, illiberal ideals need not be automatically excluded from the arena of democratic politics. Furthermore, from the standpoint of conditions of stress, if retreat from radical secularism were genuinely likely eventually to culminate in dissolution of the Turkish polity, then suppression of *Refah* would be justified. It could even be defended on grounds of militant democracy, but it would result in less democracy and less pluralism.[43]

On the other hand, if discord over secularism created conditions of stress in contemporary Turkey, but moving away from radical secularism would not risk the break up of the polity, but merely a realignment that may or may not live up to the prescriptions of the European Convention of Human Rights, then suppression of Refah would not be justified. In that case the risk of greater stress would not justify significantly curbing democracy and pluralism in the absence of actual erosion of the rights protected by the Convention.

What the preceding discussion of the *Refah* case illustrates is that conditions of stress do not necessarily call for militant democracy or an increase or decrease in democratic rights or in the reach of pluralism. Instead, the right solution requires a proper readjustment and balancing of competing rights and objectives depending on the particular circumstances involved, and on how far or near existing conditions of stress happen to be from conditions of crisis.

---

[42] *Refah Partisi* v. *Turkey*, 35 Eur. Ct. H.R. 3 (2002).

[43] It could still be consistent with comprehensive pluralism depending how close the conditions of stress happened to be in relation to conditions of crisis.

7.4.2. *The War on Terror*

If the issues surrounding militant democracy invite comparisons between conditions of stress and ordinary conditions, the issues raised by the war on terror require focus on the comparison between conditions of stress and states of crisis. Terrorism, as previously noted, can provoke a state of crisis, such as seemed to be the case in the immediate aftermath of the attacks of September 11, 2001, in the United States. In the long run, however, as also already emphasized, the war on terror, whether it be that against Al Quaeda, or those against ETA in Spain or the IRA in Northern Ireland, is more likely to produce times of stress than to sustain a state of crisis.

At first sight, the war on terror seems much more likely to affect civil rights, the rights of criminal defendants and those of detainees held without charges for long indefinite periods of time than political rights. Upon closer consideration, however, the war on terror is likely to have some effect on certain political rights, such as, for example, the right freely to associate in pursuit of a common political project. Indeed, the war on terror may, at least prima facie, justify infiltration of certain political groups and thus adversely affect their ability to compete effectively in the political arena. Moreover, to the extent that a political party is suspected of acting in concert with, or of pursuing the agenda of, terrorists, such as was the case with the Batasuna Party linked to ETA in Spain (Ferreres Comella 2004), the war on terror may give rise to genuine militant democracy concerns comparable to those raised by political parties that use democratic means to achieve antidemocratic ends.

The most significant nexus between the war on terror and the political, however, concerns the boundary between a state of crisis and conditions of stress. The more the war on terror is like a veritable war, the more emergency powers may be justified with the consequent diminution of civil and political rights. On the other hand, the more the war on terror approximates combating and prosecuting crimes, the greater is the justification for those institutions that are customarily deployed in times of stress rather than for preservation of a state of crisis.[44]

So long as the war on terror unfolds under conditions of stress, two kinds of constraints that may be suspended in states of emergency remain in force: rights-based constraints and democracy-based constraints. For example, it may be justified in times of crisis, but not in times of stress, to suspend habeas corpus rights.[45] Furthermore, whereas ordinary parliamentary democratic politics may be

---

[44] Ordinary crime does not trigger conditions of stress so long as it does not threaten to drive a wedge in the polity's collective self. Even intermittent terrorist activity, in contrast, seems likely to render that collective self more vulnerable.

[45] See, for example, US Const. Art I, § 9, cl. 2, allowing for such suspension.

suspended during a state of emergency,[46] no such suspension could be justified in times of stress.

The war on terror does not justify suspension of fundamental rights, but it does allow for recalibration of the scope of such rights to account for greater concerns regarding the polity's security and well-being. This can be accomplished through judicial deployment of ordinary balancing approaches and proportionality analysis.[47] In the context of the war on terror, the weight of the fundamental rights at stake would remain the same as those ascribed to them in ordinary times. The weight accorded to security concerns and to protection of the polity's identity, however, would be greater in the war on terror than during ordinary times. Thus, in the *Hamdi* case that arose out of the U.S. war against Al Quaeda and the Taliban in Afghanistan, the greater weight given to the state's security interests in the midst of the war on terror resulted in significantly less extensive procedural rights for a detainee claiming that he was mistakenly arrested as an enemy combatant in Afghanistan than for an ordinary domestic criminal suspect, including one believed to be a serial killer. Even if the presumed enemy combatant poses no greater threat to life than the suspected serial killer, granting the former somewhat lesser procedural rights than the latter may well be justified under a judicial balancing approach. Ordinary criminals, and even serial killers do not appear to pose polity-wide threats, or to strike against the very collective identity of the citizenry. Arguably, the threat that would-be terrorists pose against the felt unity and cohesiveness of the polity may alone justify according greater weight to the polity's security interests and hence legitimate some constriction of fundamental rights.

As already observed, terrorists, such as those who struck New York on September 11, 2001, or ETA or the IRA, are not likely to pose a danger of destroying a polity the way a foreign war or a full fledged civil war might. Nevertheless, terrorism, by its very unexpected and seemingly senseless and random nature, creates fears and anxieties that affect a polity's self-confidence and self-image. These changes, in turn, are likely to bring about conditions of stress. Under such conditions, moreover, and in connection with waging the war on terror, collective security and identity reinforcement may justify curtailing the scope of certain rights both civil and political. With respect to political rights, whereas the war on terror may call for suppression of certain political parties, such as *Batasuna* as discussed earlier,[48] just as does adherence to militant democracy, the respective reasons involved are different. In the case of militant democracy, the principal fear is that democracy could be compromised;

[46] See, for example, French Const. Art 16 giving President virtually complete power monopoly during state of emergency.

[47] See, for example, *Hamdi v. Rumsfeld*, 124 S. Ct. 2633 (2004) (U.S. Supreme Court plurality opinion used balancing test to determine validity of continued detention without charges of war on terror prisoner); *Beit Sourik Village* (2004) (Israel Supreme Court use of proportionality analysis to determine legality of separation wall designed to protect Israeli civilians from would-be Palestinian suicide bombers).

[48] See supra, at 244.

in that of the war on terror, that security will be threatened and the collective self-image of the polity destabilized.[49]

In short, to the extent that the war on terror unfolds, under conditions of stress, it does not require abolition of political rights or creation of new ones. What it calls for is proportionate readjustment that is likely to lead to some shrinking of the scope of certain civil and political rights. Which rights, and how much shrinking, will depend on the particular circumstances involved.

7.4.3. *Pacted Secession*

Attempts at unilateral secession, such as those that led to civil war in the United States in the 1860s, invariably create conditions of crisis. Efforts to achieve a pacted secession, in contrast, are likely to arise under, and/or produce, conditions of stress, but they may well avoid falling into conditions of crisis. This may seem at first paradoxical or even contradictory, given that the distinction between conditions of stress and of crisis has been cast throughout the present analysis in terms of the difference between more remote and more immediate or more imminent threats to the unity and coherence of the polity. Under further analysis, and from the perspective of comprehensive pluralism, however, no real contradiction is involved as the unity or coherence of any particular polity is not an ultimate good. Instead, a working polity that does not actually face any plausible threat of dissolution possesses a viable framework that allows for a sufficient degree of integration among the various selves and others that share the same political space. More specifically, the framework in question must provide for a well-balanced array of nodes of identification and differentiation (e.g., through federalism, political party democracy, minority rights) to allow all the selves and others involved to engage in dynamic and peaceful interaction while cohering together through identification with the common overall self that binds the polity together without unduly sacrificing adherence to more particular or local selves. For example, one should be able to be German without abandoning being Bavarian or be at once Italian and also Florentine.

Existing nation-states do not necessarily provide the best suited framework for the achievement of the optimal balance between identification and differentiation within a viable political space. Sometimes, such optimal equilibrium may require

---

[49] This latter point is vividly illustrated by the *Batistuna* case. In relation to the self-image of post-Franco Spain, where the identity of the polity depends on a delicate balance between a sense of national unity and accommodation of the diversity represented by autonomous regions such as Cataluña and the Basque region, Basque terrorism and separatism seem to pose a much greater identity-based threat than a security one. Indeed, such terrorism risks to upset the delicate balance between unity and diversity, thus raising the possibility of repressive unity such as that imposed by Franco, or that of a civil war between those that would yearn for a return to authoritarian rule to preserve Spain's unity, those who would preserve the status quo, and those who would seek secession of certain autonomous regions.

integration of other selves within a larger political space, such as that provided by a transnational polity. For example, it is quite plausible that differences between Flemish-speaking and French-speaking Belgians might better be addressed within the larger framework of the European Union than within the narrower bounds of the Belgian polity. On the other hand, at other times, such optimal equilibrium is unlikely to be achieved without disentangling selves and others that are in such constant confrontation as threatens the unity and well-being of their common nation-state. For example, approximating the requite balance between identification and differentiation was arguably better achieved by splitting the former Czechoslovak nation-state into the Czech Republic and the Republic of Slovakia.

Dissolution and reconstitution of polities to achieve better integration of identification and differentiation is thus not per se contrary to the edicts of comprehensive pluralism. *Involuntary* dissolution (from the standpoint of all or of some groups within the polity) is certain to provoke a crisis if it seems imminent, and conditions of stress if it seems plausible but more remote. On the other hand, a successfully concluded secession pact should produce neither crisis nor stress. Finally, the *prospect* of a pacted secession would most likely take place under conditions of stress inasmuch as it would indicate a willingness to negotiate a peaceful pacted secession coupled with uncertainty about the outcome of such negotiations, which, if they were to fail, could eventually culminate in a unilateral secession or civil war.

The prospect of pacted secession was considered by the Canadian Supreme Court in *Reference re Secession of Quebec*.[50] The key question before the Court was whether Quebec was legally entitled to secede unilaterally from Canada. The Court answered in the negative, but added that if a clear majority in Quebec wanted to secede, the remaining provinces had an obligation to negotiate with Quebec in good faith in order to determine whether an agreement could be reached on a pacted secession. The Court specified that considerations of democracy and federalism, among others, required that negotiations regarding secession be as serious and solemn as deliberations concerning adoption of a proposed constitutional amendment. Ultimately, these negotiations would be political in nature.

The Court indicated that the outcome of political process of negotiation at stake was uncertain and refused to speculate over what ought to follow should negotiations toward pacted secession fail. In terms of politics, negotiations with a view to pacted secession ought to be constitutional politics. Moreover, given the tension created within the Canadian polity by Quebec's separatist movement, these negotiations would seem bound to take place under conditions of stress.

As constitutional politics intended to redesign relationships between self and other within and across polities, a pacted secession, such as that contemplated

---

[50]   2 S.C.R. 217 (1998).

by the Canadian Supreme Court, deals with subject-related conflicts rather than with those regarding mere benefit or burden allocations. Accordingly, consistent with comprehensive pluralism, such pacted secession should draw directly on the second-order norms that define the pluralist ethos. In short, inasmuch as they arise in conditions of stress, pacted secessions require both enhanced consideration of the other by the self and intensification of the role of self-government. In other words, pacted secession under stress requires greater valorization and protection of the identity rights of self and other and an increased self-restraint to preserve self-government from accrued temptations to govern for self-realization to the exclusion of the other who seeks secession or from whom secession is sought.

In the last analysis, all three cases – that of hate speech and militant democracy, that of the war on terror, and that of pacted secession – indicate that there is a common task under various conditions of stress. That task is to strengthen or prevent further weakening of the bonds between the multiple selves and others that in spite of the various layer of differentiation that separate them continue to cohere as a unified whole within the bounds of relevant polity. What precisely needs to be done in any particular case depends on the circumstances. In some cases, it requires strengthening certain rights, or strengthening some and weakening others. In other cases, it may require constricting the scope of certain rights to readjust proportionately the interplay between identity and difference. In yet other cases, it requires great self-restraint and self-control to prevent outright exclusion of an other that has seemingly become too distant. In any event, conditions of stress do not call for any wholesale rejection or reinvention of the political rights suited for ordinary times. In most cases, conditions of stress merely require refinement and readjustment.

7.5. FINAL APPRAISAL ON THE ROOM FOR PLURALISM IN POLITICAL RIGHTS DURING TIMES OF STRESS

Within the ambit of comprehensive pluralism, politics and political rights are meant to steer external dealings between self and other so as to strive to a maximum possible degree of overall unity combined with accommodation of the most extensive possible diversity. In ordinary times, political rights must encourage vigorous self-government, foster or protect communal solidarity, and carve out a space for individual and collective self-realization. In times of crisis, the threat to unity is so grave that the polity may have to suspend its pursuit of diversity and temporarily cease recognition or enforcement of political rights. In the course of a genuine struggle for survival, what unifies or can unify the polity as a whole must trump what does, or could further, divide it.

What is required in times of stress is less obvious because the prime objective at such times may either be a return to ordinary times or avoidance at all cost to deteriorate inexorably toward times of crisis, or both. To the extent that the focus is on return to ordinary times, the emphasis should be on reinforcement of political rights, or of the most important ones even if that can only be done at the expense of others. Thus, if democracy is threatened, recourse to militant democracy, which intensifies commitment to democracy but somewhat restricts its scope, may be the best weapon to ward off such threat. On the other hand, if the task is to prevent at all costs falling into conditions of crisis, the primary concern should be to defuse clashes between self and other. And that may require increasing or decreasing the scope of political rights or adjusting their weight. Thus, in the war on terror, limiting certain civil and political rights may inoculate against eventually having to suspend them altogether in the face of a crisis. Furthermore, in the case of pacted secession, the goal is to narrow the range of differences within a polity, by reassigning increasingly incompatible differences to different polities.

In the end, pluralism does not furnish a list of political rights for each of the three different times discussed throughout. Instead, it provides a logic and a dialectic that allow for a determination of the particular political rights that are best suited for given circumstances. In this context, the political rights suited for times of stress are not that different from those suited for other times. Nevertheless, in times of stress, the same rights are likely to be more or less extensive and more or less intense, depending on whether the most urgent need is to strengthen bonds between self and other or to defuse conflict between them.

Consistent with the preceding conclusions, it becomes clear that the pluralist ethos is well suited for deployment during times of stress. As we have seen, political rights may have to go through certain variations in intensity or extension in the course of being fine-tuned to best fulfill their role in times of stress, but the differences involved are ones of degree rather than of kind. In other words, depending on the particular context involved, conditions of stress may leave room for more or less *plurality* through pertinent adjustments of the scope and intensity of political rights. Under certain conditions of stress, as previously noted, plurality should be increased; under other conditions, it should be somewhat decreased, but by no means suppressed or eliminated. Moreover, variable degrees of plurality are entirely consistent with the application of the pluralist ethos in both times of stress and in ordinary times. Indeed, even in the most stable of ordinary times, the optimal actual factual plurality will vary from one polity to the next in function of the respective sets of actual competing conceptions of the good involved. In all cases, the competing conceptions at play will have to be subjected to comprehensive pluralism's dialectic and second-order norms, and, inevitably, in some cases the plurality ethos will justify greater plurality than in others.

It is only at the very borderline between conditions of stress and conditions of crisis that the viability and desirability of pluralism comes into question. But under those circumstances, as evinced by the preceding analysis of political rights, pluralism fares no differently than liberalism, republicanism or communitarianism. Indeed, as conditions of stress verge on times of crisis, liberal self-realization becomes reduced to self-preservation; republican civic virtue in the pursuit of the common good becomes confined to a struggle for survival; and communitarian group solidarity becomes directed exclusively toward defeating the internal or external enemy bent on destroying the community at stake or its way of life. In sum, based on the preceding examination of political rights, because of its greater breadth and flexibility, pluralism fares better than its competitors in times of stress, while presumably faring no worse than any of the latter in times of crisis.

8

Derrida's Deconstructive Ethics of Difference Confronts Global Terrorism

Can Democracy Survive the Autoimmune Ravage of the Terror Within Us?

Beyond the threats it may pose to our security, global terrorism has had a dramatic impact on our psyche, our imagination, and the ethos of our age. As stressed since the outset, global terrorism has inscribed itself alongside a series of evolving shifts, including those toward the disenchantment of reason, toward globalization tied to balkanization, toward the politicization of religious fundamentalism, and toward the replacement of modernism by subjectivism and postmodernism. Taken together, these changes have severely jolted, if not completely derailed, the project of the Enlightenment. Moreover, whether ultimately closely linked to the aforementioned recent trends or independent from them, global terrorism stands out for the ferocity with which it apparently undercuts all the major expressions of contemporary ethos and seemingly systematically debunks the key premises upon which the latter are grounded.

Although modalities and nuances abound, there are essentially three different approaches to ethics conceived in terms of binding self to other by properly and fairly accounting for all the relevant identities and differences that emerge in the course of intersubjective dealings between the two. Post-modern ethics, as molded by Derrida's deconstructive approach, is an ethics of difference: Self and other are identical as equals, and their ethical duty to one another is to accept, take into account, and act consistent with the singularity of the other before them, hence giving recognition and respect for all the differences embraced by the latter. In contrast, ethics grounded in modernism, as exemplified by Habermas's Kantian-based discourse ethics, places paramount importance on the universal, on that which binds together humankind as a whole, and hence requires self and other to interact as ethical beings endowed with equal dignity based on bonds of identity. In other words, above all differences, there are universal links of identity that provide the grounding for equal dignity. Finally, as against Derrida's post-modern ethics of difference, which will be discussed in this chapter, and as against Habermas's modern ethics of identity to be examined in Chapter 9, comprehensive pluralism, with its commitment to confront the dialectic between identity and difference or between the one and the many, all the way up and all the way down, sketches out an ethics that is neither tilted to identity nor to difference. Instead, pluralist ethics endeavors to blend identity and difference and to preserve as much of each of the two as possible in light of the particular contextual circumstances in play.

Global terrorism, understood as a unified, indissoluble amalgam of ideology and practices, apparently strikes at the core of all three of the aforementioned ethics. In the context of an ethics of difference, global terrorism can be posited as yet one more instance of singularity and hence as being entitled to as much ethical recognition and deference as any other set of differences that mark the singularity of another. As a consequence, either global terrorism must figure as yet one more acceptable difference, or it must be excluded, which would seemingly contradict the very premise of an ethics of difference.

To the extent that global terrorism is the expression of an ethics, such as that propounded by Jihadist fundamentalist religion, it also seemingly undermines the claims to unity and universality that are essential to identity ethics. As will be further discussed in Chapter 9, discourse ethics posits a universal morality built on the links of identity between self and other. Global terrorism not only challenges the validity of such universal morality, but also claims that its own morality based on the dictates of fundamentalist religion are at once superior to all others and universally valid. Undoubtedly, proponents of identity ethics can dismiss the particular normative claims that are advanced by those who embrace global terrorism but that alone would not dispel the impression left by the challenge posed by the latter: namely, that there are no universally acceptable bonds of identity that could bind all humankind to uniform standards of ethics or morals.

Similarly, global terrorism can be perceived as undermining pluralist ethics by thwarting both its pole of identity and its pole of difference. On the identity side, global terrorism appears completely impervious to the unifying thrust of pluralism's second-order norms. In other words, there seems to be no room whatsoever for any accommodation between the former and the latter. On the difference side, on the other hand, there is arguably no room for admission of global terrorism among all the different conceptions of the good entitled to equal inclusion in the course of the first logical moment of comprehensive pluralism's dialectic. Indeed, global terrorism looms as so abhorrent and so bereft of any positive characteristic as to deserve ex ante exclusion from the realm of permissible difference as opposed to the otherwise automatically assumed inclusion within the latter. Moreover, if these observations turned out to become fully warranted, then comprehensive pluralism would not be, in the end, pluralistic all the way up and all the way down, nor could it truly mutually reconcile the one and the many.

In order more fully to assess the threat posed by global terrorism to the three kinds of ethics discussed earlier, this chapter will concentrate on Derrida's ethics of difference and compare its handling of the problems posed by global terrorism to the way pluralist ethics is poised to deal with them. In Chapter 9, the latter will be compared, in turn, with the approach toward global terrorism devised pursuant to Habermas's ethics of identity.

8.1. DERRIDA, DECONSTRUCTION, AND THE ETHICS OF DIFFERENCE

Deconstruction as an interpretive practice has an ethics of its own, a commitment to pursue relevant intertextual links wherever they may lead, regardless of how unconventional or unsettling that may be. Deconstruction, however, has another dimension that emerges as it turns to the ethical implications of major moral, social, or political issues, such as law and justice, friendship, hospitality, forgiveness, the death penalty, and most recently global terrorism. In these latter instances, Derrida engages in the deconstruction of ethics as well as in the ethics of deconstruction. And the deconstruction of ethics is ethical inasmuch as it is driven by the necessary but impossible call to reconciliation between self and other without compromising the irreducible singularity of either (Rosenfeld 1992: 158).

"Force of Law" (Derrida 1992), Derrida's profound and path-breaking deconstruction of the relationship between law and justice more than any other single work marks the advent of his ethical turn. In that seminal work, Derrida provides a radical and revolutionary deconstruction of justice and its relation to law and violence that at once inscribes itself in a tradition going back to Aristotle and stands the latter's conception on its head. For Aristotle, justice requires treating equals equally and unequals, equally (Aristotle 1980: bk. v). Consistent with this, justice requires adoption of general rules that properly account for relevant differences (i.e., those that determine who is equal or unequal to whom). General rules, however, because they have to be formulated with some degree of abstraction, may not lead to fair applications in certain exceptional cases. To deal with this problem, Aristotle suggests that rules that are prima facie universally applicable be qualified by some exceptions to allow for fairness in those relatively few cases in which a combination of certain particular factors make application of the rule in question unfair. In short, for Aristotle justice must be supplemented by equity (Id.: 1137b, lines 27–8).

Starting from the premise that justice must be predicated on the absolute equality between self and other and confronted with the irreducible differences that distinguish self from other, Derrida radicalizes and transforms Aristotle's insight. For Derrida, in every case, justice requires simultaneous compliance with the appropriate universal rule and with its exception, thus making justice both necessary and impossible (Derrida 1992: 17). Moreover, two important further consequences follow from this: Law inasmuch as it embodies general rules (or even general rules with exceptions) cannot ever be strictly speaking just, and the pursuit of justice through binding law inevitably leads to violence inasmuch as it coerces the other to act or to refrain from acting in at least partial disregard of the other's particular and irreducible identity, beliefs, and designs (Rosenfeld 1998: 60).

More generally, Derrida's deconstruction of ethics and politics draws on two clashing European philosophical traditions: that of Kant (Derrida 2003: 167–94) and that of Nietzsche and Heidegger (Derrida 1982: 109–36). To oversimplify while capturing the essential, Derrida's deconstruction of justice as necessary but impossible combines Kantian universalism and the categorical imperative, on the one hand, with the Nietzschean/Heideggerian insight that the living constantly evolving experience that confronts us in all its complex diversity and vitality can never be neatly captured much less mastered by reason, on the other. In other words, when Derrida the philosopher of difference turns to the ethical, he encounters at once the strong normative call for a common bond of identity between self and other – a bond that, already mentioned, Kant establishes at the level of transcendental idealism – and the obligation to account for the full panoply of differences of the irreducible other, though the self can at best have a partial glance into the diversity at stake.

What emerges from this is an unbridgeable gap between the ethical duty to forge common bonds of identity with the other and the equally compelling ethical duty to account for, and act in ways that accord full respect and consideration to, the differences that cast the other as a singular other self. As already noted, in the context of justice, this gap is that between law and justice. One may craft laws with the intent of achieving justice, but these laws are bound to fall short as it is impossible to give full expression at once to the relevant general rule and to all its pertinent individualized exceptions. Moreover, similar gaps emerge in the context of deconstructing other ethical relationships such as friendship or forgiveness. The gap is between self-regarding and other-regarding friendship and between proportional and hence conditional forgiveness and unconditional forgiveness. Thus, to the extent that friendship toward another is based on an expectation of receiving something in return, it cannot be true friendship as it verges on a relationship based on mutual self-interest. True friendship is therefore impossible friendship, such as friendship toward the dead who cannot be expected to provide anything in return (Derrida 1994: 322–9). Similarly, forgiveness that is proportional, such as that extended to someone who has acted to rectify a situation or to compensate for a misdeed, is barely forgiveness. On the other hand, forgiveness that is not self-regarding is disproportionate, amounts to forgiveness of the unforgivable, and is problematic if not impossible (Derrida 2001: 38–9).

8.2. GLOBAL TERRORISM'S CHALLENGE TO THE
ETHICS OF DIFFERENCE

The unbridgeable gap between the pole of identity and that of difference is problematic, particularly in relation to determining what specific norms or actions are called for. For example, laws can never be just, but does deconstruction provide the means to determine which laws are more just or less unjust than others? Clearly, laws that blatantly disregard the common ground between self and other or that consciously ignore differences that are generally recognized as constitutive of the other's identity are unacceptably unjust. But what about laws that in their own imperfect way seek to approximate justice?

One plausible answer is that the best that can be done is to craft laws with an eye to justice in good faith, or, in other words, as best as one can.[1] For example, neither laws imposing equal treatment nor those sanctioning affirmative action can promote full racial or gender-based justice. Nonetheless, some may believe in good faith that the former laws come closer to justice, while others may believe in equally good faith the latter laws do. Moreover, since none of the two kinds of law involved inherently seems significantly more unjust than the other, adoption of either would result in an acceptable good faith approximation to justice.

Such approximation, which may be acceptable in the context of justice, friendship, or forgiveness, seems clearly inadequate, however, in the context of terrorism. On the one hand, terrorism looms as inherently and unexceptionally unacceptable no matter its cause or context. The random killing of innocent civilians in New York on September 11, 2001, Madrid on March 11, 2004, London on July 7, 2005 or Mumbai on November 26, 2008, ostensibly involves utter disregard for the other and thus constitutes a direct assault against Derrida's ethics of difference. Upon further deconstruction, on the other hand, the ethical status of terrorism can become much more murky. Thus, for example, one person's terrorism is another's war of liberation. As Derrida observes, "[e]very terrorist in the world claims to be responding in self-defense to a prior terrorism on the part of the state, one that simply went by other names and covered itself with all sorts of more or less credible justifications" (Borradori 2003: 103). In terrorism linked to national self-determination, such as that of Basques in Spain, of the IRA in Northern Ireland, or of Palestinians against Israel, the struggle is against a much more powerful and formidable adversary who is perceived as systematically negating and suppressing the core collective and individual identity of the person engaging in terrorism and of all other members of that

---

[1]   This notion of "good faith" has some resemblance to Sartre's notion of authenticity. See Sartre 1966: 86 n.10 ("authenticity" is self-recovery from "bad faith"). Sartre influenced Derrida, see Derrida 1996: 587.

person's group. Moreover, even in global terrorism, such as that perpetrated by Al Qaeda, the claim is that globalization aggressively imposes an order that assaults and undermines Islam and is destructive of the core identity of those who adhere to Islam.

If pure disregard of the other is unequivocally unethical in the context of the ethics of difference, self-defense against state terrorism or global terrorism, or, in other words, against the other's attempt to deny the self treatment as another self, seems prima facie ethical. Indeed, if even the quest for justice is inevitably accompanied by violence, violence necessary to prevent eradication of the self's identity by the other seems eminently justifiable. More generally, the obligation to forge common bonds of identity with the other must be deferred when it is necessary to engage in self-defense against the other's attempts to destroy the self's identity.

Both global terrorists and those who seek to eradicate them accuse one another of seeking to destroy the other or the other's identity. Accordingly, each seeks to justify violence against the other while condemning the violence of the other. From the standpoint of deconstructive ethics, there is a similar gap between identity and difference in the context of terrorism as there is in those of justice, friendship, or forgiveness. Unlike the gap relating to justice, friendship, or forgiveness, however, the gap concerning terrorism is unacceptable and unbearable. Indeed, the gap relating to justice, for example, calls for further ethical commitment toward narrowing the divide between law and justice, but each effort in that direction seems acceptable so long as it is conducted in good faith. In contrast, the gap relating to terrorism is unacceptable and unbearable even if approached in good faith because it at once implies self-preservation and annihilation of the other, and because any excess in either direction threatens the collapse of the very pursuit of a deconstructive ethics of difference.

The unacceptable gap in the case of terrorism raises the question of whether the latter will ultimately prove to be the Achilles' heel of a Derridean ethics of difference. In other words, if each self (from its own differentiated perspective) can cast the other as the terrorist, and if there is no way to mediate between these diverse and, at least to some extent, diametrically opposed perspectives, then there can be little hope that the self will even attempt any gesture toward the other. And without such an attempt, there cannot be ethical life. To assess whether Derridean ethics is actually bound to reach such a dead end, it is now necessary to take a closer look at Derrida's deconstruction of terrorism, and in particular at how terrorism as difference fares in relation to the project of the Enlightenment.

As understood, by Derrida, global terrorism, unlike all other phenomena, is not amenable to the dialectical dynamic between identity and difference that shapes the deconstructive ethics of self and other. The reasons for this are, in turn, twofold. On the one hand, global terrorism – as symbolized by the attacks of September 11, 2001, which are encapsulated in the sign "9/11" – is not amenable to further reference through language and hence remains beyond the meaning-endowing discourse that allows for the development of ethical links between self and other.[2] On the other hand, Derrida links global terrorism to something akin to an autoimmune disease of the contemporary Western democratic polity negotiating the passage from the Cold War to globalization, and in particular of the superpower that has led this transition, the United States (Id.: 140, 150–9). If, indeed, consistent with Derrida's assessment, the United States' push toward globalization and its consequent "victimization" by, and confrontation against, global terrorism are best viewed as an autoimmune attack, then global terrorism is a product or symptom of self-destruction. To the extent that the self attacks itself, moreover, it destroys the very possibility of seeking to build bridges between self and other so as to encompass the full singularity and diversity of each, which is the paramount pursuit prescribed by a deconstructive ethics of difference. In short, by remaining beyond language, global terrorism is destructive of the prime medium of interaction between self and other. Furthermore, as part of an auto destructive process akin to an autoimmune disease, global terrorism undermines the integrity – in the literal sense of the term – of the necessary interlocutors in any genuine intersubjective ethical project.

Underlying Derrida's conclusion that global terrorism is "unspeakable," are two principal factors: one quantitative, the other qualitative. As Derrida notes, modern terrorism is not new as it traces back to Robespierre's Reign of Terror during the French Revolution (Id.: 152). What is new with today's global terrorism, however, is the magnitude of its potential destructiveness through the use of nuclear, biological, and chemical weapons (Id.: 151). Accordingly, the threat posed by global terrorism does not naturally lead to discussion, but to unspeakable fear, panic, and trauma.

From the qualitative standpoint, on the other hand, what distinguishes global terrorism from nationalist terrorism for Derrida is that the former projects an ideology that lacks any opening to the future.[3] Global terrorism, moreover, has no future in at least two different senses. First, it has no future as pure violence breeding further violence. And, second it has no future inasmuch as Bin Laden and his associates seek imposition of a fanatical pre-modern religious ideology hermetically closed to the Enlightenment, modernity, and the present, let alone the future (Id.: 113–14).

Before focusing more specifically on the relationship between global terrorism and the Enlightenment, it is necessary to take a brief look at what Derrida characterizes as America's tendency to autoimmune auto destruction in the context of

---

[2]   See Borradori 2003: 147:

  For Derrida, by pronouncing 9/11 we do not use language in its obvious referring function but rather press it to name something that it cannot name because it happens beyond language: terror and trauma.

[3]   See Id.: 113. Speaking of Bin Laden and his global terrorism, Derrida observes that "such actions and such discourse *open onto no future and, in my view, have no future*" (emphasis in original).

globalization and global terror. Essentially, at the highest levels of abstraction, the other who sets to destroy the self is located within the latter and finds its weapons of destruction within the self. Thus, the 9/11 hijackers circulated freely in the United States, attended its flight schools, and turned its scheduled commercial jetliners into deadly weapons of terror. Furthermore, by trying to protect itself from the assault of the other within itself, the self ends up becoming other than itself. Thus, an open society with enemies within like the United States, must sacrifice liberty to security to more effectively protect itself, but in so doing it chips away at its identity as a free and open society.

More specifically, Derrida focuses on the trajectory of the process of autoimmune auto destruction in the context of the evolution from the end of the Cold War to globalization and to global terror. According to Derrida, this process of auto destruction has three phases (Id.: 150–2). The first phase is traceable the Cold War itself as it is in the context of opposing the Soviets in Afghanistan that the United States nurtured and sustained Bin Laden and his mujahadeen who would later turn against it and mastermind 9/11. The second phase is located in the aftermath of the Cold War in the context of the concurrent spread of globalization and global terrorism. The collapse of the Soviet Union has led to an arsenal of unguarded nuclear weapons, which makes it all too possible that weapons of mass destruction may fall in the hands of global terrorists. In addition, globalization has opened markets and borders, and the technological revolution in cyberspace has allowed for anonymous instant worldwide communication. All of this inures to the benefit of the global terrorist who can now secretly and anonymously threaten mass destruction without any of the Cold War safeguards such as state control and reciprocal restraints based on the danger of mutual nuclear annihilation. As a consequence of this post-Cold War imbalance, global terrorism's potential for mass destruction leads to widespread trauma, panic, and terror in all polities that feel targeted. Finally, the third phase is marked by the cycle of repression that characterizes the reactions to 9/11 and subsequent global terrorist attacks or threats. To protect itself, the state must go against terrorists, and given the nature of the threat, it is often imperative that the state act preventively. But that leads to massive internal surveillance and repression and sets open societies on a course of self-destruction.

On first impression at least, globalization seems fully consistent with the project of the Enlightenment. Overall, globalization consists in the spread of liberal capitalism and the rationality it entails worldwide beyond the strictures of nation-state control or regulation. In an important sense, globalization is called for by the very logic of the rationality of liberal capitalism given existing material conditions and capacities. Consistent with all this, moreover, it is only global terrorism anchored in premodern religious fundamentalism that stands squarely against the Enlightenment ideology and against any prolongation of the Enlightenment project.

Derrida certainly shares with proponents of the Enlightenment ideology an unequivocal condemnation of global terrorism.[4] His assessment of globalization, however, is not consistent with the one suggested previously. Moreover, whereas Derrida shares certain goals of the Enlightenment project, such as the development of Kantian cosmopolitanism (Id.: 130), he remains critical of tolerance, a key Enlightenment value and tool, and of instrumental reason, another Enlightenment mainstay. More generally, Derrida's radical ethical commitment to singularity and difference in their irreducible complexity and diversity is arguably incompatible with successful pursuit of the Enlightenment project, and perhaps even undercuts the consistency of his unequivocal condemnation of global terrorism. In other words, though there is no doubt about the sincerity of Derrida's condemnation of global terrorism, is such condemnation the mere expression of personal emotion, or is it consistent with a deconstructive ethics of difference?

If one regards globalization as the culmination of the Enlightenment project, the end of the Cold War marks the end of a major split over the true legacy of the Enlightenment. Consistent with this, moreover, globalization promises the eventual breakdown of remaining barriers to the worldwide spread of instrumental rationality and tolerance; the creation of conditions conducive to cosmopolitan citizenship for all; and democracy beyond the confines of the nation-state. In a word, globalization would thus represent the triumph of reason over prejudices and passions, and global terrorism, the last stand of parochial irrationalism. More generally, the Enlightenment project has called throughout for a struggle against the darker side of humanity, and the struggle against global terrorism is but the most recent and quite probably the last chapter in this struggle.

For Derrida, in contrast, if the project of the Enlightenment is properly placed in its actual historical context, the irrational, the partial, and the parochial must be located within it, not outside of it. In other words, when viewed historically, the Enlightenment project encompasses within its bounds aporias and contradictions that pose a series of concrete, historically situated challenges. Accordingly, the Enlightenment's ultimate success depends less on repelling outside threats than on charting a course that properly confronts internal obstacles and limitations.

Deconstructive ethics is consistent with the promise of the Enlightenment, namely freedom and equality for all (Id.: 172). The question then is not whether Derrida's theory is contrary to the Enlightenment, but whether his deconstruction of the historicity of the institutions and values associated with the Enlightenment lead to negation rather than to deferral of freedom and equality for all. To be in a

---

4   See Id.: 113 (Derrida makes it clear that though he has strong reservations concerning how Europe and the United States are handling the war against terror, he remains firmly on their side against terror).

better position to answer this question, it is necessary to take a closer look at Derrida's deconstruction of globalization, tolerance, and democracy.

8.3. DERRIDA'S DECONSTRUCTION OF GLOBALIZATION, TOLERANCE, AND DEMOCRACY

In appearance both tolerance and globalization are widely encompassing, open to all, and neutral. As Derrida sees them, however, beneath the surface they are both to a significant degree exclusionary and far from neutral. Just as there is for Derrida a gap between law and justice, there is also one between tolerance and hospitality and between globalization and equal cosmopolitan citizenship for all. Finally, there also an insurmountable divide for Derrida between democracy as it is and the "democracy to come" (*à venir*) between rational pursuit of the will of the majority and the (impossible) equal treatment of the full singularity of every person within the global polity (Id.: 120).

Derrida approaches tolerance historically and emphasizes that traditionally to be tolerated did not mean being treated as an equal, but rather as an object of condescension to whom is extended no more than mere acceptance (Id.: 127). Tolerance is a Catholic virtue (Id.: 126), and as such is it accorded from a position of strength by those who are confident of possessing the truth to those perceived by those in power as living in error. Tolerance, therefore, is not for Derrida a relationship among equals, but rather a concession by the powerful to the powerless, and one that is subject to change or revocation at will.[5] Derrida contrasts tolerance to hospitality. For him, hospitality requires unconditional invitation and acceptance of all others to one's home, community, or polity (Id.: 127–30). Tolerance, on the other hand, amounts to limited hospitality as it seeks accommodation of some but not others, and as it makes such accommodation conditional (Id.: 127–8). Unconditional hospitality is ethically mandated but politically impossible – indiscriminate hospitality to all comers could prove self-destructive – whereas tolerance though an Enlightenment virtue ends up undermining the latter inasmuch as it stands in the way of, rather than promoting, equality for all.

Like tolerance, globalization purports to promote freedom and equality for all, but in fact it ends up doing the opposite. Ideally, globalization is meant to level the playing field for all humanity by turning the entire planet into a single fully integrated market and a seamlessly conjoined unified worldwide polity. In point of fact, however, globalization has consisted in imposition of the sectarian partial and highly contested institutional practices and way of life of the most powerful nation-states

---

[5]   In contrast to Derrida, Habermas is convinced that present-day tolerance can transcend its Christian origins and become a subject of dialogical give and take among equals (Id.: 17–18).

on an ever-increasing portion of the globe. Consistent with this, viewed through a Derridean lens, globalization is much less a movement of worldwide emancipation from the strictures of the nation-state than a kind of recolonization achieved though the economic might of the most powerful and through rapid spread and strategic use of sophisticated modern technologies (Id.: 121–4).

As already noted, in Derrida's view, globalization sets the globalizing polities, and the United States in particular, on a path of autoimmune self-destruction. This is done in part by unwittingly enabling the global terrorist or the enemy other within, and, in part, by alienating the self from itself through repressive actions undertaken in self-defense and through dilution of its identity in the quest for global reach.

The global terrorist is bent on resisting or countering the penetration of globalizing trends and ways of life through terrorizing violence in the name of a fundamentalist pre-modern religion. Significantly, consistent with views discussed in Chapter 5, Derrida stresses that the principal globalizing power, the United States, has also experienced a return to religion, or more precisely, a thorough politicization of religion (Id.: 117–18). To some extent, consistent with Derrida's assessment, these two convergences toward religion mirror one another as they mark a reaction against the disembodied obstructions produced by the rapidly spreading new technologies (Id.: 157). Thus, both for American and for Islamic fundamentalists, religion provides the means to reestablish links to the concrete or, in other words, to reclaim singularity in the face of the sweeping homogenizing trend spearheaded by the new technologies (Id.).

If, in spite of the convergence of America and of global terrorism toward religion, Derrida unequivocally sides with America,[6] it is that the religion that emerges in globalizing polities arises in a very different context than that in which Islamic fundamentalism prevails. Indeed, notwithstanding its contradictions, shortcomings, and pathologies, globalization loosens the barriers erected by the nation-state and thus paves the way toward cosmopolitanism and equal citizenship for all the world's inhabitants. Accordingly, even if America's religion taken by itself had no more future than that invoked by the global terrorists, America's globalizing enterprise taken as a whole is not without future provided only that it can be rechanneled away from its autoimmune pathologies.

Although religious America remains clearly preferable to Islamic fundamentalism, Derrida regards secular Europe as much more favorable terrain than present-day America for cosmopolitanism (Id.: 140). Moreover, the ideal of cosmopolitanism as conceived by Derrida derives from Kant and is thus firmly anchored in Enlightenment thought. As Derrida explains, Kant thought that "we should probably give up the idea of a 'world republic' … but not the idea of a cosmopolitical law,

[6] See supra, at note 4.

'the idea of a law of world citizenship'" (Id.: 130). Today, Europe with its extensive transnational network, its serious commitments to international covenants such as the European Convention on Human Rights, and its secular vision looms as propitious grounds for the implantation of world citizenship. In contrast, the United States with its flouting of international law[7] and hostility toward international organizations, such as the United Nations[8] and international institutions, such as the International Criminal Court,[9] does not loom as fertile ground for launching world citizenship notwithstanding its extensive globalizing activities. In the end, whereas Europe holds greater promise for world citizenship, it remains unclear whether the shortcomings and pathologies of globalization may be sufficiently overcome for genuine cosmopolitanism to take hold.

Cosmopolitanism could extend democracy worldwide, but it is insufficient according to Derrida to bring about the "democracy to come" (Id.). The latter requires going beyond the limits of world citizenship to allow all persons on the globe to live together consistent with full respect for the irreducible singularity of each and with sufficient room for such singularity to flourish (Id.). Just as deconstruction emphasizes the gaps between law and justice, tolerance and hospitality, globalization, and cosmopolitanism, so too it highlights the unbridgeable divide between actual democracy and ideal but impossible "democracy to come".

Democracy or self-rule by the *Demos* provides the best available means for reconciling self and other, identity and difference. Ordinary democracy dependent on majority rule, however, must systematically sacrifice singularity and difference to rational pursuit of common interests shared by a majority of the polity's citizenry within the constraints imposed by enforcement of fundamental rights. In democracies on the scale of the nation-state, strangers or non-citizens within and without are essentially left out. Worldwide citizenship overcomes this limitation by making it possible for all human beings to participate in self-government. Moreover, worldwide citizenship without worldwide government allows for multiple centers of democratic rule and for a wider diversity in clusters of common interests amenable to majority rule.

Nevertheless, no democracy based on majority rule can do justice to democracy in its deepest and most radical sense, the "democracy to come," which must be pursued but inevitably forever deferred. This latter democracy requires self-rule not in pursuit of majority wishes but in pursuit of what the singularity of each human being requires for that person and for all those with whom the person in question

---

[7] One notorious example concerns the treatment of the detainees in the "war on terror" held in Guantanamo. See Paust 2005: 838–45.

[8] See, for example, "US Law Makers Keep Up Criticism of the UN," *The Epoch Times*, April 21, 2005, http.//English.@pochtimes.com/admin/makeArticle2.

[9] See "United States Unsigning Treaty on War Crimes Court", *Human Rights Watch*, May 6, 2002.

does or may interact. Thus, the majoritarian compromises that shape ordinary democracy prove inimical to the "democracy to come." Moreover, only the latter democracy, if it ever could come into being, could complete and fully vindicate the Enlightenment's ultimate goal of freedom and equality for all.

Consistent with the preceding analysis, it becomes plain that for Derrida pursuit of the project of the Enlightenment is necessary, but its achievement is impossible. The historical unfolding of the Enlightenment's heritage with its aporias and contradictions is to its ultimate realization in the "democracy to come" like law is to justice. Moreover, tolerance, globalization, global terrorism, and even cosmopolitan citizenship remain far removed and many pitfalls and reversals away from even an incipient breakthrough toward democratic self-rule based on singularity.

Based on this conclusion, is Derrida's unequivocal condemnation of global terrorism and his preferences for America's globalizing mission and ever-more intrusive religiosity sufficiently justified from the standpoint of a deconstructive ethics of difference? That depends on the solidity of Derrida distinction between the global terrorists' religion as having no future and America's religion and self-destructive repression as nonetheless open to a better future. As we shall see later, further deconstruction indicates that this distinction is at best shaky.

8.4. ASSESSING THE ETHICS OF DIFFERENCE'S ACCOUNT OF GLOBAL TERRORISM

Consistent with the Enlightenment's promise of liberty and equality for all, ethical assessment pursuant to the corresponding cannons of justice requires taking proper account of relevant identities and differences. Ethics of difference, such as that based on Derridean deconstruction, however tend to pursue difference to such a degree as to make establishing a basis for common identity virtually impossible. As discussed earlier, Derrida advances an argument for condemning global terrorism from the standpoint of a deconstructive ethics of difference. Derrida's argument will be examined later in this section and found to be ultimately unsupported by the ethics of difference.

Derrida's distinction between the lack of future of the global terrorists' Islamic fundamentalism and the openness to the future of America's globalizing efforts and its further turn toward religion is at best precarious. Indeed, by subjecting this distinction to further deconstruction, it becomes apparent that further differentiation casts doubt on Derrida's claim that fundamentalist Islam has no future and on the proposition that America's turn to religion does not pose a similar threat. If global terrorism's Islamic fundamentalism has no future, it is for at least one of two reasons. First, Islamic fundamentalism is pre-modern and openness to the future requires taking the legacy of the Enlightenment into account, either as Derrida does, by trying to perfect it to meet current historical conditions, or, by trying to go beyond its contradictions and limitations and into a yet to be defined post-Enlightenment era. Second, global terrorism unlike national terrorism is bent on pure negation and destruction. Thus, an Al Quaeda suicide bomber appears bent on pure destruction, whereas a Palestinian suicide bomber or a Basque ETA terrorist appears ultimately motivated by the hope of bringing about liberation and self-government. Furthermore, by combining these two reasons, global terrorism appears to project pure negativity and to irrevocably turn its back to the future.

Further deconstruction indicates, however, that neither of these two reasons nor their conjunction necessarily supports the conclusion that global terrorism cannot be future-looking. First, even if it is conceded that Islamic fundamentalism itself cannot be open to the future, it does not necessarily follow that its political use also need be thus limited. If global terrorism is meant above all as a means of resistance against the evils of globalization, and if its use of Islamic fundamentalism is primarily intended for purposes of countering or slowing down the spread of globalizing forces, then it may well be largely oriented toward the future – a future in which globalization is limited, transformed, or transcended and in which those whom it displaces, disfavors, or ignores will enjoy greater freedom and equality.

Second, whereas it may seem that Basque, Northern Irish, or Palestinian terrorism is less nihilistic than Al Quaeda's global terrorism, careful analysis does not bear out that impression. If national terrorism or that fitted to the scale of the nation-state seems rational in relation to its ends, if not its means, it is because liberation and self-determination are worthy pursuits in the quest for freedom and equality for all. That is at least the case from the subjective standpoint of those who feel unfree and oppressed. Those who perceive themselves unfree and oppressed because of the intrusive inroads of globalization, moreover, are clearly in an analogous position even if their prospects of success are more unlikely – an assumption that is by no means obvious. In other words, if there is any hope of moving closer to liberation and self-determination at a sub-national, national, or supra-national level, then the ends pursued by global terrorists would seem as future-oriented as those motivating their counterparts who act on the scale of the nation-state.

On the other hand, if the current trend toward repolitization of religion in America is pursued to its logical culmination, then the United States may find itself plunged in a pre-modern universe that, for all relevant purposes, would be analogous to that of Islamic fundamentalism. Take for example the demand already mentioned in Chapter 5 that creationism be taught in public schools.[10] Creationism has

---

[10] See "Religion in the Science Class?," *ADL Online*, http://www.adl.org/issue_religious-freedom/ create/creationism ("proponents of religious theories of creation have recently renewed efforts to persuade public schools to teach creationism … either along side or in place of evolution").

no scientific basis,[11] and accordingly were it to supplement, or substitute for, evolution in public schools, it would violate a basic tenet of Enlightenment thought: the separation between science and religion. Moreover, if this separation were systematically eradicated, American society would return to a pre-modern state where the Enlightenment would have lost all future. Accordingly, from the standpoint of the Enlightenment, there would be little difference between Islamic fundamentalism and full implantation of Christian fundamentalism in the United States.

Consistent with the preceding observations, the deconstruction of global terrorism does not lend sufficient support to Derrida's conclusions regarding lack of openness to the future. Moreover, the gap between globalization and genuine cosmopolitan citizenship without world government and that between actual democracy and the "democracy to come" are unbridgeable and the ways to narrow them uncertain. Accordingly, absolute condemnation of global terrorism cannot be systematically justified from the standpoint of a deconstructive ethics of difference. Since even the pursuit of justice involves perpetration of violence, and since the self is not ethically called upon to forgo violence when confronting the other's threat to annihilate it or to eradicate its core identity, it is impossible to justify an unequivocal condemnation of global terrorism without a full grasp of its meaning. But such a meaning is bound to remain elusive since it cannot be fully ascertained without future interpretation (Rosenfeld 1992: 157). Thus, for example, terrorism in the pursuit of national liberation against a cruel and repressive authoritarian regime may be justified ex post if it proves to have been a necessary step in the transition to a democratic regime that is committed to freedom and equality for all. Similarly, it cannot be foreclosed that the interplay between globalization and global terrorism will lead to an institutional reorganization better suited to freedom and equality for all than would have been possible had globalization been fully realized without encountering any serious opposition or confrontation.

It becomes thus clear that a deconstructive ethics of difference cannot yield an unequivocal and categorical condemnation of global terrorism. This is because, given its aim to accommodate all differences and singularities, the ethics of difference cannot sustain a sufficiently stable common identity to sift through competing claims regarding what is required for self-preservation and for protection of the core identity of the self. In other words, as radical singularity precludes establishing a common intersubjective criterion to assess conflicting claims issuing from different perspectives, at least in the short run, each claim can only be evaluated from the standpoint of the subjective perspective from which it is made.[12] Accordingly,

---

[11] Id.
[12] The difference between the short run and the long run is attributable to the fact that the hindsight of history (through future interpretations) may clarify whether a particular past subjective claim was compatible with the ethically mandated search for reconciliation between self and other. Thus, if

without the benefit of long-term hindsight, global terrorism could only be unequivocally condemned as nihilistic and without any future if those conclusions could be drawn from within the perspective of the proponents of such terrorism. And they clearly cannot.[13]

In the last analysis, the deconstructive ethics of difference does not provide a sufficient balance between identity and difference to yield a convincing condemnation of global terrorism. I will argue in the next section that such a balance could be better struck in the context of a pluralist ethics consistent with comprehensive pluralism.

8.5. GLOBAL TERRORISM AND THE CONTRASTS BETWEEN PLURALIST ETHICS AND THE ETHICS OF DIFFERENCE

The advantage of a pluralist ethics is that whereas it seriously aims to accommodate difference, it refuses to treat irreducible singularity as an absolute, thus averting the shortcomings of the Derridean ethics of difference. Moreover, pluralist ethics does guarantee a genuine non-trivial ex ante equal hearing to all perspectives and conceptions of the good, including those of global terrorists. Because of this, I will argue that pluralist ethics offers a superior and more systematic condemnation of global terrorism consistent with striving for the best possible balance between identity and difference than does Derrida's theory. Finally, in light of the pluralist case against global terrorism, I will cast a last critical glance at Derrida's views on the subject.

In its negative moment, comprehensive pluralism is compatible with Derrida's insistence on singularity. In its positive moment, however, comprehensive pluralism is committed to limiting deference to difference to the extent necessary to sustain a minimum of common identity within the relevant unit. That minimum of identity is that required to maintain a fair and workable level of intersubjective give and take to accommodate as much diversity as possible without risking a breakdown of the polity.[14] Accordingly, in its insistence that the practical need for unity limit the

---

global terrorism were to lead to nothing but nihilism and destruction, then its subjective claim that it is necessary to the preservation of a valuable way of life would become susceptible to ex post facto refutation. Conversely, if history were to prove that global terrorism contributed, albeit involuntarily or only partially, to a better reconciliation between self and other, then its subjective claim would receive some degree of ex post facto vindication.

13   This is at least the case with respect to the "defensive" claims of Islamic fundamentalist terrorists who see the West and America in particular as the "great Satan" bent on destroying the Islamic way of life through global spread of its economy, culture and ideology. See, for example, Zettner 2004. In contrast, the "offensive" or Jihadist claims associated with global terrorism may be unequivocally condemned within an ethics of difference to the extent that even within the perspective from which they are made, they negate the "infidel's" right to self-preservation or to his or her own chosen identity and way of life.

14   As indicated in Chapter 7, this does not foreclose peaceful secession. Comprehensive pluralism is as compatible with designing institutions to share a common space or dividing political space so

extent of recognition ultimately accorded to difference, comprehensive pluralism embraces an ethics that is inconsistent with Derrida's conception of an unbreakable bond between the ethics of difference and the ontology of singularity. For comprehensive pluralism, from an ethical standpoint, singularity is only worthy of pursuit so long as it does not threaten the unity of the relevant socio-political unit.

Based on the proper integration of its two moments and on reliance on the interplay between first-order and second-order norms, comprehensive pluralism allows for a systematic condemnation of global terrorism that does not suffer from weaknesses similar to those of Derrida's condemnation. Consistent with pluralism, global terrorism must be unequivocally condemned regardless of whether it is purely nihilistic and without any openness to the future or whether it is in the name of a worthy goal that it alone appears capable of bringing about. Terrorist means are contrary to comprehensive pluralism's second-order norms and hence have no place in any polity – at least so long as one cannot justify them as the sole available means to avert personal annihilation or total destruction of a group's ability to live in accordance with the dictates of its conception of the good.[15] Globalization and American economic expansion worldwide may threaten the way of life of religious fundamentalists, but they neither seek to annihilate the proponents of fundamentalist religion nor use coercive methods or concerted violence to eradicate such religion. In fact, globalization threatens fundamentalist religion mainly through the spread of ideas and promotion of a way of life that are inimical to fundamentalist tenets. Under these circumstances, the greater threat to fundamentalism is likely to be coming from within as exposure to Western ideas and ways of life are likely to draw certain members of fundamentalist groups away from their religious traditions. Since the second-order norms of pluralism require room for open circulation of ideas among proponents of different conceptions of the good, it is entirely inconsistent with pluralism to shield proponents of particular conceptions of the good from exposure to, and possible influence by, other conceptions of the good. In short, consistent with pluralism, religious fundamentalists are not entitled to exclude other ideologies and viewpoints by peaceful means, let alone by terrorist violence.

Both the message of the global terrorist, as opposed to the means used to convey that message, and that of the proponents of globalization are entitled to full protection within a pluralist polity. Moreover, both fundamentalist religion and the ideology of global capitalism, to the extent they are compatible with the functioning

that each of two incompatible conceptions of the good can rule unhindered within its own space. Of course, at the level of global society, secession is not an option, and accommodation becomes mandatory.

[15] Although it is not possible to elaborate this line of argument any further here, presumably some instances of national liberation terrorism, particularly if directed exclusively against military targets, may be warranted under comprehensive pluralism. This may be the case in the context of a particularly oppressive colonial regime that held the indigenous population in virtual slavery.

of second-order norms, are entitled to accommodation and protection in a pluralist society. Conversely, within such society, the coercive aspects of fundamentalist religion and of globalization ought to be neutralized or rejected.

The foregoing discussion lays out an ideal pluralist blueprint for handling the clashes between globalization and Islamic fundamentalism. Proponents of global terrorism could argue, however, that, as a practical matter, there is such a huge discrepancy in power between globalizing forces and those determined to resist them that the latter will be simply swallowed up unless they use terrorism as a means to defend their core identity. In other words, in line with this argument the global terrorist is an analogous position to that of the nationalist terrorist who struggles against virtual enslavement by an authoritarian and repressive colonial regime.

Upon closer inspection, this latter argument is unpersuasive for a number of reasons. Perhaps the most important of these from the standpoint of comprehensive pluralism is that both the Western polities that promote globalization and the Islamic societies where the most concentrated and violent sources of resistance are found are pluralist-in-fact. Indeed, there are debates within globalizing polities, including the United States, concerning the proper scope and limits of globalization. For example, laid-off textile workers may have very different views on the matter than venture capitalists.[16] Similarly, there are proponents and beneficiaries of globalization in Muslim countries, and in many of these countries there have long been profound divisions among proponents and opponents of Islamic fundamentalism (Abdullah 2002). Furthermore, the tools and institutional arrangements at work in the process of globalization are radically different from those at play in a repressive colonial regime. Thus, for example, even if the economy were in fact fully globalized, there is no veritable global polity or government. This allows for coexistence of a multiplicity of overlapping clashing and competing layers of pluralist-in-fact social units in which proponents of various conceptions of the good can vie to acquire increased influence and political power. In short, the multiple opportunities for a pluralist give and take available in the evolving relevant contexts belie the claim that terrorism constitutes the sole means to resist, modify, or counter the efforts produced by the forces of globalization.

Concerning religious fundamentalism itself, from the standpoint of comprehensive pluralism, American Christian fundamentalism is no better than Islamic fundamentalism inasmuch as they both seek to impose their own truth, which they deem absolute, on the polity as a whole, be it the nation-state or the entire planet. Inasmuch as America's reaction to global terrorism has been religious, authoritarian, intolerant, and coercive, Derrida seems justified in having opted after 9/11 for

---

[16]   See, for example, Conway et al. 2003.

more secular Europe. Paradoxically, however, America may still be more open to difference than Europe. Whereas Europe may seem more homogeneous and more unaccepting of other cultures, such as that of its Muslim immigrants, America is divided, and the turn to fundamentalist religion is highly contested (Feldman 2005). Accordingly, Derrideans should not prematurely write off America. On the other hand, perhaps greater focus on Europe will underscore that from an ethical as opposed to an ontological standpoint singularity can be taken too far.

Derrida's deconstruction of ethics and the ethics of difference that it propels cast invaluable light on the struggle to bridge the gap between identity and difference and self and other. They also productively recast the Enlightenment's project by placing it in its proper historical perspective and by highlighting its internal challenges and contradictions. Whereas the unequivocal condemnation of global terrorism that Derrida derives from his ethics of difference proves to be right, the justifications he offers for it remain unsatisfactory. This is primarily due to overemphasis of the ethical import of radical singularity. By being so focused on differences, the crucial countervailing identities become blurred. I have argued that comprehensive pluralism can make up for this deficiency by striking a better balance between identity and difference consistent with the need to provide principled yet specific answers to the crucial ethical questions raised by the encounter between globalization and global terrorism.

There remains one vexing problem that arises in connection with Derrida's conclusion that the apparent vicious cycle that binds globalization, global terrorism, and repression together is the result of a process of self-destruction that mimics the progression of an autoimmune disease. The problem in question is that such autoimmune condition may render further pursuit of the Enlightenment project impossible and altogether destroy the very basis for pluralist ethics. Indeed, pluralist ethics requires constant relationships between self and other,[17] the maintenance of a dialogue between them, and the possibility of accommodation and coexistence between them – these being guaranteed by implementation of second-order norms in the context of comprehensive pluralism. If the self attacks itself and becomes its own enemy, and if it cannot avoid harboring its enemies within itself, then dialogue, accommodation, and any relationship between self and other that is not one of pure enmity become impossible. Stated differently, the autoimmune condition that Derrida has associated with global terrorism seems poised to destabilize and eventually destroy all relationships between self and other, by foreclosing dialogue and accommodation, by heading seemingly inexorably toward self-directed violence and

---

[17] Consistent with the preceding analysis, this does not preclude that self and other evolve over time, but it does require that there be at all times relationships between two or more interlocutors that regard one another as self and other.

enmity against the other within. This leaves no room for any kind of pluralism, let alone comprehensive pluralism.

Whether Derrida's autoimmune analogy is apt, and whether therefore global terrorism may be best condemned, in theory, by a pluralist ethics that it, in practice, renders inoperative are key questions that must be for the moment set aside. Indeed, in order to be in a better position to address these questions, it is first necessary to examine how global terrorism fares in the context of an ethics of identity.

9

Habermas's Discourse Ethics of Identity and Global Terror

Can Cosmopolitanism, Post-Nationalism, and Dialogue Downsize the Terrorist Threat?

9.1. TERRORISM'S CHALLENGE TO HABERMAS'S CONCEPTION OF MODERNISM

Habermas has been a formidable and undaunted defender of modernism and of the project of the Enlightenment against all odds and all foes. And these have been numerous and powerful, such as Nazism and Stalinism in history and politics, and thinkers as diverse as Weber, Heidegger, Wittgenstein, Schmitt, Adorno, and the post-moderns, in theory (Habermas 2001: 130–56). Habermas had been in particular critical of Derrida, charging the latter's deconstructive approach with fostering a reversion to a pre-Enlightenment mystique inimical to the project of modernity (Habermas 1990: 181–4). Habermas and Derrida met and joined hands against global terror, however, in the aftermath of the 9/11/01 attacks (Borradori 2003: xi), and on that occasion, as discussed in Chapter 8, Derrida made clear that he was on the side of the Enlightenment project – though as we shall see, his conception of it remains in sharp contrast to that of Habermas.

Habermas's defense of modernism is predicated on a recasting of Kant's universal moral insight and Rousseau's republican ideal within an intersubjective communicative framework. Through communicative action guided by public reason, social actors from different backgrounds and with diverse interests can arrive at a working understanding by jointly settling on universalizable normative standards meant to regulate the realm of their intersubjective interactions. As conceived by Habermas, communicative action requires each participant in a collective discussion to have an equal opportunity to present claims for consideration and a universal commitment to be swayed only by the force of the better argument.[1] In the context of contemporary pluralist societies, communicative action leads to a rule of law regime based on application of positive law legitimated by adherence to the "proceduralist

---

[1] For a comprehensive discussion of communicative action, see Habermas 1984: vol. 1, 273–337.

paradigm of law." Under this paradigm, laws are legitimate if they can be justified at once as self-imposed by those subjected to them and as satisfying universalizable normative criteria, such as those embodied in universal human rights
(Habermas 1998).

Habermas's reliance on communicative action to legitimate positive law as
both self-imposed and normatively valid for all those subjected to it is meant to
counter the two previously identified major threats confronting the project of the
Enlightenment: the instrumentalization of reason and the disenchantment with
the world associated with modernism (Habermas 2001: 138). As will be recalled,
the reduction of universal reason into instrumental reason leads to domination,
exploitation, and colonization, thus turning the means of the Enlightenment against
its ends, namely liberty and equality for all. On the other hand, the Enlightenment's
use of reason to loosen the "magical" underpinnings – based on religion and other
metaphysical commitments – of pre-modern social cohesion can lead to a crisis
in identity. Either alienated social actors are faced with retreating to individualist
isolation in futile opposition to an increasingly oppressive and meaningless social
reality (Id.: 140), or uprooted collective selves are left with a yearning for return to,
or reinvention of, pre-modern commonly shared meaning-endowing identities.

Whereas Derrida regards these pathologies as intrinsic to the Enlightenment,
Habermas insists that they are extrinsic to it (Borradori 2003: 13, 70). Consistent
with this, if universal reason can be stirred toward the rational discourse fostered
by communicative action, then the Enlightenment need not culminate in mere
instrumental reason. Similarly, if the loosening of religious and metaphysical bonds
is mediated by the solidarity of a community of equals engaged in communicative
action, then disenchantment and despair can be overcome. Indeed, the modalities
of self-government and self-realization framed by the mutual recognition of equals
engaged in communicative action are not only supposed to reinforce solidarity and
endow social actors with a common purpose but also expected to pave the way for
accommodation and harmonization of diverse conceptions of the good within the
bounds of a mutually acceptable legal regime.

As a consequence of historical factors, such as globalization of the economy,
and in reaction to pathologies that have posed a major threat to the project of the
Enlightenment, such as Nazism in Germany or destructive balkanization after the
collapse of the Soviet Union, communicative action requires increasing reliance
on transnational legal norms. This calls for transnational communal solidarity that
may lead to a veritable cosmopolitan order and to the deployment of constitutional
patriotism to supplant nationalism and all its shortcomings. Although the viability
of constitutional patriotism has been seriously questioned (Grimm 1995: Rosenfeld
2010: 258–69), Habermas has steadfastly defended it as highly compatible with the
normative implications of communicative action (Habermas 1995).

Whatever the prospects of a cosmopolitan rule of law order glued together by constitutional patriotism may have been from a late 1990s perspective (Habermas 1998a: 118–20; 2001: 58–129), the spectacular eruption of global terrorism on the world stage on September 11, 2001, and its aftermath seem to cast a potentially fatal blow to Habermas's post-national vision. Not only do reactions to global terrorism in countries like the United States and others signal palpably serious retrenchments from the rule of law (Cole & Dempsey 2002). But also, inasmuch as global terrorism seems to lack any comprehensible meaning, it presumably strikes at the very premises underlying Habermas's communicative action. National terrorism, as we have seen, can carry a specific message and purpose regardless of how improbable actual achievement of its particular political goals may be. Such national-based terrorism, therefore, may involve "distorted" communication to use Habermas's term (i.e., strategic, deceptive communication), but it is communication nonetheless, and it can be critically handled from the standpoint of communicative action. Global terrorism, in contrast, seems to have no other aim than to instill terror, fear, and uncertainty. Its random violence tends to leave those who witness it "speechless" as Derrida emphasized (Borradori 2003: 147), and hence it seemingly triggers a set of actions and reactions that remain beyond the grasp of communicative action.

By hitting at cosmopolitanism and the potential for rational communication itself, global terrorism seems to pose a grave threat to the viability of Habermas's philosophical project. The pure destructiveness of global terrorism seems irreconcilable with the aim of developing a common worldwide identity standing above all clashing national, religious, ethnic, and cultural identities through the communicative redemption of the Kantian universal normative ideal. Moreover, global terrorism, with its distant roots and links and its hidden presence within the innermost recesses of the polity, seems prone to greatly hinder, if not make impossible altogether, the meaningful pursuit of communicatively open communally developed self-governance.

Notwithstanding these ominous forebodings, Habermas regards global terrorism as yet another extrinsic threat to the project of the Enlightenment. For Habermas, global terrorism must be fought through reinforcement of commitment to communicative action and through continued construction of a cosmopolitan post-national common identity circumscribed by constitutional patriotism. For Habermas, therefore, global terrorism is the culmination of increasingly distorted communication that must be fought by renewing stress on humanity's common identity above all differences. And, by thus stressing identity over difference, Habermas carves out a position that stands at the opposite end of the spectrum of that staked out by Derrida.

In the remainder of this chapter, I provide a critical assessment of Habermas's analysis of the meaning and impact of global terrorism. This assessment concentrates both on Habermas's discussion of a post-national cosmopolitan rule of law regime and on his ethics of identity. Section 9.2 focuses on how global terrorism figures in Habermas's post-national cosmopolitan rule of law paradigm. Section 9.3 evaluates Habermas's account of global terrorism. Section 9.4 critiques Habermas's assumptions regarding global terrorism and examines the threat the latter poses for the paradigm itself. Finally, Section 9.5 examines how Habermas's ethics of identity fares in comparison to pluralist ethics.

9.2. GLOBAL TERRORISM AND THE POST-NATIONAL RULE OF LAW COSMOPOLITAN ORDER

Historically, the project of the Enlightenment was grounded within the confines of the nation-state. Although from a theoretical standpoint this project is boundless and universal, from a practical standpoint, for those living in the eighteenth century, the requisite horizon could not plausibly extend beyond the bounds of the nation-state. Consistent with this, the nation-state appears to be historically necessary but conceptually contingent from the standpoint of realization of the Enlightenment project. Moreover, as the link between the latter project and the nation-state is not intrinsic, it stands to reason that when necessary it could be undone. And accordingly, pathologies associated with the nation-state, such as the rise of Nazism in Germany, whether or not intrinsic to the nation-state, can still be cogently characterized as extrinsic to the project of the Enlightenment itself. According to Habermas, it is precisely such pathologies that require regrounding post-World War II constitutional democracy beyond the nation-state – a process that seems well on its way in the European Union (Habermas 2001: 85–112).

In view of the trial and tribulations associated with efforts to adopt a constitution for the European Union (Dorsen et al. 2010: 77–110), however, it seems fair to question the ultimate viability of post-national constitutionalism as a means of carrying out the project of the Enlightenment. If transnational identity is bound to remain too thin, then the project of the Enlightenment may prove ultimately inseparable from the nation-state. And in that case, the excesses of nationalism would amount to an intrinsic threat to that project.

A similar argument can be made regarding reason, which, as repeatedly stressed, plays a key role in the Enlightenment project. Indeed, as there are pathologies that relate to the nation-state, there are also pathologies that concern the deployment of reason. These latter pathologies, moreover, result from two principal causes that were previously discussed: disenchantment and the seemingly unstoppable expansion of instrumental reason.

Disenchantment leads to feelings of rootlessness and prompts a return to irrationalism, which may take several forms, including virulent and excessive nationalism or the embrace of fundamentalism. As already indicated, in Habermas's view, religious fundamentalism is not characterized by the beliefs involved, but by their *modality* (Borradori 2003: 72). The fact that religious fundamentalists regard the truths of their own religion as absolute, leads Habermas to conclude that fundamentalist religion constitutes a violent reaction against modernism (Id.: 78). The unconstrained deployment of instrumental reason, on the other hand, transforms it from a means to an end. And, as we have seen, this results from instrumental reason's moving away from securing the material underpinnings of liberty and equality for all to paving the road to exploitation, colonization, and economic and political domination.

Habermas regards both fundamentalism and growing disparities in wealth and power fueled by contemporary economies as external threats to the project of the Enlightenment (Id.: 2; 78). But these threats are plausibly regarded as intrinsic to modernism. Uprooted impoverished persons living in a materialistic world dominated by rampant consumerism may well be naturally driven to religious fundamentalism. Similarly, globalization of markets may be both economically inevitable and bound to exacerbate inequalities in power and wealth. Moreover, if the hypothesis of intrinsic links is justified, then the clash between runaway globalization and global terrorism as the inevitable byproduct of religious fundamentalism may well spell the doom of modernism. This would leave the world stage reduced to a clash between fragmentary and diverse post-modernism, or a schism between the latter and intransigent pre-modern dogmatism.

Habermas remains nonetheless firm in his conviction that globalization need not result in surrender to instrumental reason and that modern identity need not dissolve into an evermore fragmented array of clashing self-images or else become mired in a struggle to death among opposing fundamentalisms. Habermas's conviction stems from his belief that commitment to communicative action and to communicative rationality can stir the course of modernism away from the pathologies discussed previously. To assess Habermas's claim that communicative action provides the requisite tools to overcome the aforementioned pathologies and global terrorism, it is first necessary to take a brief look at his account of the historical events and theoretical developments that have paved the way to the present-day predicament.

The fate of post-World War II Western Europe and the efforts of the European Union to establish a veritable transnational polity provide the key to understanding Habermas's appraisal of contemporary challenges and his ideas on how to handle them. Moving beyond the strictures of the nation-state was essential for post-war Western Europe, in general, and for Germany, in particular. This was the case for two principal reasons: an economic-based reason and an identity-based one. With the Western European economies in shambles at the end of the war, reconstruction was paramount, and its success depended on the establishment of transnational markets. On the identity front, on the other hand, the Europe of national identities that had waged two world wars had to look beyond nationalism to try to avoid repeating the tragic mistakes of the past. Moreover, opening toward post-nationalism was most urgent for Germany in view of its Nazi past.

Currently, the transnational European project faces two threats, one economic, which is external, and the other, identity-based, which is internal. Globalization of the economy unhinges the fetters of the nation-state's social and political controls over economic activity and relationships. Indeed, what democratic nation-states like the United States and transnational political entities like the European Union have been able to do before globalization of the economy, was to constrain or harness economic markets for purposes of guaranteeing acceptable levels of social welfare for the relevant polity's citizenry. Globalization of the economy and free worldwide circulation of capital allows, however, for a race to the bottom as entrepreneurs can shift capital and production to locations with lower wages and taxes, less stringent environmental or safety standards, and so forth. As a consequence of this, individual nation-states as well as the European Union become increasingly unable to maintain a decent social welfare safety net for those within their boundaries.

The difficulty in articulating a common European Union-wide identity, which became evident in the attempts to establish a European constitution, poses, on the other hand, an internal threat to the project of entrenching a post-national social and political democratic order. Significantly, it has been suggested in the context of the project for a European constitution that the requisite identity might be constructed, at least in part, negatively by drawing on anti-Americanism (von Bogdandy 2005: 310), or that it might be supplanted by appeal to economic self-interest (Id.: 315). Whether these difficulties in elaborating a post-national identity are symptomatic of growing pains or indicative of the impossibility of forging a cogent and workable post-national identity remains to be seen. In any event, both the external and the internal threat pose a formidable challenge to the legitimation of a post-national order in general, and of that in the course of construction in Europe, in particular.

Habermas deals with these challenges in terms of the conceptual distinction he draws between "system" and "lifeworld." In complex modern societies, the economy and bureaucratic administration function as self-regulating systems steered respectively by money and administrative power. Thus, for example, the economic system monetarizes all needs, objectives, and relationships.[2] In other words, by ascribing to every desire, plan or problem a monetary value, the economic system tends to transform all human concerns and endeavors into subjects that can be dealt with through market transactions.[3] Similarly, in the context of the modern bureaucratic

---

[2] For an extensive discussion of the economic system's process of monetarization, see Luhmann 1990: 230–1.

[3] The economy not only monetarizes needs and desires but also shapes them as consumer demand inasmuch as a capitalist market society is to a significant extent shaped by producers' economic interests. See Galbraith 1976: 127.

state, problems of social organization are systematically transformed into issues of administrative coordination.

In Habermas's view, competing against these systems operating as self-enclosed networks is an entirely different kind of integration, namely that of the lifeworld. The lifeword endows a collectivity with distinct meaning by providing a shared collective identity, "a social integration based on mutual understanding, intersubjectively shared norms, and collective values" (Habermas 2001: 82). Moreover, the meaning-endowing function of the lifeworld is supposed to be comprehensive. In Habermas's words,

> The spatial and temporal horizons of a lifeworld ... always form a whole that is both intuitively present but always withdrawn to an unproblematic background; a whole which is closed in the sense that it contains every possible interaction from the perspective of the lifeworld participants. (Id.)

The lifeworld, which may be that circumscribed by a religious community or a modern constitutional democracy operating within the confines of the nation-state, competes against the systems it confronts. The lifeworld does so by attempting to achieve some measure of control over the relevant systems, by reinterpreting them, and by constraining them in conformity with that lifeworld's norms and values. For example, in the period between the end of World War II and the dissolution of the Soviet Union, Western democratic nation-states were able to maintain social-welfare standards for all their citizens and limit the scope of wealth-based inequalities within their societies through legislation, taxation, monetary policy, and the like, which imposed certain constraints on economic markets.

Conversely, competing systems can expand to the point of impinging on the corresponding lifeworld. Thus, as Habermas sees it, through expansion and systematic deployment of its mode of functioning, the economic market can end up "colonizing" the lifeworld (Habermas 1992). In the context of globalization, in particular, as market relations escape the fetters of nation-state-imposed constraints, they tend to encroach upon, and eventually to undermine, social-welfare policy that clashes with the dictates of worldwide competition.

As systems impinge on a particular lifeworld, the latter must open itself to changes that will better enable the relevant collectivity to cope with systemic challenges. Accordingly, to remain adaptable, the lifeworld must be subject to a dynamic process of openness and closure. In other words, the lifeworld must realign its norms and values when the prevalent ones no longer can cope with systemic challenges. Once properly realigned, however, the relevant norms and values must remain fixed so as to offer effective resistance against undue systemic incursions.

Globalization characterized by systematic escape of economic market processes from the fetters of nation-state regulation and constraint require opening lifeworlds previously adapted to a nation-state-based world order. Such opening, moreover, should be followed, consistent with Habermas's vision, by a readjustment of values and norms and a redrawing of the boundaries of the horizon of collective interaction, such that would allow for a fair and workable engagement with an ever-expanding global market system. And if the called-for readjustment and redrawing could come fully into place, then the resulting lifeworld would head toward closure, thus providing a firmly anchored vantage point from which to deal with the challenges posed by globalization.

The currently lived interim period between the no-longer apt nation-state adapted lifeworlds and the not-yet-defined post-national ones is one fraught with danger. Unhinged modernism gives way to the fragmentation of post-modernisms – fueled by a retreat into subjectivism, partiality, and a strong sense of arbitrariness pursuant to exacerbated disenchantment – competing against neoliberalism – the view that the global market economy has finally triumphed against all politics, which if true, would signal the ultimate triumph of instrumental reason. As Habermas points out, in the context of globalization, post-modernism, and neoliberalism are closely linked:

> For different reasons, [the two] ... ultimately share the vision of the lifeworlds of individuals and small groups scattering, like distinct monads, across global, functionally coordinated networks, rather than overlapping in the course of social integration in larger, multidimensional political entities. (Habermas 2001: 88)

To complete this rapid sketch, religious fundamentalism and global terrorism are like post-modernism and neoliberalism reactions to the unsettling of the realm of the lifeworld caused by globalization. Habermas considers contemporary religious fundamentalism a modern phenomenon (Borradori 2003: 18). The exacerbation of disenchantment combined with the spreading inequities produced by the global economy prompt the losers in that system to yearn for a return to a pre-modern state of affairs. Religious fundamentalism, with its rejection of the values of advanced capitalist societies, is this modern conception of what pre-modern meaning and certainty might have been. Furthermore, global terrorism, which Habermas views as primarily motivated by economic factors rather than by *Kulturkampf* (Id.: 28–36), seems like a desperate reaction to the impoverishment, dislocation, humiliation, and so forth, that globalization, which seems unstoppable, implacably inflicts upon the losers in the new worldwide economic order.

For Habermas, however, as already mentioned, the downward spiral produced by an evermore encompassing global economy and a rising spread of global terrorism is by no means unstoppable, as it can be countered and the project of the Enlightenment set back on course through commitment to a suitable communicative action-based normative framework. That normative framework, moreover, finds expression in the proceduralist paradigm of law already elaborated by Habermas in the context of the contemporary nation-state (Habermas 1996). Accordingly, the challenge is to adapt the proceduralist paradigm of law calling for all binding laws to be susceptible of legitimation as self-given and as treating all those bound by them as full-fledged equals, from a national to a post-national setting. What this requires, in turn, is devising an institutional setting allowing for a reorientation of the globalized economy from an instrument of colonization and exploitation to one of equalization and of the equitable spread of opportunities. At the same time, what is imperative from the standpoint of identity is that the process of fragmentation and of retreat into isolated post-or pre-modern ideologies be reversed through deployment of post-national lifeworld with expanded horizons within a coherent whole. Furthermore, what is to propel this post-national lifeworld toward a dynamic of ever-widening integration is the spread of constitutional patriotism. In short, in the post-national lifeworld, constitutional patriotism is meant to supplant and to surpass nationalism and to counter post-modern fragmentation and unbound neoliberalism.

In the last analysis, Habermas's hope is that by taking control over globalization through application of communicatively redeemed norms and institutional structures and processes we will be able to defeat fragmentation and global terror. At the institutional level, Habermas's vision calls for transnational government based on a vision of perfectibility of the European Union model coupled with international governance, but not international government.[4] Moreover, at the normative level, it is to the highest aspirations of the Enlightenment project itself, the rational pursuit of liberty and equality for all, that Habermas turns. Finally, to extend the lifeworld, identity, and concern for the other beyond the confines of the nation-state, Habermas has recourse to the concept of constitutional patriotism. If on the scale of the nation-state, it is national identity, ethnicity, language, culture, and a common tradition that infuse the breath of life into constitutional forms and structures, Habermas's bet is that on the transnational scale, it is commitment to constitutionalism itself that will bring a transnational constitutional order to life. Precisely because they are so severely threatened, it is the values of constitutionalism and the Enlightenment-in-and-of themselves that will be invoked to mobilize actors engaged in communicative action to embark on an attack against the evils of globalization. And, if it becomes clear that these evils can be cut down to size, then the very causes of global terror, as Habermas conceives them, will altogether disappear. In a word, thorough internationalization of the Enlightenment project and global spread of constitutional

---

[4]   For example, the World Trade Organization (WTO) provides a framework for international governance of commerce and trade, but does not constitute a "government" as that of a nation-state or as that currently in place in the European Union.

patriotism, global terror driven by religious fundamentalism should be eradicated for lack of appeal and of adherents.

As we have seen, Habermas's sketched vision maps out an ideal, but whether this ideal provides adequate guidance on how to cope with, and perhaps one day defeat, global terrorism remains to be seen. Is it plausible that we might move closer to Habermas's ideal? Or does the latter, in the end, only serve to reinforce the sense of fragmentation, disenchantment, and fear that pervades in our polities confronted with economic globalization and global terror?

9.3. HABERMAS'S ANALYSIS OF GLOBAL TERRORISM IN THE CONTEXT OF DISCOURSE THEORY

Habermas's discursive ethics and discursive theory of law and democracy grounded on communicative action all depend for their plausibility and viability on the possibility of achieving unity at the relevant level of intersubjective interaction for the relevant collectivity of normatively engaged actors. Habermas follows Kant in sundering the realm of justice and rights from that of the good. For Habermas, justice and the right must be established dialogically taking all relevant interests into account rather than ignoring them as is the case in Kantian morals, wherein the dictates of justice and morals can be monologically and solipsistically derived.[5] Therefore, whereas Kantian morals based on the categorical imperative is purely abstract, Habermas's communicative ethics seeks achieving agreement on common norms that equally accommodate all existing interests or that equally rise above them.[6] Moreover, whereas Habermas's discursive morals require a consensus that could encompass humanity as a whole (Habermas 1990: 67), discursively redeemed law only requires the assent of those affected by the legal regime at stake – which in the case of the nation-state is limited to those within its borders – and such assent may be bargained for compromise as well as the product of a genuine consensus (Habermas 1996: 459–60). Unlike discursive consensuses, which must be accepted by all actors *for the same reasons*, discursive compromises may be acceptable to different actors on the basis of *different reasons* (Id.: 119–20, 152). Finally, Habermas specifies that, in the context of law, the discourse principle extends to ethical and pragmatic questions (Id.: 452). Ethical questions ask who we are and what our goals

[5] For a succinct statement of the main differences between Habermas's communitive ethics and Kant's moral theory, see Habermas 1990: 195, 204.
[6] Thus, Habermas's consensus-based conception of justice can be viewed as standing halfway between Kant's purely abstract ideal and contractarian justice, which does not filter out bargaining advantages held by contractors who advance certain particular interests. For an account of Habermas's position as the perfection of the contractarian tradition and for a critique of his discursive proceduralism, see Rosenfeld 1998a.

are, thus dealing with the concerns of self-realization of a particular community. Pragmatic questions, on the other hand, aim at reaching an equilibrium between competing values preferences and competing interests (Id.: 119–120).

By embracing the Kantian dichotomy between justice and the good, Habermas bets that pluralistic societies with a multitude of competing conceptions of the good will nonetheless be in a position to aim for a level of unity that would enable them to share common moral and legal norms, which they could all equally accept as self-imposed and just. In multi-cultural societies, there can be no substantive consensus on values, so Habermas seeks the requisite unity through "a consensus on the procedures for the legitimate enactment of laws and the legitimate exercise of power" (Habermas 1998: 225). Unlike customs and traditions, which forge internal links within a community, and more like contracts, which allow for external relationships between contractors who seek to cooperate in the pursuit of different interests, law satisfying Habermas's proceduralist paradigm is supposed to allow for fair external relationships that afford equal recognition and respect for all within the relevant polity. Moreover, such recognition and respect is due to all as proponents of particular conceptions of the good and to the place of such conceptions in the identity and pursuit of self-realization of their proponents. By the same token, the recognition and respect in question should not be understood as endorsements on the merits of the conceptions of the good involved (Id.: 221).

In essence then, in the context of the normative universe circumscribed by communicative ethics, law and democratic politics are supposed to achieve unity amidst diversity by stressing justice and rights over the good, and procedure over substance. Moreover, at least at the level of the nation-state, the task of discourse-based law and democracy is facilitated because only those conceptions of the good with proponents within the polity need to be taken into account. Thus, for example, whereas discourse-based morality depends on reaching a consensus among proponents of all religions of the world, law and democracy in a nation-state with only two religions depends on reaching a consensus or compromise in the context of a much more limited field of differences.

Consistent with these observations, it could seem that the mono-ethnic, mono-religious, and mono-linguistic nation-states would have best chances of achieving the requisite consensuses and compromises to comply with the discursive proceduralist paradigm of law.[7] By the same token, the multi-ethnic state would seem bound to experience greater difficulties, and the transnational or global community, almost insurmountable odds. Furthermore, just law in a multi-cultural polity would

---

[7] Even in the absence of al multi-culturalism, it is not obvious that Habermas's proceduralist paradigm of law would produce the requisite consensuses and compromises. For a critique of Habermas's proceduralism based on feminist objections, see Rosenfeld 1998b.

presumably have to provide some significant measure of accommodation to all the prevalent conceptions of the good, and that would (arguably) include, where present, the kind of religious fundamentalism that is linked to global terrorism.

As noted in Section 9.2, Habermas does believe in the possibility of a rule of law transnational constitutional democracy. At the same time, he does not regard global terrorism as the product of a clash of cultures but rather as a weapon used in an economic struggle over globalization. From the standpoint of communicative action, the proceduralist paradigm of law can operate successfully beyond the nation-state through a dialectical progression that involves a transformation or "formalization" of constitutional patriotism. Global terrorism, in turn, is viewed as the product of "distorted communication" uttered in response to the "distorted communication" mustered in support of the current processes of economic globalization. To better understand Habermas's assessment of global terrorism, it is therefore necessary to take a somewhat closer look at "distorted communication" and at the dialectical progression mentioned earlier.

"Distorted communication" or "strategic action" as opposed to communicative action is the product of instrumental reason. As Habermas states,

> in strategic action the actors are interested solely in the *success*, i.e., the *consequences* or *outcomes*, of their actions, [and] they will try to reach these objectives by influencing their opponent's definition of the situation, and thus his decisions or motives, through external means by using weapons or goods, threats or enticements. (Habermas 1990: 133; emphasis in original)

Thus, the model for communicative action is that of an idealized community of scientists gathered together to ascertain dispassionately the truth of a scientific hypothesis. In contrast, the model for strategic action is that of an unscrupulous salesperson who will say anything – cajole, flatter, cause fear, or threaten – with the sole objective of obtaining a sale.

On the surface at least, the confrontation between Islamic fundamentalism and Western individualistic materialism looms as an irreconcilable clash of ideologies. This clash, moreover, may seem bound to become violent as economic globalization aggressively introduces Western materialism and consumerism to the innermost precincts of Islamic culture. Consistent with this, global terrorism could be understood as a desperate violent reaction in the face of impotence against the implacable spread of globalization and its evils. Furthermore, depending on one's assessment, global terrorism such as the 9/11 attacks may amount to an incomprehensible, meaningless political act, as Habermas believes (Borradori 2003: 34). Or, in view of the huge costs that it has imposed on Western societies, both materially and in terms of threats to civil liberties, and in view of the further polarization of the world and seeming further entrenchment of fundamentalist Islamic regimes, global terrorism may be interpreted as having a definite political payoff. Under this latter interpretation, global terrorism has made globalization more costly and painful and enhanced religious fundamentalism as a political force by demonstrating that, in spite of a huge disparity in material power, the seemingly invincible West can be seriously disrupted as 9/11 and its aftermath clearly indicate.

For Habermas, however, beneath the surface lurks an economic struggle fueled by the exacerbation of exploitation and inequality due to economic globalization. As he puts it,

> Without the political taming of an unbounded capitalism, the devastating strati-
> fication of world society will remain intractable. The disparities in the dynamic
> of world economic development would have at least to be balanced out regard-
> ing their most destructive consequences-the deprivation and misery of complete
> regions and continents comes to mind ... The so-called "clash of civilizations"...
> is often the veil masking the vital material interests of the West (accessible oilfields
> and secured energy supply, for example). (Id.: 36)

Globalization thus turns the world into winners and losers, and the masses in most of the Muslim countries end up as losers. Moreover, the rapid spread of materialism and consumerism leads to a "disenchantment" similar to that experienced earlier in the West, but with one fundamental difference. In the West, loss of traditional values was mitigated by vast social political and economic gains. In contrast, in Muslim countries, not only is the process of disenchantment much accelerated, but the vast majority of the population ends up as a clear loser in the new materialist and con-sumerist environment (Id.: 32). Under these circumstances, the turn to fundamen-talism becomes a desperate attempt to erect a barrier against forces of secularization and materialism that are proving so devastating (Id.: 32–3).

From the standpoint of communicative action, the West engages in strategic action and distorted communication when it preaches the language of universal human rights only to open markets worldwide (Id.: 33) and presents a neoliberalist picture of economic globalization as an inevitable systemic force of nature that is the only path to human well-being. For its part, Islamic fundamentalist discourse also amounts to a strategic form of distorted communication designed to mask the failures and contradictions of authoritarian governments that have resisted modern-ism and democracy to buttress the privileges of wealthy and powerful elites. In this connection, Habermas remarks that it is no coincidence that many of those drawn to "holy war" were yesterday's secular nationalists disappointed in their nationalist authoritarian regimes' policies (Id.).

These two distorted discourses feed on one another fueling distrust and eventu-ally violence. Thus, the losers in the global economy regard the West's preaching of universalism and human rights as cynical hypocrisies advanced to better entrench dominance. For its part, the West regards Islamic fundamentalism as a cynical weapon deployed to keep ignorant masses under wraps and away from the great potential benefits of modernism for the sole purpose of preserving the privileges of authoritarian ruling elites. Eventually, this cycle of mutual deception, mistrust, and violence leads to a breakdown in communication (Id.). Accordingly, global terrorism can be regarded as the culmination of a process of distorted communication taken to its logical extreme, but precisely because this breakdown can be understood in terms of a communicative logic, it may be overcome through communicative action. In Habermas's own words, "[i]f violence thus begins with a distortion in communication, after it has erupted it is possible to know what has gone wrong and what needs to be repaired" (Id.: 35).

One can imagine how, through communicative action, Islamic fundamentalism and global terrorism could be overcome. From the standpoint of the West, strategic action regarding globalization would be replaced by work on the requisite transformations of the lifeworld and of institutions on a transnational scale. The purpose of these transformations would be to allow channeling the processes of economic globalization so as to equalize opportunities and more evenly spread wealth and social welfare throughout the globe. From the standpoint of Muslim societies, on the other hand, commitment to communicative action would lead to abandonment of authoritarianism and to forgoing the use of Islam to inflame impoverished masses that are inexcusably deprived of the benefits of modernism. In the face of the potential great material gains of a process of globalization that is fine-tuned to promote equal opportunities and social justice, Muslim polities should willingly embrace globalization as being in the best interests of their citizenry. Consistent with this, moreover, Muslim societies should adjust their lifeworld, and their legal and political institutions in order to reconcile Islam, modernism, and fair and responsible globalization. The resulting Islam would not be fundamentalist, but instead accepting of pluralism, as are many of the other great religions that have adjusted to the conditions that prevail in modern multi-cultural societies.

For it to be even plausible for the clash between the West and Islamic fundamentalism to be resolved along the lines suggested here, it must be at least conceivably possible for Habermas's proceduralist paradigm of law and democracy to become operational on a transnational scale. To see if this is feasible, focus must first be brought to bear on how this paradigm and the kind of constitutional patriotism associated with it are supposed to function in the context of a multi-cultural nation-state.

To understand how one might progress from a multi-cultural national communicatively just society to a transnational or global one, it is useful to imagine the deployment of the proceduralist paradigm in successive stages from the least complex environment within which it might operate to the most complex such environment. At one end of the spectrum, in a fully integrated collectivity exclusively ruled by custom and tradition, there is no room for the proceduralist paradigm as consensus among the members of the collectivity is implicit and common norms fully internalized by one and all. Such a collectivity, however, would be a pre-modern one. In contrast, in any modern collectivity, the interests of the group would vary to some significant extent from those of its individual members. Accordingly, the proceduralist paradigm becomes plausible and conceivably functional with the advent of modernism and its call for the protection of fundamental individual rights. In an ideologically, ethnically, linguistically, and religiously homogeneous modern nation-state, therefore, the demands of the proceduralist paradigm would seem to coincide with those of liberalism. Moreover, in such a nation-state, constitutional patriotism would appear indistinguishable from liberal constitutionalism.

In a more pluralist setting, the need of self and other for recognition as belonging to a distinct group makes it necessary to go beyond classical liberalism. For example, in a polity in which the citizenry is divided between Catholics and Protestants, the proceduralist paradigm's success would depend on the reaching of consensuses, compromises, and pragmatic bargains between the two religious communities. Moreover, in such a polity the intra-communal identity of each of the two religious communities would have to be distinguished from the inter-communal identity allowing the two communities to join in a single, unified project promoting constitutional democracy at the level of the nation-state. Also, the constitutional identity giving substance to that polity's constitutional patriotism would be a Christian one that would be acceptable to both Catholics and Protestants.[8]

The more diverse and multi-cultural a polity happens to be, the more abstract the unity achievable through consensuses and compromises under the proceduralist paradigm would seem to have to be. Concomitantly, the constitutional identity corresponding to constitutional patriotism in a thoroughly multi-cultural polity would presumably differ greatly from the intra-communal identity of any of the groups implicated. Furthermore, as one moves to the transnational context, in a case such as that of the European Union, as already mentioned it is difficult to elaborate a common identity. Habermas, however, does not believe that construction of a constitutional democracy is inextricably linked to the kind of common identity that can only thrive within a nation-state, albeit a multi-cultural one. As he sees it,

> A previous background consensus, constructed on the basis of cultural homogeneity and understood as a catalyzing condition for democracy becomes superfluous to the extent that public, discursively structured processes of opinion-and-will-formation make a reasonable political understanding possible, even among strangers. (Habermas 2001: 73)

---

[8]   Consistent with this, as Habermas notes, in Germany freedom of religion is deemed constitutionally compatible with institutional guarantees to Christian churches. See Habermas 1998: 218.

In other words, the exigencies brought about by the seemingly uncontrolled advance of economic globalization require strangers (i.e., actors coming from different nation-states) to cooperate and find solutions consistent with the proceduralist paradigm. It becomes imperative to agree in spite of differences in ethical self-perception, and thus the strictures of communicative action drive the political agenda rather than merely guiding it consistent with the self-identity and collective goals of a distinct ethical and/or political community. For example, in the face of a grave environmental danger that threatens the planet as a whole, all the earth's inhabitants have an interest to set national and cultural differences aside and to negotiate a workable solution. This they can do presumably from either a strategic or communicative action perspective. And if they were to choose the latter, their solidarity as strangers facing a common danger would derive from the dictates of the proceduralist paradigm of law and democracy.

Under these transnational conditions, moreover, a dialectical reversal transforms constitutional patriotism from nation-state scale nationalism mediated by appropriate constitutional constraints to the elevation of constitutional essentials themselves to serve as the glue that binds together strangers interacting across national boundaries with the requisite solidarity to confront together with equanimity and fairness the common problems that transcend their respective boundaries. In a word, strangers must be patriotic concerning the constitutional essentials that emerge from the proceduralist paradigm in order to be able to confront fairly and successfully the transnational and global problems that besiege them (Id.: 73–4).

Transnational constitutional patriotism is not meant to supplant patriotism or nationalism, only to supplement them. Indeed, Habermas does not envision a world government replacing national, transnational, and sub-national government (Id.: 70–1). Instead, what he seems to have in mind is a layered system of interlocking centers of political organization, law, and democracy, with federal or quasi-federal features allowing for integration of various levels of identity.[9] Within this vision, constitutional patriotism is to play a limited but crucial role: It is supposed to expand the lifeword to make it suitable to properly channel the systemic spread of economic globalization toward greater social justice and fairness.

In the last analysis, the combination of communicative action, the proceduralist paradigm of law and democracy, and the extension of constitutional patriotism beyond the nation-state present a prima facie conceptually plausible way to approach globalization and global terror as external threats to the project of the Enlightenment. Moreover, Habermas indicates, through his adaptation of constitutional patriotism for supra-national use, how the project of the Enlightenment

---

[9] See, for example, Habermas 1998: 220 (discussing how Canada's use of federalism could reconcile national identity with the distinct identity of Quebec).

might transcend the bounds of the nation-state. In the course of building his case, however, Habermas makes several contestable assumptions, including the crucial one that the fundamentalism that leads to global terror is at bottom the product of distorted communication. To properly evaluate Habermas's assessment of global terrorism and the latter's impact on Habermas's theory of law, ethics, and democracy based on communicative action, it is now necessary to take a closer look at some of Habermas's key contestable assumptions.

9.4. A CRITIQUE OF HABERMAS'S ASSUMPTIONS REGARDING GLOBAL TERRORISM AND CONSEQUENT IMPLICATIONS FOR HABERMAS'S POST-NATIONAL DISCOURSE-THEORY MODEL

The key to Habermas's analysis and ideal reconstruction of the Enlightenment project's continued viability in the context of globalization and the threat of global terror is the ability to postulate modalities of unity emanating from communicative action at all requisite levels of intersubjective interaction. The conditions of unity involved depend, however, on assumptions that often seem at least intuitively unwarranted. And chief among these assumptions is Habermas's belief that the roots of fundamentalism are ultimately economic in nature.

Fundamentalism, which Habermas acknowledges has taken hold in democracies in the West as well as in societies that are thus far clear losers in the progression of globalization (Habermas 1998: 224), amounts for him to distorted communication. This is true for at least two different reasons. First, fundamentalism masks its ultimate economic causes as it emphasizes a clash of cultures instead of facing up to feelings of powerlessness in connection with the injustices perpetrated by globalization. And, second, as already noted, fundamentalism – for Habermas a modern phenomenon – refuses to even acknowledge the existence of other world views. From the standpoint of Habermas's discourse theory,

> Fundamentalist worldviews are dogmatic ... they leave no room for reflection on their relationship with the other worldviews in which they share the same universe of discourse and against whose competing validity claims they can advance their positions on the basis of reasons. They leave no room for "reasonable disagreement." (Habermas 1999: 224)

Both of these claims are, however, questionable. First, whereas it is plausible that fundamentalism has economic roots, this is by no means obvious, and at least in some cases of fundamentalism it seems downright counterintuitive. Take, for example, a fundamentalist view that considers abortion and homosexuality absolutely wrong and hence not subject to any compromise. Are such views, particularly in wealthy Western democracies, in any way based on economic differences or issues? Is it not more convincing to regard these views as part of deeply held beliefs that belong to the core identity of certain religious worldviews?

Consistent with considering debates about abortion or homosexuality as part of cultural clashes over conflicting worldviews, moreover, it seems highly debatable that fundamentalist discourse need amount to distorted communication. It is indeed quite possible to imagine, for example, that a sincere person who is convinced that life begins at conception holds in all honesty the view that abortion amounts to murder. Such a person could also be envisioned as participating in communicative action, and hearing out the arguments of proponents of the right to abortion being inextricably linked to the achievement of women's equality. Yet even then, it would seem perfectly compatible with the strictures of communicative action for our religious abortion foe to conclude, after fair and full hearing of all views on the matter, that no consensus is possible and that there is no room for compromise.

Habermas seems to foreclose this latter possibility by restricting communicative action and the proceduralist paradigm to post-metaphysical worldviews, which would exclude all positions grounded on religious ideology or dogma.[10] Furthermore, Habermas also in effect excludes from the dialogical process worldviews based on inegalitarian ideologies (Rosenfeld 1998b: 101). Indeed, such ideologies would find the very structure of communicative action incompatible with their deeply held views, as they would become automatic losers in the throes of discursive proceduralism.

What these latter observations reveal is that Habermas's discursive proceduralism ultimately rests on substantive presuppositions that in effect exclude certain worldviews, including fundamentalist ones, from the dialogical process of legitimation. This casts a strong doubt on both Habermas's assertion that the breakdown in communication associated with global terrorism may be overcome and on his confidence in the feasibility of multinational and transnational consensuses and compromises based on a purely abstracted and uprooted conception of constitutional patriotism.

This last point may not be immediately apparent, but it should become so on the basis of the following example. Suppose – as happens to be the case at this writing – that Catalans and Castillians disagree as to how much autonomy, linguistic and otherwise, Cataluña should have from the central government of Spain. One can well imagine this dispute – which is a purely secular one involving no inherently inegalitarian ideology – being subjected to communicative action with no eventual agreement on the kind of autonomy and federalism that would equally comport with the respective self-understanding and identity of the two communities

---

[10] See Rosenfeld 1998b: 101 for a discussion of the kinds of views that would be in fact excluded from Habermas discursive legitimation of law and democracy.

involved. In other words, in such a case, a particular consensus or compromise that both sides could consider just and legitimate is certainly conceivable. But for that to occur would seem more a contingent matter than a necessary byproduct of communicative action.

On the other hand, the complete breakdown in communication surrounding global terrorism does seem to call into question Habermas's communicative approach much more radically than do challenges coming from different positions, including non-violent fundamentalism. There is a difference in kind between post-metaphysical and egalitarian worldviews on one side, and metaphysical and anti-egalitarian ones, on the other side. The former are clearly susceptible to accommodation and to the formation of requisite consensuses and compromises within the communicative model. The latter, in contrast, are not as flexible, even though they may happen as a contingent matter to be amenable by coincidence to certain particular consensuses and compromises. Thus, for example, a religion with an ideology that is anti-secularist may be comfortable within a secular state to the extent that as a matter of religious dogma it maintains that a strict separation ought to be maintained between the realm of heaven and that of earthly rule.

Furthermore, as already noted, there is a difference in degree between non-fundamentalist religion and fundamentalist religion. Specifically, the difference is that whereas the former admits the fact of pluralism and can act jointly with those who do not (fully) share its worldview (e.g., Catholics can work together with non-believers to fight poverty or with Protestants and Jews to combat secular biases against religion), fundamentalism, at least by Habermas's definition, remains closed to all other viewpoints. Nevertheless, if fundamentalism is turned inward rather than in active war against other ideologies, it can be, at least in part, dealt with within the communicative model. Indeed, even if fundamentalists refuse to engage in communicative action, those who do engage in it are called upon to consider fundamentalists as beings with their own sense of identity and self-realization. Accordingly, at least arguably, those engaged in communicative action ought to try to accommodate fundamentalists to the extent that would be compatible with reaching the appropriate consensuses and compromises with those who have agreed to abide by communicative action. Once fundamentalists opt for violence and global terror, however, all communication and communicative action with, or directed to, them becomes impossible. In that case, it seems that the only sensible way to respond to the fundamentalist terrorist is with deeds rather than words, and, in some cases, even with acts of violence.

It follows from the preceding analysis that global terrorism poses a far greater threat to Habermas's discursive model and procedural paradigm of law than all the other previously discussed obstacles to their successful deployment. Moreover, global terrorism poses a serious threat even if it were a contingent aberration at the margins of the Enlightenment project. It poses, however, a devastating threat if it turns out to be a natural culmination of global capitalism's creation of ever-greater inequalities and of the bottomless disenchantment caused by the all-pervasiveness of instrumental reason. In other words, if the Enlightenment leads to global terrorism, then communicative action seems much more a utopian dream than a useful and inspiring ideal.

9.5. COPING WITH GLOBAL TERRORISM BEYOND THE ETHICS OF IDENTITY: PLURALISM AS AN ALTERNATIVE TO HABERMAS'S PROCEDURALISM

In the end, Habermas's treatment of global terrorism falls short for two principal reasons. First, his proceduralist approach in effect leaves out fundamentalism ex ante, and, second, it seems highly unlikely that global terrorism is ultimately, or evenly predominantly, economically motivated. Accordingly, Habermas projects identity and achieves unity at a price of unwarranted exclusion and reductionism. Habermas's excessive suppression of difference thus proves in the end as unsatisfactory as Derrida's refusal to place any curbs on difference. Furthermore, as I will argue, pluralism can avoid the pitfalls of exclusionist identity just as it can, as discussed in Chapter 8, avoid those of unbound difference.

Whereas for Habermas there appear to be two types of conception of the good – those consistent with modernism and those like fundamentalism that are not – for comprehensive pluralism there are three as pluralism as a conception of the good in its own right is distinguishable from the other two. For Habermas, in addition to the two types of conceptions of the good, there are procedural devices belonging to the realm of justice to mediate among conceptions that are consistent with modernism. Moreover, comprehensive pluralism plays a similar role of mediator as between a plurality of competing conceptions of the good as does Habermas's discursive proceduralism. What then, is the difference between the two? In essence, as already emphasized, comprehensive pluralism makes no claim of neutrality and is, in the last analysis, more inclusive of difference without abandoning a working identity than is Habermas's proceduralism.

The fact that, as previously discussed, comprehensive pluralism can accommodate fundamentalist religion to the extent that it is peaceful and inwardly oriented[11] illustrates how the latter is more inclusive than Habermas's discursive proceduralism, which justifies downright exclusion of fundamentalism on account of its modality of belief. On the other hand, unlike the ethics of difference, comprehensive pluralism, through systematic deployment of second-order norms, does not allow for

---

[11] See supra, at Section 1.8.

unlimited difference or singularity. It calls for sustaining a minimum of common identity within the relevant socio-political unit. That minimum is what is required to maintain a fair and workable level of intersubjective give and take to accommodate as much diversity as possible without risking the breakdown of the socio-political unit in question. Furthermore, in its endeavor to foster the best possible equilibrium between identity and difference along the lines suggested earlier, comprehensive pluralism is agnostic as to number, composition, or relationship among different socio-political units. Thus, as underscored in Chapter 7, comprehensive pluralism is equally compatible with federalization of diverse units into a larger whole and with, where appropriate, peaceful secession, allowing highly incompatible groupings with conflicting worldviews to separate and relate to one another externally rather than constantly feud within the same common socio-political unit.

Consistent with contemporary exigencies, the optimal arrangement, from the standpoint of comprehensive pluralism, would be a series of layered, interlocking and overlapping socio-political units ranging from the purely local to the truly global. Indeed, on the one hand, globalization and the advent of issues better settled on a global scale, such as those pertaining to the planet's environment, call for some level of political organization on a worldwide basis. On the other hand, given the great proliferation of cultural diversity, through travel and migration, and given the corresponding increased prevalence of identity politics, there are greater demands for local or intra-group opportunities for meaningful self-government and self-realization. Accordingly, comprehensive pluralism could optimize the requisite equilibrium between identity and difference through integration of various levels of political ordering, by applying its second-order norms within each such level and among all the different levels involved.

In the end, this arrangement should allow for the greatest possible accommodation of diversity with preservation of the necessary conditions for unified action at all the requisite levels of intersubjective exchange. In terms of overlapping and layered levels of government, going from the local to that of the nation-state, to the transnational and to the global, what comprehensive pluralism envisions is not all that different than what Habermas elaborates pursuant to his discursive proceduralism. There is, however, an important difference between the two, and it concerns their respective approaches to the relationship between identity and difference within the various relevant realms of socio-political interaction. This difference should become plain based on the following pluralist assessment of the challenges posed by global terrorism.

To provide a proper pluralist account of global terrorism, an initial distinction must be drawn between the fundamentalist ideology that purports to justify terrorist violence and the violence of global terrorism itself. Fundamentalist religion and its exclusivist claim to a monopoly over all truth is entitled to prima facie recognition as do all other conceptions of the good in the negative stage of the dialectic of comprehensive pluralism. Moreover, as already noted, fundamentalist religion may be entitled to partial recognition in the positive stage of comprehensive pluralism so long as it is peaceful and predominantly inward looking, and it is properly constrained from exerting coercion on its own members[12] or from engaging in coercive proselytizing.

Conversely, to the extent that fundamentalist religion is violent in a Jihadist sense (i.e., that it justifies aggression against its non-conforming members or non-members who refuse conversion), it is equally deserving of unequivocal condemnation under comprehensive pluralism as under Habermas's discursive proceduralism. If fundamentalist religion uses violence in a *defensive* sense, however, to ward off what it perceives as a mortal danger to its survival, matters seem more complex given that, as noted in Chapter 8, comprehensive pluralism does not foreswear all uses of violence.

In the broadest terms, comprehensive pluralism's second-order norms justify the use of violence in self-defense to ward off violence that threatens the life of a person or that substantially and imminently threatens to destroy a person's or a group's means to pursue self-realization within the confines of pluralism's second-order norms. Thus, for example, use of violence may be legitimate consistent with comprehensive pluralism if necessary to eliminate slavery or to counter extreme forms of religious persecution that clearly threaten the very survival of the targeted religion. Moreover, along the same lines, as already pointed out in Chapter 8, it is at least arguable that domestic terrorism may be justifiable under comprehensive pluralism in the context of a struggle for national liberation from a brutal and oppressive authoritarian colonizing power, where absolutely no other viable alternatives are at hand.

The best defensive case for global terrorism is that globalization and the spread of Western materialism, consumerism, and decadence is destroying the way of life prescribed by fundamentalist Islam in Muslim countries. Moreover, within this perspective, recourse to global terrorism rather than to other less devastating means to combat economic globalization is justified because of the huge disparity in power between Western industrialized nations and economically disadvantaged Muslim countries. Given this huge disparity, it would be argued, Islamic culture would be simply swallowed up in the course of globalization if it were not for the use of global terrorism as a means of resistance and of protecting Islamic fundamentalism's core identity.

Even upon a cursory examination, this defensive argument is utterly unpersuasive. This is not because, as Habermas sees it, global terrorism is a meaningless act

---

[12] What may amount to "coercion" over a member of a closely knit isolated group is likely to be a matter of debate that remains beyond the scope of the current discussion. For present purposes, "coercion" will be understood to be limited to that which is perceived as such by affected members of the relevant group as opposed to what is thus perceived by outsiders.

inasmuch as the religious fundamentalists who perpetrate it have no chance whatsoever to defeat the West or ward off economic globalization. Quite to the contrary, as noted in Chapter 8, global terrorism can be viewed as highly successful inasmuch as it has managed to exact a very high price in terms of fear, uncertainty, the huge increased cost of security, and the erosion of civil liberties in many Western countries. Moreover, even if the terrorists cannot win in the sense of defeating the West, they can achieve significant victories in the ideological wars within Muslim societies.

Actually the defensive argument is unpersuasive, for purely normative reasons tied to comprehensive pluralism, even if global terrorism could succeed. Unlike in the case of domestic terror used as a last resort against an oppressive authoritarian regime, there is no world government or world army and police that could uproot Islamic fundamentalism by force in the Muslim countries in which it has achieved the greatest success. As a matter of fact, both the countries that promote globalization, such as the United States, and the countries in which the most virulent Islamic reactions against globalization have taken place are pluralist-in-fact. As already indicated in Chapter 8, there are debates about the proper scope and limits of globalization in countries that lead the way in its spread. Similarly, there are proponents and beneficiaries of globalization in Muslim countries as well as opponents of it and persons adversely affected by it. Also in many of these countries, there have been long and profound divisions among proponents and opponents of Islamic fundamentalism (Abdullah 2002).[13] Finally, and this is most important from the standpoint of comprehensive pluralism, at bottom the main defensive argument of the fundamentalist is that the introduction of Western ideology and ways of life through globalization undermines the grip that fundamentalism has over Muslim populations. But openness to different ideas, ideologies, and ways of life is, as emphasized throughout, one of the principal imperatives deriving from comprehensive pluralism's second-order norms. Fundamentalist Islam may be entitled to some protection in a pluralist polity,[14] but it cannot shield members of its religious communities from receiving and trying different ideas. Fundamentalism can use persuasion to dissuade dissension among its ranks, but it cannot resort to violence to repel views and ideas with which it vehemently disagrees. That is the minimum required by the precepts of comprehensive pluralism.

The case against any possible legitimacy for fundamentalist violence is an easy one for comprehensive pluralism, Habermas, or any view that is consistent with the Enlightenment project. What is much more difficult, one the other hand, and this

---

[13] See, for example, Ghassan F. Abdullah, *New Secularism in the Arab World*, http://secularism.org/skeptics/secularism.htm.

[14] This is on the assumption that any violence that may be associated with it is severable from its core ideology.

has been repeatedly noted, is dealing with the non-violent spread of fundamentalism. For Habermas, as discussed earlier, fundamentalism is altogether excluded, so allowing the spread of its ideas is not an issue. The problem with this view is that leaving out fundamentalism and other conceptions of the good tends to undermine discursive proceduralism as a whole. For comprehensive pluralism, in contrast, fundamentalism should be afforded some recognition and protection, but that leads to the danger that through peaceful lobbying or persuasion, fundamentalists will succeed in entrenching anti-pluralist norms that will eventually threaten the integrity of second-order norms by interfering with their deployment and functioning.

To illustrate the dangers posed by non-violent fundamentalism, let us focus briefly on Christian fundamentalism in the United States. Such fundamentalism has not taken arms or incited to terror as has its Islamic counterpart. But through dogged and concerted intervention in the political arena, as mentioned in Chapter 5, Christian fundamentalism has targeted an essential tenet of the Enlightenment: the separation between science and religion. Indeed, Christian fundamentalists have recently waged a highly visible campaign to have creationism, which lacks any scientific basis, taught in public schools instead of, or alongside, evolution theory.[15] If to this is added American Christian fundamentalism's fight against abortion, contraception, homosexuality, same sex marriage, and secularism in general, then in the end, if left to its own devices and allowed to push for its project to its logical conclusion, even non-violent fundamentalism seemingly poses a grave threat not only against the Enlightenment project but also against pluralism itself.

The greater the success of non-violent fundamentalism, the less it ought to be tolerated pursuant to the second-order norms of comprehensive pluralism, and up to a certain point, pluralism could protect itself by entrenching its second-order norms in the relevant constitution. But pushing this line of reasoning to its very end, a completely successful peaceful fundamentalism would be completely intolerable from the standpoint of pluralism. This conclusion, moreover, may seem at first to buttress Habermas's decision to exclude fundamentalism altogether from the process of discursive proceduralism designed to lead to normative unity and a common identity. Upon closed scrutiny, however, the conclusion in question actually underscores the inadequacy of Habermas's treatment of fundamentalism and points to an even more serious problem.

Habermas not only excludes fundamentalism but also reinterprets it in a way that makes it fairly convenient to simply make it go away. Indeed, fundamentalism itself is excluded, but behind its intransigent façade, there are economic issues. Moreover, though fundamentalism is not allowed in the communicative arena, it is

---

[15] See ADL Online, Religion in the Science Class? http:/www.adl.org/issue_religious_freedom/create/creationism_QA.asp.

but the extreme culmination of a process of distorted communication. Consistent with this, fundamentalism's façade should be susceptible to being dismantled in the course of achieving greater economic justice. Concurrently, the breakdown in communication is attributable to the seemingly unstoppable spread of economic disparity, a process that can be presumably reversed through rechanneling globalization to minimize unconscionable disparities in social welfare. And this, in turn, should do much to allow undoing the breakdown in communication and to grant those who formerly identified with fundamentalism sufficient recognition to convince them that they may be able to participate as equal partners in communicative action.

But what if fundamentalism is ultimately opaque, not necessarily a symptom of economic discontent, and not a product of communicative breakdown or distortion, being instead an easy-to-communicate bundle of norms and values that are utterly unacceptable to non-fundamentalists and pluralists. In that case, fundamentalism poses a much more radical problem, for it not only forecloses unity, but also, as underscored in Chapter 8, threatens pluralism by progressively eliminating all space for difference and diversity. In other words, pluralism depends on constant interaction between self and other, a dialogue between them, and the possibility of mutual accommodation and peaceful coexistence – all under the aegis of comprehensive pluralism's second-order norms. If triumphant fundamentalism is the other who refuses to dialogue or compromise with all non-fundamentalists (and fundamentalists committed to other absolute truths), then self and other seem bound to remain split. As positions harden, moreover, pluralism, multi-culturalism, and religious diversity, among others, are likely to recede in favor of individualistic liberalism and strict secularism as core fallback positions for embattled Enlightenment values. Under these circumstances, globalization and the rise of fundamentalism, which seem linked, would perhaps not destroy the Enlightenment project but they would eradicate all the progress and greater inclusiveness it has achieved through many generations, thus sending the Enlightenment virtually back to its starting point. That would not necessarily destroy the Enlightenment project, but it would amount to a huge setback for it.

It is by no means certain that fundamentalism will strengthen or triumph as globalization spreads and deepens. But it is clear that fundamentalism, particularly as it becomes linked to violence and global terrorism, poses a formidable threat to the Enlightenment project and undermines Habermas's identity ethics based on discursive proceduralism as it does Derrida's ethics of difference. Habermas's analysis of the relationship between globalization, fundamentalism, and global terrorism provides many sharp insights and useful observations. In addition, Habermas is right in insisting that the solution to these new daunting problems will in all likelihood depend on developing and strengthening post-national spheres of governance and properly linking them to national and infra-national democratic self-government.

What does remain most problematic about Habermas's account, and ultimately renders his diagnosis of the current situation and his recommendations on how to cope with it difficult to accept, however, is his serious underestimation of how much fundamentalism and global terrorism are rooted in identity politics bound to culminate in culture wars.

Fundamentalism and global terror also threaten to undermine comprehensive pluralism, but for entirely different reasons. Comprehensive pluralism does not underestimate the identity politics associated with fundamentalism. What threatens pluralism, therefore, has nothing to do with its assessment of the situation. Its stems, instead, from the potential polarization of the polity into fundamentalists and anti-fundamentalists, which would sap the very basis upon which pluralism rests. Indeed, the aggressive fundamentalist – whether with or without violence – is set to eradicate difference, and that position must be rejected as incompatible with pluralism. On the other hand, the more the fundamentalists are aggressive, the more the anti-fundamentalists must rally to each other's aid and stress identities at the expense of differences, thus veering ever closer to liberalism than to pluralism.

In the end, comprehensive pluralism looms as better suited than Habermas's discursive proceduralism to cope with the challenge that fundamentalism and global terrorism pose to the Enlightenment project. This is because pluralism is at once more inclusive and more attuned to the difficulties stemming from the identity politics involved in the confrontation between fundamentalists and non-fundamentalists. Moreover, broader inclusiveness is not only more consonant with pluralism, but it also increases the chances – all things being equal – that fundamentalism will retreat rather than advance. Indeed, the core of the pluralist ideal is openness to ideas and viewpoints, and although fundamentalism is hermetically closed to any outside perspectives, fundamentalists and those subjected to them are not.

The focus on global terrorism in this chapter and the preceding one has shed light on the vulnerabilities and limitations of the ethics of difference, the ethics of identity and the ethics deriving from comprehensive pluralism. I have argued that the latter is better suited to cope with the challenges posed by global terrorism than either of its two rivals. But by the same token, it has become clear that there are conditions besides the war of all against all that pose a serious threat to the viability and ultimate relevance of comprehensive pluralism. In view of this, in the concluding chapter, I will assess the scope and limitations of comprehensive pluralism and its potential for recharting and redirecting the project of the Enlightenment based on the insights garnered throughout the preceding analysis.

10

Conclusion

The Hopes of Pluralism in a More Unified and More Fragmented World

The philosophical case for comprehensive pluralism advanced throughout the pre-ceding pages is based on the conviction that normative pluralism is best under all circumstances, ranging from the non-pluralist polity to the increasingly pluralist-in fact multi-national, multi-ethnic, multi-cultural polity and the transnational arena. Even in a purely homogeneous social setting, encouragement and protection of the pursuit of multiple paths to self-realization and self-fulfillment is a clear normative imperative for comprehensive pluralism. Indeed, there are bound to be enough rele-vant differences among individuals even in the most non-pluralistic of socio-political settings to allow for each to fine-tune her personal journey toward self-realization, and thus enrich her experience of the good life as well as that of others who may use or build upon the conception of the good she helped to forge for her own pur-pose. In the best of all possible worlds, priority would be given to singularity and all conceivable differences promoted and celebrated. Moreover, by thus thrusting singularity to the fore, not only would each person be encouraged to find the best for himself, but also in the course of pursuing the call originating in his singularity, he would be likely to expand horizons and contribute to the needs or aspirations of others. If one seeks self-fulfillment in music and becomes a superb performing musician, for example, she is likely to end up enriching the experience of those who listen to her and prompt some of the latter to explore previously unthought of more well-suited paths to their own self-realization and self-fulfillment.

In the best of all possible worlds, the first negative moment of comprehensive pluralism would become the only one, and pluralism would merge into an ethics of difference akin to that propounded by Derrida. But down to earth, including in the best of all plausible intrasubjective settings, leaving the entire realm of the norma-tive to comprehensive pluralism's negative moment or to a Derridean ethics of diffe-rence would simply not do. And, this is the case not just because of the failings of the ethics of difference in tackling the normative challenge posed by global terrorism, which were detailed in Chapter 8. Indeed, inherent harmony among competing conceptions of the good is virtually impossible even in the most ordinary of times, and that for two principal omnipresent reasons. First, inevitably some conceptions of the good seek restriction or destruction of others as repeatedly alluded to in the course of the preceding analysis. And, second, coexistence among conceptions of the good that bear no ill will toward one another cannot continue for long without competition for scarce resources resulting in at least partial frustration of the designs of some of the conceptions involved.

Paradoxically, precisely because all singularity cannot be fully accommodated, there arises a need for unity. At a minimum, that unity should provide a cogent and principled way to account for as much singularity and difference as possible given the particulars at play under the prevailing circumstances. And, the second, positive, logical moment of comprehensive pluralism coupled with the latter's second-order norms supply the requisite criteria. Moreover, optimally, the operative measure of unity carved out through deployment of the latter criteria should lead to more than the securing of a shared space for mere coexistence. It should also foster, through internalization of second-order norms, greater inner openness and greater acceptability and empathy within each singular self toward all different others with whom the self in question is bound to come across. The idea, as repeatedly emphasized, is not to merge conceptions of the good or to fudge differences among them but to emphasize that the self's relation to her conception of the good is similar to the other's relation to his. And also, to seek to understand how particulars in the conception of the good of the other, which one may find alienating or indifferent, appeal to needs or aspirations of the other just as other particulars within one's own conception contribute to meeting one's own needs and aspirations.

For example, one may seek spiritual solace by praying, another by reading poetry, yet another by fighting cruelty against animals or joining the battle to eradicate poverty. It may well be, moreover, that from the religious perspective of one who considers prayer essential to spiritual well-being reading poetry and other sources of comfort could not be deemed acceptable substitutes. At a minimum, pluralism requires that the religious believer leave room for those who forgo prayer to turn to other means in the search for spiritual fulfillment. At best, the spread of the pluralist ethos will enable the religious believer in question, without weakening her commitment or beliefs, to understand and appreciate that to certain others, reading poetry, eradicating animal cruelty, or combating poverty may occupy the very place that prayer does in the case of the believer.

Comprehensive pluralism, unlike value pluralism, which was examined in Chapter 1, is pluralistic all the way up and all the way down and does not subordinate the one to the many or vice versa. Comprehensive pluralism's negative moment ensures that all differences count whereas its positive moment and the second-order norms it deploys allow for its core unity to permeate the many and to provide the latter with the requisite normative apparatus for orderly coexistence. Comprehensive pluralism's two pronged dialectical process, unlike Rawlsian pure procedural justice or Kantian or Habermasian rights-based proceduralism, does not purport to be neutral or to rise above the good. Although comprehensive pluralism's dialectic necessarily relies on procedure – the competing conceptions of the good at play in each concrete setting must be measured against one another according to the criteria provided by pluralism's second-order norms – it is at all times guided and molded by substantive values issued by particular conception of the good that is distinct from all its monistic and relativistic counterparts.

As most strongly exemplified by typically prevailing circumstances in times of crisis and in times of stress, such as those discussed in Part III of the book, the actual plurality and diversity yielded though recourse to comprehensive pluralism's dialectical process is prone to great variations. In grave crises, when fear for one's own survival becomes all pervasive, pluralism may have to end up siding with one position against all others, and thus produce a result that is in all appearances equivalent to that which would have been produced under liberalism or some other monistic ethos. From a strictly philosophical perspective, the latter result does not detract from the integrity or coherence of comprehensive pluralism. In grave crises, a common collectively shared identity may have to be promoted above all differences, lest the minimum space needed for a pluralist way of life be in danger of complete elimination. This is consistent with the logic of pluralism and with its extending all the way up and all the way down.

Upon inspection, the most troubling problem concerning pluralism under conditions marked by a severe decrease in openness between self and other does not have to do with pluralist philosophy, but with its application. As became manifest in the preceding examination of times of stress and of the challenges posed by global terrorism, it is difficult to draw the line between when an adherent to the pluralist ethos ought to focus exclusively or primarily on identity and when she should insist on opening up to greater plurality. This difficulty is compounded, moreover, by the natural tendency to retrench from those who are different when one feels that one's very identity is under threat.

From a practical standpoint, it seems reasonable to expect that openness to pluralism would be prevalent in ordinary times in a well-integrated polity that is pluralistic-in-fact. As long as the differences at stake are not too far ranging, and as long as the various selves involved are accustomed to the others they encounter and know what to expect from the latter, then the life of the polity would seem to have much to gain and little to lose from a policy of inclusion and tolerance. Under such circumstances, undoubtedly many would be pragmatically pluralistic even if they had no inclination to embrace philosophical pluralism. On the other hand, the more one feels that one's identity is under threat, the less likely it seems that one would veer toward a policy of inclusion.

It is precisely in the latter class of cases that theory and practical application may in the end clash. Thus, for example, as the result of the perceived failure of integration of the Muslim minority in the United Kingdom, France, and Germany, coupled with the ongoing threat and prospect of Islamic militancy and its links to global terror, the British Prime Minister, the German Chancellor, and the French President have denounced "multi-culturalism" and multi-culturalist policies, such as those implanted in the United Kingdom in the 1960s, as having paved the way for extremism and violence.[1] Such sentiments are hardly surprising in an era of economic retrenchment and profound changes in Western Europe's cultural and religious landscape. Nevertheless, these anti-pluralist stances clearly seems to run counter to the normative precepts associated with pluralist philosophy. If, as seems most likely, the great majority of Muslims in Western Europe seeks acceptance by, and integration in, the polity in which it resides provided respect for its religious and cultural differences is widely granted, then the pluralist ethos clearly commands inclusion in spite of the fears and uneasiness that such policy would instill in the country's majority. On the other hand, if, as sounds most improbable, claims to Muslim difference were inextricably linked to promotion and institution of Islamist militancy and the politics of global terror, then pluralist philosophy would call for reinforcement of majority identity and restrictions on, if not exclusion of, actually threatening Muslim-based differences.

To cope with difficulties concerning application, such as those that arose in the context of the last example, comprehensive pluralism ought to insist on a strong presumption in favor of openness toward the other. This presumption, moreover, should be assessed in the context of the dynamic triggered by the dialectic associated with comprehensive pluralism. In other words, the presumption of openness considered here is one that is introduced in an evolving dynamic setting in which improvements to mutual understanding and mutual acceptance are possible though not inevitable. Provided there is some general internalization of second-order norms throughout most of the polity, betting on openness, save in virtually unmistakable cases, thus seems the optimal way to seek to reconcile pluralist theory and its application.

Thus far, the difficulties encountered in the passage from theory to application stemmed from a dichotomy between the likely reaction to perceived threats involving one's identity and the optimal pluralist response, all things considered. There is, however, a seemingly much deeper problem that results from a key paradox, if

[1]   See John F. Burns, "Prime Minister Criticizes British 'Multiculturalism' as allowing extremism." *New York Times*, February 6, 2011, A6.

not a contradiction, at the very heart of comprehensive pluralism. Indeed, as already emphasized, for comprehensive pluralism to be workable and coherent, it is necessary that at least some non-pluralistic conceptions of the good with associated first-order norms maintain a dynamic presence within the polity ruled by the pluralist ethos. In other words, as specified from the outset, comprehensive pluralism is parasitic on the existence and pursuit of other conceptions of the good. As we have seen, that does not pose a theoretical problem since, from the standpoint of comprehensive pluralism, first-order norms that are inconsistent with its second-order norms are acceptable so long as they are not incompatible with the latter. Nevertheless, the fact that many acceptable conceptions of the good are inherently non-pluralistic does pose a potentially vastly disruptive practical problem.

Suppose, for example, that under conditions of stress, comprehensive pluralism counsels boosting multi-culturalism, but that proponents of conceptions of the good that embrace limited pluralism, such as liberalism, and their anti-pluralist counterparts, such as Christians in Western Europe who wish to deny Muslims in their midst everything beyond mere toleration, advocate drastic curtailment, if not eradication, of multi-culturalist policies. In such a case, comprehensive pluralism seems impotent when it comes to closing the gap between theory and application. And in this regard, comprehensive pluralism stands in sharp contrast to monist conceptions, such as liberalism, which are not parasitic on other conceptions. Indeed, if liberal theory prescribes a particular application, there appears to be no intrinsic impediment to consistent and successful execution.[2]

There are obvious measures that may help narrow the gap between theory and application in the context of comprehensive pluralism. One such possibility is to have recourse to institutional mechanisms, like those that can be set in place through constitutionalization of second-order norms, as already mentioned on several occasions throughout the preceding discussion. Moreover, the constitutionalization in question can be achieved through a combination of adoption of constitutional provisions that enshrine second-order norms and of interpretation of pertinent existing constitutional provisions and interpretive standards, such as that of proportionality, consistent with the dictates of second-order norms.

To the extent that constitutional means are used for purposes of application of pluralist norms, they impose external constraints on the non-pluralistic conceptions of the good upon which they impinge. Such non-pluralist conceptions become thus enlisted in the application of the pluralist ethos through compliance with applicable

---

[2] This is not to say that there may not be genuine issues of interpretation, leading to a diversity of opinions within liberalism, such as the ones between libertarians and egalitarians discussed in Chapter 6. There may also be questions relating to how best to harmonize means and ends. None of that, however, detracts from the fact that there is no liberal impediment that prevents going from a liberal prescription to its consequent implementation.

constitutional norms. Furthermore, because the constraints involved are external, the non-pluralists affected ought to be able to preserve their intra-communal ethos for the most part intact. In short, in this case, external steering toward pluralism would leave the particular non-pluralist ethos involved virtually internally unaffected. And that would seem to guarantee maintenance of the requisite tension between pluralist and non-pluralist conceptions of the good upon which comprehensive pluralism depends.

External constraints, however, are highly unlikely to be sufficient to produce a satisfactory alignment between theory and practice. As already pointed out, for pluralism to become more than a mere counterfactual, it is necessary that it make certain internal inroads in order to be to some extent intra-communally internalized. As we have seen, this can be accomplished, at least in part, through education and through integration and accommodation of multifaceted selves within a particular community. For example, the German Catholic feminist woman of our example literally brings external commitments, such as her feminism, into her internal intra-communal relationships, such as those that she actively pursues within her Catholic community (and also conversely, she brings with her "external" Catholic values to her feminist community). This is likely to lead to greater interaction and greater interpenetration among distinct and even, at times, antagonistic conceptions of the good, hence expanding the reach and scope of pluralism from "within" non-pluralist conceptions of the good.

But "internal" penetration by "external" values, taken to its logical conclusion would eventually result in the elimination of tension among conceptions of the good, as all formally mutually antagonistic conceptions would end up in one big indistinct blend. And therein lies the paradox: It appears that if it were to achieve complete success, comprehensive pluralism would end up doing away with all genuine plurality.

In theory, comprehensive pluralism requires the maintenance of an equilibrium between itself and other conceptions of the good, but in practice it would seem geared to the eventual elimination of all other such conceptions. Is that inevitable? Is pluralism's aim to accommodate difference and diversity likely to culminate in a unity based on dull and dispirited uniformity? Or worse, is it either the latter, in case of success, or the war of all against all, as hinted by the critics of multi-culturalist policies in Western Europe, in case of failure?

Although neither of these two possibilities can be logically discarded, they are highly unlikely to come about, or to be precipitated, *as a consequence of* the deployment of the pluralist ethos. As repeatedly emphasized, comprehensive pluralism proceeds dialectically, by aiming at fostering the best possible equilibrium between unity and plurality. Moreover, once unleashed, the dialectic in question operates both at the inter-communal and at the intra-communal levels. Communities must become more open to one another: One religion should not view another exclusively as an enemy of the truth, but rather as a religious community like one's own that aims at fulfilling the spiritual needs of its believers. In so doing, moreover, the other religion (from the standpoint of one's own) may either fail to reach the truth or, as became Catholicism's assessment of Judaism after Vatican II, to reach the truth only in part (Rosen 2005). Similarly, the pluralist dialectic requires greater intra-communal openness. Feminism, for instance, has undoubtedly had an effect on religion, though that effect has thus far been uneven. Some religions have opened up the clergy to women, whereas others have not (Corbin 2007: 1967, fn. 3). Be that as it may, religions have had to adjust, to revisit, or to reinterpret some of their fundamental tenets and prescriptions. Throughout this process, however, whether at the inter-communal or at the intra-communal level, religions have not retreated from their truth or distinct identity. Catholicism, which shares the Old Testament with Judaism, may evolve to perceive the latter as a holder of part of the truth, but it has not, and need not, thereby yield in its assertion that it is the superior religion as the holder of the whole truth (Adler 1990: 40–1). Similarly, Catholicism may conceivably become more open to feminist goals, but it would have to achieve this within the normative and interpretive confines of the Catholic religion as opposed to within those of religion defined generically, or of a broad-based humanism spanning across a wide range of conceptions of the good.

More generally, the operation of the dialectic is supposed to increase openness, and thus foster greater acceptance of the other. At the same time, if the differences of the other become more acceptable, then so should mine be to the other, and if the other can proclaim his openly, so should I. Challenges require not only greater acceptance of the other but also renewed assertion and expression of the self. Catholicism can confront the challenge of feminism, either by rejecting it outright or by accommodating it as far as possible within its own normative system, in which case the Catholic religion would integrate some aspects or versions feminism within its self-conception. Inter-communal and intra-communal boundaries may shift and so may the relationships within and among them. The dialectic, however, does preserve all along the basic dynamic between the self and the other. In addition, the tension between unity and plurality as animated by the constant work of the negative and positive moments of comprehensive pluralism remains consistent. Who is included, to what extent, who is not included, and what kind of unity is prevalent at a particular point in time are always subject to change. But the fact that no perfect or final unity or diversity is ever likely to be achieved, and that there is always room for better alignments and adjustments remains constant.

There is inevitably a gap between the potential and the workings of pluralism. What pluralism prescribes under particular circumstances and what recourse to its ethos can achieve cannot fully coincide because pluralism's other must per force resist or else not only it but pluralism itself would disappear. Ontologically, plural-ism assumes that both the self and the other have an insatiable need to maintain their own distinct identity while at the same time needing some measure of unity only achievable though mutual recognition. Comprehensive pluralism does not con-template any great Hegelian synthesis in which unity and plurality would become totally and definitively integrated as part of the comprehensive self-definition and self-mastery of being-as-such which is in-itself and for-itself completely unified and exhaustively differentiated. Consistent with this, comprehensive pluralism con-ceives its own dialectic as an unending evolving process with no culminating ending point. There will always be, therefore, a gap between what ought to be done and what can be done, between the theory and its application. Moreover, it is because of the constant presence of this gap that comprehensive pluralism must maintain its edge as a critical counterfactual all the while it keeps urging for greater perfection in light of shifting horizons of possibilities.

Once the workings of the dialectic of comprehensive pluralism are properly understood, it should become evident that threats to the viability of the pluralist ethos seem bound to be external rather than internal. It may be that globalization and the leveling of cultural diversity that it fosters coupled with the tendencies toward subjectivism and religious fundamentalism, triggered by the disenchant-ment of reason and intensified by global terrorism, will end up making pluralism unworkable. As we have seen, one imaginable scenario is a total war between neo-liberal capitalism and religious fundamentalism, with each of the two contenders completely closed to the other or to any form of pluralism. But, in that case, it would be neither pluralism not its logic nor its dialectical process that would lead to its own demise. Indeed, the push to global markets and the attraction toward religious fundamentalism stem primarily, respectively, from the evolution of cap-italism and from various forms of disenchantment and frustration associated with the implementation of the project of the Enlightenment. Accordingly, globaliza-tion and belligerent religious fundamentalism may conceivably sweep pluralism away for the duration of their all-encompassing and all-consuming struggle, but this would certainly not result from anything intrinsic to comprehensive pluralism or to its deployment.

On the other hand, a plausible narrative links the Enlightenment to the strug-gle between globalization and belligerent fundamentalism through relativism. If the Enlightenment and modernism necessarily lead to post-modernism, and if post-modernism is ultimately inextricably linked to relativism, then the struggle in ques-tion may be understood in terms of the culmination of the surge of a strong reaction against relativism. And if this inference is warranted, then the previously discussed threat to pluralism may be traceable to relativism, which, as stressed from the outset, is distinct from, and antagonistic toward, comprehensive pluralism.

These observations do raise, however, a larger question: What is, at bottom, the relationship between comprehensive pluralism and the Enlightenment project?

As recounted in Chapters 8 and 9, both Derrida and Habermas have placed themselves on the side of the project of the Enlightenment and have characterized globalization and global terrorism fueled by religious fundamentalism as posing serious threats to the survival of that project. As will be remembered, Derrida posited that post-modernism is consistent with the Enlightenment and that the preceding threats were intrinsic to the unfolding of the project of the Enlightenment in the course of history. Habermas, for his part, consistent with his unshakable adherence to modernism, has concluded that the same threats were extrinsic to the realization of the Enlightenment project.

I have argued that comprehensive pluralism is better equipped than Derrida's ethics of difference and than Habermas's ethics of identity for purposes of combating the foregoing threats. As will be recalled, the ethics of difference fails to produce a cogent condemnation of its own of global terrorism, whereas the ethics of identity unduly sacrifices plurality in its confrontation against terrorism fueled by religious fundamentalism. I endeavored to demonstrate that comprehensive pluralism overcame both of these shortcomings, but I did not specify how comprehensive pluralism may figure in the trajectory of the Enlightenment project in the face of the threats addressed by Derrida and Habermas. I now briefly turn to that task with a view to buttress the proposition that the pluralist ethos is best suited to guide the Enlightenment project through the perils posed by globalization and global terrorism.

The Enlightenment project seems best understood dialectically as an evolving one, confronting different obstacles over time, and adapting its trajectory to meet the particular challenges and contradictions that spring up before it as it edges its way forward having overcome or finessed the contradictions of the past, which inevitably pave the way to the formation of new ones. Within this perspective, Derrida looms as being right against Habermas in his understanding of the threats to the Enlightenment project posed by globalization and global terror as being intrinsic rather than extrinsic. The relevant sequence leads from the emergence of instrumental reason as paramount to the disenchantment of reason, subjectivism, post-modernism, and the spread and politicization of religious fundamentalism as a reaction against globalization, an all-encompassing materialistic culture, and the rampant spread of relativism. And that sequence, particularly if viewed dialectically, seems by far best understood as stemming from a series of evolving internal struggles and contradictions, as encompassing the symptoms and pathologies produced by the latter, and as defining the reactions and directions formulated with an aim to overcoming the obstacles posed by each of the succeeding sets of contradictions.

Both that which stands against the Enlightenment and that which it forges ahead toward are bound to change in relation to the shifting points of consideration

and changing horizons of possibility that punctuate the internal unfolding of
the Enlightenment project. At its beginnings, in eighteenth-century France, the
Enlightenment stood against the hierarchical feudal order and against the Catholic
Church as the institutional actor determined to maintain the constraint of reason
in the name of faith. As detailed in Chapter 5, by the end of the twentieth century,
the Enlightenment project confronted an all together different set of obstacles that
arose in the course, and as a consequence, of its own evolution. On the one hand,
secularism has achieved dominance in the inter-communal arena, and on the other
hand, in a form of return of the repressed, strong and fundamentalist religion was
reclaiming the political arena. Accordingly, just as secularism loomed as the proper
antidote to the stranglehold held by the Catholic Church at the dawn of the French
Revolution, so too, consistent with the preceding analysis, comprehensive pluralism seems particularly suited to stir the contemporary conflict between secularism
and repoliticized strong religion toward a course that would recalibrate the tension
between faith and reason and the relationship among the principal existing competing conceptions of the good. Such recalibration, moreover, should enable continuation of the Enlightenment project's pursuit of liberty and equality for all.

Being directly confronted by feudal hierarchy, initially the Enlightenment
needed to endorse a conception of individual liberty and individual equality geared
to the leveling of the intricate web of privilege and subordination that entrenched
the feudal system. After implantation of individual liberty and equality through the
spread of liberalism and the consequent piecemeal eradication of certain particular
instances of illiberalism accompanied by devaluation of group-regarding concerns
and conceptions of the good, however, both the negative and positive orientation of
the Enlightenment project had to shift. As argued throughout the book, against the
excesses, insufficiencies, and pathologies of liberalism, comprehensive pluralism
offers a conception of liberty and equality that better encompasses the contemporary
range of self-perception and diversity. On the other hand, on the positive side, comprehensive pluralism provides a better conception of equal liberty as envisioned by
the Enlightenment project under prevailing current conditions. Through comprehensive pluralism, individual liberty and equality is supplemented with, and eventually superseded by, equal liberty among selves as possessors of conceptions of the
good and in the function, as much as possible, of the particular content of the latter.
In short, comprehensive pluralism aligns itself with the Enlightenment project in
the pursuit of equal liberty for all, but it transforms the particular content of the
latter in order to overcome internal contradictions that developed over time and to
take advantage of newly created opportunities that arise upon its triumphs over past
obstacles and its adjustments to meet new ones.

One potential serious obstacle to comprehensive pluralism contributing successfully to the reorientation and furtherance of the project of the Enlightenment stems

from pluralism's embrace of post-modernism. If post-modernism ends up being inextricably linked to relativism, and if it thoroughly undermines the modernist conception of reason, by postulating that all existing and potential discourses are in fact equivalent, then any embrace of post-modernism, including that by comprehensive pluralism, would seem more prone to derailing than to buttressing the advancement of the Enlightenment project. Because of this, it is imperative to briefly consider whether, in the last analysis, post-modernism can be successfully disentangled from relativism and from complete devaluation of the discourse of reason.

Derrida's ethics of difference is not relativistic as recognition and respect for the singularity of the other is not equivalent to considering that all conceptions of good can only be normatively assessed from their own internal perspective. Nevertheless, under certain exceptional circumstances, such as those involving global terrorism, as we have seen, the ethics of difference operates as the functional equivalent of relativism. In contrast, as explained in Chapter 8, comprehensive pluralism is open to both post-modernism and to the accommodation of the other's singularity, but, in either case, only insofar as this does not result in incompatibilities with pluralism's second-order norms.

If post-modernism is understood as leveling all hierarchies among all discourses, then it would seem ultimately incompatible with furtherance of the Enlightenment project. Indeed, in that case, the discourse of reason and that of science would be on a par with that of magic or superstition, let alone with that of religion. Assuming for the sake of argument that this interpretation of post-modernism is warranted, it does not follow, however, that comprehensive pluralism would countenance embracing such post-modernism all the way down. As underscored in Chapter 5, comprehensive pluralism because of its internal imperatives as put in action in the context of the current predicament of contemporary societies, institutes a bifurcation between the realm of facts and that of norms. Prima facie, comprehensive pluralism remains open to all discourses and adopts initially what could be characterized as a post-modern receptivity toward them. In reprocessing these discourses under its second-order norms, however, comprehensive pluralism, for the reasons elaborated in Chapter 5,[3] determines that the optimal way to handle the tension between unity and plurality under prevailing circumstances requires preservation of key elements of the modern discourse of reason and science within what may be roughly characterized as the realm of fact while, at the same time, continuing to accept use of the full range of possibilities opened up by post-modern discourse in the context of normative self-definition and self-expression.

By thus subjecting singularity and its post-modern discourses to its unifying second-order norms, and by best managing its handling of the competition among

---

[3] See supra, at Section 5.3.

prevailing contemporary conceptions of the good by setting a boundary between the empire of the modern and that of the post-modern, comprehensive pluralism does pave the way for reinvigoration and continuation of the Enlightenment project. Thus, as I have argued throughout, comprehensive pluralism does better than any of its current competitors. But whether it can continue doing this for long, and whether the Enlightenment project will endure and prosper well into the future, only time will tell. After all, even if fully guided by the normative precepts of comprehensive pluralism, the Enlightenment project, based on its history, seems bound to confront new internal contradictions and new external threats. How comprehensive pluralism's dialectic may adapt, and whether it or the Enlightenment project might be transformed beyond recognition as a result, can only be at present matters of pure speculation. The most one can hope for now is that comprehensive pluralism will meet the current challenges that confront it and that it will help steer the Enlightenment project toward the enhanced and enriched conception of equal liberty that pluralism has helped to articulate.

Bibliography

Abdullah, Ghassan F. 2002. New secularism in the Arab world. *Minbar Ibn Rushd: Forum for freedom of thought.* http://www.ibn-rushd.org/forum/Secularism.htm.

Ackerman, Bruce. 1991. *We the people: Foundations.* Cambridge, MA: Harvard University Press.

2004. The emergency constitution. *Yale Law Journal* 113: 1029.

Adler, Mortimer J. 1990. *Truth in religion: the plurality of religions and the unity of truth.* New York: Macmillan.

Anderson, Benedict. 1991. *Imagined communities: Reflections on the origin and spread of nationalism.* New York: Verso.

Arato, Andrew. 2000. Law and interpretation. *Cardozo Law Review* 21: 1929.

Aristotle. 1946. *Politics,* trans. E. Barker. Oxford: Clarendon Press.

1980. *The nicomachean ethics,* trans. Martin Oswald. New York: Oxford University Press.

Arkoun, Mohammed. 1994. *Rethinking Islam: Common questions, uncommon answers.* Boulder, CO: Westview Press.

2002. *The unthought in contemporary Islamic thought.* London: Saqi.

Balibar, Etienne. 1998. *Spinoza and politics,* trans. Peter Snowdon. London: Verso.

Beiner, Ronald. 1995. *Theorizing citizenship.* Albany: State University of New York Press.

Bentham, Jeremy. 1970. *An introduction to the principles of morals and legislation.* New York: Hafner.

Berlin, Isaiah. 1970. *Four essays on liberty.* New York: Oxford University Press.

1997. *The crooked timber of humanity,* ed. Henry Hardy. Princeton, NJ.: Princeton University Press.

2000. *Three critics of the Enlightenment: Vico, Hamann, Herder,* ed. Henry Hardy. Princeton, NJ.: Princeton University Press.

2001. *Against the current,* ed. Henry Hardy. Princeton, NJ: Princeton University Press.

2002. *The power of ideas,* ed. Henry Hardy. Princeton, NJ: Princeton University Press.

Birnbaum, Pierre. 2009. On the secularization of the public square: Jews in France and the United States. *Cardozo Law Review* 30: 2431.

Borovali, Murat. 2009. Islamic headscarves and slippery slopes. *Cardozo Law Review* 30: 2593.

Borradori, Giovanna. 2003. *Philosophy in a time of terror: Dialogues with Jürgen Habermas and Jacques Derrida.* Chicago: University of Chicago Press.

Breitung, Barrett. 1996. Intervention and eradication: National and international responses to female circumcision. *Emory International Law Review* 10: 657.

Brennan, Katherine. 1989. The influence of cultural relativism on international human rights law: Female circumcision as a case study. *Law and Inequality: A Journal of Theory and Practice* 7: 367.

Brugger, Winfried. 2003. Communitarianism as the social and legal theory behind the German constitution. *International Journal of Constitutional Law (I. CON)* 2: 431.

Casanova, Jose. 1994. *Public religions in the modern world.* Chicago : University of Chicago Press.

Clinton, Robert N. 1993. Redressing the legacy of conquest: A vision quest for a decolonized federal Indian law. *Arkansas Law Review* 46: 77.

Cole, David & James X. Dempsey. 2002. *Terrorism and the Constitution: Sacrificing Civil Liberties in the Name of National Security.* Los Angeles: The New Press.

Conway, Patrick, et al. 2003. The North Carolina textiles project: An initial report. *Journal of Textile and Apparel, Technology and Management* 3: 3.

Corbin, Caroline Mala. 2007. Above the law? The constitutionality of the ministerial exemption from antidiscrimination law. *Fordham Law Review* 75: 1965.

Cord, Robert L. 1982. *Separation of church and state: historical fact and current fiction.* New York: Lambeth Press.

Derrida, Jacques. 1982. *Margins of philosophy*, trans. Alan Bass. Chicago: University of Chicago Press.

    1992. Force of law: The "mystical foundation of authority." In *Deconstruction and the possibility of justice*, ed. Drucilla Cornell, Michel Rosenfeld & David Grey Carlson. New York: Routledge.

    1994. *Politiques de l'amitié.* Paris: Editions Galilée.

    1996. Il courait mort: salut, salut. *Les Temps Modernes* 587: 7.

    2001. *On cosmopolitanism and forgiveness*, trans. Mark Dooley & Michael Hughes. London: Routledge.

    2003. *Voyous.* Paris: Editions Galilée.

    2003a. Deconstructing terrorism. In *Philosophy in a time of terror: Dialogues with Jürgen Habermas and Jacques Derrida*, ed. Giovanna Borradori. Chicago: University of Chicago Press.

Descartes, René. 1998. *Meditations and other metaphysical writings*, trans. Desmond Clarke. London: Penguin.

DeWolf, David K. 2009. The "teach the controversy" controversy. *University of St. Thomas Journal of Law and Public Policy* 4: 326.

Dorsen, Norman, et al. 2010. *Comparative constitutionalism: Cases and materials.* Minneapolis: West Group.

Dumont, Louis. 1977. *From Mandeville to Marx.* Chicago: University of Chicago Press.

Dworkin, Ronald. 1978. *Taking rights seriously.* Cambridge: Harvard University Press.

    1985. *A matter of principle.* Cambridge: Harvard University Press.

    1986. *Law's empire.* Cambridge: Belknap Press.

    1993. *Life's dominion.* New York: Knopf.

    1996. *Freedom's law: The moral reading of the American Constitution.* Cambridge, MA: Harvard University Press.

    2003. Response to overseas commentators. *International Journal of Constitutional Law (I. CON)* 1: 651.

Eberle, Edward J. 1997. Public discourse in contemporary Germany. *Case Western Reserve* 47: 797.

Ely, John Hart. 1980. *Democracy and distrust: A theory of judicial review*. Cambridge, MA: Harvard University Press.

Epstein, Richard A. 1992. *Forbidden grounds: The case against employment discrimination laws*. Cambridge, MA: Harvard University Press.

Evans, David C. 1960. Problems of teaching evolution in the secondary schools. *The American Biology Teacher* 22: 221.

Farer, Tom J. & Gaer, Felice. 1993. The UN and human rights: At the end of the beginning. In *United Nations, Divided World*, ed. Adam Roberts & Benedict Kingsbury. Oxford: Clarendon Press.

Feldman, Noah. 2005. *Divided by God: America's church-state problem and what we should do about it*. New York: Farrar, Straus and Giroux.

Ferreres Comella, Victor. 2004. The new regulations of political parties in Spain, and the decision to outlaw Batasuna. In *Militant democracy*, ed. A. Sajo. Amsterdam: Eleven International Publishing.

Fineman, Martha Albertson. 2004. *The autonomy myth: A theory of dependency*. New York: New Press.

Fish, Stanley. 1994. *There's no such thing as free speech*. New York: Oxford University Press.

Fukuyama, Francis. 1992. *The end of history and the last man*. New York: Free Press.

Galbraith, John Kenneth. 1976. *The affluent society*. Boston: Houghton Mifflin.

Gallie, W. B. 1965. Essentially contested concepts. *Proceedings of the Aristotelean Society* 56: 167.

Galston, William A. 2009. What value pluralism means for legal-constitutional orders. *The San Diego Law Review* 46: 803.

Garlicki, Lech. 2008. Cooperation of the courts: The role of supranational jurisdictions in Europe. *International Journal of Constitutional Law (I. CON)* 6: 509.

Gilligan, Carol. 1982. *In a different voice: Psychological theory and women's development*. Cambridge, MA.: Harvard University Press.

Ginsburg, Ruth Bader. 1985. Some thoughts on autonomy and equality in relation to Roe v. Wade. *North Carolina Law Review* 63: 375.

Gough, J. W. 1957. *The social contract*. Oxford: Clarendon Press.

Greenawalt, Kent. 2009. Secularism, religion, and liberal democracy in the United States. *Cardozo Law Review* 30: 2383.

Grimm, Dieter. 1995. Does Europe need a constitution? *European Law Journal* 1:282.

2009. Conflicts between general laws and religious norms. *Cardozo Law Review* 30: 2369.

Haarscher, Guy. 2009. Religious revival and pseudo-secularism. *Cardozo Law Review* 30: 2799.

Habeck, Mary. 2006. *Knowing the enemy: Jihadist ideology and the war on terror*. New Haven, CT: Yale University Press.

Habermas, Jürgen. 1984. *The theory of communicative action: Reason and the rationalization of society*, trans. Thomas McCarthy. Boston: Beacon Press.

1990. *The philosophical discourse of modernity*, trans. F. Lawrence. Cambridge, MA: MIT Press.

1992. Further reflections on the public sphere. In *Habermas and the public sphere*, ed. Craig Calhoun. Cambridge, MA: MIT Press.

1996. *Between facts and norms: Contributions to a discourse theory of law and democracy*, trans. William Rehg. Cambridge, MA: MIT Press.

1998. Paradigms of law. In *Habermas on law and democracy: Critical exchange*, ed. M. Rosenfeld & A. Arato. Berkeley: University of California Press.

1998a. Reply to symposium participants. In *Habermas on law and democracy: critical exchange*, ed. M. Rosenfeld & A. Arato. Berkeley: University of California Press.

1999. Struggles for recognition in the democratic state. In *Inclusion of the other*, ed. Ciaran P. Cronin & Pablo de Greiff. Cambridge, MA: MIT Press.

2001. *Jürgen Habermas, the postnational constellation: Political essays*, ed. & trans. Max Pensky. Cambridge, MA: Polity Press.

2003. Reconstructing terrorism. In *Philosophy in a time of terror: Dialogues with Jürgen Habermas and Jacques Derrida*, ed. Giovanna Borradori. Chicago: University of Chicago Press.

Hartney, Michael. 1995. Some confusions concerning collective rights. In *The rights of minority cultures*, ed. Will Kymlicka. Oxford: Oxford University Press.

Hegel, G. W. F. 1952. *Philosophy of right*, trans. T. Knox. Oxford: Oxford University Press.

1977. *Phenomenology of spirit*, trans. A. V. Miller. Oxford: Clarendon Press.

1999. *Hegel's science of logic*, trans. A.V. Miller. Amherst, NY: Humanity Books.

Hobbes, Thomas. 1973. *Leviathan*. New York: Every Man's Library.

1978. The citizen: Philosophical rudiments concerning government and society. In *Man and citizen*, ed. B. Gert. Atlantic Highlands, NJ: Humanities Press.

Huntington, Samuel. 1996. *The clash of civilizations and the remaking of the world order*. New York: Simon and Schuster.

Hyppolite, Jean. 1946. *Genèse et structure de la phénoménologie de l'esprit de Hegel*. Paris: Aubier.

Johnston, Darlene M. 1995. Native rights as collective rights: a question of group self-preservation. In *The rights of minority cultures*, ed. Will Kymlicka. Oxford: Oxford University Press.

Kant, Immanuel. 1969. *Foundations of the metaphysics of morals*, ed. Robert P. Wolff, trans. Lewis W. Beck. Indianapolis: Bobbs-Merrill.

1970. Perpetual peace: a philosophical sketch. In *Kant's political writings*, ed. Hans Reiss. Cambridge: Cambridge University Press.

Kelman, Mark. 1981. Interpretive construction in the substantive criminal law. *Stanford Law Review* 33: 591.

Kumm, Mattias. 2008. Why Europeans will not embrace constitutional patriotism. *International Journal of Constitutional Law (I-CON)* 6: 117.

Kymlicka, Will. 1995. *Multicultural citizenship: A liberal theory of minority rights*. New York: Oxford University Press.

1995a. Introduction. In *The rights of minority cultures*, ed. Will Kymlicka. Oxford: Oxford University Press.

Ladeur, Karl-Heinz. 2009. The myth of the neutral state and the individualization of religion: The relationship between state and religion in the face of fundamentalism. *Cardozo Law Review* 30: 2445.

Levy, Leonard W. 1986. *The Establishment Clause: Religion and the First Amendment*. New York: Macmillan.

Linz, Juan and Alfred Stepan. 1996. *Problems of democratic transition and consolidation: southern Europe, South America, and post-communist Europe*. Baltimore: Johns Hopkins University Press.

Locke, John. 1960. The second treatise of government. In *Two treatises of government*, ed. P. Laslett. New York: Mentor Books.

Luban, David. 2004. A theory of crimes against humanity. *Yale Journal of International Law* 29: 85.

Luhmann, Niklas. 1990. *Essays on self-reference*. New York: Columbia University Press.

Lukes, Steven. 1973. *Individualism*. Oxford: Basil Blackwell.

Macedo, Stephen. 1995. Homosexuality and the conservative mind. *Georgetown Law Journal* 84: 261.

Macherey, Pierre. 1979. *Hegel ou Spinoza*. Paris: F. Maspero.

Mahlmann, Matthias. 2009. Freedom and faith: Foundations of freedom of religion. *Cardozo Law Review* 30: 2473.

Mancini, Susanna. 2009. The power of symbols and symbols as power: Secularism and religion as guarantors of cultural convergence. *Cardozo Law Review* 30: 2629.

Mansfield, Anna Morawiec. 2003. Ethnic but equal: The quest for a new democratic order in Bosnia and Herzegovina. *Columbia Law Review* 103: 2052.

March, Andrew F. 2009. Are secularism and neutrality attractive to religious minorities? Islamic discussions of Western secularism in the "Jurisprudence of Muslim minorities" (fiqh al-aqalliyyat) discourse. *Cardozo Law Review* 30: 2821.

Marcuse, Herbert. 1965. Repressive tolerance. In *A critique of pure tolerance*, ed. Robert Wolff, Barrington Moore & Herbert Marcuse. Boston: Beacon Press.

Marx, Karl. 1964. Economic and philosophical manuscripts. In *Early writings*, ed. & trans. T. B. Bottomore. New York: McGraw-Hill.

Masters, Roger. 1968. *The political philosophy of Rousseau*. Princeton, NJ.: Princeton University Press.

McGoldrick, Dominic. 2004. The interface between public emergency powers and international law. *International Journal of Constitutional Law (I. CON)* 2: 380.

Michelman, Frank I. 1988. Law's republic. *Yale Law Journal* 97: 1493.

—— 2000. Modus vivendi postmodernus? On just interpretations and thinning of justice. *Cardozo Law Review* 21: 1945.

Mill, John Stuart. 1869. *The subjection of women*. London: Longmans, Green, Reader, and Dyer.

—— 1961. On liberty. In *The philosophy of John Stuart Mill*, ed. M. Cohen. Indianapolis: Hackett.

—— 1962. *Utilitarianism*. London: Collins/Fontana.

Minow, Martha. 1987. Justice engendered. *Harvard Law Review* 101:10.

Moore, Shelby. 1997. Doing another's bidding under a theory of defense of others; shall we protect the unborn with murder? *Kentucky Law Journal* 86:257.

Mostefai, Ourida & Scott, John. 2009. *Rousseau and l'infâme: Religion, toleration and fanaticism in the age of enlightenment*. Amsterdam: Rodopi.

Mouffe, Chantal. 2004. The limits of liberal pluralism: Towards an agonistic multipolar world order. In *Millitant democracy*, ed. A. Sajo. Amsterdam: Eleven International Publishing.

Munzer, Stephen. 1977. Right answer, pre-existing rights and fairness. *Georgia Law Review* 11: 1055.

Nagel, Thomas. 1986. *The view from nowhere*. New York: Oxford University Press.

Neuhaus, Richard John. 1984. *The naked public square: Religion and democracy in America*. Grand Rapids, MI: W.B. Eerdmans.

Nozick, Robert. 1974. *Anarchy, state, and utopia*. New York: Basic Books.

Pateman, Carole. 1988. *The sexual contract*. Stanford, CA: Stanford University Press.

Paust, Jordan J. 2005. Executive plans and authorizations to violate international law concerning treatment and interrogation of detainees. *Columbia Journal of Transnational Law* 43: 811.

Perry, Michael J. 1998. *The idea of human rights: Four inquiries*. New York: Oxford University Press.

Pitkin, Hannah. 1967. *The concept of representation*. Berkeley: University of California Press.

Popper, Karl. 1966. *The open society and its enemies: The spell of Plato*. Princeton, NJ: Princeton University Press.

Poscher, Ralph. 2003. Spinoza and the paradoxes of toleration. *Cardozo Law Review* 25: 715.

Posner, Richard. 2002. *Economic analysis of the law*. New York: Aspen Publishers.

Raday, Frances. 2003. Culture, Religion and Gender. *International Journal of Constitutional Law* 1: 663–715.

Radford, Mary F. 2000. The inheritance rights of women under Jewish and Islamic law. *Boston College International and Comparative Law Review* 23: 135.

Rawls, John. 1971. *A theory of justice*. Cambridge, MA: Belknap Press.

1993. *Political liberalism*. New York: Columbia University Press.

1997. The idea of public reason revisited. *Chicago Law Review* 64: 765.

2005. *Political liberalism: Expanded edition*. New York: Columbia University Press.

Raz, Joseph. 1972. Legal principles and the limits of law. *Yale Law Journal* 81: 823.

Resnik, Judith. 2008. Law as affiliation: "foreign" law, democratic federalism, and the sovereigntism of the nation-state. *International Journal of Constitutional Law (I-CON)* 6: 33.

Reule, Deborah A. 2001. The new face of Creationism: The Establishment Clause and the latest efforts to suppress evolution in public schools. *Vanderbilt Law Review* 54: 2555.

Ricoeur, Paul. 1990. *Soi-même comme un autre*. Paris: Éditions du Seuil.

Roach, Kent. 2004. Anti-terrorism and militant democracy. In *Militant democracy*, ed. A. Sajo. Amsterdam: Eleven International Publishing.

Rorive, Isabelle. 2009. Religious symbols in the public space: In search of a European answer. *Cardozo Law Review* 30: 2669.

Rosen, David. 2005. "Nostra aetate": Forty years after Vatican II. *Conference of the holy see commission for religious relations with Jewry*. Rome, October 27, 2005 Present & Future Perspectives. Available online at http://www.vatican.va/roman_curia/pontifical_councils/chrstuni/relations-jews-docs/rc_pc_chrstuni_doc_20051027_rabbi-rosen_en.html.

Rosenfeld, Esther. 1995. Jewish divorce law. *University of California, Davis Journal of International Law and Policy* 1: 135.

Rosenfeld, Michel. 1985. Contract and justice: The relation between classical contract law and social contract theory. *Iowa Law Review* 70: 769.

1989. Hegel and the dialectics of contract. *Cardozo Law Review* 10:1199.

1989a. Decoding Richmond: Affirmative action and the elusive meaning of constitutional equality. *Michigan Law Review* 87: 1729.

1991. *Affirmative action and justice: A philosophical and constitutional inquiry*. New Haven, CT: Yale University Press.

1991a. Metro Broadcasting, Inc. v. FCC: Affirmative action at the crossroads of constitutional liberty and equality. *University of California Law Review* 38: 583.

1992. Deconstruction and legal interpretation: conflict, indeterminacy and the temptations of the new legal formalism. In *Deconstruction and the possibility of justice*, ed. Drucilla Cornell, Michel Rosenfeld & David Gray Carlson. New York: Routledge.

1994. Modern constitutionalism as interplay between identity and diversity. In *Constitutionalism, identity, difference and legitimacy: Theoretical perspectives*. Durham, NC: Duke University Press.

1998. *Just interpretations: Law between ethics and politics*. Berkeley: University of California Press.

1998a. A pluralist critique of contractarian proceduralism. *Ratio Juris* 11: 291.

1998b. Can rights, democracy and justice be reconciled through discourse theory? Reflections on Habermas' proceduralist paradigm of law. In *Habermas on law and democracy: Critical exchange*, ed. M. Rosenfeld & A. Arato. Berkeley: University of California Press.

1999. A pluralist critique of the constitutional treatment of religion. In *The law of religious identity: Models for post-Communism*, ed. Andras Sajo & Shlomo Avineri. The Hague: Kluwer Law International.

2001. The rule of law and the legitimacy of constitutional democracy. *Southern California Law Review* 74: 1307.

2003. Hate speech in constitutional jurisprudence: A comparative analysis. *Cardozo Law Review* 24: 1523.

2003a. The philosophy of free speech in the United States. In *Mensch und Staat*, ed. Peter Hänni. Friboury: University of Friboury Press.

2008. Rethinking constitutional ordering in an era of legal and ideological pluralism. *International Journal of Constitutional Law (I. CON)* 6: 415.

2009. Introduction: Can constitutionalism, secularism and religion be reconciled in an era of globalization and religious revival? *Cardozo Law Review* 30: 2333.

2010. *The identity of the constitutional subject: selfhood, citizenship, culture and community*. New York: Routledge.

Rosenthal, Michael A. 2001. Tolerance as a virtue in Spinoza's ethics. *Journal of the History of Philosophy* 39: 535.

Rousseau, Jean-Jacques. 1947. *The social contract*, ed. C. Frankel. Riverside, NJ: Hafner Press.

Sajo, Andras. 2009. Constitutionalism and secularism: the need for public reason. *Cardozo Law Review* 30: 240.

Samuelson, Paul. 1976. *Economics*. New York: McGraw-Hill.

Sandel, Michael. 1982. *Liberalism and the limits of justice*. Cambridge: Cambridge University Press.

Sapir, Gidi & Statman, Daniel. 2009. Religious marriage in a liberal state. *Cardozo Law Review* 30: 2855.

Sartre, Jean-Paul. 1966. *Being and nothingness*, trans. Hazel E. Barnes. London: Methuen.

Schlink, Bernard. 2003. Hercules in Germany? *International Journal of Constitutional Law (I. CON)* 1: 610.

Schmitt, Carl. 1985. *The crisis of parliamentary democracy*, trans. E. Kennedy. Cambridge, MA: MIT Press.

1996. *The concept of the political*, trans. G. Schwab. Chicago: University of Chicago Press.

Slaughter, M. M. 1993. The Salman Rushdie affair: Apostasy, honor and freedom of speech. *Virginia Law Review* 79: 153.

Smith, Adam. 1976. *An inquiry into the nature and causes of the wealth of nations*, ed. E. Cannan. Chicago: University of Chicago Press.

1976a. *The theory of moral sentiments*. Indianapolis: Liberty Classics.

Smith, Steven B. 1997. *Spinoza, liberalism and the question of Jewish identity*. New Haven, CT: Yale University Press.

Spinoza, Benedict de. 1951. *A theologico-political treatise and a political treatise*, trans. R. H. M. Elwes. New York: Dover.

1955. The ethics. In *On the improvement of the understanding/ The Ethics/ Correspondence*, trans. R. H. M. Elwes. New York: Dover.

1955a. Correspondence. In *On the improvement of the understanding/ The Ethics/ Correspondence*, trans. R. H. M. Elwes. New York: Dover.

Stein, Eric. 1986. History against frees speech: The new German law against the "Auschwitz" and other "lies." *Michigan Law Review* 85: 277.

Stone, Suzanne L. 1991. Sinaitic and Noahide law: Legal pluralism in Jewish law. *Cardozo Law Review* 12: 1157.

Sunstein, Cass. 1993. *The partial constitution*. Cambridge, MA: Harvard University Press.

Taylor, Charles. 1975. *Hegel*. New York: Cambridge University Press.

Tribe, Laurence H. 1980. The puzzling persistence of process-based constitutional theories. *Yale Law Journal* 89: 1063.

1992. *Abortion: The clash of absolutes*. New York: Norton.

Troper, Michel. 2009. Sovereignty and laïcité. *Cardozo Law Review* 30: 2561.

Ullmann, Walter. 1967. *The individual and society in the Middle Ages*. London, Methuen.

Unger, Roberto. 1983. The critical legal studies movement. *Harvard Law Review* 96: 561.

Vatican II. 1965. http://www.vatican.va/archive/hist_councils/ii_vatican_council/index.htm

Von Bogdandy, Armin. 2005. The European constitution and European identity: Text and subtext of the treaty establishing a constitution for Europe. *The International Journal of Constitutional Law (I. CON)* 3: 295.

Waldron, Jeremy. 2007. Status versus equality: The accommodation of differences. In *Multiculturalism and law: a critical debate*, ed. Omid A Payrow Shabani. Cardiff: University of Wales Press.

Wallace, E. Gregory. 2009. Justifying religious freedom: the western tradition. *Penn State Law Review* 114: 485.

Weber, Max. 1930. *The Protestant ethic and the spirit of capitalism*, trans. Talcott Parsons. London: G. Allen & Unwin.

1968. *Economy and society*, ed. Guenther Roth & Claus Wittich. Berkeley: University of California Press.

Weithman, Paul. 1997. Natural law, morality and sexual complementarity. In *Sex, preference and family*, ed. D. M. Estlund & M. C. Nussbaum. Oxford: Oxford University Press.

West, Robin. 1997. Symposium: Fidelity in constitutional theory: Fidelity as integrity: Integrity and universality: A comment on Ronald Dworkin's freedom law. *Fordham Law Review* 65: 1313.

Yin, Tung. 2007. Punish or surveil. *Transnational Law and Contemporary Problems* 16: 873.

Yovel, Yirmiyahu. 1989. *Spinoza and other heretics*. Princeton, NJ: Princeton University Press.

Zizek, Slavoj. 1989. *The Sublime Object of Ideology*. London: Verso.

Zetner, Scot J. 2004. A just war: Friends, enemies and the war in Iraq: A view from the founding. *Nexus, A Journal of Opinion* 9: 27–45.

Index

Abortion
  confrontation between universalism,
    particularism and relativism, 99
  the constitutional treatment of the relationship
    between religion and the state, 164
  Dworkin's theory, 206
  in homogeneous and heterogeneous
    societies, 58
  pluralist constitutional approach to
    religion, 182
  Rawls's Kantian contractarianism, 23
Abstraction
  dialectic of equality, 75–76
  dynamic between identity and difference,
    83, 86
  human rights, 99, 125
  Rawls's Kantian contractarianism, 33
Ackerman, Bruce, 213, 216
Adler, Mortimer J., 303
Affirmative action
  the contrast between homogeneous and
    heterogeneous societies, 59
  Dworkin, 198–97
  minority rights under the U.S.
    Constitution, 104
Anderson, Benedict, 181
Arato, Andrew, 52
Aristotle, 16, 70, 215, 253
Arkoun, Mohammed, 165, 176
Australian Capital Television Pty Ltd v.
  Commonwealth, 237

Balibar, Etienne, 126, 128, 133, 134, 143
Beauharnais. v. Illinois, 105
Beiner, Ronald, 2
Bentham, Jeremy, 36

Berlin, Isaiah, 37–42
Bill of Rights, 53, 107, 237
Birnbaum, Pierre, 170
Board of Educ. v. Grumet, 159
Borovali, Murat, 155
Borradori, Giovanna, 255, 271, 272, 273, 275,
    278, 282
Bowers v. Hardwick, 75
Bradwell v. Illinois, 69, 74, 83, 104
Brandenburg v. Ohio, 114
Braunfeld v. Brown, 93
Breitung, Barrett, 118
Brennan, Katherine, 118
Brown v. Board of Education, 198
  Dworkin's theory, 198
Brugger, Winfried, 176

Casanova, Jose, 6, 149, 162
Citizenship
  dialectic of equality, 72
  gap between globalization and equal
    cosmopolitan citizenship, 253, 265
Clinton, Robert N., 107
Collins v. Smith, 105
Common law
  Dworkin's thesis, 184–85, 189, 191, 195–96
Communicative action
  critique of Habermas's assumptions regarding
    global terrorism, 287–90
  global terrorism and the post-national rule of
    law cosmopolitan order, 278–80
  Habermas's analysis of global terrorism in the
    context of discourse theory, 280–84, 286–87
  pluralism, 295
  terrorism's challenge to Habermas's conception
    of modernism, 273, 275

Communitarianism
defined, 12–13
comparing liberal, republican and
communitarian political rights, 227, 231–33
compatibility with limited pluralism, 233,
249–50
contrasted with comprehensive pluralism,
109–10
Dworkin's thesis, 200
minority group rights, 95
minority rights under the U.S.
Constitution, 109
overriding values and pluralism, 223–26
Comprehensive pluralism
defined, 11–16
as an alternative to Habermas's proceduralism
to cope with global terrorism, 290–96
areligious counterfactual, 152
clash between deprivatized religion and
relativized secularism, 150
the Constitution and group rights, 109–14
constitutional framework and pluralist
politics, 216
contrast between homogeneous and
heterogeneous societies, 57
contrasting Dworkin's theory and pluralism in
terms of the one and the many, 205–07
global terrorism and the contrasts between
pluralist ethics and the ethics of difference,
266–70
hate speech and militant democracy, 239, 241–42
Hegelian dimension of comprehensive
pluralism, 42–51
from liberalism to pluralism, 79–81
liberalism's, republicanism's, and
communitarianism's overriding values,
225–26
limited liberalism, republicanism and
communitarianism, 234
minority group rights, 93–95
from the modern to the postmodern and from
homogeneous to heterogeneous societies,
51–52
modern versus the postmodern, 55–56
nexus between human rights and constitutional
rights, 112–21
pacted secession, 246–48
pluralist account of the constitutional
treatment of the relationship between
religion and the state, 164–66, 172–78
pluralist constitutional approach to religion,
178–81

pluralist political rights in times of
stress, 238
political rights and the struggle between self
and other, 217, 219
political rights in times of stress, 248–50
priority of the good over the right, 59–62
Rawls's *Political Liberalism*, 62–67
relational and contextual pluralist political
rights and free speech, 237
Spinoza's theory and tolerance and pluralism
in a postmodern world, 144–48
teleological monism, 35
constitutional identity, 285
Constitutional patriotism
defined, 20
global terrorism and the post-national rule of
law cosmopolitan order, 279–80
Habermas's analysis of global terrorism in the
context of discourse theory, 282, 284–87
terrorism's challenge to Habermas's conception
of modernism, 272–74
Constitutionalism
areligious, 153–51
comparing liberal, republican and
communitarian political rights, 229, 231
constitutional framework and pluralist politics,
215–17
global terrorism and post-national
constitutionalism, 274, 279–80
pluralist account of the constitutional
treatment of the relationship between
religion and the state, 174–77
pluralist constitutional approach to religion,
178–81
recent historical changes and new trends,
161–64
Contract
freedom of contract, 54, 194
Habermas's dialogical Kantian proceduralism,
34–35
Kant's pure social contract proceduralist
approach, 29–31
problematic nexus between unity and
plurality, 24
Rawlsian contractarianism, 31–34
Conway, Patrick, 268
Corbin, Caroline Mala, 303
Cord, Robert L., 179
Cosmopolitanism
Derrida, 259, 260, 261–63, 265
global terrorism and the post national rule of
law, 274–80

terrorism's challenge to Habermas's conception of modernism, 273
Counterfactual reconstruction
Dworkin's theory of interpretation, 191–97
Dworkin's thesis, 184–85
law as integrity, 201
Critical legal theory, 184, 185, 187, 188, 189

Deconstruction
assessing the ethics of difference's account of global terrorism, 263–66
Derrida and the ethics of difference, 253–54
Derrida's deconstruction of globalization, tolerance and democracy, 262
global terrorism's challenge to the ethics of difference, 256
Derrida, Jacques, 255–53
assessing the ethics of difference's account of global terrorism, 263–66
in conflict with Habermas, 271–74
deconstruction and the ethics of difference, 253–54
deconstruction of globalization, tolerance and democracy, 255–56
the Enlightenment project as evolving, 305
global terrorism and the contrasts between pluralist ethics and the ethics of difference, 266–70
global terrorism's challenge to the ethics of difference, 255–60
Descartes, René, 135
DeWolf, David K., 151
Dorsen, Norman, 217
Dred Scott v. Sanford, 69
Due process, 53, 54, 194, 195, 201, 202, 203
Dumont, Lewis, 24
Dworkin, Ronald, 149–83
contrasted with pluralism in terms of one and the many, 204–07
counterfactual reconstruction and theory of interpretation, 156–97
moving from concept to conception and law as integrity, 197–204
rivals and the distinction between principle and policy, 185–91
thesis and one law principle, 183–85

Eberle, Edward J., 241
Economics
Posner's law and economics, 183–84, 186, 189–91

Employment Division Oregon Dept. of Human Resources v. Smith, 158
Employment Division v. Smith, 106
Epstein, Richard A., 194
Equal Protection Clause, 57, 59, 85, 99, 103, 108, 195, 199
Equality, 1, 3, 8, 16
accommodating cultural difference, 88–89
comparing liberal, republican and communitarian political rights, 228
contrast between homogeneous and heterogeneous societies, 59
Derrida, 253, 259, 263
designing a legal and institutional framework to accommodate cultural difference, 90–91
dialectic between identity and difference, 68–70
Dworkin's one law principle, 183, 198–92, 202, 203, 204
dynamic between identity and difference, 82–86
global terrorism, 260, 263–65, 305–06
Habermas, 272, 275, 279, 283, 288
from liberalism to pluralism, 77–81
liberalism's, republicanism's and communitarianism's overriding values, 223–24
minority group rights, 92–93, 103, 118, 121
Rawls's *Political Liberalism*, 64–65
Rawls's Kantian contractarianism, 32, 33
religion, 160, 161, 166, 169
single status society and the federalization of difference, 86–87
three stage progression of the dialectic of equality, 70–77
value pluralism, 38–39
Ethics, 11
approaches to ethics, 251–53
contrast between pluralist ethics and ethics of difference, 266–70
Derrida, deconstruction and the ethics of difference, 254
Derrida's deconstruction of globalization, tolerance and democracy, 263
distinguished from morality, 27, 28, 31
ethics of difference and global terrorism, 251–66
ethics of identity and difference contrasted with comprehensive pluralism, 290, 295–96, 297, 305, 307
global terrorism's challenge to the ethics of difference, 255–60

Ethics (*cont.*)
  Habermas's discursive ethics, 281
  Rawls's *Political Liberalism*, 62
  Spinoza, 128, 136
European Convention of Human Rights, 4,
  242–43, 262
European Union
  discourse theory, 285
  post-national rule of law, 274, 275–76, 279
Evans, David C., 150
Exchange value, 25–26, 30

Farer, Tom J., 96
Feldman, Noah, 269
Feminism, 44, 45, 168, 302–03
  John Stuart Mill, 77
Ferreres Comella, Victor, 244
Fineman, Martha Albertson, 65
Fish, Stanley, 188
Freedom of expression, 78, 143, 213, 216, 227, 228
Freedom of speech, 104, 114, 119, 141, 237
Fukuyama, Francis, 129

Galbraith, John Kenneth, 276
Gallie, W.B., 199
Galston, William A., 15, 38
Garlicki, Lech, 4
Gender-based equality, 32, 64, 69, 73–74, 83, 89,
  160, 166
Gilligan, Carol, 35
Ginsburg, Ruth Bader, 76
Globalization, 2, 9–15
  Derrida's deconstruction, 260–63
  ethics of difference's account of global
    terrorism, 264–65
  global terrorism and the contrasts between
    pluralist ethics and the ethics of difference,
    267–70
  global terrorism and the post-national rule of
    law, 275–76, 277–80
  global terrorism's challenge to the ethics of
    difference, 256–59
  Habermas's discourse theory, 282–87
  pluralism to cope with global terrorism, 292–96
  recent historical changes and new trends,
    161–63
Gough, J.W., 29
Greenawalt, Kent, 155, 162
Grimm, Dieter, 159, 272
Griswold v. Connecticut, 114

Haarscher, Guy, 14, 159, 160
Habeck, Mary, 3

Habermas, Jürgen
  analysis of global terrorism in the context of
    discourse theory, 280–87
  critique of comprehensive pluralism, 52
  critique of Habermas's assumptions
    regarding global terrorism and consequent
    implications for Habermas's post-national
    discourse theory model, 287–90
  dialogical Kantian proceduralism, 34–35
  the Enlightenment project as evolving, 305
  global terrorism and the post-national rule of
    law, 274–80
  Kantian universalism, 31
  pluralism as an alternative to Habermas's
    proceduralism, 290–96
  reciprocal recognition, 50
  terrorism's challenge to conception of
    modernism, 271–74
Hartney, Michael, 101
Hate speech
  defined, 239
  militant democracy, 239–43
  pacted secession, 248
Hegel, G.W.F.
  Hegelian dimension of comprehensive
    pluralism, 42–51
  Kant's morals, 28
  overcoming contradictions, 128
  Spinoza's dialectic, 133
Hobbes, Thomas, 29, 30, 31, 35
Homosexuality, 64, 75, 171, 218, 287, 288, 294
Human rights
  comprehensive pluralism and the nexus
    between human rights and constitutional
    rights, 115–21
  confrontation between universalism,
    particularism and relativism, 95–97
  Habermas's analysis of global terrorism, 283–84
  Habermas's conception of modernism, 272
  minority group rights, 95
Huntington, Samuel, 14
Hyppolite, Jean, 48, 49

Illiberalism, 7, 58, 64, 79, 95, 165, 232–33,
  242–43, 306

Johnston, Darlene M., 106, 107, 108

Kant, Immanuel
  Derrida's deconstruction of ethics and
    politics, 254
  Dworkin and the distinction between principle
    and policy, 190

Habermas's defense of modernism, 271
Habermas's dialogical Kantian
  proceduralism, 34–23
Habermas's embrace of the dichotomy between
  justice and the good, 280–81
ideal of cosmopolitanism as conceived by
  Derrida, 262
pure social contract proceduralist approach,
  27–28
Rawls's Kantian contractarianism, 34
severing unity from plurality, 27–28
Spinoza's dialectic, 128
Kelmanm, Mark, 187
Kumm, Mattias, 4
Kymlicka, Will, 96, 100
  liberal defense of group rights, 109–10

Ladeur, Karl-Heinz, 158
Lawrence v. Texas, 75
Legal realism, 184, 186, 187, 189
Levy, Leonard W., 179
Liberal egalitarianism, 184, 188, 194, 195–97
Liberalism, 3, 5, 6–7, 10–14
  accommodating cultural difference, 89
  clash between deprivatized religion and
    relativized secularism, 149
  comparing liberal, republican and
    communitarian political rights, 229, 231–15
  compatibility with pluralism, 225
  comprehensive pluralism, the constitution, and
    group rights, 109–10
  contrasted with illiberalism, 58
  dialectic between identity and difference,
    68–70
  dialectic of equality, 77
  dynamic between identity and difference,
    82, 84
  Habermas, 285
  Hegel, 42
  from liberalism to pluralism, 77–81
  minority group rights, 92–95, 121
  neoliberalism, 278–79
  overriding values, 223–24
  pluralism and limited liberalism, 234
  pluralism to cope with global terrorism, 295,
    296, 299, 301, 306
  pluralist account of the constitutional
    treatment of the relationship between
    religion and the state, 165
  pluralist conceptual framework for political
    rights, 216
  pluralist constitutional approach to religion, 180

political rights in times of stress, 212
problematic nexus between unity and
  plurality, 24
Rawls's *Political Liberalism*, 59, 62–65
value pluralism, 38–39
Linz, Juan, 26
Lochner v. New York, 54, 55, 194, 195
Locke, John, 29, 228
Luban, David, 226
Luhmann, Niklas, 276
Lukes, Steven, 24, 37
Lynch v. Donnelly, 179

Macedo, Stephen, 218
Macherey, Pierre, 128
Mahlmann, Matthias, 158
Mancini, Susanna, 93, 155, 156, 157, 179
Mansfield, Anna Morawiec, 163
March, Andrew F., 5, 159, 168, 176
Marcuse, Herbert, 141
Marketplace of ideas, 70, 161
Marx, Karl
  clash between Marxist communism and liberal
    capitalism, 1
  overcoming contradictions, 128
  Spinoza's dialectic, 133
Masters, Roger, 225
McGoldrick, Dominic, 212
Michael M. v. Sonoma County Superior Court, 75
Michelman, Frank I., 14, 47, 52, 57
  distinction between the right and the good,
    59–63
Mill, John Stuart, 36
  feminism, 77
Minow, Martha, 74
Models of constitution making, 155–56, 164, 167
Modern polity
  defined, 10–11
Monism
  defined, 13–14, 26
  and communitarianism, 231
  contrasted to value pluralism, 37–42
  contrasted with comprehensive pluralism,
    42–51, 116, 204–05, 299, 301
  contrasted with pluralism and relativism,
    24, 125
  deontological monism, 29, 31
  Dworkin, 183
  minority group rights, 95
  Spinoza, 129
  teleological monism, 35–37
Moore, Shelby, 98

Morality
distinguished from ethics, 27, 28, 31
Dworkin, 196
global terrorism, 252
Habermas, 34, 281
Spinoza, 135
Mostefai, Ourida, 161
Mouffe, Chantal, 238
Munzer, Stephen, 183

Nagel, Thomas, 38, 56
Nebbia v. New York, 194
Neuhaus, Richard John, 6, 158
Nozick, Robert, 77, 227, 228

Paradox of tolerance, 129, 146, 240
Pateman, Carole, 32
Paust, Jordan J., 262
Perry, Michael J., 116, 118
Pitkin, Hannah, 36
*Planned Parenthood of Southeastern
Pennsylvania v. Casey*, 114
Plessy v. Ferguson, 59, 69, 104, 198
Pluralism
defined, 11
accommodating cultural differences, 88–89
communitarianism, 226, 233
conceptual framework for political rights,
212–15
constitutional framework, 215–17
contrasted with liberalism, 12
contrasted with republicanism, 12
designing a legal and institutional framework to
accommodate cultural differences, 90
dialectic of equality, 77
distinction between ordinary times, times of
crisis and times of stress, 221–22
Dworkin, 185, 205
dynamic between identity and difference,
82, 84
free speech, 236–37
global terrorism, 267
Habermas, 284, 289
Habermas's dialogical Kantian
proceduralism, 34
hate speech and militant democracy, 239,
241–42, 243
illiberalism, 233
liberalism, 211
from liberalism to pluralism, 77–81
limited liberalism, republicanism and
communitarianism, 234–36

nexus between unity and plurality, 23–24
pluralist constitutional approach to religion,
178–81
political rights and struggle between self and
other, 221
political rights in times of stress, 211–12, 238–39,
248–50
relationship between religion and the state, 166
religious critique of pluralism, 171–78
religious pluralism, 17, 154, 162
republicanism, 223–24, 225–26, 230
single status society and the federalization of
difference, 86
value pluralism, 37–42
Popper, Karl
paradox of tolerance, 129
Spinoza's dialectic, 142
times of stress, 240
tolerance and pluralism, 146
Poscher, Ralph, 127
Posner, Richard
Dworkin and the distinction between principle
and policy, 190–91
Dworkin's thesis and one law principle, 184
wealth maximization, 189
Postmodern polity
defined, 11
Spinoza, 148
Proceduralism
Habermas's critique of comprehensive
pluralism, 52
Habermas's dialogical Kantian proceduralism,
34–35
Habermas's discursive proceduralism, 288
pluralism as an alternative, 290

R.A.V. v. City of St Paul, Minnesota, 105
Raday, Frances, 118, 159
Radford, Mary F., 64
Rawls, John
comprehensive pluralism and *Political
Liberalism*, 62–67
critique of utilitarianism, 36
Dworkin's thesis and one-law principle, 156
Habermas's dialogical Kantian
proceduralism, 34
Kantian contractarianism in A Theory of
Justice, 31–34
secular versus the "areligious", 151–52
Raz, Joseph, 38, 186
Refah Partisi v. Turkey, 243
Regina v. Adams, 114

Regina v. Keegstra, 105
Relativism
 defined, 8–9
 confrontation with universalism and
  particularism, 98–99
 contrasted with monism, 125
 Hegel, 47, 50
 human rights, 96–97
 pluralism, 115, 119, 125, 304, 305, 306–07
 postmodernism, 52
 Spinoza, 126, 141, 145
 value pluralism, 37–39
Religious pluralism, 17, 154, 162
Republicanism
 defined, 12
 accommodating cultural difference, 93–95
 comparing liberal, republican and
  communitarian political rights, 231–33
 compatibility with pluralism, 225–26
 overriding values, 223–24
 pluralism and limited republicanism, 234–35
 political rights in times of stress, 250
Resnik, Judith, 4
Reule, Deborah A., 151
Reynolds v. United States, 158
Richmond v. J.A. Croson, 104
Ricoeur, Paul, 197
Roach, Kent, 241
Roe v. Wade, 114, 159, 182
Rorive, Isabelle, 160
Rosen, David, 303
Rosenfeld, Esther, 64
Rosenthal, Michael A., 126
Rousseau, Jean-Jacques, 12, 30, 225, 229
 overriding values of republicanism, 224

Sajo, Andras, 6, 14
Samuelson, Paul, 26
Sandel, Michael, 225
Santa Clara Pueblo v. Martinez, 73,
 106, 108
Sapir, Gidi, 156, 168
Sartre, Jean-Paul, 255
Schlink, Bernard, 183
Schmitt, Carl, 226, 231
Secularism, 2, 5, 8–11, 14
 clash between deprivatized religion and
  relativized secularism, 149–51
 constitutional jurisprudence, 156–61
 constitutional models, 155–56
 global terrorism, 294, 295
 Habermas, 283, 289

hate speech and militant democracy, 243
 pluralism, 164, 177, 178–80, 226, 306
 recent historical changes and new trends,
  161–64
 secular versus the areligious, 151
 Spinoza, 147–48
Slaughter, M. M., 113
Smith, Adam, 24–26
Smith, Steven B., 137
Spinoza, Benedict de, 125–36
 contrasted with Dworkin, 182, 207
 guiding principles for structuring a
  constitutional regime, 224
 in relation to Marx and Hegel, 130–33
 tolerance, 126–29
 tolerance and pluralism in a postmodern
  world, 144–48
 tolerance in a political context, 133–44
Stein, Eric, 240
Stone, Suzanne L., 5, 97, 176
Sunstein, Cass, 225

Taylor, Charles, 38, 47
Tolerance
 communitarianism, 233
 comprehensive pluralism, human rights and
  constitutional rights, 116–17, 119
 comprehensive pluralism, the Constitution and
  group rights, 111–12
 constitutional models, 155
 Derrida, 259–61, 262–63
 hate speech, 239–42
 liberalism, 78
 pluralism, 180, 207, 216, 299
 relationship between religion and the state,
  165, 172, 175–65
 relativism, 13
 secular versus the areligious, 152
 Spinoza. *See* Spinoza, Benedict de
Tribe, Laurence H., 53, 159
Troper, Michel, 93, 155, 157

Ullmann, Walter, 24
Unger, Roberto, 187

Value pluralism, 37–27, 42, 50, 298
von Bogdandy, Armin, 276

Waldron, Jeremy, 16
 cultural difference, 70, 79, 81, 90
Wallace, E. Gregory, 64, 153
"War on terror"

distinction between ordinary times, times of crisis and times of stress, 222

pacted secession, 248

pluralist conceptual framework for political rights, 213

pluralist political rights in times of stress, 244–46

political rights in times of stress, 211, 249

Wealth maximization, 37, 55, 189, 190, 191

Weber, Max, 23, 82, 271

Weithman, Paul, 218

West Coast Hotel Co. v. Parrish, 194

West, Robin, 218

Wisconsin v. Yoder, 106

Yin, Tung, 212

Yovel, Yirmiyahu, 126, 128, 130, 132

Zizek, Slavoj, 47